# SOCIAL WO
# PRIMARY HE

# SOCIAL WORK AND PRIMARY HEALTH CARE

Edited by

## Anthony W. Clare
## Roslyn H. Corney

*Institute of Psychiatry*
*Denmark Hill, London*

1982

## ACADEMIC PRESS

*A Subsidiary of Harcourt Brace Jovanovich, Publishers*

London   New York
Paris   San Diego   San Francisco   São Paulo
Sydney   Tokyo   Toronto

ACADEMIC PRESS INC. (LONDON) LTD.
24/28 Oval Road
London NW1

*United States Edition published by*
ACADEMIC PRESS INC.
111 Fifth Avenue
New York, New York 10003

*British Library Cataloguing in Publication Data*
Social Work and Primary Health Care.
1. Medical social work
2. Family medicine
I. Clare, A.W.
II. Corney, R.H.
362.1'6424    HV687

ISBN 0-12-174740-9

LCCCN 82-72333

Printed in Great Britain by
Whitstable Litho Ltd., Whitstable, Kent

# LIST OF FIRST NAMED AUTHORS

**Butler, J.,** (Deceased) *Dept. of Sociology and Social Administration, University of Southampton, Southampton.*

**Clare, A.W.,** *General Practice Research Unit, Institute of Psychiatry, Denmark Hill, London. S.E.5.*

**Cooper, B.,** *Zentralinstitut für Seelische Gesundheit Mannheim, Postfach 5970, 6800 Mannheim 1.J5, Germany.*

**Corney, R.H.,** *General Practice Research Unit, Institute of Psychiatry, Denmark Hill, London. S.E.5.*

**Creer, C.,** *MRC Social Psychiatry Unit, Institute of Psychiatry, Denmark Hill, London. S.E.5.*

**Dingwall, R.,** *Centre for Socio-legal Studies, Wolfson College, Oxford.*

**Gibbons, J.S.,** *Dept. of Sociology & Social Administration, University of Southampton, Southampton.*

**Gilchrist, I.C.,** *Broomfields, Hatfield Heath, Bishop's Stortford, Herts.*

**Goldberg, E.M.,** *Policy Studies Institute, 1/2 Castle Lane, London. S.W.1.*

**Herbert, M.,** *School of Social Work, 107 Princess Road East, Leicester LE1 7LA.*

**Rushton, A.,** *3 Galveston Road, South Norwood. Croydon.*

**Shepherd, M.,** *General Practice Research Unit, Institute of Psychiatry, Denmark Hill, London. S.E.5.*

**Weissman, M.M.,** *Depression Research Unit, Dept. of Psychiatry, Yale University.*

**Williams, P.,** *General Practice Research Unit, Institute of Psychiatry, Denmark Hill, London. S.E.5.*

# FOREWORD

I have been fortunate in working in one team with social workers in an inner city practice for many years. Any other form of collaboration seemed inferior before that experience and seems more obviously inferior now. But that is a personal impression.

This book raises the question whether problems of ill-health presented in primary care, inextricably bound up with social need and difficulty, are neglected without social work attachments to general practices; whether physically and mentally ill patients receive a better, more integrated service when their social worker is attached than when he or she operates within a separate, independent social service department. It seeks systematic answers, not impressions; careful observations and measured comparisons, not personal prejudices.

The authors seek to do this by bringing together those papers (in most instances already published) which throw the clearest available light on these questions and on others which relate to them — how does the role of a social worker in a general practice differ? How effective is social work in the general practice setting?

The papers reprinted are, of course, a selection; it is made both on grounds of their quality as convincing enquiries and because they were judged to be the best available answers to the questions at issue. They are arranged in logical sequence like a loosely-linked chain. But the linkages are made stronger and clearer by short commentaries, each of which introduces the next major question to which a small group of papers offers answers.

I believe that this carefully selected sequence of published studies will not only prove conveniently useful, but will also serve to reveal the interest and importance of an overlapping area where our health and social services have so far largely failed in exploiting their exceptional opportunity. Failed or been prevented?

John P. Horder

# FOREWORD

It is fashionable to exhort doctors and social workers to co-operate and to work together for the benefit of their patients or clients, but so far as we know exhortation is quite ineffective. It does not create reasons for co-operation, nor change the structures which impede it nor settle the question of when it is worthwhile. Rather it tends to obscure the complexities of co-operation in a cloud of good intentions so that when co-operation breaks down personal relationships are blamed.

If we believe that inter-disciplinary co-operation is important we must be able to say why and that will involve a consideration of the costs as well as the benefits. For costs there certainly are and it cannot be taken for granted that in all circumstances co-operation is necessarily worth its cost. There is always a price in terms of time and often in emotional stress since co-operation inevitably involves alterations in the existing balance of power. In fact co-operation, far from being dependent only on good will, may more accurately be described as a market place activity in which information, knowledge, time and power are the medium of exchange.

The editors, through their selection of papers, help us to address some of the complexities of co-operation and in particular suggest reasons why they consider it not only desirable but also essential. Their argument rests upon the connection which research has established between social factors and some psychological illness and upon the fact that clients are ready to talk to social workers who are attached to a general practice when they would not have approached a Social Services department.

The authors also consider possible structures for promoting co-operation when they ask where social service teams and social workers should be sited. There is a fierce debate taking place in the social services, which has been fuelled by the Barclay Report and its minority statements, about the relative merits of patch based teams as opposed to other forms of organisation. The editors suggest that a general practice might come to be seen as a patch based multi disciplinary team. Patch basing however implies, for its adherents, more than setting a team in the relatively small population group it is to serve. It also suggests ideas of client participation, if not control, of the services provided and a preventive rather than a remedial approach to problem solving. Such a shift in ideology makes considerable demands upon a social service team, and raises questions not only of power sharing but of the social workers' social control functions. To implement a similar ideology in general practice would demand an even greater shift in values although it would not raise, as it does for social services, the question of the role of elected representatives. It is interesting to speculate about the alternative possibility — that of attaching doctors, nurses and health visitors to social service teams. The editors do not consider such ideas but their collection raises in my mind questions about the structure of the health service as well as that of the social services, and about the roles of medical staff as well as the roles of social workers. These are questions which must be addressed if a firm base is to be built for interprofessional co-operation. This collection of papers provides a starting point for the work which still remains to be done.


Phyllida Parsloe

# PREFACE

The purpose of this collection is to focus attention on the extent of the
social component of ill-health identified and managed in the primary care
setting. It does appear clear to us that while there is a growing recognition
of the theoretical and practical difficulties involved in teasing apart the
physical, psychological and social components of ill-health, this is not
reflected in the structure and content of the services currently provided to
meet health and social needs. In our selection of papers, we have concentrated on the social needs of those individuals and groups with psychological
symptoms and disorders because we believe that it is in this area that the
fragmentation of the health and social services is at its most obvious and
damaging. However, many of the findings reviewed in this collection are of
relevance to the wider issue of the optimum relationship between social
work and medicine.

In choosing the twenty-one papers which make up this collection, we
have adopted the policy which underpinned the selection of papers in a
companion volume to this one, "Psychosocial Disorders in General
Practice" (Williams and Clare, 1979). We have brought together these
papers because we believe that it will be a useful service to social workers,
general practitioners, psychiatrists, health visitors, and others interested
in the medico-social aspects of primary health care. These papers
reveal not merely the extent of the current level of general practice-social
work collaboration, but also the immense potential for collaborative
research which this field possesses. The contribution to research and clinical
work in primary care is genuinely multi-disciplinary, a fact which carries
with it the disadvantage that much of the published work originating from
the field is scattered through a very disparate range of professional journals.
Nor is it always easy on reading these individual papers to obtain any overall
views of the context within which the paper is sited. By providing an overview, in the form of an introduction to each section or group of papers, we
hope to provide the reader, particularly the social worker or general
practitioner in training, with a more informed idea of the place of the
individual paper in question in the overall schema of psycho-social team
work in primary care.

Inevitably, our selection of papers has had to be influenced by such
factors as availability, clarity and precision. We would have liked to include
more papers from North America but, regrettably, the number of papers
published concerning the application of social work within the growing field

of family medicine is quite small. Inevitably, our choice is personal and also draws heavily on work undertaken by ourselves and our colleagues at the General Practice Research Unit at the Institute of Psychiatry in London over the past ten years under the direction of Professor Michael Shepherd. This collection of papers, together with the references they provide, embody some of the most productive and provocative aspects of research and practice in this area. They bear witness to the feasibility of social work research at a time when doubts are expressed concerning this very issue. While they clarify the present situation and even take it a number of steps further these papers by no means exhaust the possibilities. Indeed, this entire volume should serve not merely to indicate what has already been achieved but to point ahead to what could be undertaken if the will, enthusiasm and professional collaboration were to be available.

Anthony W. Clare and Roslyn H. Corney
September, 1982

# CONTENTS

List of Contributors v
Foreword by John P. Horder vi
Foreword by Phyllida Parsloe vii
Preface ix

## Section 1
## Social Problems and Ill-health

Introduction 3

Social aspects of ill-health in general practice 9
 *A. W. Clare*

The extent of mental and physical ill-health of clients referred 23
to social workers in a local authority department and a general
attachment scheme
 *R. H. Corney*

Referrals to social workers: a comparative study of a local 31
authority intake team with a general practice attachment
scheme
 *R. H. Corney and B. A. Bowen*

Towards accountability in social work: One year's intake to 45
an Area Office
 *E. M. Goldberg, R. W. Warburton, B. McGuinness and J. H. Rowlands*

## Section 2
## The Social Worker and the Primary Care Team

Introduction 71

Problems of teamwork in primary care 81
 *R. Dingwall*

Social workers in primary health care: the general practitioner's 105
viewpoint
 *P. Williams and A. W. Clare*

Social work in general practice 115
*I. C. Gilchrist, J. B. Gough, Y. R. Horsfall-Turner, E. M. Ineson,*
*G. Keele, B. Marks and H. J. Scott*

Health visitors and social workers 133
*R. H. Corney*


Section 3
Social Work Intervention

Introduction 143

Social workers'\interventions: A comparative study of a local 151
authority intake team\with a general practice attachment
scheme
*R. H. Corney*

Task-centred casework with marital problems 163
*J. Butler, I. Bow and J. Gibbons*

A social work method for family settings 179
*M. Herbert and B. O'Driscoll*

Casework, psychotherapy and social work 199
*A. W. Clare*

Social work with patients and their families 213
*C. Creer*

Group work with single parents — 229

a single and separated parents' group
*A. Rushton and J. Winny*

— the consumer's viewpoint: participants' impressions 237
*R. H. Corney*


Section 4
Evaluation of Social Work

Introduction 247

Evaluation of a social work service for self-poisoning patients 255
*J. S. Gibbons, J. Butler, P. Urwin and J. L. Gibbons*

Treatment effects on the social adjustment of depressed patients 265
*M. M. Weissman, G. L. Klerman, E. S. Paykel, B. Prusoff and B. Hanson*

Mental health care in the community: an evaluative study 283
*B. Cooper, B. G. Harwin, C. Depla and M. Shepherd*

Social work and the primary care of mental disorder 295
*M. Shepherd, B. G. Harwin, C. Depla and V. Cairns*

The effectiveness of social work intervention in the management    311
of depressed women in general practice
  *R. H. Corney*

Client perspectives in a general practice attachment    325
  *R. H. Corney*

## Section 5
## Social Work and Primary Care

Social work and primary care: problems and possibilities    337
  *A. W. Clare and R. H. Corney*


Subject Index    345

# SECTION 1

# SOCIAL PROBLEMS AND ILL-HEALTH

# INTRODUCTION

Any discussion which concerns itself with the possibilities for collaboration between social workers and other professionals working in the primary health care area must be founded on the premise that there is a close and intimate relationship between social problems, disturbances, difficulties and needs on the one hand, and physical and mental ill-health on the other. Such a proposition may appear obvious to anyone familiar with the research literature. Many social workers, however, most of whom currently labour to meet a very varied constellation of personal and social service demands, may not feel the need to add to their burdens by contemplating an active primary care role. Social workers will, understandably, wish to be convinced that such is the extent of the social component of health problems in primary care that is inconceivable that the services should be so designed and function in a way that excludes them from an active, constructive contribution. It is the central point of the four papers in this opening section that *the problems of ill-health presented within the ambit of primary care are in a fundamental and often inextricable way bound up with social need and difficulty.* The implications of such findings for the appropriate detection and optimum management of such conditions are considered in later sections of this volume.

The first paper, by Clare, documents the accumulated and accumulating evidence testifying to what one North American medical commentator somewhat inelegantly describes as the "bio-psycho-social" nature of disorders presenting in primary care [Engel, 1977]. The sheer weight of the evidence is in stark contrast to the relative failure of community care services in Britain, Europe and America to develop appropriate professional and organizational responses [Musto, 1977; Fink and Weinstein, 1979; Scharfstein, 1980]. The extent, however, of the reorganization of primary care with the sharp trend towards multi-disciplinary working located in health centres is not always recognized. It has been a slow but steady development, largely unheralded and not part of any conscious national plan. There is evidence [Clare and Lader, 1982] that GPs in general are well aware of the enormous contribution made by social problems to the overall burden of morbidity presented in their surgeries. Where there is less agreement amongst general practitioners is what to do when confronted by such problems [Cartwright and Anderson, 1981]. There is widespread dissatisfaction concerning the tendency to rely on psychotropic and other medication and the limitations placed on more thorough exploration and response by the practical realities of general practice, such as the pressure on time. The international initiatives referred to in Clare's paper [Regier *et al.*, 1979] serve to sharpen the issue and underline the challenge to current primary care services implicit in research uncovering the extent of the social component of morbidity.

The second paper, documenting the extent of morbidity in clients attending social workers reminds us that the argument favouring greater collaboration between primary care physicians and social workers is not one-way. The implications of Corney's work is that the general practitioner and other members of the primary care team can also be of value to the social worker. The high proportion of clients found to have physical and/or mental ill-health amongst those referred by GPs to social workers in an attachment scheme may not be so surprising but the remarkable degree of such morbidity in clients referred to social workers working in the orthodox setting of a social service department is noteworthy. This high percentage of illness (40% of intake clients) is likely to be an under-estimate and a further study is underway in which more precise information is being recorded. Few studies have attempted to assess the health status of social service clients [Richards *et al.*, 1976; Corney and Briscoe, 1977]. However, those studies in which reasons for referral to social workers are carefully recorded, as in Goldberg's study described in the fourth paper in this section, also suggest that high proportions are indeed ill. In Goldberg's study, 30% were referred for problems associated with physical disability, illness and ageing and 7% for problems related to emotional disorder. This is a less surprising finding when one remembers that the statutory responsibilities of the social services involve the chronically sick and disabled, the mentally ill and those with serious child care problems. Corney's paper, more disturbingly, reveals the almost total inadequacy of the official returns provided by the Department of Health and Social Security quantifying the morbidity component of social work; only 4% of the intake clients were assessed by the social workers as mentally ill, physically ill or mentally handicapped according to these returns.

Whereas Corney's paper concentrates on the health characteristics of clients referred to social workers, whether working in a primary care attachment scheme or in a social service department, the third paper, that by Corney and Bowen, focuses on other details such as the age and sex of the referred individual, the reasons for referral and the problems presented. The purpose of this study was to discover whether attaching social workers alongside general practitioners significantly affected the quality and quantity of the social work case load. Would referrals from the primary care team increase? Would clients referred to attached social workers differ from those referred to and presenting at social service departments? In fact, the attachment did indeed lead to a sharp increase in the amount of referrals from the primary care sector to social work. The nature of the problems referred altered too: before the attachment such clients as were referred to social workers were in the main those in need of practical assistance (provision of aids, disability allowances etc.) whereas after the attachment began a much wider variety of clients, and particularly those with problems affecting their personal relationships and seeking advice and counselling, were referred.

Perhaps the most dramatic difference between referrals in the two settings concerned the large number of women referred to the attached social workers complaining of anxiety and depression, reflecting the high proportion of such patients who attend general practitioners (as discussed in the opening paper). Such women more often than not had a number of associated social problems and the fact that they figured prominently in patients selected for social work intervention by GPs suggests that doctors are favourably disposed to seeking the professional assistance of social workers in the management of such patients.

There is evidence in this third paper that attachment schemes draw a wider section of the population with social problems than does the orthodox arrangement of the social worker located in the social services department. There is clearly overlap between the populations referred but there is a strong suggestion, supported in other studies [Goldberg and Neill, 1972] that locating social workers in primary care may well facilitate contact with social workers for sections of the population which normally do not avail of it. It may well be that there is stigma attached to social service departments and ignorance amongst the public as to their function. There is much less, if any, stigma attached to visiting one's doctor and people of all social classes will bring problems to the primary care surgery especially if these problems are associated with ill-health. It may well be that a social worker working within the context of a primary care facility is seen in a more favourable light than in the context of a social service department but to date that aspect of primary care social work attachment has not been studied.

The final paper, that by Goldberg and her associates, describes the results of a study in which referrals to social workers in an intake team at a social service department were carefully monitored over a period of one year using a case review system designed by this group (Goldberg and Fruin, 1976). In the paper included in this collection, the authors demonstrate a more harmonious relationship between the primary care services and the social services than has tended to be reported. Yet the finding of a difference in pattern of referral between those clients referred in the attachment scheme and in this study persists. In Goldberg's study, it is from amongst the elderly and the disabled that referrals are most common whereas those patients referred with psychological disturbances were clients "mainly referred at a crisis point when the mental handicap or the chronic psychiatric illness seriously upset the family equilibrium". Such a picture contrasts sharply with that portrayed by the attachment arrangement in which the majority of patients referred with mental ill-health were less severely ill with the strong implication that their referral had occurred before a crisis had arisen. In addition, in the majority of the cases described by Goldberg, the referring doctor had requested specific services which could be carried out routinely whereas in the attachment scheme patients were very often referred for more time-consuming, supportive and exploratory counselling. The lack of basic demographic data concerning age, sex, type of housing etc. in the Goldberg study makes a more comprehensive comparison difficult but the information collected by this group concerning the actual social work undertaken is discussed in the introduction to Section 3 (pp. 143–150).

It might legitimately be argued that pressures on the social service department in the Goldberg study militated against the social workers involving themselves in what might be seen as the comparative therapeutic luxury of counselling. Yet, in this regard, it is interesting to note that Goldberg and her colleagues themselves suggest that a shift of emphasis might be made "from an information and social casualty service towards a more community-oriented preventive endeavour" and they add that more help might be given "to families and individuals who show early signs of stress, which without intervention may reach crisis point or develop into more chronic and intractable conditions". It is precisely these families which constitute a large proportion of referrals to attached social workers.

It would appear reasonable to conclude on the basis of the above papers that whereas the elderly and physically disabled make up a high proportion of referrals to social workers in both settings, the numbers of mentally ill (especially those with minor illness) referred to local authority settings are far fewer, *suggesting that their social needs are neglected in the absence of social work attachments in general practice.*

However, lest it be imagined that what is being advanced here is a largely uncritical and euphoric argument on behalf of the attachment of social workers in primary care, we should point out that such schemes are not without their problems, attempts to establish them have occasionally ended in failure and many professional and organizational difficulties need to be overcome for them to work with any degree of success [Ratoff *et al.*, 1974; Huntingdon, 1981]. The attachment scheme described in this section has been a highly successful one yet it too has had its difficulties [Rushton and Briscoe, 1981]. The difficulties involved in such collaboration are discussed in more detail in Section 2 (pp. 71–139).

## References

Cartwright, A. and Anderson, R. (1981). "General Practice Revisited". Tavistock Publications, London.

Clare, A. and Lader, M. (1982). "Psychiatry and General Practice". Mental Health Foundation Conference Proceedings, Oxford, 1981. Academic Press, London.

Corney, R. and Briscoe, M. (1977). Social workers and their clients: A comparison between primary health care and local authority settings. The Team – 2. *Journal of the Royal College of General Practitioners* 27, 295–301.

Engel, G. L. (1977). The need for a new medical model: a challenge for biomedicine. *Science* 196, 4286, 129–136.

Fink, P. J. and Weinstein, S. P. (1979). Whatever happened to psychiatry? The deprofessionalization of community mental health centers. *American Journal of Psychiatry* 136, 406–409.

Goldberg, E. M. and Fruin, D. J. (1976). Towards accountability in Social Work: A case review system for social workers. *British Journal of Social Work* 6, No. 1, 3–22.

Goldberg, E. M. and Neill, J. E. (1972). "Social Work in General Practice". George Allen & Unwin, London.

Huntington, J. (1981). "Social Work and General Medical Practice". Allen & Unwin, London.

Musto, D. (1977). Whatever happened to community mental health? *Psychiatric Annals* 7, 30–35.

Parish, P. (1982). *In* "Psychiatry and General Practice". (Eds A. Clare and M. Lader. Academic Press, London.

Ratoff, L., Rose, A. and Smith, C.R. (1974). Social workers and GPs. *Social Work Today* 5, 16, 497–500.

Regier, D.A., Kessler, L.G., Burns, B.J. and Goldberg, I. ). (1979). The need for a psychosocial classification system in primary care settings. *International Journal of Mental Health* 8, 16–29.

Rickards, C., Gildersleeve, C., Fitzgerald, R. and Cooper, B. (1976). The health of clients of a social services department. *Journal of the Royal College of General Practitioners* 26, 237–243.

Rushton, A. and Briscoe, M. (1981). Social work as an aspect of primary health care: the social worker's view. *British Journal of Social Work* 11, 61–76.

Sharfstein, S.S. (1980). Community mental health centres. *Journal of the Royal Society of Medicine* 73, 219.

# SOCIAL ASPECTS OF ILL-HEALTH IN GENERAL PRACTICE

ANTHONY W. CLARE

## Introduction

In the conditions of the British National Health Service from its inception, the general practitioner is the physician of first contact, the professional figure who is the gate-keeper to all medical facilities. From the very outset, the service has been organized around the GP who occupies a central position in the health service structure, a structure which differs radically from that encountered in most other developed countries. Given that the general practitioner keeps records of his consultations, it seemed reasonable to researchers in the late 1950s and early 1960s to try and assess the amount and the nature of the mental disorders with which the GP is concerned. Initially, however, the prevalence rates of psychiatric disorders in this setting showed enormous variation (Table 1).

TABLE 1

Psychiatric referral rates from general practice and community surveys in England and Wales

| Author | Year | Size of population | Survey period (years) | Referral rate per 10,000 at risk | Proportion of psychiatric cases referred |
|---|---|---|---|---|---|
| Bodkins et al. | 1953 | 14,000 | 1 | 72.9 | — |
| Hopkins | 1958 | 1,400 | 3 | 160.6 | — |
| Martin et al. | 1957 | 17,250 | 1 | 29.0 | 5.3 |
| Fry | 1959 | 5,500 | 1 | 61.8 | 5.0 |
| Rawnsley and Loudon | 1961 | 18,500 | 9 | 17.7 | — |
| Taylor and Chave | 1964 | 40,000 | 3 | 31.5 | 5.4 |
| Shepherd et al. | 1966 | 15,000 | 1 | 71.4 | 5.1 |

From Kaeser and Cooper [1971] with permission.

However, what seemed to be less variable was the proportion of patients regarded by the GP as suffering from psychological problems which was referred to a psychiatrist. The finding that only about 5% of psychiatric patients presenting in general practice are referred onwards is one which persists in relevant studies to this day [Williams and Clare, 1981]. It was originally placed on a more secure foundation by the first systematic study of psychiatric ill-health in general practice undertaken by Shepherd and his colleagues, a study which involved 46 general practitioners in the metropolitan area of London [Shepherd *et al.*, 1966]. When these workers first started, their first inclination was to employ or adopt the standard International Classification of Diseases in the diagnosis of conditions which they identified. However, after a very brief experience of the clinical problems encountered, it became apparent that neither the ICD (then in its 7th edition) nor any available alternatives did justice to the situation. Accordingly, they were compelled to design a more relevant system of their own to meet the needs of the GP by distinguishing between so-called "formal" psychiatric illness, familiar to hospital psychiatrists and hospital-based social workers, and what they called "psychiatric-associated disorders" which constituted the bulk of the psychiatric morbidity identified and managed by GPs. Summarizing the results of the 1966 study, we can say:

> Of some 15,000 patients at risk during a 12-month period, rather more than 2000, or approximately 14%, consulted their doctor at least once for a condition diagnosed as entirely or largely psychiatric in nature. The bulk of these patients would have to be classified in the International Classification of Diseases as suffering from minor affective or personality disorders, which therefore take their place among the commoner conditions in practice.

> No more than 1 in 20 of the patients identified in the survey had been referred to any of the mental health facilities despite what the family practitioners freely admitted to be the unsatisfactory nature of the treatment they were able to provide.

> The demographic, social and diagnostic contours of the population are quite different from those provided by hospital statistics. Corresponding discrepancies are found in respect to outcome and therapeutic responses. Thus the data showed that a large proportion of psychiatric morbidity in general practice is made up of chronic disorders and in a seven year follow-up study more than half of the cohort exhibited a very poor outcome in terms of recurrence or chronicity.

> Emotional disorders were found to be associated with a high demand for medical care. Those patients identified as suffering from psychiatric ill-health attended more frequently and exhibited higher rates of general morbidity and more categories of illness per head than the remainder of patients consulting their doctors.

For each psychiatric case identified in this study, the general practitioners were asked to record the social factors which they regarded as relevant, in the sense of being implicated in either the onset, course or severity of the patient's illness (Table 2). Although no factors were specified for a minority of cases, it appeared that in general the doctors regarded social factors as important in the aetiology of psychiatric illness. They tended to report concurrent factors such as marital disharmony, housing problems and work difficulties rather than remote difficulties such as childhood experiences and there was a surprising conformity of opinion amongst the survey doctors as to which factors were more common and more important. Apart from "occupational and employment problems", all the social factors were more

TABLE 2
Social factors associated with psychiatric illness

| Medical and social factors | Psych-otic[1] | Neur-otic[1] | Psycho-somatic[1] | Other[1] [2] |
|---|---|---|---|---|
| | % | % | % | % |
| Early environment and upbringing | 3.0 | 2.9 | 1.9 | 1.5 |
| Adolescent stress, engagement, premarital problems | – | 2.3 | 2.1 | 1.0 |
| Sexual problems | 3.0 | 3.4 | 1.5 | 3.0 |
| Marital problems | 8.3 | 14.5 | 10.7 | 27.2 |
| Child management | 3.0 | 4.5 | 3.4 | 5.4 |
| Dependent relatives | 2.3 | 5.7 | 6.0 | 7.4 |
| Housing and other domestic problems | 4.5 | 6.8 | 4.1 | 10.4 |
| Bereavement and widowhood | 3.8 | 9.1 | 7.1 | 7.9 |
| Occupational and employment | 2.3 | 9.0 | 11.1 | 11.4 |
| Overwork, studying, examination stress | 0.8 | 3.8 | 3.0 | 1.0 |
| Other factors | 4.5 | 7.2 | 7.1 | 11.9 |
| None mentioned | 36.4 | 32.8 | 40.5 | 17.8 |
| No. of psychiatric patients (100%) | 132 | 1249 | 466 | 202 |

[1] Percentages add to more than 100% since in many cases more than one factor was recorded.
[2] "Other" includes patients with psychosocial problems and multiple psychiatric diagnoses.

From Shepherd *et al.* [1966] with permission.

commonly recorded for female patients and the distribution of the factors varied considerably with age.

If a prediction had been made from these findings as to the kind of treatment most favoured by the general practitioners it would surely have been that advice, counselling and some forms of psychotherapy have a value at least as important as that of drugs, and that a considerable utilization of the resources and skills of personnel in social agencies might be anticipated. The findings, however, provided a sharp contrast (Table 3). The vast majority of patients received prescriptions for one or more type of drug, combined in only one-quarter of the cases with some form of superficial counselling. Although social factors were implicated by the doctors in over half of the 2000 patients identified as suffering from psychiatric ill-health, in only 27 cases was there any recorded mention of referral to or liaison with any social or welfare agency.

This study has served as a catalyst for research in the whole area of primary health care and in the intervening years since it was first published the picture concerning the prevalence, nature, treatment and outcome of psychiatric ill-health in the primary care setting has been considerably clarified. However, the central findings of the study have been confirmed repeatedly not merely in Britain but also in the United States [Regier *et al.*, 1979; Pardes and Regier, 1981], in Europe [Strotzka, 1969] and the developing world [Giel and Van Luijk, 1969; Holmes and Speight, 1975; Harding *et al.*, 1980]. Such research findings have also strengthened the argument,

TABLE 3
Treatment and management of psychiatric patients

| Treatment and management | Psych-otic[1] | Neur-otic[1] | Psycho-somatic[1] | Other[1] [2] |
|---|---|---|---|---|
| | % | % | % | % |
| Sedatives | 18.2 | 32.6 | 26.4 | 26.8 |
| Tonics and placebos | 2.3 | 5.4 | 6.0 | 8.9 |
| Stimulants (amphetamine, etc.) | 4.5 | 6.5 | 2.8 | 4.9 |
| Tranquillizers and/or antidepressant drugs | 32.6 | 19.8 | 5.8 | 14.8 |
| Reassurance, discussion, counselling | 6.8 | 25.1 | 22.3 | 33.2 |
| General practitioner psychotherapy | – | 1.6 | 1.7 | 0.5 |
| Referral to psychiatrist and/or mental hospital admission | 25.0 | 4.8 | 0.6 | 4.9 |
| Referral to non-psychiatric consultant | 6.8 | 2.3 | 6.6 | 9.4 |
| Recommendation or referral to social or welfare agency | 2.3 | 1.0 | 0.2 | 4.9 |
| Symptomatic | 6.1 | 7.0 | 25.7 | 20.8 |
| "Other" or not known | 0.8 | 0.5 | 0.9 | 1.0 |
| No treatment recorded | 34.8 | 27.8 | 27.9 | 22.8 |
| No. of psychiatric patients (100%) | 132 | 1249 | 466 | 202 |

[1]  Percentages add to more than 100% since in a number of cases more than one form of treatment and management was recorded.
[2]  "Other" includes patients with psychosocial problems and multiple psychiatric diagnoses.
From Shepherd et al. [1966] with permission.

put forward in the 1966 study report, to the effect that at the level of primary care social factors enter so closely into what physicians call "psychiatric disorder" as to justify the descriptive term "psychosocial disorder", and the need for further study of these conditions in their own right and in their role as potential pathways for intervention.

## Social Factors and Psychiatric Ill-Health

The 1966 morbidity survey indicated that substantial social morbidity was associated with psychiatric disorder in general practice but the measurement of social morbidity was entirely subjective, i.e. the general practitioner's opinion. With the development of a standardized instrument, specifically designed to provide a more objective assessment of an individual's objective material circumstances, social management and subjective satisfaction [Sylph et al., 1969; Clare and Cairns, 1978], it proved possible to investigate this association more objectively.

Cooper [1972] described a study which aimed to clarify the relationships between social factors and psychiatric ill-health in the community and to these ends a case control study was carried out involving patients from eight general practices in South London. The index cases were selected from amongst those given a psychiatric diagnosis by the general practitioner and in whom the duration of ill-health exceeded one year. Control patients were selected from the clinic attenders with no known psychiatric symptoms and individual pairs were matched for sex, age, marital status, occupational status and social class. Patients thus selected were given a standardized psychiatric interview [Goldberg *et al.*, 1970] and any index patient not confirmed as psychiatrically ill and any control patient found to have significant psychiatric symptoms were rejected. Eighty-one matched pairs were thus generated and each patient was seen individually at home and given the standardized social interview.

Mixed affective disorder (i.e. anxiety and depressive symptoms coexisting together) accounted for 80% of the psychiatric conditions seem. Anxiety, depression, insomnia, fatigue, irritability and loss of concentration were the most commonly reported symptoms while depressed mood, depressive thoughts and anxiety were the most commonly observed clinical abnormalities at interview. With regard to the social interview scores, serious social dysfunction was much more frequently identified in the index group. The intergroup differences extended across all areas of social functioning (Fig. 1)

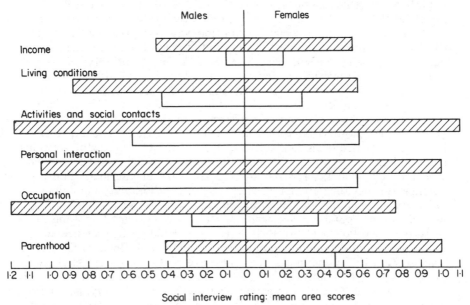

Social interview rating: mean area scores

**Fig. 1**   (From Cooper [1972] with permission.)

but when the ratings were grouped into the three broad categories of objective material conditions, social management and role satisfaction, the differences were more striking for the two latter categories than for the first. (However, the matching of the pairs almost certainly modified the extent to which material differences could show up between the groups.)

These findings provided more reliable support for the view that the problem of chronic non-psychotic illness in the community is largely bound up with affective disorder. So much is this so indeed that Cooper [1972] has argued that anxiety and depression can be viewed as "the normal psychological response to certain types of stress situation much as inflammation and fever are normal physiological responses to infection". What chiefly distinguishes the chronically psychiatrically ill patient in general practice is less the nature of his/her reaction than the frequency and persistence with which it is manifested. Intrinsically abnormal reactions dominated by compulsive, phobic or grossly hypochondriacal features comprise only a small fraction of the total. Hence, medical care devolves largely on the treatment of anxiety and depression.

Whilst the presence of social problems amongst psychiatric patients does not necessarily imply that social welfare agencies should be mobilized in every case, the detailed assessment and management of social problems is often time consuming. Some general practitioners do devote more time to patients presenting with psychosocial problems [Raynes and Cairns, 1980] but it seems clear that the effective management of a significant proportion of such patients does require the involvement of a social agency of some kind. In a pilot study carried out with the first 20 of the 81 matched pairs described above, a research team re-examined each index case to determine whether, in their opinion, social intervention was appropriate. In 12 out of the 20, social intervention was thought likely to have been beneficial, and in half of these such intervention was considered an urgent priority.

In the light of the evidence linking social difficulties and stresses in the environment with psychiatric ill-health [Cooper and Sylph, 1973; Hesbacher *et al.*, 1975; Corney and Briscoe, 1977; Williams and Clare, 1979], attention has focused on the need to provide stressed individuals with social supports or buffers. Psychosocial transitions have been identified (R.C.G.P., 1981] in which the individual is confronted with "a major discrepancy between his old world and the new one with which he is faced". Such transitions include separation from parents, relatives and friends, bereavement, marital breakdown, pregnancy, migration, retirement, sickness or disability in family members and the birth of a handicapped child. The extent to which any individual can negotiate such transitions without developing symptoms of physical or psychological distress is in part attributed to the presence of family and social supportive relationships [Cassel, 1974; Henderson, 1977; Kaplan *et al.*, 1977] and in part to the massive quality of the stressful event or difficulty itself. Vulnerability factors, which influence a person's reaction apart from his or her ability to cope with the event or difficulty, have been described [Brown and Harris, 1978] and include low socio-economic status, the presence of several young children at home, unemployment, overcrowded housing conditions and lowered self-esteem.

## Social Factors and Physical Ill-Health

During the past 30 years various studies have suggested that there is an association between mental and physical disorders. The findings of the 1966 general practice survey lent support to the concept of a true link between chronic psychiatric disorder and other forms of chronic ill-health, a view in line with the conclusions of Hinckle and Wolff that "clustering of illness occurs in some individuals with all forms of morbidity being involved" [Hinckle and Wolff, 1957]. Eastwood and Trevelyan [1971], in a carefully conducted study, confirmed the association between mental and physical ill-health in general practice patients, the link being most marked in subjects suffering from cardiovascular and respiratory disease. An independent study of patients with chronic airways obstruction reached the same conclusion [Faulkner, 1969].

A three-way link, between psychiatric and physical ill-health and social problems, is also strongly suggested. At least one large-scale American study has shown that psychosocial factors must be considered in the context of physical disorder. [Shaffer *et al.*, 1972]. The authors investigated a population for disability benefits under the US Social Security Administration's disability programme, made psychiatric assessments of such patients suffering from physical disorders and assessed the mental health of more than 1000 individuals matched with 14,000 patients attending a medical clinic. The results showed a marked difference between the two groups, giving an estimate of up to 44% of individuals with moderate or severe psychological difficulties or personality disorders among the applicants for disability benefit. Murphy and Brown [1980] found a significant association between severe life events and the onset of organic illness in women who were 50 years or younger. This did not appear to be a direct causal association but was mediated by an intervening psychiatric disturbance of an affective kind, all occurring within a six month period.

Whether social factors act causally or merely aggravate physical or psychological morbidity when it appears is unclear. What is relatively well established, however, is that disruptive events in people's lives can contribute to the risk of their succumbing to a wide range of physical illnesses [Totman and Kiff, 1979]. Over the past decade there has been a proliferation of research studies examining the role of stressful life experiences in precipitating episodes of serious physical ill-health [Dohrenwend and Dohrenwend, 1974; Rabkin and Struening, 1976; Rowland, 1977]. Traumatic life experiences and emotional conflicts have been shown to precede heart disease and also influence the course of the disease. While patients appear to function in a relatively calm and restrained manner, many live in a constant state of psychological tension such as to make clear the necessity of attending for the relief of emotional tension and the development of tolerance of stress in any therapeutic plan aimed at restoring such patients to useful and satisfying lives [Wolff, 1966; Pilowsky *et al.*, 1973]. An association has also been demonstrated between psychological factors, particularly psychosocial stress, and neuroendoctrine activity [Selye, 1946; Froberg *et al.*, 1971; Frankenhaeuser, 1975] and Bradley [1979] has illustrated some of the practical implications of this work by showing that stressful experiences may be associated with the disruption of diabetes control in diabetic patients.

Social factors may operate in surgical conditions too. Harding [1962] reported that 62% of appendix specimens removed from girls aged 11–20 were histologically normal and although he accepted that pain from the ovary might mimic appendicitis he believed that there might be a large psychological element because of the important changes that occur in adolescent girls. However, it is recognized that true appendicitis may occur within hours of an emotional upset or at a time of considerable stress [Paulley, 1955], the most famous example of this association being the operation on King Edward VII on the eve of his proposed coronation. In a recent study of life events in relation to appendicectomy, Creed [1981] found that appendicectomy patients with a normal or mildly inflamed appendix post-operatively were more likely to have experienced a severe and stressful life event and to continue to experience pain in the first post-operative year than those in whom the appendix was found at operation to be acutely inflamed.

Social factors have been implicated in a wide range of other diverse conditions and groups including physically and psychiatrically ill elderly patients [Harwin, 1973], children [Rutter and Shaffer, 1980], and women suffering from puerperal depression [Paykel et al., 1980] and menopausal symptoms [Greene and Cooke, 1980]. At the level of primary care social factors enter closely into the matrix of physical and mental ill-health, a fact underlined by the findings of a study of the health status of 2300 consecutive patients referred by 8 general practitioners to their attached social workers in the course of their routine clinical practice [Corney and Briscoe, 1977]. The ratings were made by a medical member of the research team and demonstrated that the health of the population was generally poor; only 7% of referrals were without a somatic or a psychiatric diagnosis and more than 25% suffered from both mental and physical ill-health [Fig. 2]. So impressed has one group of international research workers with such findings that they have proposed a tri-axial system of problem classification for testing and use in the setting of primary care [Regier et al., 1982], composing a distinct axis for the recording of physical and psychological symptoms and syndromes and social problems.

A further point concerning the inter-relationship between social, physical and psychological factors relates to the impact upon social functioning of physical and mental ill-health. The impact not merely of handicap and disability but also of acute and chronic morbidity is reflected in the long-standing collaboration between medicine and social work within the specialized secondary and tertiary levels of health care, namely the hospitals, long-stay asylums, homes for the elderly and hospices for the terminally ill.

## Implications for Management

Despite the impressive literature testifying to the intermeshed nature of much ill-health and social difficulties, the response, in terms of the organization of the appropriate services is far from co-ordinated. While general practitioners are independent contractors to the National Health Service, the social services are administered by the local authorities. The Seebohm Report, which was crucially influential regarding the decision that each local authority should establish a social service department, did emphasize the need for liaison between the general medical and social services. "We regard teamwork between general practitioners and social workers as vital", the

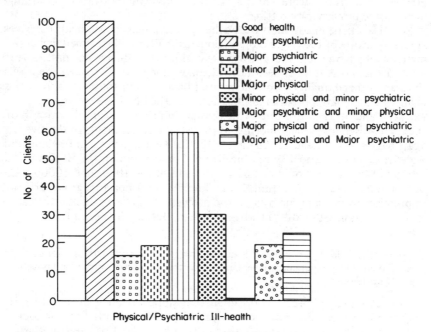

Fig. 2    Health status of clients

Report declared. "It is one of our main objectives and the likelihood of promoting it is a test we would like to see applied to our proposals for a social service department".

By such a test, however, it is hard to contest the view that the Seebohm proposals have not been entirely successful. At the time of the Report, there was considerable evidence of the lack of liaison between general practitioners and social workers [Harwin *et al.*, 1970], a state of affairs later confirmed by a national survey of Area Directors of Social Services [Ratoff *et al.*, 1973] which revealed that while the Seebohm Committee had recommended that social workers be specifically attached by GPs, only 1.5% of social workers in the country were actually deployed in this fashion.

Since then, however, the situation has somewhat improved and the literature is replete with reports of various kinds of attachment and liaison schemes involving the two professional groups [Cooper, 1971; Gilchrist *et al.*, 1978; Corney, 1980]. Yet the relationship is far from that envisaged by Seebohm to judge by the comments of social workers responding to researchers investigating the social work task [Parsloe and Stevenson, 1978]. The general practitioner was seen as someone with little knowledge of what social workers did, who was critical of the professional standing of social work and treated social workers in a patronizing fashion. While caution must be exercised in interpreting what is little more than anecdote and opinion, it is interesting to note that those social workers who were more favourably inclined towards GPs were working within some form of attachment arrangement in the primary care setting.

Social workers, in common with other professionals in the health services, appear unaware of the remarkable organizational and educational developments which have been underway in general practice during the past 15 years. Such changes will, it must be conceded, take time to work through to affect the standard and quality of primary care in general but they are, nonetheless, changes which have potential implications for the involvement of social workers, and other health care professionals in primary care. The growth of the multi-disciplinary health centre is one such development. In the five years between 1972 and 1977, the number of health centres in England and Wales rose from 212 to 731 and the Royal Commission on the Health Service estimated that there would be 900 by the end of the 1970s and 1000 by the early 1980s. At the present time, if one includes multi-partner group practices in premises owned and run by GPs themselves, it can be estimated that at least one in four GPs works in a health centre defined in a recent DHSS circular as:

> premises provided by an area health authority where primary health care services are provided by general practitioners, health visitors and district nurses and possibly other professions.

The reference to "other professions" may appear somewhat tentative. It may also be a recognition of the ambivalent position adopted by the social work profession towards primary care in general. It is of course true that social work faces heavy demands particularly in the areas of child care and the provision of social services to the elderly and the handicapped. But it is doubtful that the enormity of the current social work load is the only or the complete explanation for the persistence of the split in the provision of psychosocial care between the primary care and social services. It is also true that many GPs, particularly older ones and those accustomed to working single-handedly, are not particularly enamoured by the notion of working in a collaborative team exercise with social workers, or indeed with other professionals. There is widespread criticism too, within the medical profession, of the allegedly low level of knowledge and expertise relating to physical and mental ill-health possessed by post-Seebohm social workers [B.M.J., 1980; Brewer and Lait, 1980] which undoubtedly militates against closer collaboration.

It may well be that these various obstacles will serve to frustrate the growth of social-worker-GP collaboration from the experimental and largely *ad hoc* attachment schemes scattered throughout the country to a comprehensive primary care social service and health collaborative programme. There are signs that many GPs are able and willing to turn to other professionals within the primary care team, most notably the health visitor and the district nurse, for assistance in the management of psychosocial disorders. Whether this is an appropriate solution is a question which social workers might be expected to address themselves to and answer over the coming decade. But it is difficult to ignore the fact that the opportunity for social work as a profession to play a more significant role in the development of the primary care service has never been more obvious than at the present time. In addition to the operational developments which make it physically easier to locate other professionals alongside the GP, there are developments in the vocational training of general practitioners [Pereira Gray, 1979; R.C.G.P., 1979], a growing realization concerning the need for a more appropriate range of therapeutic responses to the demands of psychosocial disorders [Clare and Lader, 1982] and a greater awareness of the shortcomings in the quality and competence of the primary care services at the present time [Cartwright and Anderson, 1981] which, taken together, all underline the need and the opportunity for professionals with social knowledge and skills to be deployed within primary care.

## Summary

The complex inter-relationship between physical and psychiatric ill-health on the one hand and social difficulties and stresses on the other has been the subject of considerable research over the past 25 years. The implications for the optimum provision of primary health care include the need for a more comprehensive and multi-disciplinary professional response. In view of the extent to which social problems and factors are enmeshed with health and morbidity, a greater involvement of appropriately trained social workers in primary care would appear indicated. Trends in the organization of general practice services, the education of general practitioners and the classification of psychosocial disorders in primary care all suggest that the opportunity exists for greater collaboration and lend urgency to the need for a resolution of the issues which currently stand in the way of closer social work — general practice working arrangements.

## References

Bradley, C. (1979). Psychophysiological effects of stressful experiences and the management of diabetes mellitus. *In* "Research in Psychology and Medicine" (Eds. D.J. Oborne, M.M. Gruneberg and J.R. Eiser), pp. 133–140. Academic Press, London.
Brewer, C. and Lait, J. (1980). "Can Social Work Survive?" Temple Smith, London.
British Medical Journal (1980). Prescription for social work. Editorial, 2, 890–891.
Brown, G.W. and Harris, T.O. (1978). "The Social Origins of Depression". Tavistock, London.
Cartwright, A. and Anderson, R. (1981). "General Practice Revisited." Tavistock, London.
Cassel, J. (1974). Psychosocial processes and "stress": theoretical formulation. *International Journal of Health Services* 4, 471–482.
Clare, A.W. and Cairns, V.E. (1978). Design, development and use of a standardised instrument to assess social maladjustment and dysfunction in community studies. *Psychological Medicine* 8, 589–604.
Clare, A.W. and Lader, M. (1982). "Psychiatry and General Practice." Edited proceedings of Mental Health Foundation Conference, Oxford, 1981. Academic Press, London.

Cooper, B. (1971). Social work in general practice: the Derby scheme. *Lancet* 1, 539–542.

Cooper, B. (1972). Clinical and social aspects of chronic neurosis. *Proceedings of the Royal Society of Medicine* 65, 509–512.

Cooper, B. and Sylph, J. (1973). Life events and the onset of neurotic illness: an investigation in general practice. *Psychological Medicine* 3, 421–435.

Corney, R.H. (1980). Factors affecting the operation and success of social work attachment schemes in general practice. *Journal of the Royal College of General Practitioners* 30, 149–158.

Corney, R.H. and Briscoe, M. (1977). Investigation into two different types of attachment schemes. *Social Work Today* 9, 15.

Creed, F. (1981). Life events and appendictomy. *Lancet* 1, 1381–1385.

Dohrenwend, B.S. and Dohrenwend, B.P. (1974). "Stressful Life Events: Their Nature and Effects." Wiley, New York.

Eastwood, M.R. and Trevelyan, M.H. (1971). Relation between physical and psychiatric disorder. *Psychological Medicine* 2, 363–372.

Faulkner, M.A.L. (1969). The Psychiatric Status of Patients With Chronic Bronchitis. M.Phil (Psych.) Dissertation, University of London.

Frankenhauser, M. (1975). Sympathetic adreno medullary activity, behaviour and the psychosocial environment. *In* "Research In Psychophysiology." (Eds. P.H. Venables and M.J. Christie), pp. 71–94. Wiley and Sons, London.

Froberg, J., Karlsson, C.G., Levi, L. and Lidberg, L. (1971). Physiological and biochemical stress reactions induced by psychosocial stimuli. *In* "Society, Stress and Disease." (Eds. L. Levi), Volume I. Oxford University Press, London.

Giel, R. and Van Luijk, V.N. (1969). Psychiatric morbidity in a small Ethopian town. *British Journal of Psychiatry* 115, 149–162.

Gilchrist, I.C., Gough, J.B., Horsefall-Turner, Y.R., Ineson, E.M., Keele, G., Marks, B. and Scott, H.J. (1978). Social work in general practice. *Journal of the Royal College of General Practitioners* 28, 675–679.

Goldberg, D.P., Cooper, B., Eastwood, M.R., Kedward, H.B. and Shepherd, M. (1970). A standardized psychiatric interview for use in psychiatric surveys. *British Journal of Preventive and Social Medicine* 24, 18–23.

Greene, J.G. and Cooke, D.J. (1980). Life stress and symptoms at the climacterium. *British Journal of Psychiatry* 136, 486–491.

Harding, H.E. (1962). A notable source of error in the diagnosis of appendicitis. *British Medical Journal* ii, 1028–1029.

Harding, J.W., Arango, M.V. De, Baltazar, J., Climent, C.E., Brahim, H.N.A., Ladrigo-Ignacio, L., Srinivisa Murthy, R. and Wig, N.N. (1980). Mental disorders in primary health care: A study of their frequency and diagnosis in four developing countries. *Psychological Medicine* 10, 231–241.

Harwin, B. (1973). Psychiatric morbidity among the physically impaired elderly in the community. *In* "Roots of Evaluation – the Epidemiological Basis for Planning Psychiatric Services." (Eds. J.K. Wing and H. Hafner), pp. 269–278. Nuffield Provincial Hospitals Trust. Oxford University Press.

Harwin, B.G., Cooper, B., Eastwood, M.R. and Goldberg, D.P. (1970). Prospects for social work in general practice. *Lancet* ii, 559–561.

Henderson, S. (1977). The social network, support and neurosis. *British Journal of Psychiatry* 131, 185–191.

Hesbacher, P.T., Rickels, K. and Goldberg, D. (1975). Social factors and neurotic symptoms in family practice. *American Journal of Public Health* 65, 2, 148–000.

Hinkle, L.E. Jr., and Wolff, H.G. (1957). The nature of man's adaptation to his total environment and the relation of this to illness. *Archives of Internal Medicine* 99, 442–460.

Holmes, J.A. and Speight, A.N.P. (1975). The problem of non-organic illness in Tanzanian urban medical practice. *East African Medical Journal* 52, 225–236.

Kaplan, B.H., Cassel, J.C. and Gore, S. (1977). Social support and health. *Medical Care* 15, 47–58.

Kaeser, H.C. and Cooper, B. (1971). The psychiatric patient, the general practitioner, and the outpatient clinic: an operational study and a review. *Psychological Medicine* 1, 312–325.

Murphy, E. and Brown, G.W. (1980). Life events, psychiatric disturbance and physical illness. *British Journal of Psychiatry* 136, 326–338.

Pardes, H. and Regier, D.A. (1981). Incidence of mental illness. *Archives of General Psychiatry* 38, 365.

Paulley, J.W. (1955). Psychosomatic factors in the aetiology of acute appendicitis. *Archives of the Middlesex Hospital* 5, 35–41.

Parsloe, P. and Stevenson, O. (1978). "Social Service Teams: The Practitioner's View." D.H.S.S., HMSO.

Paykel, E.S., EMMS, E.M., Fletcher, J. and Rassaby, E.S. (1980). Life events and social support in puerperal depression. *British Journal of Psychiatry* 136, 339–346.

Pereira Gray, D.G. (1979). A System of Training for General Practice. Occasional Paper No. 4, Royal College of General Practitioners, London.

Pilowsky, I., Spalding, D., Shaw, J. (1973). Hypertension and personality. *Psychosomatic Medicine* 35, 50–56.

Rabkin, J.G. and Struening, E.L. (1976). Life events, stress and illness. *Science* 194, 1013–1020.

Ratoff, L., Cooper, B. and Rockett, D. (1973). Seebohm and the N.H.S.: A survey of medico-social liaison. *British Medical Journal* (Suppl.) 2, 51–53.

Raynes, N.V. and Cairns, V. (1980). Factors contributing to the length of general practice consultations. *Journals of the Royal College of General Practitioners* 30, 496–498.

Regier, D.A., Kessler, L.G., Burns, B.J. and Goldberg, I.D. (1979). The need for a psychosocial classification system in primary care settings. *International Journal of Mental Health* 8, 16–29.

Regier, D.A., Burns, B.J., Burke, J.D., Clare, A., Lipkin, M. Jnr., Spitzer, R., Wood, M., Bulbinet, W. and Williams, J.B.W. (1982). Proposed classification of social problems and psychological symptoms for inclusion in a classification of health problems. *In* "Psychosocial Factors Affecting Health." (Eds. M. Lipkin, Jnr., W. Gulbinat and K. Kupka). Praeger, New York (In press).

Rowland, K.F. (1977). Environmental events predicting death for the elderly. *Psychological Bulletin* 82, 349–384.

Royal College of General Practitioners. (1979). Trends In General Practice. R.C.G.P., London.

Royal College of General Practitioners. (1981). Prevention of Psychiatric Disorders In General Practice. Report from General Practice No. 20. R.C.G.P., London.

Rutter, M. and Shaffer, D. (1980). DSM III: A step forward or back in terms of the classification of child psychiatric disorders. *Journal of American Academy of Child Psychiatry* 19, 371–394.

Selye, H. (1946). The general adaptation syndrome and diseases of adaptation. *Journal of Clinical Endocrinology and Metabolism* 6, 117–230.

Shaffer, J.W., Nussbaum, K. and Little, J.M. (1972). MMPI profiles of disability insurance claimants. *American Journal of Psychiatry* 129, 403–408.

Shepherd, M., Cooper, B., Brown, A.C. and Kalton, G. (1966). "Psychiatric Illness In General Practice." Oxford University Press, London.

Strotzka, H. (1969). "Kleinburg: eine sozial psychiatrische feldstudie." Austrian State Publishers, Vienna and Munich.

Sylph, J.A., Kedward, H.B. and Eastwood, M.R. (1969). Chronic neurotic patients in general practice. *Journal of the Royal College of General Practitioners* 17, 162–170.

Totman, R.G. and Kiff, J. (1979). Life Stress and Susceptibility to Colds. *In* "Research In Psychology and Medicine." (Eds. D.J. Oborne, W.M. Gruenberg and J.R. Eiser), Vol. 1, pp. 141–148. Academic Press, London.

Williams, P. and Clare, A. (1979). "Psychosocial Disorders In General Practice." Academic Press, London.

Williams, P. and Clare, A. (1981). Changing patterns of psychiatric care. *British Medical Journal* 282, 375–377.

Wolff, S. (1966). Emotional stress and the heart. *Journal of Rehabilitation* 32 (2), 42–45.

# THE EXTENT OF MENTAL AND PHYSICAL ILL-HEALTH OF CLIENTS REFERRED TO SOCIAL WORKERS IN A LOCAL AUTHORITY DEPARTMENT AND A GENERAL ATTACHMENT SCHEME

ROSLYN H. CORNEY

## Synopsis

Information regarding the physical and mental health of clients referred to social workers in a local authority intake team and to a general practice attachment scheme was collected over a 3-month period. Although returns to the Department of Health and Social Security during this period indicated that a very low proportion of clients were physically or mentally ill, it is clear that these figures greatly underestimate the extent of illness present. While social workers operating outside hospital and general practice attachments have been shown to have little contact with medical staff, in this study high proportions of their clients were ill and their social problems were often associated with their illness.

## Introduction

The mental and physical ill-health of the population has previously been measured by the numbers of admissions to hospital and attendance at out-patient departments and doctors' surgeries. However, relatively little is known about the physical and mental health of the community, many of whom do not attend any medical services. General practice surveys have indicated that a high proportion of minor psychiatric disorders is found in conjunction with social difficulties [Shepherd *et al.*, 1966; Cooper, 1972], and a similar association is found between physical ill-health and social problems. Therefore, it seems likely that a high proportion of patients referred to agencies with social problems are also suffering from physical or mental ill-health or a combination of the two.

The purpose of this study was to monitor referrals to social workers in two settings: a local authority social services department intake team and an attachment scheme to 4 general practices covering approximately the same area. Data were collected on the health status of clients and the types of problems presented as a further indicator of their health.

Reprinted, with permission, from the *Psychological Medicine* 9, 585–589, 1979.

## Previous Work

In the United Kingdom official and local authority statistics give inadequate information on the health status of clients referred to social workers in social service departments. In most local authorities social workers are asked to classify each of their referrals under one category only, e.g. elderly, child in care, physically handicapped, mentally ill. Statistics, including those sent to the Department of Health and Social Security, are then based on these figures. These returns furnish an under-estimate of the extent of ill-health in the population, as they include only clients who are assessed by the social worker as having illness as their major problem and exclude all other clients referred for other types of problems who are also suffering from physical and mental ill-health.

A previous study [Richards *et al.*, 1976] investigated the physical and mental ill-health of clients referred to social workers in local authority and hospital departments in an outer London borough. The social workers were asked to make an assessment of the client's state of health, based on any information obtained on medical treatment and on their own observations made at interview. The research team, including psychiatrists, reviewed the material recorded and made their own ratings of physical and mental ill-health on a 3-point rating scale (none, minor, major). A subsequent study also obtained health status data on the first 300 referrals to a social worker attachment scheme to 8 group practices in the same borough [Corney and Briscoe, 1977]. Medical information was obtained in this second study by a psychiatrist who independently recorded information from the medical notes and also interviewed the doctors concerned. This information was then compared with the health data of referrals to the area offices of the social services department obtained in the previous study. The results showed that 45% of these referrals to the area offices were diagnosed by the research team as suffering from minor or major psychiatric illness and approximately 45% from a physical illness. Of the referrals to the "attached" social workers, 65% has been given a diagnosis of mental ill-health by their family doctor and 46% a diagnosis of physical ill-health. The amount of mental ill-health of the clients referred to the attached social workers was significantly higher than the figure obtained from the referrals to the area offices ($P < 0.01$).

The two groups of clients in Corney and Briscoe's study were not strictly comparable, however, as the information was collected over two different time periods from teams operating in different areas. In addition, the local authority social workers recorded only limited information on their referrals. In the present study more detailed information was collected on referrals to an attachment scheme and to a local authority intake team covering the same area and over the same period of time. The attachment scheme had been operating in the practice for 3 years and had become well established when the data were collected.

## Method

Information was collected on referrals over a 3-month period to (*a*) 3 social workers in an intake team ("intake group") and to (*b*) 4 part-time social workers in an attachment scheme to 4 general practices (the "attachment group"). The social workers were asked to fill in 3 specially designed forms on every client referred to them; the information included the physical and mental health status of the client, the reason for referral, and the social worker's assessment of the client's problems. They were asked to record the health status of the client according to all the information available regarding medical or hospital treatment, but not to include their own assessment of physical or psychiatric ill-health. To supplement the data obtained from the intake team, the author recorded any diagnosis made in the medical notes of the clients in the intake group who were registered at the health centre where the attachment scheme was in operation (the "intake subsample"). In the attachment group, the social workers recorded any diagnosis made in the medical notes of the clients as well as any comments regarding diagnosis made by the doctor on referral or during subsequent discussions.

## Results

During the 3-month period of data collection, 119 cases were referred to the 3 social workers in the intake team, 82 to the attachment group. Both samples contained many more females than males. In the attachment group, 80% of the referrals were women; in the intake group, women accounted for just over 60% ($P < 0.01$). Women predominated in all age groups but particularly in the attachment group for the age group 20–44 where 95% of the clients referred were female.

The age distribution of the clients referred to the groups is shown in Table 1. A higher proportion of clients over 65 were referred to the intake group. While the attachment group received a higher proportion of clients aged up to 44, the proportions of middle-aged clients (45–64) were similar in both groups.

Only 1 case was referred to intake by the primary care team in comparison with 85% of the attachment group referrals.

TABLE 1
Age/sex distribution of referrals to both settings

| | Intake | | | | GP attachment | | | |
| | Male | | Female | | Male | | Female | |
| Age group | No. | % | No. | % | No. | % | No. | % |
| --- | --- | --- | --- | --- | --- | --- | --- | --- |
| Under 20 years | 7 | 5.9 | 11 | 9.2 | 2 | 2.4 | 5 | 6.1 |
| 20–44 | 15 | 12.6 | 23 | 19.3 | 2 | 2.4 | 34 | 41.5 |
| 45–64 | 5 | 4.2 | 11 | 9.2 | 4 | 4.9 | 11 | 13.4 |
| 65+ | 13 | 10.9 | 32 | 26.9 | 8 | 9.8 | 15 | 18.3 |
| Not known | 0 | 0 | 2 | 1.7 | 1 | 1.2 | 0 | 0 |
| Total | 40 | 33.6 | 79 | 66.3 | 17 | 20.7 | 65 | 79.3 |

TABLE 2

Mental ill-health of clients referred to the two settings (the subsample of intake clients registered at the health centre in parentheses)

| Mental illness | Intake | | GP | |
|---|---|---|---|---|
| | No. | % | No. | % |
| Minor mental illness | 6 (2) | 7.5 (8·0) | 23 | 31.1 |
| Major mental illness (inc. senile dementia) | 4 (1) | 4.9 (4.0) | 4 | 5.4 |
| Alcoholism | 0 (0) | 0 (0) | 3 | 4.1 |
| Mental handicap | 1 (0) | 1.2 (0) | 2 | 2.7 |
| No diagnosis | 70 (22) | 86.4 (88.0) | 42 | 56.8 |
| Total | 81 (25) | 100.0 (100) | 74 | 100 |

Mental health was not known in 38 intake cases and 8 attachment cases.

## Health Status

The information collected on the medical diagnosis of intake clients was incomplete, and in approximately one-third of intake cases, the diagnosis was not known. The intake social workers had little contact with medical agencies and no access to medical notes. As the author recorded any recent diagnosis written in the medical notes of the 25 intake clients registered at the health centre, the information on this sample of intake clients was more complete than for intake clients registered elsewhere.

Where the medical diagnosis was known, 41% of the intake cases were suffering from physical ill-health (44% of the intake subsample registered at the health centre) and 38% of the attachment cases. The slightly higher proportion of clients with physical ill-health in the intake group could be due to the larger numbers of elderly clients referred to this group: clients aged 65 and over accounted for approximately two-thirds of the physical illness in both groups.

In the attachment group, nearly 45% of clients were regarded as mentally ill and this percentage was even higher for clients aged below 65. The majority of these clients were seen as suffering from depression or anxiety. Only 6 out of the 23 elderly clients referred to the attachment scheme were suffering from mental ill-health; 4 of those were suffering from senile dementia and 2 from depression.

Of the intake clients registered at the health centre, only 12% had a diagnosis of mental ill-health recently recorded in the medical notes. This was a similar percentage to that of the intake group as a whole. A very small proportion of clients were regarded as suffering from minor psychiatric illness. Of the 4 clients referred with major mental illnesses, 2 were over 65 and had been given a medical diagnosis of senile dementia and 2 were on the 20–44 age group with a diagnosis of schizophrenia.

*Reason for Referrals and the Client's Problems*

The reasons for referral and the problems presented by the client to the social worker also give some indication of the health status of the client. One-third of intake clients were referred for a relationship or emotional problem (this includes marital, child care and relationship problems as well as problems of bereavement, social isolation and mental illness) and over 20% with problems of physical disability or managing in the home. This latter category is used for elderly clients who cannot cope adequately at home; in the majority of cases this is due to illness. In the attachment group, nearly 60% were referred for relationship or emotional problems and a further 18% for problems associated with physical disability.

The social workers also assessed the problems of each client referred. In the intake group, just over half the referrals had relationship and emotional problems and over 40% had problems associated with physical disability. In the attachment group, nearly 80% had relationship or emotional problems and nearly 40% had problems associated with physical disability.

The social workers were also asked to make their own assessment of whether the client was suffering from emotional problems or mental ill-health. Of the intake group, 16% were regarded by the social workers as having these types of problems, while this figure was nearly 60% for the attachment group.

Table 3 indicates the entries in the official classification system used by the social workers, the figures which are sent to the Department of Health and Social Security for their statistics. With this system, each referral can be placed in one category only.

Although 11 clients referred to the intake group were diagnosed as suffering from mental illness, only 4 clients were classified by the social worker as either mentally ill or handicapped. Only 1 client was classified as physically handicapped, although 34 had a diagnosis of physical ill-health, and 7 of them were partially sighted or hard of hearing.

TABLE 3
Local authority classification of referrals to both settings

| | Intake | | GP attachment | |
|---|---|---|---|---|
| *Local authority classification* | *No.* | *%* | *No.* | *%* |
| Families with children | 45 | 37.8 | 31 | 37.8 |
| Physically handicapped | 1 | 0.8 | 3 | 3.7 |
| Mentally handicapped | 1 | 0.8 | 0 | 0 |
| Mentally ill | 3 | 2.5 | 5 | 6.1 |
| Elderly | 46 | 38.7 | 18 | 22.0 |
| Individual/adult | 22 | 18.5 | 14 | 17.1 |
| Marital | 1 | 0.8 | 11 | 13.4 |
| Total | 119 | 100 | 82 | 100 |

No clients were placed in 5 other categories in the local authority classification which are as follows: children in care, care orders, C.P. fostering, matrimonial and supervision orders.

In the attachment scheme, 5 clients were classified as mentally ill by the social worker out of a total of 32 with a diagnosis of mental illness. Although only 2 clients were classified as physically handicapped, 27 clients had a diagnosis of physical illness, 10 of them were either deaf, blind, partially sighted or hard of hearing.

## Discussion

Although the figures for ill-health among the intake clients were high, they are likely to underestimate the amount of morbidity. The information regarding health in the intake subsample was obtained from the medical notes at the health centre and these are often incomplete. The reasons for referral and the problems of the intake clients is a further indication of morbidity; over 40% of intake clients were assessed by the social worker as having problems associated with physical disability and over half had relationship and emotional problems.

The assessment of ill-health found in the "attachment group" clients is likely to be more accurate. Assessment was collected both from the medical notes and from information obtained by the social worker when she discussed the case with the doctor concerned. Moreover, over 90% of the "attachment group" clients had been in recent contact with their doctor.

These figures do show, however, that the returns to the Department of Health and Social Security greatly underestimate the morbidity of clients seen by social workers either in social services departments or in attachment settings. Clients with multiple handicaps may be classified by the social worker under "elderly" rather than "physically handicapped", and a mother with severe depression under "families with children" rather than "mentally ill".

The results of this study, together with those of Corney and Briscoe [1977], indicate that many of the clients seen by social workers are clearly ill and that their social problems are often associated with their illness. Whereas in attachment schemes there is usually close contact between social workers and primary care staff regarding these clients, this is often lacking when social workers are based elsewhere, as in social services departments [Harwin et al., 1970; Jenkins, 1978; Bursill, 1978]. This lack of contact between social workers and primary care staff has probably worsened since the Seebohm reorganization when social workers were transferred from the mental health, welfare (both formerly under the medical officer of health) and child care departments to the newly set-up social services department [Jenkins, 1978; Brooks, 1977].

This study highlights the need to obtain more accurate prevalence data on the physical and mental health of social work clients, using more objective assessments.

## Acknowledgements

This study was carried out as part of a research programme planned by the General Practice Research Unit and the Institute of Psychiatry, under the direction of Professor Michael Shepherd and with the support of the Department of Health and Social Security.

## References

Brooks, D. (1977). Social workers have not helped ir care in general practice. *Update* 14, 1395—1398.

Bursill, M. (1978). "Assessment of Social Work Attachment — Stage 2". Research Section, Kent County Council.

Cooper, B. (1972). Clinical and social sspects of chronic neurosis. *Proceedings of the Royal Society of Medicine* 65, 509—512.

Corney, R. H. and Briscoe, M. E. (1977). Social workers and their clients: a comparison between primary health care and local authority settings. *Journal of the Royal College of General Practitioners* 27, 295—301.

Harwin, B. G., Eastwood, M. R., Cooper, B. and Goldberg, D. P. (1970). Prospects for social work in general practice. *Lancet* ii, 559—561.

Jenkins, M. E. (1978). "The Attachment of Social Workers to G.P. Practices". Research Section, Mid Glamorgan County Council.

Rickards, C., Gildersleeve, C., Fitzgerald, R. and Cooper, B. (1976). The health of clients of a social services department. *Journal of the Royal College of General Practitioners* 26, 237—243.

Shepherd, M., Cooper, B., Brown, A. C. and Kalton, G. W. (1966). "Psychiatric Illness in General Practice". Oxford University Press, London.

# REFERRALS TO SOCIAL WORKERS: A COMPARATIVE STUDY OF A LOCAL AUTHORITY INTAKE TEAM WITH A GENERAL PRACTICE ATTACHMENT SCHEME

ROSLYN H. CORNEY and BARBARA A. BOWEN

## Summary

We studied clients seen by social workers in two settings, one a conventional intake team in a social service department and another where clients were referred to social workers attached to a primary health care team.

In both groups a high proportion of clients were either physically ill or disabled and the attachment group had a high proportion of clients with mental ill health. A large proportion of both groups were elderly and in general they had similar characteristics.

However, clients referred to intake teams were more likely to be un-employed, to be living on benefits in council or rented accommodation, and to have had some contact with social services before. The attachment group consisted of more women who were either housewives or working, living on either their own earnings or their husbands', and were more likely to own their own homes and not to have had previous contact with social services.

Clients referred to attached social workers were more likely to have an emotional or relationship problem, and many had practical problems as well. The implication is that attachment schemes will tap a wider section of the community and that the additional clients will have as many and as severe problems as clients referred to intake teams.

## Introduction

Several different schemes for social work attachment to general practice have recently been developed throughout the country [Gilchrist et al., 1978]. However, at a time when most social service departments are struggling to maintain a service fulfilling their statutory commitments, there are reservations about the appropriateness of allocating social workers' time to the primary care team. It is thus important to evaluate the usefulness of placing social workers at the primary care level and to compare their work

Reprinted, with permission, from the *Journal of the Royal College of General Practitioners* **30**, 139–147, 1980.

with that of the social workers in local health authority teams. To this end, a necessary first step is a comparison of the client population referred to social workers in both settings.

An earlier study [Rickards et al., 1976] provided information on the health of clients referred to the "intake" teams of an outer London borough. The social workers were asked to record information on the health status of their clients and their recent vitis to the doctor. The results indicated that a high proportion of the social service clients were suffering from ill health and that nearly half of these clients had consulted their family doctors in the month before referral. Nevertheless, although so many of the intake clients had seen their doctor recently, only five per cent had been referred by their doctor to the social services. This study confirmed the findings of a previous report by Harwin and colleagues [1970] that although general practitioners are consulted for a wide range of social and psychological problems, most doctors have very little contact with social agencies and refer very few patients directly to them.

Studies of social work attachment schemes show that referral patterns alter considerably when social workers are allocated to general practice, for the doctors then refer a wide variety of cases to them [Collins, 1965; Forman and Fairnbairn, 1968; Ratoff and Pearson, 1970; Cooper, 1971; Goldberg and Neill, 1972]. In a preliminary study we compared referrals to the social workers in a general practice attachment scheme with referrals to the local intake teams [Corney and Briscoe, 1977]. We used the area office data collected from Rickards and colleagues [1976], and compared it with data from the first 300 referrals to an attachment scheme operating in the same London borough. We found that the populations were similar in terms of sex, age, and proportion suffering from physical ill health.

The psychiatric morbidity of clients referred to the attached social workers was significantly higher, however, than those referred to the intake team and their problems were generally more likely to need casework help rather than practical measures. These differences were considered to be due mainly to the different types of referral agencies operating in the two settings and their perceptions of the social worker's role.

Our preliminary study was limited in several respects. The data from the two settings were collected over different periods of time and the information recorded from the intake referrals, having been collected in a previous study, was restricted in scope. It was, therefore, decided to repeat the study but to collect more detailed information from both teams on cases feferred over the same period of time. Furthermore, the attachment scheme had been operating in the practice for three years and had become well established when the data were collected.

## Aim

We wished to collect data on all the referrals to four social workers in an attachment scheme and to three social workers in an intake team during the same three-month period and within the same local health authority area in order to compare the client population referred to the two settings.

## Method

The four "attachment" social workers involved in this study spent about two thirds of their time on cases referred by four group practices. The remaining third of their time was spent working in the local authority area team. Three of the group practices are housed within a health centre and the fourth practice, which has three principals, is about a mile away. Together, the practices cover a population of approximately 27,500. The social workers deal with all referrals from the primary health care team and take on both long-term and short-term work.

The local authority social workers cover an area which coincides almost exactly with the area covered by the general practices. The area office has a long-term team of six social workers and an intake team of five social workers, and covers a population of approximately 47,000. Three of these intake social workers co-operated in the study and the seven social workers involved completed three precoded forms on all clients referred to them during a period of just over three months.

## Results

### Number of Referrals

During the three-month period of data collection 201 clients were referred, 119 of these to the intake team and the remaining 82 to the general practitioner attachment scheme. Very few cases were referred directly to the long-term team, except where care or supervision orders were made by the Courts.

### Demographic Features of the Population

Both samples contained many more women than men. In the health centre sample, 80 per cent of the referrals were women; in the intake group women accounted for just over 60 per cent ($p < 0.1$). Predominance of women occurred in all age groups but particularly in the attachment group for the 20 to 44 year age group where 95 per cent of the clients referred were women.•This is probably a reflection of the higher female attendance at the doctor's surgery and at the clients, as women visit their doctor not only on their own behalf but also on behalf of their children.

The age/sex distribution of the clients referred to both groups is shown in Table 1. A higher proportion of clients over 65 was referred to the intake group. While the attachment groups received a higher proportion of clients aged up to 44, proportions of middle-aged clients (45 to 64) were similar in both groups. It is possible that the total proportion of elderly was slightly higher than usual as the cases were collected from 1 January to mid-April, a period when the elderly are especially at risk.

The marital status and household composition of the clients referred to both groups were very similar. The slight differences between the two groups were due to the different age distributions. The intake team received a

TABLE 1
Age/sex distribution of referrals to both settings

| Age group | Intake team | | | | General practitioner attachment | | | |
|---|---|---|---|---|---|---|---|---|
| | Male | | Female | | Male | | Female | |
| | Number | Percent-age | Number | Percent-age | Number | Percent-age | Number | Percent-age |
| Under 20 years | 7 | 5.9 | 11 | 9.2 | 2 | 2.4 | 5 | 6.1 |
| 20 to 44 | 15 | 12.6 | 23 | 19.3 | 2 | 2.4 | 34 | 41.5 |
| 45 to 64 | 5 | 4.2 | 11 | 9.2 | 4 | 4.9 | 11 | 13.4 |
| 65 plus | 13 | 10.9 | 32 | 26.9 | 8 | 9.8 | 15 | 18.3 |
| Not known | 0 | 0 | 2 | 1.7 | 1 | 1.2 | 0 | 0 |
| | 40 | 33.6 | 79 | 66.3 | 17 | 20.7 | 65 | 79.3 |

slightly higher proportion of clients living alone and widowed clients (the majority were over 65); a higher proportion of married clients living with their families were referred to the attachment group. The two populations were very similar to each other in terms of their clients' racial origins. Approximately 85 per cent of each sample was British, 10 per cent were from Africa and the West Indies, and only ond per cent were of Asian origin. When compared with the distribution of the racial groups in the area as a whole, it appears that the West Indians and Africans make much use of the social work services.

## Source of Referral

Table 2 shows that the doctors and other health workers operating outside the attachment scheme referred very few people to the intake team during the three months of the study. This has also been recorded in previous studies [Harwin et al., 1970; Rickards et al., 1976; Corney and Briscoe, 1977]. In 40 per cent of the intake cases, the date of the client's last contact with his doctor was recorded. Where this was known, 90 per cent of the intake clients had seen their doctor in the three months before referral, implying that the doctors' low rate of referral was not due entirely to lack of contact with the client. Seventy per cent of the intake cases were either self-referrals or referrals made by relatives or friends. The agencies referring to intake were predominantly non-medical, such as the Education Department, the DHSS and the Housing Department.

In the attachment scheme, the patients were not encouraged to refer themselves but were asked to go through their doctor or another member of the primary care team. The majority of self-referrals were clients who already had some contact with the sociel workers and had been told to contact them again if necessary. Doctors referred nearly two thirds of the cases to the attached social workers, while health visitors and district nurses referred just over 20 per cent. The doctors referred patients of all ages; the health visitors tended to refer women under 44 (mostly with children) and district nurses to refer the elderly.

TABLE 2
Referral agents to the two settings

| Referral agent | Intake team | | General practitioner attachment | |
|---|---|---|---|---|
| | *Number* | *Percentage* | *Number* | *Percentage* |
| General practitioner | 1 | 0.8 | 52 | 63.4 |
| Health visitor | 0 | 0 | 12 | 14.6 |
| District nurse | 0 | 0 | 6 | 7.3 |
| Self | 50 | 42.0 | 7 | 8.5 |
| Friends/relatives | 35 | 29.4 | 2 | 2.4 |
| Education department | 5 | 4.2 | 0 | 0 |
| Other local authority department | 9 | 7.6 | 1 | 1.2 |
| Other agency | 19 | 16.0 | 2 | 2.4 |
| | 119 | 100.0 | 82 | 100.0 |

## Re-referrals

All the referrals were checked for previous contact either with the social services department or the attachment scheme. Clients who had any previous contact with either were designated "re-referrals". Table 3 shows that a much higher percentage of new referrals was referred to the attachment scheme ($p < 0.01$). In general, clients made contact with the same scheme as in their previous contact; thus the local authority clients would go back to the social services department, while attachment group clients would revisit the health centre.

TABLE 3
Referral status in both settings

| Type of referral | Intake team | | General practitioner attachment | |
|---|---|---|---|---|
| | *Number* | *Percentage* | *Number* | *Percentage* |
| New referrals | 57 | 47.9 | 65 | 79.3 |
| Re-referrals | 62 | 52.1 | 17 | 20.7 |
| Total | 119 | 100.0 | 82 | 100.0 |

## Reason for Referral

The social workers were asked to record the reasons why the case was referred using a shortened and modified version of the problem classification developed by Fitzgerald [1978]. These 23 categories were simplified into three categories (Table 4).

Table 4 shows that a higher proportion of clients were referred to the intake team with practical and material problems, whereas the attachment group were referred with more relationship and emotional problems. These differences in reason for referral occurred mainly in the clients under 65; in the elderly the reasons for referral to both facilities were similar.

TABLE 4
Reason for referral

| Reason for referral | Intake team | | General practitioner attachment | |
|---|---|---|---|---|
| | Number | Percentage | Number | Percentage |
| Material/practical problems | 46 | 38.6 | 19 | 23.2 |
| Relationship, emotional problems and minor mental ill health | 40 | 33.6 | 46 | 56.1 |
| Problems associated with physical disability | 27 | 22.7 | 15 | 18.3 |
| Other | 6 | 5.0 | 2 | 2.4 |
| Total | 119 | 100.0 | 82 | 100.0 |

Fewer than 15 per cent of the elderly in either group were referred with relationship or emotional problems. Approximately 50 per cent of the elderly in both groups were referred with problems of home management and physical disability. Housing and financial problems were also prominent. Some of these old people were referred for a social work assessment for Part 3 accommodation, others for services such as home help or meals on wheels. Among the younger clients (those under 65), just over 40 per cent of the intake group were referred with housing and financial problems compared with less than 15 per cent of the attachment group. By contrast, just over 40 per cent of intake clients were referred with relationship or emotional problems compared with 70 per cent of the attachment group.

## Housing — Nature of Tenure

Table 5, presenting the nature of housing tenure in the two groups, shows that there was a much higher proportion of owner occupiers referred to the attachment service than those referred to the intake team. However, this difference between groups occurred only with clients under 65 ($p < 0.01$) as the elderly clients referred to both groups had similar housing tenure. The differences were greatest in the 20 to 44 age group, where less than 10 per cent of those in the intake group were owner-occupiers compared with over 60 per cent in the attachment group.

The percentage of owner-occupiers in the attachment group was similar to the percentage of owners-occupiers in the area as a whole, whilst council tenants were over-represented in both social work groups.

## Financial Situation and Employment Status

Table 6 shows that the attachment group has a much higher percentage of employed clients than the intake ($p < 0.01$) and this difference is also reflected in their financial situation ($p < 0.01$). Many more of the intake group under 65 were living on social benefits, while a higher percentage of the clients in the attachment group were either living on their earnings or

TABLE 5
Nature of housing tenure in the two groups

| Tenure | Intake team | | General practitioner attachment | | Percentage composition of area covered by the schemes* |
|---|---|---|---|---|---|
| | Number | Percentage | Number | Per entage | |
| Owner occupied | 25 | 26.6 | 43 | 58.1 | 54.2 |
| Council | 32 | 34.0 | 16 | 21.6 | 11.7 |
| Rented | 29 | 30.9 | 12 | 16.2 | |
| Hotel/boarded out and other | 7 | 7.4 | 3 | 4.1 | 33.8 |
| Homeless | 1 | 1.0 | 0 | 0 | 0.3 |
| | 94 | 100.0 | 74 | 100.0 | 100.0 |

Housing tenure was not known in 25 intake cases and eight attachment cases.
* Figures taken from 1961 census.

TABLE 6
Employment status of the under-65s in both groups (where known)

| Employment | Intake team | | General practitioner attachment | |
|---|---|---|---|---|
| | Number | Percentage | Number | Percentage |
| Employed | 11 | 17.5 | 20 | 36.4 |
| Unemployed | 22 | 34.9 | 11 | 20.0 |
| Retired | 6 | 9.5 | 2 | 3.6 |
| Housewife, schoolchild or student | 24 | 38.1 | 22 | 40.0 |
| | 63 | 100.0 | 55 | 100.0 |

Employment status was not known in 11 intakes cases and four attachment cases.

dependent on others (i.e., housewives and children). The great majority of clients over 65 in both groups were retired and living on pensions.

## Physical and Mental Health of Clients

All social workers were asked to record any medical diagnosis of physical or mental illness, or handicap mentioned by the referral agent or the client. The social workers did not include their own assessment of the client's health except where a handicap was obvious (e.g., blindness or deafness). In addition, the attached social workers had access to the medical records of their clients and recorded any diagnosis written in their notes. All these diagnoses were then classified to indicate severity according to the system developed for this purpose by Eastwood and Trevelyan [1972].

The information collected on health status of intake clients was incomplete as the intake social workers had little contact with medical agencies and no access to medical notes. To supplement this, the research worker recorded any diagnosis written in the medical notes of the 25 intake clients who were registered at the health centre. Thus, information on this sample of intake clients registered at the health centre was more complete than for intake clients registered elsewhere.

Table 7 shows the high proportion of clients referred to both settings with

TABLE 7

Physical ill health of clients referred to the two settings (figures in brackets for sub-sample of intake clients registered at health centre)

| Health | Intake team | | General practitioner attachment | |
|---|---|---|---|---|
| | Number | Percentage | Number | Percentage |
| Slight ill health | 6   (2) | 7.2   (8.0) | 3 | 4.2 |
| Moderate ill health | 19   (5) | 22.9   (20.0) | 12 | 16.9 |
| Severe ill health | 9   (4) | 10.9   (16.0) | 12 | 16.9 |
| No ill health | 49 (14) | 59.0   (56.0) | 44 | 62.0 |
| | 83 (25) | 100.0 (100.0) | 71 | 100.0 |

Physical ill health was not known in 36 intake cases and 11 attachment cases.

physical ill health. The sample of intake clients registered at the health centre had a higher percentage of the physically ill than those referred to the attached social workers, suggesting that the intake group as a whole had a slightly higher proportion of physically ill clients. This could be due to the higher proportion of elderly referred to the intake group: the over-65s accounted for approximately two thirds of the physical illness in both groups.

In the attachment group, 50 per cent of clients below the age of 65 were regarded as mentally ill. The majority of these clients were seen as suffering from depression, none of them falling into the category of major ill health. Only six out of the 23 elderly clients referred to the attachment scheme were suffering from mental ill health; four of these were suffering from senile dementia and two from depression.

Of the intake clients registered at the health centre, only 12 per cent had a diagnosis of mental ill health recorded in the notes (Table 8). This is a similar percentage to that of the intake group as a whole. A very small proportion of clients were regarded as suffering from minor psychiatric illness. Of the four clients referred with major mental illnesses, two were over 65 and had been given a medical diagnosis of senile dementia and two were in the 20 to 44 age group with a diagnosis of schizophrenia.

## Social Workers' Assessments of Clients' Problems

The social workers were asked to record all the problems in each case using a checklist and to indicate which was the client's major problem. They recorded the severity of each problem on a three-point scale using set guide-lines as discussed in the pilot study.

In the under-65s over 85 per cent of the attachment group had relation-ship or emotional problems. Over 55 per cent of the group also had practical problems but few had problems associated with physical illness or disability. In the intake group these percentages were also high; approximately two thirds of the clients had practical problems and rather fewer had relationship problems.

The over-65s in both groups had a high percentage of clients with problems of physical disability and practical problems. Over 55 per cent of the elderly in the attachment group had relationship problems in comparison with one third of the intake group.

These differences between groups are not as large as those found when "reason for referral" was considered. This is due to the large proportion of both groups who had more than one category of problem.

Table 9, indicating the major problems of the clients in both groups, also shows similarities between the groups. The higher proportion of clients in the intake group with physical disability as their main problem is probably due to the greater degree of physical ill health in this group and to the larger proportion of over-65s.

Both groups had similar proportions of cases where child care was their major problem, whilst the attachment group had a significantly higher proportion of clients with marital and emotional problems as their major problem and the intake group had higher proportions of other types of relationship problem and educational problems as their major problem.

Clients under 65 who owned their own homes were more likely to have relationship or emotional problems as their major problem than clients in other types of accommodation. For example, 80 per cent of the owner occupiers under 65 in the attachment group had relationship and emotional problems as their major problem in comparison with less than 50 per cent of clients who rented their houses or were in council accommodation. The same difference occurred in the intake group but not to such a large extent.

No major differences were found between the two groups in terms of severity: the problems encountered by the attachment social workers were just as severe as those seen by the intake.

## Discussion

There are obvious methodological problems inherent in a study of this kind. It is very difficult to obtain all the data necessary for an adequate comparison to be made between groups of social work clients. It is also difficult to ensure that the social workers complete the forms in a uniform manner, for the busy social worker has little time to fill up forms additional to those of the local authority. She may have very little information about a client, especially where her only contact is with the referral agent or with the client over the telephone. The intake social workers also had little contact with medical agencies and no access to medical notes. For these reasons comparisons between the intake and attachment groups could not be made on certain important factors such as chronicity of problems and the occupation of the head of the household, owing to the incompleteness of the data.

An additional problem lies in the decision about which member of the family may best be regarded as the "client". In some cases, information

TABLE 8

Mental ill health of clients referred to the two settings (figures in brackets for sub-sample of intake clients registered at health centre)

| | Intake team | | General practitioner attachment | |
|---|---|---|---|---|
| *Mental illness* | *Number* | *Percentage* | *Number* | *Percentage* |
| Minor mental illness | 6  (2) | 7.4   (8.0) | 23 | 31.1 |
| Major mental illness | 4  (1) | 4.9   (4.0) | 4 | 5.4 |
| Alcoholism | 0  (0) | 0   (0) | 3 | 4.1 |
| Mental handicap | 1  (0) | 1.2   (0) | 2 | 2.7 |
| No diagnosis | 70 (22) | 86.4  (88.0) | 42 | 56.8 |
| | 81 (25) | 100.0 (100.0) | 74 | 100.0 |

Mental ill health was not known in 38 intake cases and eight attachment cases.

TABLE 9

Social workers' assessments of clients' major problems

| | Intake team | | General practitioner attachment | |
|---|---|---|---|---|
| *Category of problem* | *Number* | *Percentage* | *Number* | *Percentage* |
| 1. Relationship/ emotional/mental illness | 46 | 38.7 | 42 | 51.1 |
| 2. Practical | 40 | 33.6 | 23 | 28.1 |
| 3. Associated with physical disability/ illness | 33 | 27.7 | 17 | 20.8 |
| | 119 | 100.0 | 82 | 100.0 |

about the child may be recorded; in others, it may be the mother. In view of this difficulty, the social workers were asked to fill up individual sheets for each member of the family with whom they worked. In practice, however, only one individual form was completed per referral after the first week of the study.

Before the pilot study, the completion of the forms had been discussed amongst the social workers concerned. "Pen portraits" were used to discuss how the problem classification should be used. Despite this, it is likely that some of the differences between the two groups can be attributed to the orientations of the social workers concerned and the way the case was presented to them. Most of the cases in the attachment group were referred by professionals whose major concern was the clients' health. This would affect their reason for referral as well as their expectations of how the social worker should handle the case. This in turn would affect the social worker's attitudes towards the client and her selection of the client's major problem. Clients presenting themselves to social workers in a local authority setting are perhaps more likely to stress their practical or material problem at first rather than their physical or mental health, thus affecting the reason for referral.

Data on health status were also limited and the difference in mental ill health diagnosed in the two groups could be due to a number of factors. Although the majority of intake clients had probably visited their doctor in the last three months, they may have presented symptoms other than those of mental ill health. Doctors may also be unwilling to make a diagnosis of this sort especially when confronted with a depressed patient who is unemployed or is living in bad housing conditions. Doctors may be more likely to diagnose minor mental ill health when a patient complains of marital problems or difficulties with the children. Medical notes are also unreliable and the attachment social workers also included information passed on during referral as well as that recorded in the medical notes. They found that in many cases doctors would make a verbal diagnosis but not record it in the medical notes.

Despite the problems encountered, many important similarities and differences between the two groups emerged. Although the intake team encountered a large proportion of clients over 65, the elderly referred to both groups were similar in many respects. The majority were retired and living on pensions. Approximately one third of both groups lived in their own homes, one third in council accommodation and the final third in rented rooms or flats. The elderly were also similar in their reasons for referral, the types of problems presented, and the high proportion of each group who were physically ill or disabled.

The younger group also had similarities in terms of the social workers' assessments of their problems. The severity of the clients' problems (as judged by the social workers) was similar in both groups. Both groups had a high number of clients with either practical or relationship problems and a substantial proportion of both groups had both types of problems. However, more attachment than intake clients had relationship and emotional problems alone and more intake than attachment clients had practical problems alone.

There were, however, differences in the under-65s. Intake clients were more likely to be unemployed, living on benefits in council or rented accommodation. Many already had had some contact with social services before. Most referred themselves with a practical problem but would be assessed by the social worker as having other types of problems as well. The attachment group, on the other hand, referred more women who were either housewives or working, living on either their own earnings or their husbands'. They were more likely to own their homes and not to have had contact with social services. Although these clients were likely to have been referred by doctor or health visitor for an emotional or relationship problem, many had practical problems as well.

Another finding was the high proportion of clients in both groups who were either physically ill or disabled. This is similar to previous findings [Rickards *et al.*, 1976; Corney and Briscoe, 1977]. Moreover, approximately 40 per cent of both groups were judged by the social workers to have problems associated with their physical illness of disability. The amount of illness in the intake group is high considering that the intake social workers in the study had little contact with the doctors concerned and received very few referrals directly from the primary care team.

Are attachment schemes referred a different section of the population than intake teams? With the elderly, very similar clients were referred to both schemes. In the under-65s the attachment scheme was referred a much wider section of the community, more representative of the area as a whole in terms of housing tenure. Referrals thus included wives of professional men with marital problems as well as unsupported mothers on social security. This is probably due to the doctor and health visitor seeing people of all social classes with all types of problems. Without a special scheme in operation, very few of these people will be referred directly by the health care team to the social services. In this study, the intake group received only one referral from medical agencies although a high proportion of the referrals were physically ill and many had visited the doctor in the last three months.

The intake social worker, on the other hand, sees a smaller section of the community. Those who refer themselves must know about the service and feel that it is appropriate for them. This may account for the high proportion of re-referrals. Other studies indicate that there is a stigma attached to seeing a local authority social worker [Rees, 1974] and more middle-class clients may be willing to see only a social worker who is based in the surgery and recommended by the doctor.

In this study, no evidence was obtained showing that attachment clients had substantially different types of problems or less severe problems than intake clients. This implies that, although the setting up of attachment schemes will tap a wider section of the community, their clients have as many and as severe problems as clients seen by intake social workers.

## Acknowledgements

This study was carried out as part of a research programme planned by the General Practice Research Unit of the Institute of Psychiatry, under the direction of Professor Michael Shepherd and with the support of the DHSS.

We would like to thank the six other social workers involved in this study: Miss G. Clark, Mrs Y. Davis, Mr T. Jones, Mrs A. Rushton, Mrs J. Tombs, and Mrs J. Winny. We are particularly grateful to Mr D. Wiggins and Mr D. Kirkman for their help on the initial stages of the study.

## References

Collins, J. (1965). "Social Casework in a General Medical Practice". London, Pitman Medical.
Cooper, B. (1971). Social work in general practice: the Derby scheme. *Lancet* 1, 539–542.
Corney, R. H. and Briscoe, M. E. (1977). Social workers and their clients: a comparison between primary health care and local authority settings. *Journal of the Royal College of General Practitioners* 27, 295–301.
Eastwood, M. R. and Trevelyan, M. H. (1972). Relationship between physical and psychiatric disorder. *Psychological Medicine* 2, 363–372.
Fitzgerald, R. (1978). The classification and recording of "social problems". *Social Science and Medicine* 12, 255–263.

Forman, J. A. S. and Fairbairn, E. M. (1968). "Social Casework in General Practice", London, Oxford University Press for Nuffield Hospitals Trust.

Gilchrist, I. C., Gough, J. B., Horsfall-Turner, Y. R., Ineson, E. M., Keele, G., Marks, B. and Scott, H. J. (1978). Social work in general practice. *Journal of the Royal College of General Practitioners* 28, 675–686.

Goldberg, E. M. and Neill, J. E. (1972). "Social Work in General Practice". London, George Allen and Unwin.

Harwin, B. G., Eastwood, M. R., Cooper, B. and Goldberg, D. P. (1970). Prospects for social work in general practice. *Lancet* 2, 559–561.

Ratoff, L. and Pearson, B. (1970). Social casework in general practice: an alternative approach. *British Medical Journal* 2, 475–477.

Rees, S. (1974). No more than contact: outcome of social work. *British Journal of Social Work* 4, No. 3, 255–280.

Rickards, C., Gildersleeve, C., Fitzgerald, R. and Cooper, B. (1976). The health of clients of a social service department. *Journal of the Royal College of General Practitioners* 26, 237–243.

# TOWARDS ACCOUNTABILITY IN SOCIAL WORK:
## ONE YEAR'S INTAKE TO AN AREA OFFICE

E. MATILDA GOLDBERG, R. WILLIAM WARBURTON,
BRENDAN McGUINNESS and JOHN H. ROWLANDS

## Summary

Monitoring one year's referrals to an area of a social services department, we found that of the 2,436 referrals representing 2,057 cases, about half were already known to the area office. Demographically the clientele fell largely into three groups — the elderly, young families and children. The main problem groupings consisted of those with physical disabilities or suffering from frailty in old age, those with financial and environmental problems, and families with disturbed relationships and child care problems. Most of the clients had short-term help and at the end of six months only 11% of the referrals were still open.

Distinctive profiles emerged when comparing the routes by which clients with different types of problems reached the area office and the help they got once they had passed its threshold:

(a) The elderly and disabled, mainly referred by the health services, received predominantly practical help.
(b) Those with financial and material problems, largely self-referred, received information, advice and referral to other agencies.
(c) The disturbed families, referred by many different sources, received detailed exploration, assessment and casework.

Those clients who were passed on for more extended help to the long-term teams — some 10% of the intake — were mainly the very vulnerable elderly and disabled persons, and children who had been taken into care or who were in need of surveillance and protection for other reasons.

The study raises questions about the methods of service delivery in response to the demands made on the area office and discusses possible changes in approach towards more community-oriented preventive work.

In a previous article we argued the need for social workers to develop more systematic and informative ways of accounting for their ordinary day-to-day activities. We described the potentialities of a case review system (CRS)

Reprinted, with permission, from the *British Journal of Social Work* 7, 257–284, 1977.

as developed in one area office of a social services department designed to meet this need. We suggested that among other functions such a system could monitor staff resources, and practical and counselling help allocated to different client groups (Goldberg and Fruin [1].

In this article we want to demonstrate these monitoring properties of the CRS by using the data held on it to report on all client referrals to the area office during one year. We shall examine the characteristics of these clients, how they came, what their problems were, what they wanted, what they received in terms of practical services and non-material help, what modes of intervention the social workers engaged in and with which outside agencies they were in contact on the clients' behalf; we shall also show how long these cases remained open and for what reasons they were closed. We shall explore whether typical patterns emerged for different client groups. Finally, we shall consider how such service responses fit into the practical organization of the services and the theoretical knowledge available to social work.

This monitoring exercise describes "what happened" and is thus concerned mainly with input rather than evaluation of outcome. We do not know how typical the emerging picture is, since as far as we are aware, no similar information exists at present for other areas. Our impression from contacts with other areas offices in social services departments is that neither the composition of the client population (Camden [2], Cheltenham [3], Kensington and Chelsea [4], Wiltshire [5] ), nor the kind of help received are unique to this particular office. However, one of the reasons for reporting these findings is to encourage other social services departments to use similar monitoring devices in order to discover what they are doing.

## Method of Data Collection

The data on the year's referrals were collected on a referral form which contains information on the age and sex of the client, his address, his living group, the source, method and date of referral, problems presented and the nature of the request made. The "no-carbon-required" form was adapted from the referral document already in use in the department. Subsequent reviews were coded onto the case review form but the intake team used a shortened version for the majority of cases they closed. This procedure was adopted because at this experimental stage the case review form was *additional* to all the other obligatory paper work and we could not expect the intake workers to fill in a detailed form on the many enquiries with which they dealt in a single contact, often on the telephone only. The continuous stream of information was then transferred onto punch cards and magnetic tape for computer processing.

The referral and case review forms were filled in reasonably well considering the number of clients dealt with; but inevitably the pressure of work, the scant information on some of the casual referrals and the fleeting "one-off" contacts with many clients resulted in incomplete information. While we tried our best to retrieve missing data, we accepted some deficiencies since we wanted to learn how much systematic information can be gained in a routine manner under ordinary working conditions.

## The Setting

The area office serves a socially mixed district of Southampton of approximately 73,000 people, constituting a third of Southampton's population. Its demographic composition is very similar to that of Southampton.

The area contains a mixture of neighbourhoods ranging from a bedsitter/ lodging, grey type of district near the docks, through fairly stable "respectable" working-class neighbourhoods, to owner-occupied housing in tree-lined avenues.

Three neighbourhoods stand out as producing many social problems: a pre-war local authority housing estate, which still lacks amenities such as piped hot water in a substantial number of dwellings; an immediately post-war local authority housing estate, built in barrack style with little sense of "community", which has a high delinquency rate and a higher than average number of care orders; and a very modern local authority housing estate which contains half of the new dwellings being erected in Southampton and half the warden-controlled purpose-built housing for the elderly and disabled in Southampton. This area produces new community problems, such as the sense of social isolation of transplanted families and of old people, financial problems related to expensive housing amenities and lastly the substantial service needs of the frail aged living in the warden-controlled flats.

Most incoming cases are dealt with by an intake team comprising the equivalent of five and a half social workers and a part-time occupational therapist, led by a senior social worker. The senior is readily accessible for advice and consultation and he endorses all closures. During the study year staff shortages occurred which at one time reduced the intake team to four workers in all. The intake team as a rule only undertakes short-term work, estimated to last three months or less, but this does not always work out in practice. Cases requiring longer-term care are usually passed on to the two long-term teams, each having the equivalent of six full-time social workers and two ancillary staff.

## Numbered Referred — Old and New Cases

Data collection began on 1 February 1975 and during the subsequent year there were approximately 2,500 referrals representing some 2,200 cases (Table 1).

The number of referrals ranged from 170 to 240 per month, averaging about 200 — roughly just under 50 referrals per week. A referral was defined as "any incoming case requiring some social work input which is neither currently on an allocated nor on the agency review caseload". Comparing the number of referrals in 1975 and 1973, when we undertook a detailed study of referrals (Neill [6]), there was an increase of one-fifth. However, just under half of the referrals in 1975 were re-applications from clients who had previously been in contact whereas in 1973 only one-third of the referrals were old cases. This trend is also reflected in the figures we have been able to collect from other social services departments (Cheltenham [7], Kingston-upon-Thames [8]. Certain questions arise.

TABLE 1
Referrals and cases (year beginning 1 February 1975)

| Number of times referred | Number of cases | Percentage of cases | Number of episodes |
|---|---|---|---|
| 1 | 1,747 | 85 | 1,747 |
| 2 | 255 | 12 | 510 |
| 3 | 44 | 2 | 132 |
| 4 | 8 | – | 32 |
| 5 | 3 | – | 15 |
| Totals | 2,057* | 100 | 2,436 |

* Includes 804 cases known to be in contact with the department before 1 February 1975.

First, has the area office discovered most of its potential clients? This seems unlikely, although there are some indications of a broad coverage. For instance the area teams, at a conservative estimate, are in touch with one-eighth of the area's population aged over 65, including one-fifth of the over 75s. This estimate excludes clients receiving home help or meals-on-wheels services only. Similarly the number of cases of physical disability and frailty compare favourably with those expected on the basis of the national survey of the handicapped and impaired (Harris [9]): the social workers were in contact with about 30% of the estimated number of very severely, severely or appreciably handicapped in the over 65s, and about 45% in the over 75s. In contrast, however, contact with the younger handicapped adults, estimated on the same basis, could be as low as 5%. Finally, a study of the spatial distribution of cases shows differences in rates which correlate with indicators of need, particularly the standard and tenure of accommodation; the areas of higher need accounted for proportionately more referrals and long-term cases consistently over a range of client groups (McGuinness [10]).

The second question is: has the record keeping improved so that the administrative staff are now better able to retrieve information on old cases? A better filing and central record system supported by the CRS improved efficiency in tracing old client records.

Thirdly, has the area policy changed with regard to closure of cases? This is a likely hypothesis. Since the formation of the intake team in the autumn of 1974, the aim is to deal mainly with explicit requests on a short-term basis unless there are clear indications for more intensive and longer-term involvement, for example a child at risk or a vulnerable elderly person living alone. The result of this policy was that approximately 75% of all incoming cases were closed within two months, as we shall show below (Table 4). At the same time, clients were encouraged to come back if they experienced further problems.

## Age and Sex

In describing the client population we have taken the case as the unit of analysis and confine ourselves to client characteristics at first referral during the study year.

As one would expect, the age and sex distribution of the client population differed from that of the area, particularly in relation to the elderly. At least 20% of the clients were aged 75 and over compared with 5% in the general population in the area. On the other hand the middle-aged were under-represented compared with the general population. This is presumably a phase when children have grown up, when financial and family problems have eased and the more serious disabilities associated with growing old have not yet begun.

The sex ratio of this client population showed two unusual features: first, boys predominated in the young age group because of their proneness to delinquency. Secondly, contrary to expectations, there were equal propor-tions of men and women in the 65–74 age group. Further exploration showed that a considerable number of men living in two-person pensionable households came to the area office in the winter months with financial problems, many of them related to fuel bills.

Unfortunately, it was not possible to collect reliable data on social class, family size, or housing amenities, as this would have imposed too many demands on the social workers. Hence we cannot determine whether the clients differed in these social characteristics from the local population. We did collect data on marital status and living group and we shall refer to these social characteristics in the appropriate contexts.

## Problems Presented on Referral

Nearly a third of the main problems given by the referrer or identified by the social worker were associated with physical disability, illness or ageing (Table 2). Financial and material problems (17%), delinquency (15%) and other child behaviour and family relationship problems (14%) constituted the other large groups.

When we tried to compare the problem distribution with those of other referral studies, we encountered several difficulties. First, some analyses did not distinguish between types of problems and client group. Secondly, in some studies referrals for domiciliary services only were included, while in

TABLE 2
Main problems given at first referral (year beginning 1 February 1975)

| Main problem | No. | (%) |
|---|---|---|
| Physical disability/illness/ageing | 614 | 30 |
| Financial/material | 337 | 17 |
| Housing/accommodation | 217 | 11 |
| Child behaviour/family relationships/etc. | 284 | 14 |
| Mental/emotional disorder | 152 | 7 |
| Delinquency | 296 | 15 |
| Other | 119 | 6 |
| Total | 2,019* | 100 |

* Problem not known in 38 cases.

others, like our own, only social work referrals are enumerated. This greatly
affects the proportion of frail elderly in the total referrals. Thirdly, some
authorities treat casual requests and automatic notifications of delinquents
by the police as purely administrative matters. The only percentage of
referrals which occurs with astonishing regularity is that for mental or
emotional disorder — between 6% and 9%. Thus, until more uniform
problem classifications and definitions are adopted in social service departments, it would be hazardous and misleading to compare referral information
on problems in different areas.

Since we had referral data for 1973 it was possible to study trends. In
both years just under a third of all cases were referred because of problems
of physical disability or ageing. In 1975 twice as many clients presented
financial and material difficulties as in 1973. Many of these were referred
several times during 1975 — in fact, of the substantial number coming back
to the office within three months of closure, 27% presented financial and
material difficulties. This large increase was also noted in a study of social
services consumers in the same city and probably reflects the consequences
of rising unemployment and inflation (Glampson and Goldberg [11]). The
comments of the consumers also suggested that the social services department is increasingly used as an information and advice centre and as a
referral agency, particularly in relation to financial difficulties. In contrast,
there has been a fall in the proportion of cases referred with housing and
accommodation difficulties which is associated with the transfer of responsibility for homelessness to the district housing authority in February 1975.

A slightly higher proportion of delinquents were notified by the police.
The proportion of child behaviour and family relationship problems has
remained the same at 14% for both years, which is somewhat surprising in
view of the growing concern with children at risk.

Finally, referrals concerned with mental or emotional disorders had
decreased slightly. This decrease is probably related to the establishment of
a specialist team operating from a different base in close association with the
local psychiatric services.

### Problems and Social Characteristics

When we relate the problems presented to certain demographic variables
some features stand out. We have already mentioned that the preponderance
of boys under the age of 16 was almost entirely due to their frequent
referrals for delinquency. In contrast, among the 175 girls referred, only a
third were notified for their delinquent behaviour; a further third came with
other behaviour problems, of which a substantial proportion centred around
adolescent difficulties.

Single people between the ages of 17 and 44 came with a variety of
problems. This was the group with the highest proportion of mental and
emotional disturbances (24%), possibly illustrating yet again that single
people are more at risk of developing mental disorder than the ever-married.

There was a notable difference in the types of problems presented by
single people living alone and those living in families. Those living on their

own tended to come with housing and financial problems whilst those living with their families were often referred by their relatives for emotional troubles.

Among young families financial difficulties predominated and occurred in over a third of all cases. There were instances of unpaid electricity bills, wrangles with the DHSS over social security payments, deserted spouses who found themselves left with heavy debts and so on. Just over a quarter of the young families presented problems related to family relationships or behaviour disturbance in their children. This category includes cases of serious family disruption and child neglect. A further 17% of the families were referred on account of housing and accommodation difficulties.

Almost half of the middle-aged presented problems of physical disability which included serious illness such as terminal cancer or progressive diseases such as multiple sclerosis. A further fifth of these clients came with financial difficulties and 14% were referred because of mental illness or emotional problems.

As we move up the age range, problems of frailty and disability increase proportionately. Of those aged 65–74 living in family groups, three-quarters came into contact with the area office because of needs arising from frailty or disability. A further fifth came with either housing or financial difficulties – for instance, a man in his early 70s, who had lived with his married daughter, wanted to move to a place of his own as his daughter's marriage was breaking up; subsequently, he returned to the office with requests for furniture and floor covering for his new flat. Proportionately more clients in this age bracket who lived alone experienced financial problems – 26 % – compared with those living with their families – 10%. Correspondingly fewer had needs resulting from physical disability – 57% – compared with 74% of clients in family settings. These observations confirm the findings of a socio-medical study of the needs of elderly welfare clients in 1969, when those who lived alone were found to be fitter but financially worse off than those living with families or friends (Goldberg *et al.* [12]).

Among the very old needs arising from infirmity and physical disability were the main reason for referral in three-quarters of the cases, whether they lived with their families or alone. We observed that financial need as a main problem occurred less often among the very old than in any other adult client group. Possibly financial entitlements have been sorted out by that time whilst the problems of physical disability and day-to-day living assume increasing importance. Many of the referrals in this age group reflected the mounting burden on relatives who were themselves ageing. Not infrequently, a short stay in an old persons' home was requested to enable the family to take a holiday, or during an emergency when the caring relative suddenly fell ill. Problems of bereavement and depression also occurred, sometimes coupled with the request for a recuperative holiday. Needs for services such as meals-on-wheels may arise in otherwise stabilized situations because a small accident, such as a fall, can for a while completely incapacitate an old person living alone.

## The Referral Route

Almost a third (32%) of the clients came on their own initiative; if one adds the 14% referred by relatives and friends, nearly half made contact with the area office through informal channels (Table 3). This large proportion of self referrals represents a small but significant increase compared with 1973 and may be associated with the intake team's policy to respond quickly to immediate problems and to encourage clients to come back if further need arose. The next largest group, 21% of referrals, came from health personnel. Police notifications of young delinquents accounted for most of the 18% of referrals from legal sources.

Comparing informal sources of referral and referrals by health personnel with other studies, we found similarities. In over half of the 13 studies we traced, clients who came on their own initiative or on the suggestion of relatives and friends comprised about 50%, and the referrals by health personnel in most areas amounted to roughly 20%.

Four distinct configurations stand out if we relate mode of referral to type of problem: those who experienced financial and material troubles and to a lesser extent housing problems came largely on their own initiative; just under half of the frail elderly and physically disabled were referred by health agencies; delinquents were practically all referred by the police; whilst those with child behaviour or family relationship problems were referred by a variety of agencies.

Age trends were also observable in relation to source of referral. Self referrals peaked among young families (61%), their troubles being mainly financial, decreased among the middle aged (50%), fell steeply among the recently retired (27%), and were lowest among the very old (17%). There was a corresponding rise in referrals by health personnel. It is worth noting though that when it comes to financial problems even the very old tend to make the first move.

## The Request of the Referrer

We distinguished between three types of request: (1) information and advice, (2) specific services, and (3) investigation. Unfortunately, this categorization is so broad and open to interpretation by the intake workers that it tells us comparatively little, although some conceptual progress in referral categorization was made by disentangling client characteristics, problems and requests. One finding is firm: in 40% of all cases a request for specific services was made and this rose to 76% among the elderly and physically disabled. The consumer study also showed that the majority of these clients came to the department expecting some form of practical help.

The category of information and advice (27%) masks a multiplicity of financial, personal and legal problems which families tend to bring and the so-called "request" might be very vague and hardly formulated. "Investigation" (31%) can mean an administrative check to discover whether a client is known, as in the automatic police notifications in relation to delinquency, or a need for thorough exploration and assessment in a case of child neglect or an elderly person at risk.

## TABLE 3

Referrer and main problems at first referral (year beginning 1 February 1975)

| Referrer | Main problems | | | | | | | |
|---|---|---|---|---|---|---|---|---|
| | Physical disability/ ageing (%) | Financial/ material (%) | Housing/ accommodation (%) | Child/ family (%) | Mental/emotional disorder (%) | Delinquency (%) | Other (%) | All cases (%) |
| *Informal channels* | | | | | | | | |
| Self | 20 | 72 | 56 | 27 | 18 | 1 | 34 | 32 |
| Family/friends/neighbours | 20 | 9 | 16 | 19 | 22 | 2 | 13 | 14 |
| *Formal channels* | | | | | | | | |
| Health personnel | 45 | 4 | 8 | 19 | 31 | – | 10 | 21 |
| Police/probation/courts/ solicitors | 1 | 2 | 1 | 11 | 7 | 94 | 24 | 18 |
| Other local authority departments — including Housing | 7 | 7 | 16 | 15 | 13 | 2 | 4 | 9 |
| Other — including D.H.S.S. | 7 | 5 | 3 | 9 | 9 | 1 | 15 | 6 |
| Base (= 100%) | 607 | 335 | 216 | 279 | 149 | 294 | 119 | 1,999* |

* Referrer or problem not known in 58 cases.

### Area Policy and Type of Disposal

Prior to analysing the case review data, we asked the area staff and, in particular, the members of the intake team, to describe what criteria determined the type of help clients received. For incoming cases five possible ways of disposal were identified.

First are *cases in which a minimal social work service is given.* These include police notifications of delinquent behaviour where court enquiry reports are not needed or where the case is not currently known or does not present a serious risk; disabled people applying for parking discs and travel concession permits; persons requesting a home help service only; and physically disabled people requiring aids or adaptations whose situations are comprehensively assessed by the occupational therapist who will then arrange for the appropriate devices to be supplied.

Secondly, *applicants who receive CAB type of information and advice.* This group includes those who need help in sorting out their welfare benefits. In these cases, the area office often mediates between the client and the DHSS. There are also people with fuel debts who may be given advice on budgeting and on whose behalf the intake workers sometimes get in touch with the DHSS over allowances or with the electricity or gas boards to arrange repayment schedules; and lastly clients with marital problems seeking advice. (Occasionally these applicants are referred to marriage guidance counsellors or taken on for short-term casework.)

The third method of disposal is *short-term social work within the intake team.* Such work is undertaken where the supportive structure of the client is threatened; where the welfare of children is endangered by family break-up; or where elderly clients are at serious risk and immediate action is necessary.

Fourthly, some *cases are transferred to the long-term teams.* These include children coming into care; children whose family situations place them at risk of neglect or injury or cause serious child disturbance; blind or partially sighted clients, some of the very vulnerable or disabled elderly and some younger persons with serious progressive disabilities. Supervision orders go to the long-term teams as a matter of course.

Finally, after the intake team has arranged a service some cases will be put on *agency review* in order to assess, say, in three months time, whether the intervention has been appropriate.

In general, the staff said that the clearer the client's problem the more likely he was to receive attention compared to people whose problems were initially hidden or ill defined because of inadequate referral information.

### Flow of Clients Through the System

We now want to explore what actually happened to applicants from the time when they were identified as potential clients and how far their disposal reflects the area's policy. The flow diagram (Fig. 1) traces the complex disposal channels which the case review system enabled us to disentangle successfully.

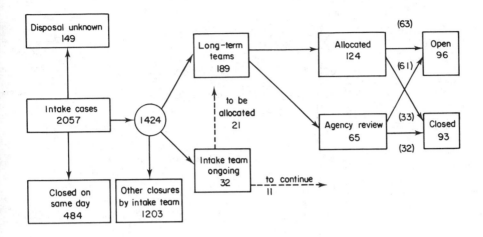

**Fig. 1.** Flow of clients referred between 1 February 1975 and 31 January 1976. (first episode only: cases followed up to 30 June 1976).

Of the 2,057 incoming cases in 1975, 149 (7%) could not be traced — an acceptable loss compared with other studies in the health field; 484 (roughly 25%) were closed on the day of referral. Of the remaining 1,424 cases, 1,203 were closed by the intake team, 11 cases were still being dealt with by the intake workers and 210 were passed on to the long-term teams. Of these 124 were allocated to individual social workers, 65 were put on agency review for occasional check up and surveillance, and 21 had yet to be reviewed. By June 1976, a further 93 cases had been closed by the long-term teams. Thus, five months after the end of the study year, of the 2,000 intakes roughly 128 cases or 6% were still receiving continuous social work help from the date of this original referral. (A study of referrals to an area office with an intake team in Buckinghamshire has produced an identical proportion of client survivals after a similar time period (James Robinson, personal communication). It should be remembered, however, that an unknown number of clients were still having home help or meals-on-wheels services and still using aids and adaptations provided by the department and benefiting from other services.

### Client Survival

An examination of the length of time cases remained open (Table 4 and Fig. 2) shows that 47% were closed within one week of referral, 64% within a month and 81% by three months. By six months, only 11% of the referrals were estimated to be open but thereafter the closure rate slowed down, and by nine months 8% were still open. We are now witnessing what our medical colleagues would call the build-up of a "chronic population". Among these long survivors were the very young and the very old; in contrast, the highest closure rates were found among the families and young single people. One

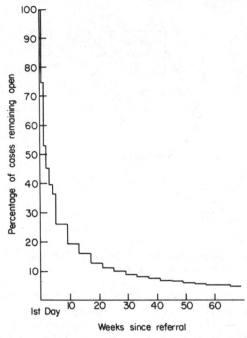

**Fig. 2.** Survival curve for clients since first referral (year beginning 1 February 1975) (n = 1902).

explanation for these trends is that speed of closure is correlated with the type of problems presented. Among the young survivors were children coming into care, delinquents under supervision orders, children at risk and a few mentally or physically handicapped children.

Physical disability was clearly associated with longer client survival among the elderly. Comparing the elderly aged 75 and over with those under 75, we observed certain differences in closure rates which are associated with the domestic unit in which the clients lived. Thus, contrary to expectations, elderly people under 75 who lived alone were closed earlier, on average, than those living with their families. The explanation is that clients in this age range who lived alone were on the whole fitter and less disabled than those who lived with their families. However, after the age of 75 the degree of disability seems to be the overriding factor and closure rates were almost identical for those living on their own and those living with others.

The speedy closure of young family cases mainly asking for help with financial and material difficulties, reflects the area's policy to deal with these problems by advice and referral to the appropriate agencies, such as the DHSS, Housing Department and so on. This intake team strenuously resisted the temptation to use their powers under Section 1 of the Children and Young Persons Act 1963 for bailing out families in debt, and instead used them towards more truly preventive purposes, for example subsidizing children attending playgroups and nurseries.

TABLE 4

"Survivorship" of clients on first referral (year beginning 1 February 1975)

| Problem | No. | Percentage remaining open after: | | | | | | |
|---|---|---|---|---|---|---|---|---|
| | | One day | One week | One month | Three months | Six months | Nine months | Twelve months |
| Physical disability/ageing | 564 | 87 | 73 | 52 | 28 | 17 | 13 | 9 |
| Financial/material | 319 | 49 | 30 | 15 | 5 | 3 | 1 | 1 |
| Housing/accommodation | 202 | 52 | 34 | 22 | 11 | 4 | 3 | 3 |
| Child behaviour/family relationships | 260 | 79 | 60 | 48 | 28 | 17 | 14 | 12 |
| Mental/emotional disorder | 135 | 84 | 71 | 57 | 35 | 20 | 13 | 8 |
| Delinquency | 284 | 94 | 36 | 15 | 5 | 2 | 1 | 1 |
| Other | 104 | 72 | 57 | 46 | 20 | 9 | 7 | 7 |
| All referrals | 1,902* | 75 | 53 | 36 | 19 | 11 | 8 | 6 |

* Includes 34 cases where problem not specified; and excludes 6 cases where closure date not given and 149 cases where disposal not known.

### The Social Work Clients Received

What kind of help did clients with different kinds of problems receive? The case review form records information on practical help provided and tangible changes effected, outside agencies in contact with the social worker, type of social worker activities, type of social worker dealing with the case and the number of contacts made with, or on behalf of, the client.

In the following analysis, we examined cases reviewed up to the end of June 1976. This cut-off point ensures that cases referred in January 1976 had a chance of being reviewed up to five months after referral. The analysis includes all those cases referred in the study year which were still open on their most recent review and a one in twelve random sample of closures for which the intake workers undertook to complete full reviews.

Looking at the general picture of help for all the clients before examining the different problem groups in detail we note (Table 5) that three types of social worker activities predominate. Exploration and assessment was recorded for over three-quarters of the cases — clearly an essential part of intake; information and advice was given to nearly half the clients and a variety of resources were mobilized in over a third of the cases. The problem-solving activity most frequently associated with social work — namely casework — was only recorded for a fifth of all clients. Over half the applicants received some form of practical service, help with applications, mostly for welfare benefits, topping the list. Social workers were in contact with a wide variety of outside agencies, most often health agencies, on behalf of four-fifths of their clients. Finally, in only a third of the cases did the social workers feel that they had achieved the aims they had set themselves. In nearly a third of all cases the department withdrew, either because they did not have the appropriate resources to meet the client's needs or because other cases were deemed to have higher priority. A fifth were passed on to other agencies.

All in all, a clear picture emerges of much information, advice, practical help and inter-agency contact for these 1,900 clients: but as we shall see below the "service packages" for different client groups contained different ingredients according to their specific needs.

### Old Age and Physical Disability

We have already noted that the health services were the largest source of referral for this frail and disabled group. The service package received by these clients reflects their needs for an array of practical support which enabled them to live reasonably independent lives in the community. Eighty-four per cent received some form of practical help, the highest percentage of any client group. These services ranged from aids and adaptations (received by 36% of cases), meals-on-wheels (23%) and home helps (22%) to a mere handful who had a holiday arranged (3%) or were referred to a voluntary visitor (3%).

For the longer-term cases, those 61 elderly and disabled people who were still open at the end of the study period, the practical help was even more

# TABLE 5
## Summary of help given and reasons vor closure

| | All cases (%) | Physical disability/ageing (%) | Financial/material (%) | Housing/accommodation (%) | Child/family (%) | Mental/emotional (%) |
|---|---|---|---|---|---|---|
| **Social workers' activities\*** | Inform'n/advice 46<br>Mob. resources 36<br>Problem solving 21<br>Review visiting 19<br>Sustaining 10<br><br>Assessment 78 | Mob. resources 69<br>Inform'n/advice 46<br>Problem solving 29<br>Review visiting 14<br>Sustaining 10<br><br>Assessment 69 | Inform'n/advice 72<br>Problem solving 26<br>Advocacy 25<br>Mob. resources 22<br>Review visiting 11<br><br>Assessment 82 | Inform'n/advice 77<br>Mob. resources 47<br>Review visiting 16<br>Problem solving 16<br>Sustaining 15<br><br>Assessment 62 | Problem solving 56<br>Inform'n/advice 31<br>Review visiting 26<br>Mob. resources 20<br>Educ. soc. skills 16<br>Sustaining 15<br>Advocacy 14<br>Assessment 85 | Inform'n/advice 43<br>Mob. resources 23<br>Problem solving 23<br><br><br>Assessment 99 |
| **Practical services\*** | Applications 20<br>Aids/adaptations 12<br>Home helps 11<br><br>None 47 | Aids/adaptations 36<br>Meals-on-wheels 23<br>Home helps 22<br>Applications 16<br>None 16 | Applications 43<br>Home helps 11<br><br>None 39 | Applications 31<br>Home helps 16<br>Ch. living group 15<br>Re-housing 15<br>None 45 | Applications 17<br>Ref. hosp./clinic 15<br><br>None 59 | <br><br>None 95 |
| **Outside agencies\*** | GPs 27<br>HVs/nurses 21<br>Police 16<br>Hospitals 15<br>DHSS 11<br>Housing Dept. 11<br>Education 10<br>None 17 | GPs 44<br>Hospitals 32<br>HVs/nurses 30<br>Housing Dept. 12<br>DHSS 11<br><br>None 16 | DHSS 39<br>HVs/nurses 18<br>GPs 11<br>Psych. hospitals 11<br><br>None 21 | GPs 30<br>Housing dept. 24<br>HVs/nurses 23<br>DHSS 15<br>Vol. agencies 15<br><br>None 46 | Education 38<br>HVs/nurses 36<br>Psych. hospitals 15<br>Vol. agencies 15<br>DHSS 13<br>GPs 12<br>Hospitals 12<br>Housing Dept. 10<br>Child guid. cln. 5<br>None 5 | GPs 59<br>Psych. hospitals 23<br>HVs/nurses 22<br>Education 22<br><br>None — |
| | Base (100%) 1,908 | Base (100%) 564 | Base (100%) 321 | Base (100%) 202 | Base (100%) 261 | Base (100%) 137 |
| *For closed cases only* | | | | | | |
| **Reasons for closure** | Aims achieved 33<br>Dept. withdraws 31<br>Referred on 22 | Aims achieved 53<br>Dept. withdraws 13<br>Referred on 13 | Referred on 41<br>Aims achieved 30<br>Dept. withdraws 22 | Referred on 38<br>Dept. withdraws 27<br>Aims achieved 20 | Aims achieved 32<br>Dept. withdraws 29<br>Referred on 18<br>Client withdraws 10 | Dept. withdraws 29<br>Aims achieved 25<br>Referred on 22<br>Client withdraws 10 |
| | Base (100%) 1,752† | Base (100%) 497 | Base (100%) 314 | Base (100%) 191 | Base (100%) 214 | Base (100%) 124 |

\* The percentages are estimated based on all Open Cases and a one in twelve sample of Closures — only aspects of social work recorded for at least 10% of cases within each group are shown.  † Reason for closure not known in 28 cases.  *Abbreviations* : Mob. resources (mobilizing resources), Educ. soc. skills (education in socials and physical skills), Applications (assistance with application), Ch. living group (changes in living group), Ref. hosp./clinic (admission/referral for assessment/treatment), Child guid. cln (child guidance clinic).

widespread. The average number of services supplied was 2.6 per client compared with 1.2 for those who had been closed by the end of the study period. Practically all — 93% — had received some practical service, over half aids and adaptations, a third home help, and nearly two-fifths had had help with applications concerned with holidays, special supplementary benefit allowances and occasionally with short or long-term admission to a welfare home. Altogether we estimate that about 3% — 18 of the 560 old people referred — went into a welfare home for long-term care during the year.

Apart from exploration and assessment on referral, mobilizing resources, that is to say, arranging practical help and supports to daily living, formed part of the intervention in over two-thirds of the cases. Information and advice was given to nearly half these clients.

Certain differences emerge in the pattern of intervention between the relatively short-term cases closed during the study year and those still open. For the relatively short-term and less complex cases assessment, advice and mobilizing resources for a practical service were the main activities. For the more vulnerable and severely disabled longer-term cases, regular surveillance (41%), some form of counselling (39%) and support (33%) were also part of the social work intervention.

Table 5 indicates that social workers were in contact with an outside agency on behalf of over four-fifths of this client group. The three agencies most frequently involved strongly reflect the central importance of disablement in the lives of these clients. GPs head the list in over two-fifths of the cases, hospitals follow in about a third of the cases and health visitors and district nurses were contacted in nearly a third of the cases. For the longer-term clients these proportions were even higher, particularly the contacts with the GP which occurred in almost two-thirds of these cases. In only 3 of the 61 open cases (5%) was no contact with an outside agency recorded. The average number of agencies contacted on behalf of the open cases was 2.3 per case compared with 1.4 for the shorter-term case. It is clear that these contacts, even if they only consist of a printed notification to the GP of the type of aid supplied or a short 'phone call to the health visitor took up a sizeable part of the social workers' time.

Finally, what about outcome? As yet we have only developed very crude and basic categories of outcome since initially the main emphasis of the CRS was on problems tackled, input and aims. Also the reliability and validity of subjective assessments of outcome are questionable. We see from Table 5 that in over half the cases in this problem group the aims, which were mainly directed towards bringing about small changes in the personal/social environment by providing a service or practical aid, have been achieved. It will also be noted that this achievement rate is almost twice as high as in other problem categories. These assessments, made by the social workers themselves, correspond well with the findings of our independent study of a random sample of consumers of social services in the same area in which the elderly and physically disabled emerged as the group who had received most practical help and were the most satisfied.

## Clients with Financial and Material, Housing or Accommodation Problems

Table 5 shows that clients walking through the door of this area office with predominantly financial and material problems, received a very different social services package. They were in the main young families, often beset by many other environmental and interpersonal difficulties. As already mentioned, the large majority (four-fifths) came on their own or on their relatives' or friends' initiatives. Contrary to general belief very few, less than 5%, were formally referred by the DHSS, though in some instances they may have suggested to clients to consult the social services department. Half of these cases were closed on the day of referral and 85% by the end of one month (see Table 4). The average case was closed within one week and received two to three contacts. The main form of practical help was assistance with applications for supplementary benefits and special grants (43%). Information and advice was recorded in 72% of these cases and advocacy in a quarter, almost always with the social security officers of the DHSS. Hence it comes as no surprise that the DHSS was the main outside agency with which the social workers were in contact on behalf of these clients. Observations in the area office and study of case records showed that the initiative for contact with the DHSS came almost entirely from the area staff, who often acted as a go-between. The area staff have suggested that this time-consuming mediation would be unnecessary if the DHSS staff themselves were better able to communicate with claimants by patient and clear explanation. The other agencies contacted most often on behalf of these clients — health visitors (in 18% of the cases), GPs (11%) and psychiatric hospitals (11%) — indicate that child care, health and emotional or psychiatric problems were not uncommon in this client group. This possibly explains why some form of casework was attempted in a quarter of this group.

In stark contrast to the elderly and disabled, only 30% of the cases relating to financial and material difficulties were closed because the social workers considered that their aims had been achieved, and over two-fifths were referred on to other agencies, mainly the DHSS. In a fifth of these cases, the social workers decided to withdraw, presumably because it was not in their power to produce the financial and other social resources necessary to put these families on their feet again. Many closure notes refer to family relationships and environmental problems which were detected but not pursued. Among these families were a number who repeatedly found themselves in financial and other crises and the area team's policy was to deal with them on an ad hoc short-term basis, rather than to get involved in long lasting, supportive relationships with very uncertain outcomes. However, when the CRS revealed the frequent re-appearance of certain families in a variety of crisis situations a small sample of these "repeater" families was selected with the aim of getting to grips with their more basic problems. The social workers found it very difficult to obtain a clear mandate from these clients to explore beyond the obvious trigger events and eventually it was decided to continue with the short-term crisis help.

The pattern of social services response was very similar for another group

of environmental problems for which the social services department did
not command the appropriate resources — the 200 cases in which housing
difficulties and problems about accommodation were the main reason
for referral. Again a substantial proportion were young families, although
a quarter were over retirement age. In this elderly group the difficulties
centred around unsuitable living conditions, rather than homelessness.
Assistance with applications was the main form of practical help (31%)
and over three-quarters in this problem group received information and
advice. Mobilization of resources, mostly in relation to housing and health,
were recorded in half these cases. These activities, as well as the frequent
contacts with the GP (30%) and the health visitor (23%), indicate that
other problems besides housing became evident in a substantial number
of cases. The homeless young families and single people often faced family
break-up and financial problems. Some old people experienced loneliness,
depression, and consequently tended to neglect themselves and their homes.

As in the group with predominantly financial troubles about two-fifths
of those with housing problems were referred to other facilities which
were either already in touch with the clients or considered to be the more
appropriate agency. In only 20% of cases did the social workers consider
that their aims had been achieved.

If we compare this comparatively gloomy picture conveyed by the social
workers of short-term advice, some practical assistance and referral on to
other agencies resulting in little or no change of the referred problems with
the statements made by consumers to independent interviewers, astonishing
differences in perception become apparent. The consumer study in this
area showed that clients who approached the area office with financial and
housing problems emerged along with the elderly as the most satisfied client
group. Clients did not expect the social services department to provide
money or a house, but to act as an advice and information centre which
would direct them to the appropriate resources. This the intake team was
able to do, thus fulfilling their clients' modest expectations.

## Problems in Family Relationships and Child Care

This group consisted mainly of grossly disturbed families in which desertion,
separation, divorce, conflict over who is to have the care of children, marital
violence, child neglect and adolescent revolt were common occurrences.
Almost every referral presented a complex situation in which several other
agencies might already be involved.

As Table 3 showed almost half the families came on their own initiative
or on that of their relatives and friends, a fifth via medical agencies, mainly
health visitors and GPs who were worried about children at risk. Schools
were also frequent referring agents, suspecting family problems or neglect
and the police referred absconders from community schools, children who
had run away from home and cases of serious parental neglect affecting
smaller children.

In these circumstances it is not surprising that the social workers were in
contact with a great variety of outside agencies on behalf of these families

(Table 5): schools and health visitors topped the list, followed by psychiatric hospitals and voluntary agencies. In only 5% of these referrals was no contact with any outside agency recorded. The average number of agencies involved in the 34 cases still open at the end of the study period was nearly 4 whilst it was under 2 for the shorter-term cases, most of which were closed within three months.

The average number of contacts per case among these very vulnerable families was the highest for any client group, about one per week. A great deal of emphasis was put on exploration and assessment, and a casework approach was recorded for over half these families. There was correspondingly less stress on practical help. In the cases still open at the end of the study year and likely to be long-term, surveillance and regular support also played a considerable part in the intervention repertoire. Mobilizing of resources, such as finding placements for children, some financial help under Section 1 of the 1963 Children Act, help with clothing and furniture, arranging outings and camps, was recorded for half these long-term situations. In the large majority of short-term cases practical help — given in 37% of cases — was concerned with applications for supplementary allowances, arrangements for temporary accommodation and holidays, and lastly with referrals to psychiatric hospitals and clinics.

In only a third of the family and child care cases did the social workers feel that they had achieved the aims they had set themselves. These aims were usually very modest — for instance, to help someone to reach a decision whether or not to embark on a certain course of action, or to clarify a complex situation by acting in a consultative capacity to another agency. In a slightly smaller proportion of these cases the intake team decided to withdraw mainly because they considered that they had not got the resources in personnel or the community facilities to enter more closely into these precarious family situations. In accordance with area policy once they had sorted out the immediate crisis and ensured that the family had a roof over their heads, some basic income and their children were not neglected or otherwise at serious risk, they closed the case, often aware that many stresses and problems were still present and had remained untouched by their intervention. The intake team also considered that when other agencies, such as probation, health visitors or general practitioners, were involved on a regular basis, they could rely on them to alert the social services if and when necessary.

## Mental and Emotional Disorders

The 137 cases of mental and emotional disorder were mainly referred at a crisis point when the mental handicap or the chronic psychiatric illness seriously upset the family equilibrium. The care of children might be endangered, and in a small proportion of cases the care of the chronically mentally handicapped was in question because of an elderly parent's incapacity to carry the burden any longer. Table 5 shows that exploration and assessment played an important part in most interventions and so did information and advice. Casework was mainly undertaken with those few

(12 cases) who were still current at the end of the study period. Outside agencies were contacted on behalf of every single case in this group, in particular GPs (in 59% of the cases).

Only a quarter of the cases referred with problems of mental or emotional disorder were closed because the aims had been achieved. In a substantial proportion — 29% — the social workers withdrew, sometimes because they considered that the situation was not amenable to social work help, or because other agencies such as psychiatric hospitals or clinics and GPs were involved. One wonders whether lack of specialist training and of familiarity with mental illness or handicap played a part in the social worker withdrawals. (Since the time of the study the area team have arranged for regular consultation with a psychiatrist and a psycho-geriatrician.)

## Delinquency

As already indicated in accordance with area policy most of the automatic police notifications were scrutinized as to the severity of the problems referred and checked whether the case was currently known. Most of the cases were then closed after the relevant information had been passed on to the police.

## Conclusions

What accounts for the service responses to the demands of clients who walked through the door of this area office?

The area social workers themselves suggest that their responses were largely shaped by legislative mandates embodied in the Local Authority Social Services Act 1970 and the Chronically Sick and Disabled Persons Act 1970. Their first priority, therefore, is to provide protective services for the most vulnerable groups — the very young and helpless and the very old and disabled. These two groups emerged as those most likely to receive long-term care.

The question then arises whether skills and resources were optimally deployed to fulfil these overall mandates as well as the many other requests made for advice and help.

We saw that the intake team spent a great deal of their time in four ways: (1) screening incoming demands, many of them for straightforward practical services; (2) providing practical help of all kinds for the elderly and disabled; (3) acting as a kind of Citizen's Advice Bureau for a great variety of material and inter-personal problems; and (4) taking on the role of a go-between or advocate vis-à-vis the DHSS, the Housing Department and other statutory bodies.

We also observed that in about a third of the cases the social workers withdrew mainly because resources had to be allocated to other urgent casualties. Among this third were families with a variety of material and relationship problems. Early and containable manifestations of family stress of various kinds, and non-material problems of the elderly, were rarely taken on.

A third feature clearly apparent was the area's policy to deal with specific episodes as they arose — much as a general practitioner would treat episodes of common or serious ailments — and to encourage clients to return should the need arise. In our consumer study clients, and especially the elderly, expressed feelings of reassurance and security that a social services department was there in the background in times of need.

If this analysis of a year's intake into an area office and the social workers' responses to it are at all typical, two further issues arise. Should the aims and functions of social services departments be as diverse and all embracing as they are at present, or should they be concentrating on more specific areas of human misery? Secondly, do social workers have the requisite skills for the roles which they are currently taking on, are they equipeed to act as information givers and advisers on such a broad front, or are they not landing themselves between several stools, being neither information experts, nor advocates, nor caseworkers?

Even at a time in which no additional resources are likely to become available it may yet be possible to think of more appropriate solutions to some of the dilemmas outlined above, which would have considerable implications for the organization of area offices, for the redeployment of skill resources and for the training of social workers. The unitary approach to social work which provides a wider, more flexible framework for viewing and tackling social problems than the older, individually oriented theories of social work, may show the way towards more appropriate solutions to the problems which confront social services departments. This approach helps us to distinguish more sharply those problem situations in which only a structural or organizational change can offer any solution, those in which a community or group response may yield possible solutions and those in which individual advice, counselling or casework seems the appropriate answer.

For example, homelessness is such a broad, structural problem for which the skills of the social services department cannot provide solutions. In Southampton, where the study was carried out, the Housing Department has now taken over these responsibilities. It has also been suggested that many financial problems landing at the door-step of the social services department cannot be appropriately dealt with by them. It is to be hoped that the current enquiry into the organization of the Supplementary Benefits Scheme will lead to a simplified and more readily understood claiming procedure, thus possibly saving many hours of inter-agency consultation and advocacy.

A new housing development in our study area, which accommodates both the young and the aged, is a good example of how a group and community approach, rather than the occasional social work visit and a routine meals-on-wheels service, might be a more appropriate form of intervention for some elderly people who are disabled, lonely and depressed. Observation and case discussion suggested that some of these old people, if stimulated by caring volunteers, might have been able to prepare their own meals. One also observed that the community facilities in these sheltered flats were empty, while the old people ate their meals in isolated silence in their little flats.

Another example was the similarity of the problems in home management, budgeting and child care, many of the young families shared. Once more it seemed that a group approach which enabled them to learn together how to make more appropriate use of the welfare system or how to draw on their own potential skills and ability, may have been more rewarding than hurried advice and referral to the DHSS. Indeed, information supplied by the CRS on the concentration, characteristics and problems of one-parent families in one particularly deprived district in our study area, has helped to stimulate plans for group work with these families (Warburton and Willmott [13]). Similar attempts at mutual help in groups have been reported from other areas (Thayer [14]).

Casework as a method of intervention at the individual and family level may be most profitably used in the early stages of inter-personal and social stress rather than as a last resort in intractable situations.

Apart from a fresh look at methods of intervention and at what level in the social system they may have their optimal impact other possibilities of redeploying resources suggest themselves. For example, requests for specific domiciliary services might as a matter of routine be channelled directly to social service officers without using social workers as assessors of need but devoting some resources to training the social service officers to spot those clients who appear to need help beyond the specific service requested. Only at that point would the trained social worker enter the case. It is also worth exploring how to develop an optimal information and advice service. Would it be more helpful to clients to create a special information and advice section manned by information officers with additional specialized training, either within the social services department or outside it by transferring some resources to Citizen's Advice Bureaux. Inherent in these suggestions is the concept of delineating clearer tasks in response to specific needs within the context of a social services team, abandoning the idea of the intake worker as a Jack of all trades.

Such a redeployment of resources and division of skills may enable some social workers to give more help to families and individuals who show early signs of stress, which without intervention may reach crisis point or develop into more chronic and intractable conditions. Time may even become available to engage in some of the preventive activities outlined in the Seebohm report, for example, providing support of various kinds to families with several children under five. Brown's work (Brown et al. [15]) has drawn dramatic attention to the vulnerability to depression of working-class women with children under five at home.

Finally, there are considerable implications for the training of social workers. The approaches outlined here demand a broad, sociological frame-work for assessing social factors in the occurrence of problem situations and greater clarity and specificity about the most appropriate methods and loci of intervention. Inherent in these suggestions is a more pragmatic model of community work which combines knowledge about the needs of an area and skills in mobilizing its resources with knowledge about the needs of special client groups and how to activate their potentialities. The framework of the unitary approach demands also that considerable emphasis, especially in postgraduate training, should be given to the function of indirect service, to the role of the social worker as an enabler and consultant to others, be they social service officers, volunteers or other community groups (Specht and Vickery [16] ).

These are some of the issues thrown up by monitoring the fate of some 2,500 referrals to one area office, which was made possible by the introduction of an easily retrievable information and review system.

The outlines of a consistent area policy emerged within the constraints of the statutory mandates and available resources but raised questions about the appropriateness of methods of tackling social problems and the deployment of social work skills. We have suggested that even within the present legislative and economic constraints, some redeployment of resources and changes in methods of intervention may shift the emphasis from an information and social casualty service towards a more community-oriented preventive endeavour.

## References

1. Goldberg, E. M. and Fruin, D. J. (1976). Towards accountability in social work: A case review system for social workers, *The British Journal of Social Work* 6, No. 1.
2. Camden Social Services Department: Planning Unit (1975). "Referrals to the Department — Area Summaries" (Background Notes).
3. Wetton, Kate (1976). The Cheltenham intake team: an evaluation. *In* "Clearing House for Local Authority Social Services Research", No. 2. University of Birmingham.
4. Kensington and Chelsea Social Services Department: Research Section (1975). "Report on New Referrals to the Social Work Division Northern Area Office".
5. Wiltshire Social Services Department: Research Unit (1975). "Intake Referral Study".
6. Neill, June E. (1974). "Study of Referrals". National Institute for Social Work Research Unit — internal publication.
7. Wetton, Kate (1976). The Cheltenham intake team: an evaluation. *In* "Clearing House for Local Authority Social Services Research", No. 2. University of Birmingham.
8. Kingston-upon-Thames Social Services Department: Development Section (1976). "Referral Statistics".
9. Harris, Amelia I. (1971). "Handicapped and Impaired in Great Britain", Part 1. H.M.S.O.
10. McGuinness, Brendan (in preparation).
11. Glampson, A. and Goldberg, E. M. (1976). Post seebohm social services: the consumer's viewpoint, *Social Work Today* 8, No. 6.
12. Goldberg, E. M., Mortimer, Ann and Williams, B. T. (1970). "Helping the Aged: A Field Experiment in Social Work", Allen & Unwin, London.
13. Warburton, R. W. and Willmott, R. R. (1976). "Referrals of Single-parent Families to an Area Office". National Institute for Social Work Research Unit — internal publication.
14. Thayer, Pamela (1976). Child minding and day care, *Social Work Service*, No. 10.
15. Brown, G. W., Bhrolchain, M. N. and Harris, T. (1975). Social class and psychiatric disturbance among women in an urban population, *Sociology* 9, No. 2.
16. Specht, Harry and Vickery, Anne (1977). "Integrating Social Work Methods". Allen & Unwin, London.

# SECTION 2

## THE SOCIAL WORKER AND THE PRIMARY CARE TEAM

# INTRODUCTION

In spite of the fact that research over the past two decades has helped to clarify and emphasize the extent to which physical and psychological ill-health are interwoven with social problems and factors, the organization of the health and social services, at least in Britain, has not adequately reflected such a development. In the area of primary health care, the general practitioner and the social worker carry out their professional activities largely separate from each other and rarely making more than a passing contact. While there are signs here and there that such a situation may be changing, it would be a sanguine observer who would maintain that there has been a significant shift in thinking or in organization since 1975. In that year there was held a joint meeting involving representatives of the Association of Directors of Social Services, the Royal College of General Practitioners and the Royal College of Psychiatrists. Widespread agreement was reached amongst the participants concerning the need for a better informed relationship between the GP and the social worker. However, at the same meeting, one general practitioner expressed the not uncommon view that the average family doctor does not understand social work and hankers after "the good old days of the mental welfare worker or the almoner rather as others complain of no servants or no longer getting the groceries delivered" [Lancet, 1975].

Such a comment gives credence to complaints by social workers to the effect that family doctors do not understand and do not value their contribution [Parsloe and Stevenson, 1978]. Resentment about being treated as "dogsbodies", whose task is to provide domiciliary, residential and other social resources without question, has been so widely and vehemently expressed as to make one wonder at times whether there is any realistic long-term possibility of the two professions working together on more than the current, piecemeal and relatively unstructured basis.

The first paper in this section, by Robert Dingwall, raises in greater detail the many obstacles to effective "teamwork" between social workers, health visitors and general practitioners in primary care. Part of the difficulty is a consequence of the differences in status between the members of these three professional groups. An additional problem is that the general practitioner is an independent contractor with a varying commitment to working in anything resembling a team. Other factors include the influence in the training of doctors of traditional hospital models of practice, and the sex and class background of the various team members. Attachments of social workers and of health visitors to general practices have of course proved satisfactory but it is difficult to contest the argument, put forward elsewhere by Dingwall, that such successes have occurred in pilot schemes with research and development-minded practices and involving people who are self-professedly pioneers [Dingwall, 1977].

Clearly there are difficulties in the relationship between health visitors and doctors but in one important respect the situation is a little less fraught than that between doctors and social workers. Health visitors, by virtue of their training as nurses, experienced in medicine and the hospital setting, are more familiar with the language and orientation of contemporary medicine and almost certainly more sympathetic to its style and activities. Social workers, however, have a very different training, are no more familiar with the language and preoccupations of medical practice than any educated lay-person and, in the main, adopt an understandably sceptical view of the average doctor's interest in and awareness of social factors in relation to illness [Huntingdon, 1981]. General practitioners, in the main, concentrate on the health or sickness of individual patients [Cartwright and Anderson, 1981], although a greater emphasis in training suggests that the new generation of practitioners may be more aware of the wider family and community aspects of their work. While some doctors clearly do wish to work in a multi-disciplinary setting, others remain happier and possibly more efficient when they see themselves as relatively isolated practitioners, having access to specialist services when they require them but not routinely exchanging information with members of other disciplines, nor indeed seeing the necessity for the involvement of other disciplines other than in a very small proportion of cases [Anderson, 1972]. In contrast, social workers appear more likely to lay emphasis on the client's social functioning, his wider relationships with family and community and the need for a steady collaboration involving representatives of many professions and agencies with which the client has or is likely to have contact.

Not surprisingly, therefore, there are even difficulties in those arrangements in which there is a measurable degree of co-operation between these two professional groups. Doctors report frustration concerning the paucity of information fed back to them from social workers to whom they have referred patients. The time taken by social workers to arrive at management decisions, together with the decisions themselves, are often a source of friction [Theophilus, 1973; Ratoff *et al.*, 1974; Brooks, 1977; Jenkins, 1978]. Indeed, differences in working tempo are a particular problem. Doctors often become impatient when immediate action is not taken by social workers to alleviate difficulties whereas the social worker, trained to take a more long-term perspective, sited within a complex and often slow-moving bureaucracy, and answerable to administrative supervisors, can rarely take decisions with quite the same degree of facility and lack of interference [Parsloe and Stevenson, 1978; Huntingdon, 1981].

Enthusiasm, therefore, for greater inter-professional co-operation in primary care should not blind us to the inherent difficulties. The inclusion of Robert Dingwall's paper serves to protect us against the charge that we have underestimated the problems involved. Yet given such problems, it is somewhat surprising to find favourable reports concerning individual schemes. The second paper, by Paul Williams and Anthony Clare, describes the successful operation of just such an attachment as seen from the standpoint of the doctors involved. The paper suggests that doctors stand to derive unexpected benefits from the attachment. General practitioners, it needs to be remembered, are under heavy attack at the present time for allegedly neglecting the social aspects of health problems and for indiscriminately prescribing psychotropic drugs to patients whose problems merit a social rather than a pharmacological response [Dunlop, 1970; Cooperstock, 1974; Trethowan, 1975]. However, GPs might legitimately counter such criticisms by questioning the value of uncovering social problems, be they causal or contributory, if they, the GPs, lack the resources with which to alter and alleviate them. However, social work attachment, if the Croydon-based experiment is a reliable indicator, assists general practitioners to be not merely more sensitive to and aware of the role of social problems but also better able to respond to them. Several of Dingwall's doubts to seem to be potentially resolvable in such a scheme; face-to-face meetings of an informal nature between different professionals can help to eliminate the more disreputable stereotyped beliefs and problems of rivalry and hold out the possibility of arriving at a more consistent, comprehensive and agreed programme of patient management.

Caution, however, has to be exercised in interpreting the accounts of individual attachment arrangements and the Croydon experiment is no exception. The opinions of the participating general practitioners were obtained indirectly by two medical colleagues from the Institute of Psychiatry's General Practice Research Unit. Nowhere in their responses do the general practitioners mention any problems of rivalry, status, authority, communication or decision-making despite the fact that such problems have been identified by their social work colleagues in the scheme. [Bowen *et al.*, 1978; Rushton and Briscoe, 1981]. This discrepancy may be due to a lack of awareness on the part of the general practitioners. It may be a consequence of doctors interviewing doctors about new methods of inter-professional co-operation. The general practitioners may well have wished to provide an enthusiastic endorsement of the arrangement because it does indeed represent a genuine advance in the organization of good primary care services and criticism, however minor, would have served only to obscure the value of the initiative. Or it may well be that such attachments have more to offer the "senior" and well-established medical professional than the "junior" and professionally insecure social worker, a point emphasised in the third paper in this section, that by Iain Gilchrist and his colleagues.

Whereas the paper by Williams and Clare is a relatively detailed account of one attachment scheme, that by Gilchrist and his colleagues provides the results of a survey of the working arrangements and the problems encountered by 219 social workers working in some form or another in the area of primary health care. The average number of problems per scheme was 4, the most common being the lack of preliminary discussion, lack of regular structured meetings and the referral of problems that are professionally unsatisfying to the social worker. It is worth considering these three problems in more detail.

The lack of discussion between social workers, area office staff and general practitioners prior to the setting up of an attachment arrangement bodes ill for the ultimate success of the venture. Beales [1978] had drawn attention to the lack of prior discussion between practices coming together to occupy a new health centre and his comments on the fact that many health centres at the present time are occupied by practices whose fundamental ethos, orientation and attitudes are fundamentally incompatible are relevant to the problem of GP-social worker co-operation. The Derby Scheme, one of the first GP-social worker schemes in the country, arose partly from historical opportunism and partly from "the enthusiasm of a few individuals" and a family doctor "keenly interested in social problems" [Cooper, 1971]. The Croydon attachment, in so far as it has worked, has benefited from careful selection of general practitioners and attached social workers whose tolerance of the differences in outlook suggests that they can work reasonably harmoniously. Without such precautions, attachments come to grief even before they start their clinical work.

As for the objection concerning the lack of discussion meetings, this is an area in which the general practitioner is going to have to be educated. Dingwall argues persuasively that GPs attend meetings only to sell a decision they have already made; otherwise, attendance is seen to be a wase of time. However, the real reason may well be the prosaic one that doctors, trained to dispense their time in sharply demarcated and relatively miniscule portions, and trained too to pack into such fractions of time a concentrated melange of exploration, diagnosis and treatment, tolerate poorly an attitude to time which strikes them as unduly wasteful and costly. Social workers, on the other hand, are used to a slower pace, spending a longer time with each client and taking decisions after much thought and deliberation.

The third problem, that of the referral of professionally unsatisfying problems, may be related to the social workers' objections to being treated like a "handmaiden" [Parsloe and Stevenson, 1978] rather than a competent professional colleague. Doctors may be more likely to ask attached social workers to provide clients with practical help, meals-on-wheels, residential placement etc. rather than asking for psychosocial assessment or counselling. Again, social workers may need to be willing to handle practical problems at the beginning of an attachment before the doctors learn to refer more complex problems to them [Marshall and Hargreaves, 1979; Corney, 1980].

Apart from such problems, the respondents in Gilchrist's survey appear not to have experienced serious barriers to satisfying practice. Indeed, two in every three said that they had enjoyed a rewarding professional experience. This does suggest that although difficulties are very common they are not insurmountable. It is also heartening to note that about one-third of the replies commented on the growth of understanding of each other's roles as a result of working together.

One problem not discussed in any detail concerns the extent to which social workers in primary care, whether in an "attached" or a "liaison" arrangement, manage all the referrals or in turn refer onwards. In those schemes where the practice social worker takes overall responsibility, the referral, discussion and feedback process is very much easier. If, however, the cases are passed onwards to others within the social work sector, feed-back can be delayed and discussions between practice staff and the social worker involved can become fragmented. The practice social worker may also have considerable difficulty in handing over cases. Such arrangements can have serious effects on the type of referrals; other members of the primary care team will not know the social workers actually handling their cases and will be wary of referring, for example, complex psychosocial problems [Corney, 1980]. As a result, those clients may only be referred to social workers who the doctors and health visitors have learnt to trust.

There is a tendency in discussions of social work attachments to forget the fact that inter-disciplinary work is not new to general practitioners. There are in Britain some 7000 health visitors, the great majority attached to general practitioners. Their apparent lack of professional rigidity together with their traditional freedom to take independent initiative have suggested to some the possibility that they might function as "a front line mental health worker" [Marsh and Meacher, 1979]. Williams and Clare illustrate the extent to which such a notion may be less fanciful than it might appear. To many general practitioners, and indeed to some hospital-based social workers [Parsloe and Stevenson, 1978], the overlap between health visitors and social workers is more striking than the demarcation between them. If social workers are tempted to regard the brief of the health visitor as more limited than their own, they would be well advised to consider the literature on what it is that health visitors do [Marris, 1969; Clark, 1972]. The unpublished Mayston Report [1969], attempting to provide a job description for health visitors, drew up a list of some 60 separate items, ranging from the provision of health education and advice to all families and individuals visited at home or seen in clinics to specific responsibilities for the health and treatment (including psychological treatment and social management) of nursing mothers, young children, the elderly, and immigrants. Hicks [1976], com-menting on the report, observed that it had drawn up a formidable list of tasks "requiring a wide-ranging knowledge and rare gifts of presentation and persuasion". A leaflet on "The function of the health visitor", issued by the Council for the Education and Training of Health Visitors [CETHV, 1977], while drawn in more general terms, covers just as extensive a field.

Social workers share with health visitors a diverse and demanding brief, if statements relating to training and curricula can be taken as evidence [Seebohm, 1968; Younghusband, 1974; B.A.S.W., 1977]. Despite the obvious fact that both professions consider themselves responsible for similar functions, the Seebohm Committee took the view that the functions of health visitor and social worker were distinct and possibly even incom-patible in one individual. This Committee disagreed fundamentally with the view that the health visitor could act as a social worker in general practice, an opinion which lives uneasily beside the fact that at least in one South London health centre over half the general practitioners regard such problems as bereavement, family break-up and marital problems, long thought to be the preserve of social workers, as suitable for health visitor intervention. One cannot help but wonder whether the problems of social dysfunction, physical ill-health and psychological distress which commonly present in primary care can be neatly disentangled and handed piecemeal to appropriate but separate groups of professionals in quite the way that those responsible for training them and for organizing our health and social services appear to believe.

Another aspect of the way such multi-disciplinary teams work in practice, and yet another that is neglected, relates to the personal relationships and knowledge of each other possessed by the various team members. Doctors often refer more in terms of the personal aptitudes, interests and qualities of individual social workers and health visitors than in terms of their respective education, technical knowledge and qualifications [Brooks, 1973]. Such a factor can be expected to operate to a greater extent in those areas, such as social work, counselling and health visiting, where the personal characteristics of the practitioner may matter as much to the doctor referring the case as her theoretical knowledge and specialist skills rather than those areas, such as surgery and gynaecology where knowledge and technical skills are at a higher premium.

In the Croydon attachment, remarkably few problems arose from the overlap in activities between the attached health visitors and social workers. In the fourth paper in this section by Roslyn Corney, health visitors in one area were asked about their contacts with social workers. Those health visitors who were attached to the Croydon health centre, which also had a social work attachment, had developed close working relationships with the social workers. Discussions were common and decisions made jointly (often with the doctor as well) regarding case management. This paper also indicates, however, that much of the work carried out by the health visitors overlapped with that of the social workers. The health visitors gave advice on a wide range of social problems, contacted agencies on behalf of their clients, and also supported those with emotional and personal problems. The health visitors working in the health centre did not regard this overlap with social work as a problem; while they did try to manage their clients' social problems themselves, they did refer on to the social workers when the problems became too complex or time-consuming.

The basic point which emerges from these papers is that social workers *can* work alongside general practitioners and health visitors in general practice settings. Whether they *should*, however, is a question considered elsewhere in this book and one upon which a number of commentators have expressed forthright opinions [Jeffreys, 1973; Goldberg, 1979; Brewer and Lait, 1980]. It does not appear reasonable to oppose such a development on the grounds that the ideological differences between GPs and social workers, their very different training experiences, the organizational arrangements which currently influence their working lives and their mutual suspicion make such co-operation impossible. It is perfectly true that such attachments raise as many awkward questions as they answer. Does the establishment of a social work attachment actually offer a "better" service to the patient/client or is it only the professionals who benefit from such an arrangement? Is such an attachment a more economical use of scarce resources? Is there less duplication of work or is more time spent on case conferences, joint visiting and working through hurt feelings? Can the primary team evolve so that the health visitor, by virtue of her contact with the healthy as well as the ill, acts to screen and detect early signs of ill-health and social dysfunction with the social worker and general practitioner providing a more comprehensive physical/psychological and social response for those who turn out to require them? And, finally, the whole discussion of the relative importance of such professionals as health visitors and social workers, raises the prickly question of efficacy. Given the solemn insistence that the tasks of social worker and health visitor can indeed be separated to some measurable extent, what is the evidence of their efficacy in those areas in which they and they alone are trained to intervene?

On the answers to some if not all of these questions, the precise composition of the ideal primary health care team turns. It would seem reasonable in the light of the findings of the literature already mentioned, that the factors influencing the team composition should include the interests and the abilities of available personnel, the number of general practitioners involved, the age, sex and socio-economic profile of the population served by the practice or health centre, and its location [Brooks, 1973]. The range of possible professionals who could and indeed are involved is extensive, ranging from psychiatrists and community psychiatric nurses, clinical psychologists and paediatricians to marriage guidance counsellors, pastoral counsellors and volunteers attached to lay organizations. There is a danger in this proliferation. Increasing the number of actual people involved in primary care may well defeat one of the principal aims of an integrated response, namely the improvement of communication. The crucial question, implicit in all this multi-professional interest, is one which social work ignores at its peril. Other professionals and non-professionals are clearly anxious to become more involved in primary care work. The social component of so much of what presents to primary care facilities does suggest that if social workers are the appropriate group to tackle such problems then some of them at least should be where this action is. But once again the issue of where best to deploy social workers returns us to that crucial question – what is it that social workers do? It is one of the ironies of primary care that in the enthusiasm with which it beckons social work (and other orientations) into its ambit it should further intensify the scrutiny currently being focused on what precisely it is that constitutes the core knowledge of social work itself [Butrym, 1976; Parsloe and Stevenson, 1978; Goldberg and Warburton, 1979; Barclay Commission, 1982].

## References

Anderson, D. (1972). Working with the family doctor: A programme for mental health. *British Medical Journal* 4, 781–784.

Barclay Commission (1982). Social Workers: their role and tasks. National Institute for Social Work. Bedford Square Press, London.

Beales, J. G. (1978). "Sick Health Centres". Pitman Medical, London.

Bowen, B., Davies, Y. A., Rushton, A. and Winny, J. (1978). Adventure into health. *Update* 6, 1512–1515.

Brewer, C. and Lait, J. (1980). "Can Social Work Survive?" Temple Smith, London.

British Association of Social Workers. (1977). "The Social Work Task". BASW Publications.

Brooks, D. (1977). Social workers have not helped in care in general practice. *Update* 14, 1395–1398.

Brooks, M. B. (1973). Management of the team in general practice. *Journal of the Royal College of General Practitioners* 23, 239–252.

Butrym, Z. (1976). "The Nature of Social Work". Macmillan, London.

Cartwright, A. and Anderson, R. (1981). "General Practice Revisited". Tavistock, London.

Clark, J. (1972). What do health visitors do? *Nursing Times* 68, Occasional Papers, 117.

Cooper, B. (1971). Social work in general practice: The Derby scheme. *Lancet* 1, 539–542.

Cooperstock, R. (1974). Some factors involved in the increased prescribing of psychotropic drugs. *In* "Social Aspects of The Medical Use of Psychotropic Drugs". (Ed. R. Cooperstock), pp. 21–34. Addiction Research Foundation, Ontario.

Corney, R. H. (1980). Factors affecting the operation and success of social work attachment schemes to general practice. *Journal of the Royal College of General Practitioners* 30, 149–158.

Council for the Education and Training of Health Visitors. (1977). "An Investigation Into the Principles of Health Visiting: a Report of a Working Group". Council for the Education and Training of Health Visitors, London.

Dingwall, R. (1977). "The Social Organization of Health Visitor Training". Croom Helm, London.

Dunlop, D. (1970). The use and abuse of psychotropic drugs. *Proceedings of the Royal Society of Medicine* 63, 1279–1282.

Goldberg, E. M. (1979). The role of social work in relation to general practice in the mental health field. *In* "New Methods of Mental Health Care". (Ed. Meacher, M.). Pergamon Press, Oxford.

Goldberg, E. M. and Warburton, R. W. (1979). Ends and means in social work. "National Institute Social Services Library, No. 35". George Allen & Unwin, London.

Hicks, D. (1976). "Primary Health Care". HMSO, London.

Huntingdon, J. (1981). "Social Work and General Medical Practice". George Allen & Unwin, London.

Jeffries, M. (1973). The social worker and the health visitor. *Health Bulletin* XXXI, 2, 72–75.

Jenkins, M. E. (1978). "The Attachment of Social Workers to GP Practices". Research Section, Mid Glamorgan County Council.

Lancet. (1975). Psychiatrists, social workers and family doctors. *Lancet, Editorial* 2, 805–806.

Marris, T. (1969). "The Work of Health Visitors in London: A Department of Planning and Transportation Survey". Greater London Council, Research Report No. 12. GLC, London.

Marsh, G. and Meacher, M. (1979). The primary health care team: The way forward for mental health care. *In* "New Methods of Mental Health Care". (Ed. Meacher, M.). Pergamon, Oxford.

Marshall, M. and Hargreaves, M. (1979). So you want to try GP attachment. *Social Work Today* 10, 42, 25–26.

Mayston Report. (1969). "Report of the Working Party on Management Structure in the Local Authority Nursing Services". HMSO, London.

Parsloe, P. and Stevenson, O. (1978). "Social Service Teams: The Practitioner's View". HMSO, London.

Ratoff, L., Rose, A. and Smith, C. (1974). Social workers and GPs: problems of working together. *Social Work Today* **5**, 16, 497–500.

Rushton, A. and Briscoe, M. (1981). Social work as an aspect of primary health care: the social worker's view. *British Journal of Social Work* **11**, 61–76.

Seebohm Report. (1968). "Report of the Committee on Local Authority and Allied Personal Social Services". HMSO, London.

Theophilus, A. (1973). General practitioners and social workers, collaboration or conflict. *Clearing House for Local Authority Social Services Research* **10**, 29–53.

Trethowan, W. H. (1975). Pills for personal problems. *British Medical Journal* **3**, 749–751.

Younghusband, E. (1974). The future of social work. *Social Work Today* **6**, 33–37.

# PROBLEMS OF TEAMWORK IN PRIMARY CARE

## ROBERT DINGWALL

Teamwork is a concept which has played an increasing part in discussions of the health and personal social services over the last 20 years or so. The very familiarity of the metaphor employed, however, may make its meaning in such discussions that much more problematic. Given its established place in English usage,[1] it is easy to employ the term without an explicit awareness of its meaning and to generate confusion as the same term is used to cover a number of different senses. I shall begin this chapter by making certain suggestions about the way in which the concept of teamwork might be analysed. From this, I shall seek to demonstrate how it may be invoked to solve certain sorts of everyday occupational problem. Finally, I shall apply this analysis to some empirical data[2] on the relations between general practitioners (GPs), health visitors and social workers in the primary care team. Obviously this can only give a selective picture omitting as it does, for example, any discussion of hospital doctors, district nurses and other practice staff. However, in an account of this length compromise seems inevitable.

## Teamwork as a Concept

In our everyday social activities we generally find it convenient to treat the social world as if it had the same objective reality as we conventionally ascribe to the material world. Such a fiction is indeed essential to the possibility of acting. Were we to reflect constantly on our mundane activities, we would rapidly be reduced to a state of paralysis. For many social scientists, however, social relationships, organisations, institutions, collectivities or whatever are not treated as though they had such a material existence. On the contrary, they are seen as human products created and sustained against a background of more or less shared cultural knowledge. This perspective gives a particular role to language as the principal medium of inter-subjective communication by which these processes of reality construction can be jointly executed. "Team" is one linguistic term which is available to participants in such an enterprise.

Reprinted, with permission, from "Teamwork in the Health and Social Services" (Eds T. Briggs, A. Webb and F. Lonsdale), pp. 111–137, Croom Helm, London, 1979.

It would, however, be a mistake to regard "team" as a term which had any definite and determinate sense. The view of language adopted here has much in common with that of the later work of Wittgenstein [1972]. In this, he rejects the view that words picture the world, as a direct representation of phenomena, and that the task of philosophy is to repair the failings of ordinary language and to draw better and more accurate pictures. On the contrary, he sees words as *used* to picture the world. One of his central metaphors depicts words as tools which may be used now this way, now that way according to the purposes of the user. In a second key metaphor, of language as a game, or set of games, Wittgenstein extends this point. In talking of a game, he is not implying that language use is a frivolous activity. Rather, he is stressing that words are used to do things with; they do not just stand as self-contained and isolated phenomena. Words always occur in a context to which they relate, and which helps us to understand how they should be interpreted. In the present discussion, this suggests a series of questions about what people might be trying to do by invoking the concept of a team rather than simply legislating a definition and drawing ironic contrasts with observable events.

Some of these questions are developed further in Bittner's [1965] paper on the concept of organisation. In this, he criticises traditional approaches to the study of organisations for drawing misleading and ironic comparisons between normative idealisations of "formal organisation" and empirically observable "informal organisation". The programmatic constructions which constitute the idealised formal organisation are borrowed from participants, or at least some of them, and then used to describe what is observed. "Organisation" in Bittner's view is a term which any society member may employ as a means of yoking together individual pieces of social action and presenting them as a stable and concerted whole. Where we are most conscious of the regularity of this process we may give the resulting collection a unique name — Area Health Authority, Social Services Department or whatever — to substitute for the generic term "organisation". The sociologist who studies an organisation is studying a phenomenon which is already given to him by its members who are ordering their own actions, or interpreting those of others as ordered, by reference to the very concept which the sociologist then uses to evaluate them. Like the view of philosophy criticised by Wittgenstein, this approach neglects the empirical usage which members find wholly adequate for their practical purposes in favour of an abstracted idealisation which is given normative priority.

What Bittner and others have argued is that, if we are to understand organisations, then we must direct our attention to the mundane instances of action from which they are constituted. How do actors themselves link actions so as to make them apparently stable and concerted? The formal schemes of the managerial technician are treated as merely one way of using the concept of organisation, moves in one language game with a tool that may be put to many uses. Organisational schemes in the minds of actors are generalised formulae to which a variety of everyday events may be brought for interpretation and recognition as organisationally relevant or irrelevant. The formula is a practical way of resolving problems which arise from the indeterminacy of the social world.

How might we use this to advance our analysis on teamwork in primary care? In a sense, we can merely substitute "team" for "organisation" in the foregoing discussion. I would suggest that attempts by analysts to legislate a definition of "team" which can be used to repair the deficiencies, by that standard, of members' concepts are unlikely to be profitable. It is more important to examine actors' definitions and the uses to which they are put. I would stress the plural nature of "definitions" here. "Team" is a term which is widely available to primary-care personnel as a linguistic tool. As such it may be employed in a number of ways, the variety of which is obscured by the use of a single term. Like "organisation", "team" is used to concert separate pieces of action by reference to a conceptual formula. Various mundane problems are brought to it for resolution and in their solution give teamwork its distinctive meaning.

The following sections of this account explore in more detail the nature of the problems which teamwork is asked to resolve in primary care. I shall begin by looking at some issues raised by investigations into the classic sociological topic of the division of labour and more recent work in the sociology of occupations. From this I shall proceed to an analysis of the concrete situations of the three main occupations in the primary care team and the way in which these contribute to the social reality of teamwork.

## Why Teamwork?

As a concept in the domain of health and social services, "team" has gone in and out of fashion. In a personal communication, Noel Timms has remarked on its currency in the early days of the child care service. For present purposes, though, I am more interested in its revival over the last decade or so, although some of my arguments, particularly on the relationships between this revival and the creation of social services departments, might well have implications for our understanding of this earlier period.

I have already suggested that "team" can be thought of as a device for con-certing action. People can refer to "the team" as a way of co-ordinating a set of individual activities. By implication, it seems plausible to suggest that the term came into use because it was felt that actions were not being concerted which ought to be. How might this come about? On the one hand, it might be that some previous device lost its original legitimacy or, on the other, it might be that some new set of activities emerged from which no existing device could be invoked. These possibilities are not, of course, mutually exclusive.

Talking about problems of co-ordinating action is, however, another way of describing a classical sociological concern: the division of labour.[3] Durk-heim, Weber and Marx all saw this as one of the problematic features of modern societies. Primitive societies, in their view, were marked by an organic unity of labour, such that any member could, in principle, turn his hand to any task. Even where craft specialisation developed, the craftsman still experienced his work as an organic whole under his own control. With the emergence of capitalist modes of production, this unity became fragmented. The classic authors emphasise different aspects of this process and its consequences.

Durkheim saw the division of labour as a spontaneous evolutionary process. It created new possibilities for human emancipation since increasing specialisation meant increasing social inter-dependence and, at the same time, increased individual choices. Primitive societies had an organic unity of labour but a merely mechanical unity of members, while modern societies offer the possibility of organic forms of social unity at the price of the division of labour. Durkheim saw one of the key social problems of his time as establishing a new form of moral order which would develop an awareness of the inter-dependence of society members and create the new sense of organic solidarity. This theme preoccupied him, not just in his writings on the division of labour but in his work on suicide, education and religion, as he sought to define a new basis of moral legitimacy.

In this task, he gave a prominent role to organised trade associations, linking employers and employed in a mutual aid corporation. The medical profession may not be a bad example of what he had in mind. Although it epitomises the advance of specialisation, and is by no means free of the consequent conflicts as new specialities emerge and the division of labour is renegotiated, there is never the less some underlying organic unity. Problems arising within the medical division of labour can be resolved internally by reference to a fundamental consensus on the social importance of doctoring. Specialisation, as Durkheim observed, has enhanced the unity of medicine b by its creation of inter-dependence. Nevertheless, Durkheim's account is rather weak on the ways in which occupational corporations would themselves be linked in a wider organic solidarity. While an occupation might have an indefinite border, there is no reason to suppose that it necessarily has an open one. Teamwork may be seen as one way of achieving this linkage, but the foregoing implies that medical concepts of the team are likely to have an essentially moral basis. Their grounds lie in professional mysteries rather than purposive-rational calculation.

Durkheim is also rather vague about the mechanisms by which the division of labour takes place. His evolutionism makes it a rather obscure process. Weber and Marx, however, devote a good deal of space to discussions of the social context in which these processes develop. Weber links the division of labour to the general spread of purposive-rational thought in the modern world. As part of this, traditional modes of working were scrutinised and broken down into component tasks which might be performed more efficiently. The resulting problems of co-ordination were dealt with by the development of purposive-rational bureaucratic forms of management. Weber, on the whole, regards this as a socially beneficial process. Marx, however, tends to treat it as a central pathology of capitalism. The division of labour is one way to enforce the subordination of the working class. Since tasks are dispersed and fragmented, workers lose sight of the surplus value of thei production which is expropriated by the capitalist. The continuing evolution of the division of labour places the worker in a situation of permanent change and insecurity which divides him from his fellows. In this account the workplace is a locale for struggle over issues of control as workers attempt to regain rights over their working lives which have been usurped by the capitalist.

These analyses help us to account for certain features of social work
and community nursing. In their contemporary forms, both represent the
application of purposive-rational thought to traditional modes of working.
In the case of social work, this has led to the collection of a number of
previously discrete occupations into a single occupation administered by a
rational bureaucracy. Community nursing has been similarly reorganised
in recent years. Both are involved in continuing problems of control; social
work in demarcating an occupational mandate and community nursing
in the context of the overall dependency strategy of nursing. For reasons
explored elsewhere by Davies [1976] nursing has, unusually, been marked
by a strategy of conceding rather than expanding work control.

One consequence of the division of labour is the emergence of occupations,
more or less organised bodies of workers. "Occupation" is itself a device
like "organisation" for concerting pieces of social action in a stable manner.
Occupations are ways in which we break down and classify the world of
work. In this process of classification two sets of issues emerge. I have
discussed these more fully elsewhere [Dingwall, 1977d] but broadly there
are two sets of questions; those of *exclusion* and those of *inclusion*. The
former relate to the problem of defending some bundle of tasks as
establishing the unique character of the occupation and warranting its claim
to a distinctive existence. The latter relate to the jostling for social esteem
as occupational members attempt to assert relationships of superiority over
some occupations and equality with others. Neither of these processes need
involve the establishment of "objective" differences or similarities between
occupations, so much as being able to appeal to indefinite sets of criteria to
justify claims to similarity or difference [Moerman, 1974; Dingwall, 1976].
Such criteria may, of course, involve the creation of apparently "objective"
distinctions. The more organised the occupation, then the more strongly
these questions are likely to arise. As Freidson [1977] observes, organised
occupations encourage workers' commitment to and identification with,
their occupation, their occupational co-workers and their work. Social
work and health visiting can both be regarded in their modern form as
organised and committed occupations. Teamwork is a way of resolving
certain consequent problems related to these issues of inclusion and
exclusion.

We can begin to sketch out this process. Given the recognition of the
social context of illness which has re-emerged in recent years it seems
necessary to yoke medical and social intervention together. At one time
this might have been achieved by straightforward appeals to professional
dominance. As Webb [1975] notes, most paramedical and social-work
occupations were originally created under medical tutelage. However,
such appeals, like most straightforward class-based appeals, have lost
legitimacy in recent years. No existing device was available for the exercise
and a new one was created. Teamwork can also address the problems of
occupational boundary maintenance, exclusion, by placing them on an
*ad hoc* basis and claim, thereby, to transcend the problem. For this to
work, however, there must be a degree of social equality between the parties
such that *ad hoc* agreements on the division of tasks are not read as merely

shuffling dirty work around. If one of the parties linked together here is medicine then the whole situation gets caught up in the claims to a special work status, that of "profession", which equality would imply.[4]

This general characterisation remains to be linked with the practical exigencies of everyday work. The next three sections of this paper attempt to do this by examining the occupational predicaments of medicine, health visiting and social work to explore the actual manifestations of these theoretically identifiable problems.

## Doctors and the Team

With the decline of simple class-based modes of domination, new bases for the social status of the medical profession have been formulated. Two of these will be of particular interest to us here. Both are essentially purposive- rational appeals to expertise but while one is a narrow appeal to technical competence at biological engineering, the other is an holistic vision of the doctor as a generalised expert in the problems of living. The first of these stalks the periphery of the present account. It is articulated with a particular version of teamwork found most commonly in high-technology hospital medicine. When talking about the heart team, the neurosurgical team or the theatre team, there are no egalitarian connotations. These are groups of people oriented to narrow and specific tasks, in which the doctor is the acknowledged expert, and they work under his direction. This is not to say that there are not occupational conflicts of various kinds but the ground tends to be undercut by the specificity of the work. Para-doxically, such a narrow conception of medicine can leave other staff a great deal of room for initiative once medical tasks are completed, as Jobling's [1978] work on dermatology shows.

The second, holistic, version of medicine has emerged most clearly in four specialties: psychiatry [Goldie, 1977], paediatrics [Armstrong, 1977], geriatrics [Fairhurst, 1977], and general practice. These are the areas where medical and social problems interpenetrate most visibly. This creates a degree of instability in their practice. In principle, these specialists are committed to a view of themselves as both social and medical experts, since their fundamental philosophy transcends the Cartesian dualism of the biological engineers. In practice, they lack direct access to key resources for the resolution of social problems. While they can prescribe drugs, they cannot prescribe sheltered housing or take children into care.[5] They may claim overall responsibility for social care but this claim is not statutorily recognised in the way that responsibility for medical care may be.

Fairhurst [1977], and McIntosh and Dingwall [1978], analyse official ideologies of teamwork in two of these holistic specialities. These adopt a purposive-rational rhetoric of increased efficiency through co-operation. But there is a fundamental ambivalence over whether teamwork leads to  equality or whether ultimate responsibility remains with the doctor. In part, this arises because of the hortatory character of the literature, which both Fairhurst and Webb (1975) remark upon. On the other hand, generalised exhortation does allow these theorists to avoid the difficult implications of their arguments for everyday practice relationships.

These ideologies are not, however, merely printed words. One can find them directly mediated through the actual teachings of holistic specialists. Several of these from the local medical school lectured on the health-visiting course which I studied. Professor A's remarks are typical.

> It is sometimes difficult to recognise that not only are changes taking place in the world but that medicine must change too ... Technology is turning us all into specialists. This changes the relations between the doctor and the patient and between the health professions ( ... ) we shouldn't think of the doctor as the automatic leader of the health team.[6]

One must make some allowance for the settings of such remarks. Atkinson's [1977] analysis of medical education gives us no grounds for thinking that this is much affected by such ideas. It remains essentially a training for personal responsibility and a sense of self-confidence amounting to dogmatism.

This conception of the medical role has more in common with that expressed in these extracts from two lectures by a GP to the same audience.

> The GP gets help from paramedical colleagues including health visitors, district nurses, practice nurses and social workers. These people should be regarded as colleagues rather than staff. They should be treated as more or less equals. The GP must delegate — that's an unfortunate way to put it — must pass on responsibility ( ... ) The practice consists of patients, doctors, receptionists, secretaries, health visitors, nurses, premises, equipment and records. The GP sits in the middle like a spider in his web.

What are the roots of this conception of medicine? I want here to concentrate on three area: the position of GPs as independent contractors, the influence of traditional hospital models of practice and the class and sex backgrounds of the various team members.

Atkinsons's [1977] remarks on medical education as a training for personal responsibility find a striking echo in Horobin and McIntosh's [1977, 1978] account of rural general practice in Scotland. They stress the strong sense of personal obligation which many of their respondents feel towards their patients. The Bradford study of health centres throughout the North of England reports similar findings [Beales *et al.*, 1976, p. 36]. This is linked in part to the structural conditions of British general practice. Unlike hospital doctors, GPs are not salaried employees but independent contractors with the NHS. As such, a GP has a substantial individual financial commitment to his premises and equipment and to the salaries of secretaries, receptionists and practice nurses. Although many of these expenses are either rebated by the NHS or tax-deductible, it is still the GP who actually creates and provides the practice and its services. As Strong and Horobin [1977] note, the doctor/patient relationship is a private contract within which the doctor has an obligation only towards individual patients and where there is an exchange of quasi-proprietorial rights: each patient has his "own" doctor and each doctor, in another sense, owns his patients. Other doctors, and, by extension, attached workers may only become involved on license from the patient's GP. Although attached workers are separately liable, GPs may feel a deep moral responsibility for any act involving *their* patients and *their* practice.

When this sense of duty is linked to the global view of the medical mandate promoted by the holistic specialities, it is not difficult to see how doctors in primary-care practice come to claim superordinate roles. We must not, however, neglect the technical model of medicine which I mentioned at the beginning of this section. There are hints of this in Horobin and McIntosh [1977, p. 94] and we ourselves have also encountered this model. In one of our cases, Marryat, a GP had initially refused to examine a baby who was seriously underweight and distressed, relenting only after his health visitor had indicated that she would accept no part of the responsibility for any consequences. He wrote an unrecorded prescription, believed to be for a sedative, and bundled the problem out of his surgery. The child was consequently taken into care. It is easy to work up a degree of moral indignation. On the other hand, the health visitor's account reveals the logic of his position. (We were unable to interview the GP himself.)

> HV:   ( ... ) he did refer her to (consultant paediatrician) on that first, [sic]
> but again that was through insistence really, um, but there, you know,
> his attitude anyway is survival of the fittest and those that can't help
> themselves, I'm not going to help them. ( ... ) That's why y'know he
> doesn't really use a health visitor because I'm helping all the people he
> thinks shouldn't be surviving ( ... )

Social Darwinism may be unfashionable but its intellectual history, not least in sociology, is not undistinguished. It is clearly a much narrower conception of the medical mandate but it does not seem an indefensible one. Medicine cannot solve the problems of the world: hence, it should confine itself to those problems which it can solve. The role which this creates for attached workers is limited. On the other hand, once the formal requirements are satisfied, such indifference may leave more room for innovation by attached staff. In the Marryat case, for example, there was an unusually direct contact between health visitor, social worker and paediatric department.

Secondly, we have the influence of doctors' previous experiences and the reward structure of the profession itself. Celia Davies has remarked[7] on the way in which extra-hospital practice is regarded as a residual form of health-care provision. The hospital is the central focus of modern medicine and other sectors deal only with those problems which are too trivial or too intractable for it to handle. It is the locale where medical advance is seen to take place, where medical education goes on and where the networks of professional power are based. The hospital furnishes a set of role models for social relationships outside. Doctors' relationships with community nurses and social workers are coloured by their previous experience of hospital life. The nature of that relationship is one of professional dominance where doctors control the key resource, access to patients, and reserve key management decisions. Nursing and medical social work both developed in a dependency relationship with medicine, taking on subordinate and routine tasks. The latter has broken away from this to some degree in recent years with the absorption into local authority social services departments. On the other hand, our present research is showing continuing problems in the conflict between the "welfare-worker" attitudes of medical social workers and the "professional" attitudes of local authority social workers. [The terminology is from Goldie, 1977.] Medical social workers may still experience a stronger sense of loyalty to medicine than to social work. Professionalising tendencies in British nursing have had only a limited impact outside academic circles. Most doctors then will be accustomed to seeing nurses and social workers in a position of institutionalised subordination, in their training and in orienting to the most prestigious model of medical practice.

One of the more public arenas for accomplishing institutional sub-ordination is the case conference. We have not yet analysed our present data in detail, but certain features seem apparent. Hospital-based staff seldom attend conferences held outside the hospital. Medical social workers and hospital nurses seldom speak, when they are present, other than at the invitation of a doctor, even where their contribution, for example on a child's response to a new social environment, might seem germane. Desborough and Stevenson [1977] comment on the absence of both hospital doctors and GPs in their report on case conferences. We seem to be finding the latter more frequently, but the role of both groups seems essentially passive unless it is necessary to "sell" a decision. The most vigorous medical participation we have observed has occurred when the doctors involved have decided that care proceedings are warranted and the local authority is not anxious to initiate them. The doctors we have encountered tend to be rather dismissive about the value of case conferences and to regard them as a waste of time. In the context of the medical model of inter-occupational relationships, this is a rational view. We intend to argue, ultimately, that case conferences are merely occasions for ratifying decisions which have already been taken by a minority of the participants and of committing all those present to that policy. Given the assumptions of professional dominance, then it *is* a waste of time discussing decisions which a doctor has already made. It is simply a matter for others to execute. Conversely, if the decisions are made by others, then the doctor's attendance would create problems for his claims to autonomy as a ground of professional status.

Older GPs, of course, may be more remote from hospital experiences and their training would predate the substantial expansion of hospital social-work departments. In a personal communication, Horobin has drawn attention to the significance of the length of their community experience. In the remote rural areas covered in his study, social-work provision is still very thin on the ground. Long before the holistic ideology of modern general practice theorists became current, they were being pressed into that role by the demands of their own communities. The doctor, the minister of religion and the combined-duty nurse/health visitor/midwife would be the only health and welfare personnel consistently available. The arrival of social workers may be much resented particularly when, as at present, geographical difficulties make social-service provision sparse and transient.

Finally, it is worth mentioning briefly the influence of traditional patterns of class and sex inequality. The brevity of such treatment is not intended to reflect on the importance of the questions, so much as on the available data.

Navarro [1977, p. 117] draws attention to the influence of class structure on teamwork.

> this class structure and hierarchy militate against the provision of comprehensive medical care. For example, while most of the needs of patients in our populations are those of care, most of the strategies within the health team and the health sector are directed by the 'expert' in cure, the physician ... the joint provision of the care, by the patient himself, his family and all members of the team, is seriously handicapped in our class-structured society where roles and functions are not distributed according to the need for them, but primarily according to the hierarchical order prevalent in our society, dictated by its class structure and class relations.

Unfortunately, relevant data are very limited. Although we know a good deal about recruitment to medicine and its integration with *élite* groups, comparative material on nursing or social work is sparse. The unchallenged nature of medicine's claim to professional status is revealing though. Medicine, indeed, is often thought of as the archetype of the modern profession. It is difficult to assert that the claims of either nursing or social work are recognised in the same sense. Neither, for example, have an established right to act as expert witnesses before a court.

It also seems relevant to note that while the majority of GPs are male, the majority of nurses and social workers are female. There is an implicit recognition of the problems which GPs may find in forming colleague relationships with women in some of the literature of the teamwork ideologists. Unfortunately, their concern is often trivial and patronising. Gibson [in Bloomfield and Follis, 1974] canvasses support for informal team meetings by remarking how "the girls love to dress-up" and sums up the arts of a good receptionist as involving "the need for feminine tact and guile". He tries to persuade male colleagues that it is not entirely abhorrent to admit women to coffee-break discussions: "the noise level is normal, the stories are appreciated and often matched by the girls, the standard of conversation is very entertaining and stimulating." Beales *et al.* [1976, p. 37] note that GPs' claims to team leadership in the health centres he studied involved reference to their gender. Desborough and Stevenson [1977] comment on the presence of large numbers of social workers at case conferences, a finding which we have replicated. Intentionally or not, this usually has the effect of ensuring the presence of a male social worker, at some level, who can take the lead for social services. The fact that health visitors and their seniors are almost exclusively female may help to account for their relatively minor contribution to many case conferences. The limited conversational rights which Zimmerman and West [1975] suggest are available to women might well be implicated here.

We are, then, left with a picture of medicine as a predominantly upper-class and male occupation marked by a variety of occupational theories, two of the most important of which provide for views of the doctor as a technician, indifferent to co-operation, or as a generalised wise man, entitled to dominate any relationship. While the consequences of these philosophies differ, they are equally antipathetic to egalitarian or co-operative models of teamwork. This need not be critical, however, if other members of the team can act without support or are prepared to accept subordinate roles.

## Health Visitors and Teamwork

In theory, health visitors should occupy a crucial mediating role between health and social services, screening populations for incipient problems requiring specialised intervention. Health visitors have an independent responsibility for primary prevention among demographically defined sections of the population. The philosophy underlying this task derived from the nineteenth-century public health movement and is captured by Sidney Webb in his comments on evidence to the Royal Commission on the Poor Law:

> it had been a question of how to deter people from applying. The medical officers of health brought in the ideas of searching out cases, of insisting on treatment at the incipient stage, of regarding even one "missed case" as an evil and a public danger, and the Commission came to see that what was wanted was not the relief of destitution but its prevention. It was this new principle learned from the medical officers of health that the Minority Report worked out into a complete scheme. [quoted in Gilbert, 1966]

Health visitors were to be the chief agents of the MOHs in this task. The principle remains valid today as the CETHV[8] [1978, p. 26] stress:

> Our original employers sent health visitors into communities which had obvious and desperate health needs. It was left to the individual worker to search for and identify the health needs of individual families. Without this painstaking and time-consuming search the identification of individual need could not have been made with any precision nor appropriate remedies applied. Within the framework of existing values and knowledge, and in co-operation with others, this tradition of the independent practitioner initiating her own search has been continuous and has been strengthened in health visiting. *As health needs have become less overt search was, and is even more importantly now, the source of all health visiting practice.* [my emphasis]

It is perhaps worth noting that the preferred definition of health is the WHO's "state of complete physical, mental and social well-being" so that "health needs" should not be read in too narrow a sense.

Even under attachment schemes, health visitors retain this responsibility. They are the only significant group of nurses with direct access to clients rather than depending upon the selection of the medical profession. Nofication of new births is a purely administrative process with no intervening medical screen. Nevertheless, liaison with both doctors and social workers is clearly critical to the successful execution of the health visitors' occupational mandate. The former is supposed to have been secured by practice attachment; the latter lacks any formal basis and is largely a matter of individual initiative.

In keeping with these traditions health-visiting ideologists assert a substantially egalitarian model of teamwork: "The marriage between health visitor and doctor must be a modern marriage based on the principle of partnership between equals, not a Victorian marriage in which one partner expected from the other obedience and servility" [Clark, in Bloomfield and Follis, 1974]. These views are transmitted to students in their training programmes. Another paper by Clark was circulated by the tutors at the school I studied with their *imprimatur*

> Each member of the team shoul understand and respect the roles and functions
> of every other member of the team. This implies partnership not hierarchy.
> In particular, the nurse members of the team are partners with and not ancillary
> to the medical members of the team. Nursing is a professional skill in its own
> right, requiring a specific professional preparation; doctors are not in a position
> to assess nursing needs nor to supervise nursing practice [Clark, n.d.].

In their own lectures the tutors repeatedly emphasised the autonomy of health visiting, to the extent that students found it a matter for comment that they were always being told they were on a level with doctors.

Given what we have already seen of the doctors' models of teamwork, the potential for conflict is evident. The CETHV (1978) report quoted above stresses inadequacies of communication between health visitors and GPs, as perceived by health visitors and, itself, cites a report from the Health Visitors' Association complaining of the lack of understanding by GPs of the health visitors' independent responsibility. This report noted that if health visitors were unwilling to fulfil their functions in the way defined for them by the GPs then they were regarded as unco-operative. Similar findings are reported by Walker and McClure [1970] who note the prevalence of "personality clashes" between health visitors and GPs in attachment schemes and by Gilmore *et al.* [1974] on the lack of understanding and even hostility expressed by GPs about the work of their attached health visitors.

On the other hand, Jean McIntosh and I [McIntosh and Dingwall, 1978] observed relatively little overt conflict. The sheer conventions of politeness are a powerful restraint. GPs and health visitors simply tend to avoid any-thing other than strictly task-oriented contact. Where practices have common room facilities, for instance, difference occupations divide into their respective groups and there is little exchange between them. The Bradford study, indeed, found that in larger health centres few staff used the common room at all. The GPs had tea in their offices and the health visitors and district nurses had tea in their own rooms. Casual contact was very limited. [Beales *et al.*, 1977, pp. 41–42]. The reasons why health visitors appear unassertive, although dissatisfied, will bear further examination. There is little to add to my earlier discussion of class and sex as relevant factors, but the influence of hospital models and the lack of colleague support seem worth a more extended treatment.

Hospital models influence health visitors as much as GPs. Health visitors are all qualified and experienced hospital nurses and it is easy for them to adopt nursing patterns of deference when GPs adopt hospital styles of dominance. This does not mean that health visitors are impotent. On the contrary, nurses develop an impressive array of subtly manipulative inter-action skills. [Stein, 1967; Mauksch, 1973.] There are, too, the general sources of power accruing to lower participants, which sometimes catch health visitors themselves [Mechanic, 1968; Dingwall, 1974; Beales *et al.*, 1977, p. 76]. Health visitors, for instance, can have a great influence over client demand in general practice by encouraging or discouraging approaches to the GP. This strategy is also advocated by tutors when students appeared to be willing to implement independent principes. One student, for example, who suggested advising a client to change her GP since he was not giving serious attention to a child's apparent lack of hearing, was told, quite force-fully, that this would be an incorrect policy. She should simply persist with traditional nursing tactics of indirect negotiation.

This lack of support for assertiveness can also be found among health visitors' administrative superiors. The reasons for this lack of support are not well understood, but they need not concern us here. What is significant is the fieldworkers' perception of themselves as unsupported, to the point indeed where some administrators are regarded as more likely to side with a GP in any conflict than with their own staff. The tendency to treat difficulties as personal problems, evidenced by Walker and McClure's "personality clashes" cited earlier, rather than as structurally generated, does little to help. On the other hand, Beales *et al.* [1977, p. 37] report that a major source of friction in the health centres they studied was between GPs and nursing administration over the latter's refusal to allow GPs to direct health authority nurses. It seems that these GPs at least perceived the administrators to be supporting their field staff. One suspects that the consequences are that nurse administrators cannot please anybody because of the diametrically opposing demands made of them. The consequences seem worth further investigation.

Health visitors also have an uneasy relationship with social workers. It can be argued that health visiting represented the first attempt to provide a statutory social-work service. For a variety of reasons, parts of this service became neglected in the years immediately prior to the last war, giving rise to what were recognised as urgent problems in the post-war years. Most notable here were the various child care scandals which led to the Curtis Committee and the creation of local authority children's departments. Areas of work were progressively hived off, creating the proliferation of welfare provision which the Seebohm and Kilbrandon reforms sought to reverse. A few local authorities employed health visitors in all these roles until the late 1960s but this policy was rendered impractical by the new legislation. To a considerable degree, the rise of social work has been at the expense of health visiting.[9] Anxieties on this front continue to exist among health visitors and have been expressed several times in the course of our current work.

Both formal and informal contacts between health visitors and social workers are limited. Although the same institutions train both occupations, the courses are quite separate with only token interchanges. At national level the close liaison envisaged by the 1962 Health Visiting and Social Work (Training) Act which created both the CETHV and its social-work equivalent, the Central Council for Education and Training in Social Work, has declined, and the two were statutorily separated by the post-Seebohm legislation. In work situations, the dependence of health visitors on social services departments for certain statutory provisions, notably aid for the chronically sick and disabled, obliges them to make periodic referrals. Health visitors, however, perceive social workers as using these referrals to create a dependency advantage, and, in effect, to shut them out.

From the health visitors' point of view, the most successful relationships seem to occur when they, themselves, can establish a dependency advantage. There are a number of ways in which this can happen, but my research has particularly identified two. In my earlier work on health visitor training, I observed some of the students' fieldwork experience in an Inner London borough. This was marked by the usual staff shortages and multiple social problems. In the circumstances, there was little competition for extra work. Social workers were happy to be relieved of some of their burdens by allowing health visitors to take on whatever they liked. The social services department furnished whatever statutory back-up was requested without particularly questioning the referral. In other areas with a lower problem/ staff ratio and more competition for work, health visiting referrals were independently investigated and clients taken onto the books of the social services department. This often seemed like poaching to health visitors [Dingwall, 1977a, pp. 148–155], but is explicable in terms of occupational strategies for work control.

The best relationships we have observed in our present study seem to develop when social workers have access difficulties. Where abuse or neglect is suspected, it can become awkward for social workers to gain admittance to a family. Health visitors, however, can often continue to visit. Blaxter [1976, p. 34] has remarked on the differential acceptability of "health" and "welfare" services to potential clients. Two reasons can be suggested for this. Firstly, health workers tend to avoid overt moralising, which the social worker's mandate of promoting personal change requires. [Strong and Horobin, 1977; Dingwall, 1977a, pp. 217–219]. Secondly, health problems, with few exceptions, tend not to be stigmatising in the sense that anyone may suffer from them. Health visiting is an unselective total population service which does not label clients in the same way as social work.

Wherever a dependency advantage is created, social workers actively maintain liaison; where the advantage runs the other way, health visitors tend to perceive their attempts at liaison as constantly rebuffed. Instead of acting as a proactive intermediary between two services, medicine and social work, which are essentially retroactive, responding to problems, health visitors more usually end up as the piggy in the middle. Their claims to an independent role and to a unique expertise in the identification of incipient problems are discounted on both sides. They have few financial or statutory resources and an historic connection with an occupation whose major strategy has been the surrender of dependency advantages. Moreover, as an occupation, health visiting remains overwhelmingly female and with an ill-defined class position.

## Social Work and Teamwork

Freidson (1961) has observed how "new" occupations like social work emerge in the perceptions of people who make policy that some need is unmet. In the first instance, they are agents of other organisations and rely on them for their clientele with an inevitable division of loyalty between sponsor and client. The almoner, for instance, had to balance the hospital's revenue needs against clients' means. Once the occupation goes independent, however, it has to establish its own identity and attract its own clients. This is particularly difficult if it is trying to intervene at the incipient stages of a problem. Potential clients' attitudes may remain coloured by past history. Blaxter [1976, p. 31] records how she found old people describing the Supplementary Benefits Commission as the "Guardian" 40 years after the latter had been abolished. Medical social workers remained "almoners" to most of her sample, and to many doctors. We have observed lawyers and judges still referring to "welfare workers" and "the Welfare Department".

Social work, as an unified occupation, can only really be said to have existed in England since the Local Authority Social Services Act 1970. (Its Scottish counterpart was passed in 1968.) As Olive Stevenson's [1979] chapter reminds us, an heterogenous collection of personnel with widely varying qualifications and experience were brought together into a single department and expected to act in a cohesive fashion. The situation has been further complicated by a major reorganisation of local government and substantial new legislative burdens, notably under the Chronically Sick and Disabled Persons Act 1970 (extended to Scotland in 1973) and the Children Act 1975. The process of consolidation is far from complete. Medical social workers are currently being assimilated and there is still a possibility of English probation officers following their Scottish counterparts into the unified departments.

Emerging from such turmoil, the new occupation faces acutely the problems which I suggested earlier were faced by *all* occupations — demarcating a set of tasks and negotiating a status relationship with other occupations. As Freidson suggests, its area of work has to be established in competition with others who are already in the field, like GPs and health visitors. The social processes which created modern social work have not, however, left these other occupations untouched and significant sections of both have adopted a wider conception of their own role.

At the same time, as a new occupation, social work has an ill-defined social status. In earlier days such a question was less relevant. Most of the staff were women who stood in a particular relation to the labour market where their remuneration constituted recognition rather than representing the market value of their labour. Their status derived from private means and personal connections, through birth or marriage, as is traditional for women. This situation has radically changed. The financial and organisational scale of social services departments, within the rational bureaucratic context of local government, has drawn them into the market, particularly for graduate labour. Large corporate enterprises based on principles of formal rationality entail particular forms of occupational commitment. This is the converse of

Freidson's [1977, pp. 30–34] discussion of organised occupations. There, he notes how these encourage the development of occupational commitment, by offering relatively secure life-careers, of commitment to one's colleagues, by creating a shared occupational fate, and of commitment to one's work, by defining a stable set of tasks likely to be performed into an open future. Work becomes a central life-interest, often squeezing out women with other life-interests. Such commitment seems likely to generate a more serious concern for status issues. The uncommitted, in this sense, caseworker is superseded by the committed would-be professional, recruited in a market situation and sensitive to the overall monetary and non-monetary rewards of his work.

The conflicts which surround social work over the nature of its mandate and its overall role in society create a situation of considerable uncertainty for the occupation and its members. Inevitably, this throws a strain on relationships with other occupations since there are no acknowledged resolutions of the problems of inclusion and exclusion.

We have already seen the influence of traditional hospital role models on current practice. Many doctors may find it hard to come to terms with the transformation of almoners into independent workers with their own powers and resources. Conversely, social workers may find it hard to accept conduct premised on a relationship of professional dominance from with they are struggling to emancipate themselves. The Bradford health centre study, for example, notes how most of the GPs thought that liaison with social workers would only be possible if social workers were practice attached, while the social workers felt that this would place them under the GP's authority or, at the very least, concede his superior professional status. In a personal communication, Eileen Fairhurst has noted that there may be situational references to the independence of medical social workers. It seems, however, that these generally arise when doctors want to redefine a case as a social rather than a medical problem and dispose of it. "Independence" can be a useful rhetorical device in creating a dependency advantage and passing on dirty work.

Difficulties often arise in child protection cases where doctors' demands for statutory intervention are met by social workers' insistence on their own right to investigate and evaluate the situation, particularly given the holistic vision of the relevant specialists. There is a delicate balance of mutual dependence since doctors need social services to initiate care proceedings and social services need good medical evidence to succeed. The problems which these cases create for the moral neutrality of the doctor/patient relationship can act as a disincentive to the doctor to press a case vigorously throughout the period before a full hearing. If doctors feel slighted by having to debate a possible court action with social services, the latter can feel equally threatened by the need to cajole doctors into giving evidence in proceedings which they wanted brought. There are third parties involved here — the local authority legal department and the various courts, which constitute an outside adjudication on the competing professional claims of doctors and social workers. It is a source of some resentment that lawyers and courts will, to a considerable degree, accommodate themselves to the availability of medical witnesses and accord them a generally privileged status, including the right to give expert evidence, while social workers are expected to accommodate themselves to the law and are given no particular recognition.

The pattern of relationships with health visitors is rather different. Although individuals may be perceived as competent, there is a tendency to regard health visiting as an historical anachronism. Health visitors are considered to be poorly trained, insensitive to any but narrow physical factors and having doubtful judgement. I discussed one of our present cases, Evers, for instance, with a senior contact in the social services department. This case conference\had been initiated by a health visitor and at the time of our conversation my contact only had an outline of the case.

> What probably happened was that some health visitor got into a flap and didn't know what to do, so the senior or the social worker called a case conference with the idea of keeping her happy and decided there was no case to proceed on.

The CETHV [1978, pp. 56—57] also remark on the limitations of others' perspectives on health visitors:

> On the one hand, their medical and nursing colleagues and managers may appear to have little regard for the emphasis they have learned to place on social, emotional and cultural aspects of a given situation; while on the other hand they may find that other professional colleagues such as social workers tend to convey the impression that their assessment of situations is based almost exclusively on physical and medical aspects.

Again, we are dealing with a complex mixture of cultural lags, stereotypes and occupational rivalries. Health visitors trained before 1965 on the old syllabi would have been taught less about social skills than those trained since. Given the historical lags in perceptions of social work described earlier, it would be surprising if they were exempt from misperceiving others. There are, moreover, general rivalries between nursing and social work, notably in the relative roles of the two occupations in caring for the mentally ill and the mentally handicapped. There is a broad critique in some quarters of a supposed authoritarianism and narrow physical orientation to nursing with an accompanying indifference to the social and phychological needs of patients. In this light, social work can be seen as bidding for most nursing work other then technical procedures and basic physical care. This is obviously an extreme view, but it represents a spirit which may well lead social workers into discounting health visiting's expertise. It should not surprise us if this leads social workers to ascribe an inferior status to an occupation they have scored off so frequently in the past.

The portrait which I am presenting, then, is one of an uncertain and insecure occupation which is still struggling to define its place in the world. It is undergoing a transition from a pastime for women to a powerful bureaucracy dominated by men and incorporating an organised and articulate professionalist occupation. In the course of this, there is inevitable friction with occupations whose social mandates will be redrawn by this new collecting device for tasks which they have regarded as their own.

## The Work of "Teamwork"

We can, then, see something of the work which the concept of a "team" is expected to do. In the context of primary care, it is asked to link a number of occupations, three of which have been analysed in this paper. Each of these three has a particular occupational predicament, relating to its attempts to resolve the problems of exclusion, controlling some domain of tasks, and of inclusion, negotiating a status relationship with other occupations. Each occupation makes its own contribution to the difficulties of co-ordination as a result of its strategies for resolving these problems. Conflicts within the team are structurally generated and it can be seriously misleading to talk in psychologistic terms of arrogant doctors or awkward health visitors or prickly social workers.

These conflicts appear to occur very widely in westernised health and welfare systems. Rosalie Kane's paper [1979] describes the American experience of the difficulties of collaborating with doctors in terms very similar to those of this paper:

> Family practice itself is ambivalent about whether its physician products should themselves incorporate the direct counselling skills of other disciplines or whether the objective is to produce a family practitioner capable of working on a team. There is, of course, the ever-present danger that, regardless of the plans of the educator, the physician might assume a posture of omnipotence and proceed unilaterally to implement a full range of therapies.

Elsewhere [Kane, 1975], she has an extended discussion of the problems of professional autonomy in teamwork and notes the conflict between public health nurses, the nearest American equivalent to health visitors, and social workers. From Holland, de Graaf (1975) reports on a study of collaboration between GPs, social workers and district nurses. This shows a similar sense of personal responsibility on the part of GPs and similar pressures for joint action by social workers and nurses. The mutual perceptions of the team members' spheres of competence and responsibility were, again, very much as I have described here from UK data.

Two related problems occupy the centre of the stage here. Firstly, there is an unstable division of labour. There is a very large grey area of social and personal problem management which has no clearly defined owner. GPs, health visitors, social workers and, indeed, district nurses may all lay claim to this as a proper part of their occupational mandate. Unless and until a stable division of this work can be achieved by negotiation or legislation there is always an open possibility for inter-occupational rivalry. Secondly, there are status problems. In the absence of a clear division of labour, any arrangements must be of an *ad hoc* kind. For acceptable *ad hoc* settlements to be reached, however, there must be some degree of equality between the parties to them, particularly in a situation like primary care, where there is so much inter-dependency of the occupations involved. As Durkheim observed, the more stable the division of labour becomes, the greater will be this inter-dependency. Hence, any attempt to gain a dependency advantage is destructive of co-operation. The need to gain dependency advantage can, however, only be eliminated by a stable division of labour and equal status of the parties to it.

"Teamwork" as a rhetorical device attempts to overcome these difficulties but, as we have seen, ultimately fails. Its usage is inconsistent between occupations and it does not articulate any fundamental change in social organisation. For the doctors, with their strong sense of individual responsibility, the metaphor is, in Webb's terms, that of a football team where they are the captain, manager and coach. For the others, with their sense of special expertise, the metaphor is that of a tennis team, a democratic or collegiate group of complementary experts. These two metaphors are not easily compatible and indeed constitute significant barriers to institutional changes which might promote a genuine significance to teamwork. Talking about teamwork is largely a way of making certain sorts of occupational claim rather than as a way of concerting action.

## Teamwork and Future

What, then, are the prospects for the primary care team? Personally, I find it hard to be optimistic. Many hopes have been pinned on educational reform, but as Freidson [1970, 1976] cogently reminds us, education is largely irrelevant without structural change. Indeed, in this case, it may make matters worse by encouraging or reinforcing holistic views of the medical mandate, turning doctors into amateur social practitioners and making co-operation as difficult as with the biological technician. The fundamental obstacle is the divided responsibility for helping people with problems. An effectively integrated organisation would involve a stable division of labour based on complementary specialisms in preventive and reactive services in both social and medical care.

One possible way of achieving this which I have sketched elsewhere in evidence to the Royal Commission on the NHS [Dingwall, 1977b] is to give health visitors responsibility for all preventive work, both social and medical, and to regard both GPs and social workers as reactive agents. They would receive referrals both directly from client-defined problems and indirectly from health visitors acting as casefinders. This would be based on integrated groups of workers under a common management sharing responsibility for the problems of a defined geographical area.

To characterise such an organisation is to see how unlikely it is. It would mean the end of independent contractor status for GPs who would be obliged to work on a salaried and geographical basis from combined health and welfare centres. It would mean re-examining the question of the link between health visiting and nursing, if the former were to adopt a wider social prevention role, a link which is reaffirmed in the recent Act to reform the General Nursing Council. It would mean a common administration for health and social services, either bringing social work out of local government or taking health services into it. Associated with this would have to be a massive programme of public education. It would be no use professionals agreeing reforms only for these to be subverted by the public choosing inappropriate problem-solvers [Dingwall, 1974; McIntosh and Dingwall, 1978].

This is the sort of upset that only a Royal Commission could bring about.

However, the present Commission is limited to considering the NHS and it hardly seems conceivable that another would cover the same ground in the foreseeable future. As Derek Gill [Gill, 1976, 1978] has argued, the opportunity has been missed for the best part of a generation of having a comprehensive scrutiny of care services, whether delivered by "health" or "welfare" workers. The long-awaited Royal Commission on the Integration of Health and Personal Social Services must be postponed even further. Nor should we forget the disadvantages of integration. The present system may allow problems to slip through but it also leaves a good deal of room for client initiative. Clients have some choice over where to seek assistance with their troubles. This may be a limited choice within agencies in both inner cities and rural areas, but there is a real choice between agencies. Clients may have a better chance of extracting resources of information from a divided group of professionals who they can play off against each other. Overlap and duplication of provisions may be wasteful in terms of narrow economic rationality but they can be a useful means of enhancing client choice. A certain amount of bureaucratic inefficiency may lead to "missed cases": it is also a powerful safeguard of civil liberty. "Better" teamwork might only increase the power of professionals in relation to their clients and many would argue that that imbalance was already too great.

## Acknowledgements

I have learned a great deal about teamwork from many people in the agencies I have studied who must remain anonymous. I owe a considerable debt, however, to a number of academic colleagues especially Jean McIntosh, John Eekelaar, Celia Davies, Eileen Fairhurst, Phil Strong, Alan Davis and Gordon Horobin. I am also indebted to the academic and practical experience of my wife, Pamela Watson. The manuscript was deciphered and typed by Angela Palmer and Lorna Pollock.

## Notes

1. "Team" in Old English refers to a group of animals harnessed together to draw some vehicle. Its extension to human activity, to describe a group of people linked in a joint enterprise, goes back to the early sixteenth century.

2. The data in this paper are drawn from three sources: official publications by occupational leaders, and two pieces of research in which I have been involved, a study of health-visitor training [Dingwall, 1977b] and a study of decision-making in cases of alleged abuse or neglect of children on which I am collaborating with John Eekelaar. The former was supported by an MRC Research Studentship at the Institute of Medical Sociology, Aberdeen and the latter is supported by the SSRC Centre for Socio-Legal Studies, Oxford. Some of the ideas used in this paper were originally developed jointly with Jean McIntosh [McIntosh and Dingwall, 1978].

3. Although the treatment of the issue here is my own, I would like to acknowledge my debt to Celia Davies' oral discussion at the Warwick Medical Sociology Workshop for the idea of applying division-of-labour theory to teamwork.

4. In this context it is interesting to note how "team" may be used within social services departments to obscure their hierarchical and bureaucratic character and to

create a more defensibly "professional" work setting. It rhetorically asserts the equality between autonomous colleagues which is often invoked as a criterion of professional standing [cf. Dingwall, 1976]. Olive Stevenson's [1979] paper brings out something of the variety of actual organisational forms which may be encompassed.

5. Although as Blaxter's [1976] work shows, a remarkable amount of ingenuity may go into trying to circumvent the licensed agents for social resources. It is also true that doctors may play a key role in determining eligibility for social benefits, for example in the area of disability. In the area of child protection, too, the success or failure of social services' court applications is crucially dependent on enlisting medical co-operation. Nevertheless, in both these situations the ultimate responsibility does not lie with the doctor.

6. In this and the following field data ... indicates a pause, hesitation or gap in recording (...) indicates that a portion of the original text has been withheld. All extracts are edited for anonymity and all names are fictitious.

7. In the discussion cited in note 4 above.

8. Council for the Education and Training of Health Visitors.

9. This historical argument is developed more fully in Dingwall [1977c].

## References

Armstrong, David. (1977). Child development and medical ontology (presented to BSA Medical Sociology Group Annual Conference, Warwick.

Atkinson, Paul. (1977). The reproduction of medical knowledge. *In* "Health Care and Health Knowledge" (Eds Robert Dingwall, Christian Heath, Margaret Reid and Margaret Stacey), Croom Helm, London.

Beales, J. G., Etheridge, J., Field, D. and Hickson, D. J. (1977). The microcosm: health centres in practice, mimeo, University of Bradford, Management Centre.

Bittner, Egon. (1965). The concept of organisation, *Social Research* 32, 239–255.

Blaxter, M. (1976). "The Meaning of Disability". Heinemann, London.

Bloomfield, R. and Follis, P. (Eds). (1974). "The Health Team in Action". BBC Publications, London.

Clark, June. "Teamwork in Community Care: The Health Visitor's Point of View" (mimeo, n.d.).

Council for the Education and Training of Health Visitors. (1978). "An Investigation into the Principles of Health Visiting". CETHV, London.

Davies, Celia. (1976). Experience of dependency and control in work: the case of nurses, *Journal of Advanced Nursing* 1, 273–282.

de Graff, Hein. (1975). "Social Welfare and Public Health Personnel in Inter-disciplinary Groups". Netherlands Institute for Social Welfare Research, 's-Gravenhage.

Desborough, Christine and Stevenson, Olive. (1977). "Interprofessional Communication in Case Conferences and Non-Accidental Injury to Children" (mimeo).

Dingwall, Robert. (1974). A team role for ancillary staff, *Health and Social Science Journal*, 7 September.

Dingwall, Robert. (1976). Accomplishing profession, *Sociological Review* 24, 331–350.

Dingwall, Robert. (1977a). "The Social Organisation of Health Visitor Training". Croom Helm, London.

Dingwall, Robert. (1977b). What future for health visiting? Evidence to the Royal Commission on the NHS, *Nursing Times*, 2 June.

Dingwall, Robert. (1977c). Collectivism, regionalism and feminism: health visiting and British social policy 1850–1975, *Journal of Social Policy* 6, 291–315.

Dingwall, Robert. (1977d). "Atrocity Stories" and professional relationships, *Sociology of Work and Occupations* 4, 371–396.

Dingwall, Robert and McIntosh, Jean. (Eds.). (1978). "Readings in the Sociology of Nursing". Churchill Livingstone, Edinburgh.

Fairhurst, Eileen. (1977). Teamwork as a panacea: some underlying assumptions (presented to BSA Medical Sociology Group Annual Conference, Warwick).

Freidson, Eliot. (1961). "Patients' Views of Medical Practice". Russell Sage, New York.

Freidson, Eliot. (1970). "Profession of Medicine". Dodd, Mead & Co., New York.

Freidson, Eliot. (1976). "Doctoring Together". Elsevier, New York.

Friedson, Eliot. (1977). The futures of professionalisation. *In* Stacey *et al.* (Eds.).

Gilbert, Bentley B. (1966). "The Evolution of National Insurance in Great Britain: The Origins of the Welfare State. Michael Joseph, London.

Gill, Derek G. (1976). The reorganisation of the National Health Service: some socio-logical aspects with special references to the role of the community physician. *In* "The Sociology of the NHS" (Ed. Margaret Stacey). Sociological Review Monograph 22, Keele, Staffs.

Gill, Derek G. (1978). The British National Health Service: a sociologist's perspective, Report, under contract NIH–75–C573, to be published by the Fogarty International Center.

Gilmore, M., Bruce, N. and Hunt, M. (1974). "The Work of the Nursing Team in General Practice". CETHV, London.

Goldie, Nigel. (1977). The division of labour between the mental health professions: a negotiated or an imposed order? *In* Stacey *et al.* (Eds).

Horobin, Gordon and McIntosh, Jim. (1977). Responsibility in general practice. *In* Stacey *et al.* (Eds).

Jobling, Ray. (1978). Nursing with and without professional nurses: the case of derma-tology. *In* Dingwall and McIntosh (Eds).

Kane, Rosalie A. (1975). "Interprofessional Teamwork". Syracuse University.

Kane, Rosalie A. (1979). Multidisciplinary teamwork in the United States: Trends, issues and implications for the social worker. *In* "Teamwork in the Health and Social Services" (Eds T. Briggs, A. Webb and F. Lonsdale). Croom Helm, London.

McIntosh, Jean and Dingwall, Robert. (1978). Teamwork in theory and practice. *In* Dingwall and McIntosh (Eds).

McIntosh, Jim and Horobin, Gordon. (1978). General practice in remote areas: attractions, expectations and experience, *Journal of the Royal College of General Practitioners* 28, 227–232.

Mauksch, Hans. (1973). Ideology, interaction and patient care in hospitals, *Social Science and Medicine* 7, 817–830.

Mechanic, David. (1968). Sources of power of lower participants in complex organ-isations. *In* "Medical Sociology" (Ed. David Mechanic). Free Press, New York.

Moerman, Michael. (1974). Accomplishing ethnicity. *In* "Ethnomethodology" (Ed. Roy Turner). Penguin, Harmondsworth (first published, 1968).

Navarro, Vincente. (1977). "Medicine under Capitalism". Croom Helm, London.

Stacey, Margaret, Reid, Margaret, Heath, Christian and Dingwall, Robert. (Eds). (1977). "Health and the Division of Labour". Croom Helm, London.

Stein, Leonard (1967). The doctor-nurse game, *Archives of General Psychiatry* 16, 699–703. (Reprinted in Dingwall and McIntosh (Eds), 1977).

Stevenson, Olive (1979). Social service team in the United Kingdom. *In* "Teamwork in the Health and Social Services" (Eds. T. Briggs, A. Webb and F. Lonsdale). Croom Helm, London.

Strong, Phil and Horobin, Gordon. (1977). Politeness is all — the forms, causes and consequences of medical gentility (mimeo).

Walker, J. H. and McClure, L. M. (1970). Community nurses' views of GP attachment. *In* "The New General Practice, 2" (Ed. M. Ware). British Medical Association, London.

Webb, Adrian L. (1975). Co-ordination between health and personal social services: a question of quality, unpublished paper presented to European seminar on Interaction of Social Welfare and Health Personnel in the Delivery of Services: Implications for Training. Strobl-am-Wolfgangsee, Austria.

Wittgenstein, Ludwig (1972). "Philosophical Investigations" (Tr. G. E. M. Anscombe). Basil Balckwell, Oxford (first published, 1953).

Zimmerman, Don and West, Candace (1975). Sex roles, interruptions and silences in conversations. *In* "Language and Sex: Difference and Dominance" (Eds. Barrie Thorne and Nancy Hewlett). Newbury House, Powley, Mass.

# SOCIAL WORKERS IN PRIMARY HEALTH CARE: THE GENERAL PRACTITIONER'S VIEWPOINT

PAUL WILLIAMS and ANTHONY CLARE

## Summary

The success of general practitioner/social worker collaboration in primary care depends largely on how the doctors perceive the attachment.

We examined the replies of a group of general practitioners to a series of questions about such an attachment. Although the collaboration may lead to more work for the doctors, it was much appreciated by them.

## Introduction

The importance of collaboration between general practitioners and social workers is now well recognized [Department of Health and Social Security, 1968 and 1974; Lancet, 1975], and reports are available from a number of social work attachment schemes in primary care [Collins, 1965; Forman and Fairbairn, 1968; Ratoff and Pearson, 1970; Goldberg and Neill, 1972; Brook and Temperley, 1976].

However, there is a wide gap between acknowledging the importance of such schemes and their general implementation: narrowing that gap depends in part on the attitudes to and perceptions of social work by general practitioners. The Seebohm Committee (DHSS, 1968] observed: "survey after survey has shown that many family doctors do not seek help from social workers nor use social services that are available: they often do not know about them, or do not understand or value them." There seems to have been little change in this situation, as six years later, Ratoff and colleagues [1974], in a discussion of problems in general practitioner/social worker liaison, noted that "overall, relationships between general practitioners and social workers are poor".

However encouraging the results of experimental social work attachment schemes, they cannot be effective if doctors do not accept them, for it has been demonstrated that judgements are made and decisions implemented on the basis of attitudes to and perception of information, rather than on information itself [Shelly and Bryan, 1964]. It is thus vital to study general

Reprinted, with permission from, the *Journal of the Royal College of General Practitioners* 29, 554–558, 1979.

practitioners' perceptions and acceptance of social work in primary care, and this paper reports such an investigation.

The General Practice Research Unit at the Institute of Psychiatry has been operating a social work attachment scheme in collaboration with a South London health centre for the past four years. A varying number (from one to four) of part-time social workers have attended the Health Centre daily to have discussions with the doctors and other staff, to take referrals from them, and to see clients.

## Aim

Using this background, we attempted to answer five questions:

(1) How far does the doctors' perception of their use of the scheme correspond to the extent of referral?
(2) What are the doctors' perceptions of the attachment scheme?
(3) What difficulties have arisen as a result of the scheme?
(4) Do the doctors believe that the attachment scheme has influenced their management of patients with psychological and social problems, and if so, in what way?
(5) How do the doctors perceive the role of the social worker in relation to that of the health visitor?

## Method

The nine general practitioners working at the South London Health Centre were each given a semi-structured interview by one or other of the authors. Each was told that his opinion was being sought on "the management of psychological and social problems in general practice". The interview consisted of general questions about the doctor and the practice, questions about the management of patients with psychological and social problems, and questions specifically relating to the social work attachment scheme. The records of the social workers were then examined to derive figures for referrals in 1977.

## Results

Seven of the practitioners were men and two women. The median age was 50 years (range 32 to 69 years) and the median length of time in general practice was 20 years (range five to 39 years). The number of patients on the list of the Health Centre was over 20,000, and the number for which each doctor was personally responsible varied from just under 2,000 to over 3,000. Their replies are presented in terms of the five questions.

*1. How Far Does the Doctors' Perception of Their Use of the Scheme Correspond to the Extent of Referral?*

The general practitioners were asked to estimate how many patients they had referred to the attached social workers in the previous year, and these figures, with the actual referrals, are given in Table 1. The estimates ranged

TABLE 1
General practitioners' referrals to the social work attachment scheme, 1977

| General practitioner | Estimated number of referrals | Actual number of referrals | Percentage inaccuracy of estimate |
|---|---|---|---|
| A | 100 | 30 | +233 |
| B | 50 | 23 | +117 |
| C | 40 | 38 | +5 |
| D | 40 | 13 | +208 |
| E | 52 | 24 | +108 |
| F | 16 | 19 | −19 |
| G | 30 | 27 | +11 |
| H | 20 | 17 | +18 |
| I | 30 | 25 | +20 |

from 16 to 100, and there were significant negative correlations with age and years in general practice (for both correlations, Spearman's r with correction for tied ranks was $-0.73$, $p < 0.05$). Six of the doctors felt that their referral pattern had changed over the years. One doctor believed that she made fewer referrals than previously, because of her awareness of the pressure of work on the social workers, while another five felt that they were making increasing use of social work referral, the reasons given being in terms of developing confidence in them and finding the service increasingly helpful. One doctor commented that referring patients to the attached social workers had become a "habit", although he in fact referred the fewest patients in 1977.

The social workers' records showed that the nine general practitioners actually referred 216 patients in 1977, individual figures ranging from 13 to 38 (Table 1). There was no relationship between estimated and actual referrals and, unlike the estimates, the actual referrals did not correlate with age or length of time in practice. All but one of the doctors overestimated the number referred, by amounts varying from five per cent to 233 per cent. The "reasonable estimators" (Drs C, F, G, H, and I) were in an older age group, had been longer in practice (median test, $p < 0.05$, both variables), and gave lower estimates (Mann-Whitney U = 0, $p < 0.05$) than the "inaccurate estimators" (Drs A, B, D, and E).

*2. What are the Doctors' Perceptions of the Attachment Scheme?*

The unanimous opinion was that the attachment scheme had been "very helpful". Particularly valued was the "new light" which a social worker could throw on a problem, because of her different approach and the greater amoung of time she could spend with a patient. One doctor, who valued the social worker attachment particularly highly, felt that he had been able to share with them the emotional burdens engendered by particular demanding patients. On the whole, the doctors believed that young patients with acute problems, particularly marital conflict and depression, benefited the most from social worker involvement, whereas patients with chronic intractable problems were felt to benefit the least (as one doctor expressed it, "those who benefit least from any treatment"). Two doctors, however, stressed the importance of the social worker providing support for such patients, one likening this role to that of a "sherpa".

### 3. What Difficulties have Arisen as a Result of the Scheme?

The general practitioners were asked if there had been any "disagreement or conflict" between them and the social workers with regard to (a) confidentiality of information, (b) primary responsibility for patient care, and (c) arising from differing concepts of illness held by the two professions. The unanimous opinion was that no conflict had arisen, but five of the doctors referred to disagreements and differences of opinion which had been resolved by direct discussion. All the doctors felt that involvement of a social worker with a patient could lead to more time being spent, for example, in case discussions or seeing patients at the social worker's request. None of them objected to this, the extra time being regarded as well spent.

### 4. Do the Doctors Believe that the Attachment Scheme has Influenced Their Management of Patients With Psychological and Social Problems, and If So, in What Way?

The doctors were asked: "Have you found that having a social worker attached to the practice has affected your management of patients with psychological and social problems, and if so, in what way?" All of the doctors answered affirmatively. One said that he now tended to hand over patients with social problems rather than dealing with them himself, but six of the general practitioners felt that the social workers had increased their awareness of social problems generally, and in relation to specific patients, the increased knowledge and fuller understanding of the social situation derived from the social workers allowed them to provide more comprehensive care. One doctor felt that general practitioners in general tended to shy away from patients with emotional problems, but that the presence of the social workers had helped him personally to avoid doing this. Another doctor commented that collaborating with members of another profession led to increasing awareness of one's own professional standards, and helped to keep one "on one's toes".

In relation to specific methods of management of psychological and social problems, two doctors felt that social worker referral was to some extent replacing the use of psychotropic drugs, and two felt that patients who would previously have been referred to a psychiatrist were now being referred to the attached social workers. Two general practitioners believed that referrals to the health visitors had decreased since the start of the attachment scheme, but all of them believed that referral to the local authority social services team had been totally replaced by referrals to the attachment scheme.

### 5. How Do the Doctors Perceive the Role of the Social Workers in Relation to That of the Health Visitor?

Each doctor was given the list that the social workers used to classify their clients' problems. Each was asked to indicate the problems he thought could "appropriately be managed by a social worker". He was then given a similar list (the same problems, but a different order of presentation), and asked to indicate the problems he thought could "appropriately be managed by a health visitor". The number of doctors so indicating each problem was summed, so that two scores (the "social worker score" and the "health visitor score") were derived for each problem (Table 2). The social worker scores were higher than the health visitor scores (Wilcoxon matched pairs signed ranks test $T = 25$, one tail $p < 0.005$), but there was a significant negative correlation between the two sets of scores (Spearman's r with correction for tied ranks, $= -0.53$, $p < 0.05$).

A quadrant analysis about the medians revealed three problems clusters:

(1) Those with high health visitor and low social worker scores — educational difficulties, bereavement, mental handicap in the family, physical disability and handicap, psychological or social problems associated with reproduction or pregnancy, and difficulties with child care.
(2) Those problems with low health visitor and high social worker scores — financial problems, criminal problems in the family, difficulties with wider family relationships, difficulties with other social relationships, employment problems, and housing problems.
(3) Those problems with above median values for both scores — marital problems, family break-up, social isolation, and loneliness.

The remaining problems had scores on one or both of the medians, no problem receiving below median values for both scores.

### Discussion

Within the limitations of this study (the small number of respondents and the relatively subjective nature of the inquiry), it is possible to make some general observations about the impact of the social work attachment scheme from the doctors' point of view.

The scheme was perceived very positively: all the doctors thought it was "very helpful", all claimed that it had influenced their practice, and inter-professional conflict was thought to be absent. Forman and Fairbairn in their study of a North Devon attachment scheme [1968] had similar findings: the social worker was thought not to have been helpful in only 5.6 per cent of cases referred.

It is possible that these positive opinions give rise to a "halo" effect surrounding the activities of the social workers. This is suggested by the

TABLE 2
Doctors' perceptions of the appropriateness of health visitor and social worker
referral in the management of psychosocial problems

| Problem | Number of doctors regarding the problem as suitable for health visitor referral (health visitor scores) | Number of doctors regarding the problem as suitable for social worker referral (social worker scores) |
| --- | --- | --- |
| Educational difficulties | 5 | 3 |
| Marital problems | 5 | 8 |
| Bereavement | 6 | 5 |
| Mental handicap in family | 6 | 6 |
| Financial problems | 2 | 9 |
| Problems with cultural adaptation | 2 | 7 |
| Physical disability and handicap | 8 | 5 |
| Family break-up | 6 | 9 |
| Criminal problems in family | 2 | 8 |
| Emotional problems or mental illness in patient or family | 2 | 7 |
| Psychological or social problems associated with reproduction and pregnancy | 7 | 3 |
| Difficulties with wider family relationships | 2 | 8 |
| Difficulties with other social relationships | 2 | 8 |
| Child neglect | 7 | 7 |
| Social isolation and loneliness | 2 | 8 |
| Problems with home and family management | 6 | 7 |
| Employment problems | 0 | 8 |
| Delinquency in family | 3 | 7 |
| Housing problems | 1 | 9 |
| Practical problems (transport, clothes) | 1 | 7 |
| Difficulties with child care | 8 | 4 |
| Problems with formal institutions and government departments such as DHSS | 0 | 7 |

degree to which the doctors overestimated their use of the scheme (in one case, by more than 200 per cent), although the more experienced doctors were more accurate in their estimations.

The main reason that the doctors felt so positively was the personal contact that they had with the social workers: they stressed the importance of face-to-face discussion and the lack of formality in the referral procedure. More impersonal social work referral facilities are perceived rather differently. Corney and Briscoe [1977a] compared this same attachment scheme with a "liaison scheme", also in South London, in which social workers took telephone referrals from general practitioners and visited them fortnightly. They found that in the liaison scheme referrals were more formal and less flexible, whereas informal discussions with the Health Centre team were an important part of the attached social workers' activities. Also, they found that the physical presence of the social worker in the practice led to more involvement with and referrals from other members of the health care team, than when a liaison-only service was provided. These findings question the assumption that reorganizing social workers into area-based teams would in itself result in improved client access, but support the view of Smith and Ames [1976], who suggested that closer liaison between social workers and other professional groups (such as general practitioners) might be more important. This view is further supported by the effect of the attachment scheme on referrals to the local authority social workers, which have virtually ceased since the start of the scheme. Also, patients who would not otherwise receive social work help are referred to the attachment scheme [Corney and Briscoe, 1977b].

The relationships that developed between the doctors and the social workers may also have helped to reduce interprofessional conflict. The doctors made reference to differences of opinion that had been resolved by discussion, and one can speculate that similar differences of opinion arising in a less congenial setting might easily escalate into conflict, with subsequent deterioration in relationships between the two disciplines. However, it would be unrealistic to suggest that problems never arise. Graham and Sher [1976] in their account of a North London attachment scheme, reported feelings of rivalry, competition, and envy between the disciplines, but it may be that these difficulties were, at least in part, a reflection of the intensely psycho-dynamic nature of that particular working relationship.

Developing a working relationship takes time, and all the general practitioners felt that more time was expended when a social worker was involved with a patient. Forman and Fairbairn [1968] estimated that each general practitioner expended an extra one to one and a half hours each week, but commented that in the long run, the social worker would save the practitioner more time than this. It is probably ill conceived to regard the social worker's function as saving the doctor's time, implying that it is inherently more valuable or that the problems undertaken by the social worker are of secondary importance: perhaps the only justification for this is that doctors' time costs more.

The doctors' views on the relative roles of the social worker and health visitor require comment. The Seebohm Committee took the view that the functions of the health visitor and social worker were distinct, and possibly incompatible in one person, and they deprecated the view that the health visitor should act as a social worker in general practice. Conversely, dealing with social problems has long been regarded as amongst the health visitor's responsibilities [Fry *et al.*, 1965], and Hicks [1976] cites a study by Jeffreys and colleagues who found that "family problems : psychosocial" was the reason for contact in 25 per cent of patients seen by health visitors attached to a group of metropolitan practices.

In our study, many of the problems on the checklist (problems which the social workers themselves regarded as constituting the bulk of their responsibilities) were seen by the doctors as appropriate for health visitor management. Some problems (cluster three above) were seen by the majority of doctors as more appropriate for health visitor than social worker management. However, the roles of the two professions were not seen as identical, as indicated by the negative correlation between "health visitor scores" and "social worker scores", and the distinct groups of problems regarded as appropriately managed by the two professions: problems associated with physical illness (cluster one above) by the health visitors, and practical and relationship problems (cluster two above) by the social workers.

It is not only doctors who have difficulty in distinguishing between the roles of the health visitor and social worker: the same issue arises within the two professions. There is a striking degree of overlap between the responsibilities of the health visitor as detailed by the Mayston Report [DHSS, 1969], and those of the social worker as defined by a working party of the National Institute for Social Work [Goldberg and Fruin, 1976]. This highlights issues of the appropriate training and effective deployment of these two types of health worker for optimal patient management in primary care, which can be settled only by future research.

More research is also needed into other aspects of social work attachment schemes; for example, outcome [Cooper *et al.*, 1976], and the effect of such schemes on variables such as psychotropic drug prescription, psychiatric referral, and other parameters of general practice.

## Acknowledgements

Thanks are due to the general practitioners who participated in the study, and particularly to Dr M. K. Thompson, a conversation with whom initiated ideas from which the study developed. Thanks are also due to Professor M. Shepherd and other members of the General Practice Research Unit for advice and criticism.

## References

Brook, A. and Temperley, J. (1976). A psychotherapeutic approach to general practice. *Journal of the Royal College of General Practitioners* 26, 86–94.

Collins, J. (1965). "Social Casework in General Medical Practice". Pitman Medical, London.

Cooper, E., Harwin, B. G., Depla, C. and Shepherd, M. (1975). Mental health care in the community: an evaluation study. *Psychological Medicine* 5, 372–380.

Corney, R. H. and Briscoe, M. E. (1977a). Investigation into two different types of attachment scheme. *Social Work Today* 9, 15, 10–14.

Corney, R. H. and Briscoe, M. E. (1977b). Social workers and their clients: a comparison between primary health care and local authority settings. *Journal of the Royal College of General Practitioners* 27, 295–301.

Department of Health and Social Security (1968). "Report of the Committee on Local Authority and Allied Personal Social Services" (Seebohm Report). HMSO, London.

Department of Health and Social Security (1969). "Report of the Working Party on Management Structure in the Local Authority Nursing Services" (Mayston Report). HMSO, London.

Department of Health and Social Security (1974). "Social Work Support for the Health Service". HMSO, London.

Forman, J. A. S. and Fairbairn, E. M. (1968). "Social Casework in General Practice". Oxford University Press, London.

Fry, J., Dillane, J. B. and Connolly, M. M. (1965). The evolution of a health team: a successful general practitioner—health visitor liaison. *British Medical Journal* 1, 181—183.

Goldberg, E. M. and Fruin, D. J. (1976). Towards accountability in social work. *British Journal of Social Work* 6, 3—22.

Goldberg, E. M. and Neill, J. E. (1972). "Social Work in General Practice". Allen and Unwin, London.

Graham, H. and Sher, M. (1976). Social work and general medical practice: personal accounts of a three year attachment. *British Journal of Social Work* 6, 233—249.

Hicks, D. (1976). "Primary Health Care. A Review". HMSO, London.

*Lancet* (1975). Psychiatrists, social workers and family doctors. Editorial 2, 805—806.

Ratoff, L. and Pearson, B. (1970). Social casework in general practice: an alternative approach. *British Medical Journal* 2, 475—477.

Ratoff, L., Rose, A. and Smith, C. (1974). Social workers and GPs: problems of working together. *Social Work Today* 5, 16, 497—500.

Shelly, M. W. and Bryan, G. L. (1964). "Human Judgement and Optimality". Wiley, New York.

Smith, G. and Ames, J. (1976). Area teams in social work practice: a programme for research. *British Journal of Social Work* 6, 43—70.

# SOCIAL WORK IN GENERAL PRACTICE

IAIN C. GILCHRIST, JEAN B. GOUGH, YVONNE R. HORSFALL-TURNER,
EILEEN M. INESON, GED KEELE, BERNARD MARKS and HEATHER J. SCOTT

## Summary

A questionnaire seeking details of working arrangements and problems
encountered was circulated to social workers working in general practice.

The main difficulties were: insufficient preparation for the scheme, poor
communication between general practitioners and social workers, and the
inadequate provision of facilities for social workers in practice premises.

Most of the respondents had not experienced big difficulties. Two thirds
had enjoyed a rewarding professional experience, which is a testimonial to
interdisciplinary co-operation.

## Introduction

There has been increasing interest in recent years in social workers and
general practitioners working together, and several studies have been
published describing early co-operative schemes [Forman and Fairbairn,
1968; Goldberg and Neill, 1972]. Many social workers and general
practitioners are probably working in relative isolation and little is known
about how widespread co-operative schemes are. Ratoff and colleagues
reported in 1973 but since then there have been further developments.

## Aim

One aim of the General Practitioner and Social Worker Workshop is to act as
a "clearing house" for such information, and where information does not
exist, to seek it. As little has been published on the current extent of social
work in general practice, we tried to assess this, examining the type of work
done by the social workers, their mode of working, and the problems they
encountered.

---

Reproduced, with permission, from the *Journal of the Royal College of General
Practitioners* 28, 675–686, 1978.

## Method

A questionnaire was drawn up under three sections: Organization and Logistics, Structured opinion, and Unstructured opinion.

In 1976 a letter was sent to the principal officer responsible for health services liaison in each social services department in Great Britain, asking for the names and addresses of social workers involved in cooperative schemes with general practitioners. Reminder letters were sent out later to those departments who did not reply initially. Individual social workers were then sent a questionnaire about their work in general practice and asked to return it in the stamped addressed envelope which was enclosed.

A few departments refused to divulge the names and addresses of individual social workers and in these cases, the questionnaires had to be distributed through the social services department concerned. Although the total number of questionnaires sent to these departments is known, we have no means to knowing how many were actually distributed to social workers, and to what extent some departments may have over ordered copies of the questionnaire. Reminders and further questionnaires were sent to those of the first 100 social workers who had not replied to the first questionnaire after three months. Owing to the limitations of time, reminders could not be sent to the other social workers. The completed questionnaires were analysed and the results tabulated.

## Results

Four hundred and twenty questionnaires were distributed: 219 questionnaires were available for analysis, some of which were only partially completed. In some sections, social workers provided additional answers relating to two places of work and so some answers total more than 219.

The response rate was 52.1 per cent. As explained above, however, some social workers who received a questionnaire may have been overestimated by the system of sending a batch of questionnaires to some authorities. Of the 285 questionnaires posted to *individual* social workers, 181 were returned — a response rate of 63.5 per cent.

Table 1 summarizes the number of local authorities with schemes: over half the departments in Great Britain have organized links with general practitioners.

### Section A: Organization and Logistics

The first part of the questionnaire dealt with the organization and logistics of the co-operation scheme, under seven headings.

### 1. Initiation of the Scheme

*Question i)*  When did the scheme start? (Answers given in Table 2.)

*Question ii)*  When did you start work in the scheme? (Answers given in Table 3.)

TABLE 1
Number of local authorities having social work schemes*

| | With schemes | | Without schemes | | Ambiguous replies | No reply | Total |
|---|---|---|---|---|---|---|---|
| | Number | Percentage | Number | Percentage | | | |
| Metropolitan districts | 16 | 44.4 | 18 | 50.0 | 0 | 2 | 36 |
| Counties | | | | | | | |
| — England | 26 | 66.7 | 9 | 23.1 | 1 | 3 | 39 |
| — Wales | 3 | 37.5 | 2 | 25.0 | 1 | 2 | 8 |
| London boroughs | 14 | 42.4 | 18 | 54.5 | 0 | 1 | 33 |
| Scottish regions | 6 | 50.0 | 3 | 25.0 | 1 | 2 | 12 |
| Total | 65 | 50.8 | 50 | 39.1 | 3 | 10 | 128 |

* This classification is the same as that adopted by the Association of Directors of Social Services in the booklet *Directory of Local Authority Social Services Departments* [1975].

TABLE 2
Initiation of the scheme

| | 1960s | 1970 | 1971 | 1972 | 1973 | 1974 | 1975 | 1976 | No answer |
|---|---|---|---|---|---|---|---|---|---|
| Number | 8 | 4 | 9 | 17 | 34 | 41 | 66 | 15 | 25 |
| Per cent | 3.7 | 1.8 | 4.1 | 7.8 | 15.5 | 18.7 | 30.1 | 6.9 | 11.4 |

TABLE 3
Number of social workers in the scheme

| | 1960s | 1970 | 1971 | 1972 | 1973 | 1974 | 1975 | 1976 | No answer |
|---|---|---|---|---|---|---|---|---|---|
| Number | 4 | — | 2 | 5 | 18 | 47 | 104 | 26 | 13 |
| Per cent | 1.8 | — | 0.9 | 2.3 | 8.2 | 21.5 | 47.5 | 11.9 | 5.9 |

TABLE 4
Type of scheme

| | Number | Per cent |
|---|---|---|
| Permanent | 135 | 61.6 |
| Experimental — definite limited period | 4 | 1.8 |
| Experimental — to be reviewed in light of progress | 59 | 26.9 |
| Other | 12 | 5.5 |
| No answer | 9 | 4.1 |

Half the schemes have started since the end of 1973, and half the social workers have been working in them since the end of 1974.

*Question iii)* What type of scheme is it? (Table 4.)

## 2. Logistics

*Question i)*  How many hours per week do you spend working in general practice?

There were 190 valid answers; 29 did not reply. The range was from 0 to 37.5 hours; the mean was 4.59 hours; standard deviation 7.70 hours. The median time was two hours.

*Question ii)*  How many hours per week do you spend working in settings other than general practice?

There were 177 valid answers; 42 did not reply. The range was from 0 to 60 hours; the mean was 31.39 hours; standard deviation 10.94 hours. The median time was 35.5 hours.

From the facts given above, it can be seen that the majority of social workers are full time, devoting only a small part of their working week to general practice. The sum of the two median times exactly equals the standard working week. The sum of the mean is slightly smaller and can perhaps be accounted for by the relatively small number of social workers working exclusively part time in general practice. There seem to be three or four groups of social workers (in this context):

(1) Full time in general practice.
(2) Part time exclusively in general practice.
(3) Session in general practice, bulk of work elsewhere — "attachment" social workers.
(4) Liaison only — no clients seen in general practice, but communication between general practitioner and social worker.

There is naturally some overlap between groups. The other defined settings in which the social workers worked are shown in Table 5.

There is some evidence that different types of local authorities have different types of schemes (Table 6).

When Metropolitan districts and London boroughs, representing the conurbation authorities, are compared with the urban and rural English and Welsh counties and Scottish regions, the difference between the numbers of social workers in sessional and in liaison attachments is statistically significant: $\chi^2 = 14.64$, d.f. = 1, p < 0.001.

*Question iii)*  How many doctors work in the general-practice centre(s) in which you work? (Table 7.)

*Question iv)*  Do you work with all the doctors in the centre?

One hundred and eighty-seven (85.4 per cent) social workers worked with all doctors in the group; 20 (9.1 per cent) did not work with all doctors in the group; 12 (5.5 per cent) did not answer.

Comparison with the tables published by the DHSS [1975] shows that there is under-representation of single-handed, and over-representation of groups of six or more practitioners in the study, compared with national figures.

TABLE 5
Other settings in which the social workers worked

|  | *Number* | *Per cent* |
|---|---|---|
| Social services department | 160 | 73.1 |
| None | 10 | 4.6 |
| Hospital social work team | 9 | 4.1 |
| Other | 9 | 4.1 |
| No answer | 31 | 14.2 |
| Total | 219 | 100 |

TABLE 6
Social work schemes

|  | *Full time general practice* | *Part time in general practice, but no other work* | *Part time in general practice, main work elsewhere* | *Liaison only* | *Unclassified because of overlap of groups* |
|---|---|---|---|---|---|
| Metropolitan districts | — | — | 26 | 4 | 2 |
| Counties | | | | | |
| — England | 2 | 1 | 39 | 59 | 18 |
| — Wales | — | — | 5 | 2 | 1 |
| London boroughs | — | 1 | 15 | 9 | 2 |
| Scottish regions | — | 1 | 7 | 6 | 3 |
| Not known | 4 | 3 | 7 | 2 | 0 |
| Total | 6 | 6 | 99 | 82 | 26 |

TABLE 7
Number of doctors working in the general-practice centre(s)

| *Number of doctors* | *Number of general-practice centres* | *Per cent* |
|---|---|---|
| 1 | 5 | 2.3 |
| 2 | 24 | 11.0 |
| 3 | 32 | 14.6 |
| 4 | 39 | 17.8 |
| 5 | 33 | 15.1 |
| 6 | 27 | 12.3 |
| 7 | 14 | 6.4 |
| 8 | 8 | 3.7 |
| 9 | 5 | 2.3 |
| 10 | 5 | 2.3 |
| 11—20 | 11 | 5.0 |
| > 20 | 1 | 0.5 |
| No answer | 15 | 6.9 |

*Question v)*  Do your responsibilities in social work outside general practice include working in any other situations? (Table 8.)

## 3. Organization Within Practice

*Question i)*  Do the practice premises include a room which is solely for the use of a social worker? (Table 9a.)
  Those giving no as the answer to this question were asked to specify the room arrangements at the general practice. (Table 9b.)

*Question ii)*  In the room you most commonly use is there a telephone available? (Table 10a.)
  Those giving no as the answer to this question were asked if a practice telephone was available for their use. (Table 10b.)

*Question iii)*  Is secretarial help provided in the practice premises and if so by whom? (Table 11.)

*Question iv)*  Is secretarial help provided for you in premises other than the practice? (Table 12.)

*Question v)*  Are the practice receptionists used to make appointments for your clients? (Table 13a.)
  Those giving no as the answer to this question were asked to provide details for the making of appointments. (Table 13b.)

*Question vi)*  Does the local authority assist the practice financially? (Areas of financial assistance listed in Table 14.)

## 4. Communication

*Question i)*  Do you record directly onto NHS records?

*Question ii)*  Are reports from you included regularly in the NHS records?

*Question iii)*  Do members of the practice send requests (or reports that you include in your records)?

*Question iv)*  Are regular meetings with the practice staff included in your weekly timetable?
  The results are given in Table 15.
  Those social workers who do meet regularly with practice staff were asked to provide details of the number of staff with whom they have meetings. (Table 16.)
  There is no statistically significant difference between the sessional and liaison groups in respect of parts (i) and (ii) of this question. However, there is a statistically significant difference between these groups in parts (iii) and

TABLE 8
Other situations involving social work responsibilities outside general practice
(percentages in brackets)

|  | Yes | No | Not applicable |
|---|---|---|---|
| Intake team | 55 | 87 | 77 |
|  | (25.1) | (39.7) | (35.2) |
| Long-term team | 112 | 43 | 64 |
|  | (51.1) | (19.6) | (29.2) |
| Hospital team | 12 | 114 | 93 |
|  | (5.5) | (52.1) | (42.5) |
| Situation other than above | 70 | 62 | 87 |
|  | (32.0) | (28.3) | (39.7) |

Forty-nine specified that they were generic social workers in an area team.

TABLE 9A
Presence of a room used solely by a social worker at the general practice

|  | Yes | No | Not applicable |
|---|---|---|---|
| Number | 44 | 167 | 10 |
| Per cent | 19.9 | 75.6 | 4.5 |

In this question there were 221 possible answers as two respondents answered twice in respect of different general practices in which they worked.

TABLE 9B
Room arrangements for the social worker at the general practice

|  | Number | Per cent |
|---|---|---|
| Spare surgery | 49 | 29.3 |
| Records room | 1 | 0.6 |
| Other room (shared) | 40 | 24.0 |
| Room (unspecified) | 15 | 9.0 |
| No answer | 62 | 37.1 |
| Total | 167 | 100 |

TABLE 10A
Availability of telephone in room most commonly used

|  | Yes | No | Not applicable |
|---|---|---|---|
| Number | 149 | 39 | 31 |
| Per cent | 68 | 17.8 | 14.2 |

TABLE 10B
Availability of a practice telephone

|  | Yes | No |
|---|---|---|
| Number | 34 | 7 |
| Per cent | 82.9 | 17.1 |

Thirty-nine answering no, and two answering not applicable to question (ii), gave responses to this question (total 41).

TABLE 11
Provision of secretarial help in the practice

|  | Yes | No | Not applicable |
|---|---|---|---|
| Number | 46 | 145 | 28 |
| Per cent | 21 | 66.2 | 12.8 |

|  | Number | Per cent |
|---|---|---|
| Secretarial help provided by: |  |  |
| — the practice | 33 | 71.7 |
| — local authority | 8 | 17.4 |
| — area health authority | 1 | 2.2 |
| — the practice/local authority | 1 | 2.2 |
| No answer | 3 | 6.5 |
| Total | 46 | 100 |

TABLE 12
Provision of secretarial help in premises other than the practice

|  | Yes | No | Not applicable |
|---|---|---|---|
| Number | 163 | 35 | 21 |
| Per cent | 74.4 | 16.0 | 9.6 |

TABLE 13A
Use of practice receptionists in the making of appointments

|  | Yes | No | Not applicable |
|---|---|---|---|
| Number | 78 | 119 | 23 |
| Per cent | 35.4 | 54.1 | 10.4 |

One person answered twice for the two practices he works in.

TABLE 13B
How appointments are made

|  | Number | Per cent |
|---|---|---|
| Via area office | 33 | 28 |
| By social worker | 29 | 24.6 |
| Referred by general practitioner or other member of team (e.g. health visitor, district nurse) and visited at home | 20 | 17 |
| Liaison only | 20 | 17 |
| No answer | 13 | 11 |
| Separate receptionists for social workers in health centre | 2 | 1.7 |
| Message written in memo book | 1 | 0.9 |

TABLE 14
Areas in which financial assistance is provided by the local authority

|  | Number answering yes | Per cent |
|---|---|---|
| Accommodation | 14 | 6.4 |
| Use of telephone | 14 | 6.4 |
| Secretarial assistance | 10 | 4.6 |
| Local authority premises used | 5 | 2.3 |

These responses should be compared with the responses to questions 3 (i) and 3 (v) which detail the services available to the social worker.

TABLE 15
Communication between social workers and members of the practice
(figures given as percentages)

|  | Yes | No | Not applicable |
|---|---|---|---|
| (i) Direct recording onto NHS records | 6 | 90.8 | 3.2 |
| (ii) Regular inclusion of reports in NHS records | 20.2 | 74.3 | 5.5 |
| (iii) Requests (or reports) from practice members | 75.2 | 20.6 | 4.1 |
| (iv) Regular meetings with practice staff | 65.6 | 30.7 | 3.2 |

TABLE 16
Percentage of social workers meeting with doctors and other workers

| Social workers meeting with: | |
|---|---|
| — several doctors | 33.3 |
| — doctors and other workers | 29.2 |
| — one doctor | 5 |

The number of social workers working exclusively in general practice is too small to allow statistical evaluation.

(v). Social workers with a sessional attachment were more likely to receive requests or reports that they included in their own records ($\chi^2$ = 8.06, $p < 0.005$) and to have regular meetings with the practice staff ($\chi^2$ = 11.25, $p < 0.001$) than social workers with a liaison scheme.

## 5. Social Work Aspects

*Question i)* Do you accept referrals from the following? The figures given are percentages of social workers answering yes.

| | |
|---|---|
| Doctors | 97.3 |
| Health visitors | 90.4 |
| District nurses | 81.7 |
| Direct from client | 70.3 |
| Others: ranging from police, DHSS, neighbours, schools and so on | 44.4 |

*Question ii)* The following is a list of the types of referral that you might have been asked to deal with. Could you please tick those types of referral that you have actually received while working in your present attachment. Answers are given as percentages answering yes:

| | |
|---|---|
| Provision of appliances for the physically handicapped (other than the deaf and the blind) | 83.6 |
| Provision of services for: | |
| — the deaf | 35.2 |
| — the blind | 55.3 |

(In some instances the social worker accepted referral but passed it on to a specialist worker.)

| | |
|---|---|
| Advice about social benefits (for example, money) | 83.1 |
| Obtaining accommodation for clients (for example, rehousing, part III for elderly) | 90.0 |
| Assisting the client with problems arising from: | |
| — marital conflict | 87.7 |
| — marital separation | 80.4 |
| — contact with the law | 51.6 |
| — conflict with parents | 75.8 |
| — other reasons | 76.3 |
| For assistance with management of psychiatris illness: | |
| — psychotic illness (for example, schizophrenia, manic depressive illness) | 73.1 |
| — other psychiatric illnesses (for example, neurotic depression, anxiety, psychosomatic illness) | 84.0 |

## 6. Use of Statutory Powers

When based in general practice are you able to use statutory powers (for example, under the Mental Health Act)? The percentage answering yes to this question was 60.7 per cent.

TABLE 17
Qualification and background of the social workers

|  | Percentage of social workers |
|---|---|
| Qualification: |  |
| – qualified | 83.9 |
| – unqualified | 12.4 |
| – no answer | 3.7 |
| Background: |  |
| – welfare assistant grade | 0.9 |
| – basic grade | 59.6 |
| – senior grade | 27.1 |
| – other grades, ranging from trainees to |  |
|    assistant team leaders | 9.2 |
| – no answer | 3.2 |

## 7. Qualification and Background

The qualification and background of the social workers are given in Table 17.

All social workers working full time, or exclusively part time, were qualified. Of those working on a sessional basis, 81.8 per cent were qualified, 15.2 per cent were unqualified, and 3.0 per cent did not answer. Of those who had a liaison arrangement, 86.6 per cent were qualified, 12.2 per cent were unqualified, and 1.2 per cent did not answer.

There is no statistically significant difference between the sessional and liaison groups in respect of the different grades in which the social workers are employed, nor in respect of the numbers qualified and unqualified.

## Section B: Structured Opinion about Problems in Attachments

This section of the questionnaire considered factors that might cause problems in co-operative schemes between social work and general practice. In order to simplify the completion of the questionnaire a list of 12 potential problems was drawn up. Respondents were asked to list the problems that had actually occurred in their scheme. They were also given the opportunity to rate the severity of each problem. The problem list was compiled by the authors on the basis of experience, but space was included so that the respondent could add problems not mentioned on the list. The 12 problems were:

(1) Inadequate provision of accommodation for the social worker.
(2) Inadequate provision of services, for example, telephone, secretaries, and so on.
(3) Lack of preliminary discussion between attached social worker and social work seniors about the attachment.
(4) Lack of preliminary discussion between the social work agency (or social worker) and the practice team about the attachment.
(5) Absence of regular structured meetings between doctors and social workers to discuss clients' problems.

(6) Inadequate provision of opportunity for informal discussion about patients' problems.
(7) Absence of regular channels of communication with the practice so that problems arising in the attachment may be discussed.
(8) Absence of procedure for regular written communication about clients' problems.
(9) The absence of channels of communication with the senior staff in the social work agency so that problems arising in the attachment may be discussed.
(10) The referral to the social worker of problems that prove professionally unsatisfying.
(11) The impairment of communication by the problems of language (social workers and doctors use language differently and each have a technical jargon of their own).
(12) That the personalities involved in the attachment are incompatible.

## Results

Problems were rated as occurring in 170 schemes. The majority of respondents confined themselves to the problems defined in the list; no respondent added more than one further problem to the list.

### Frequency of Problems in Schemes

A histogram has been prepared to show the distribution of problems within the schemes (Fig. 1). The majority had three or fewer problems, and a

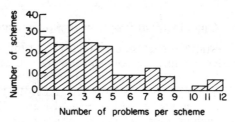

**Fig. 1**   Distribution of problems in the schemes

minority had a large number of problems (six or more). The total number of schemes was 170; the total number of problems was 697, and so the average number of problems per scheme was 4.1.

### Types of Problems in Schemes

A histogram has been constructed to show the distribution of types of problems (Fig. 2). The three most common problems were lack of preliminary discussion, lack of regular structured meetings, and referral of problems that are professionally unsatisfying to the social worker.

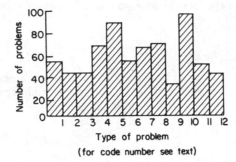

Type of problem
(for code number see text)

**Fig. 2** Distribution of type of problem

*Severity of Problems*

Scrutiny of the ratings showed that there were three categories of severity of problem. These are shown in Table 18 (the more severe the problem, the greater the number of asterisks).

TABLE 18
Severity of problem

| Severity | Problem number |
|---|---|
| * | 8, 9, 10, 11, 12 |
| ** | 1, 2, 3, 7 |
| *** | 4, 5, 6 |

## Section C. Unstructured Comments

Space was allowed at the end of the questionnaire to amplify responses in the structured part of the questionnaire. We also invited any favourable comments to counterbalance the previous section of the questionnaire (Section B).

One hundred and sixty people chose to make further comments. The most important points to emerge were:

*1. Commitment*

A high level of commitment of social service departments, management, field workers, and general practitioners is essential for the success of the scheme. This implies that social service management have given a degree of priority in their allocation of resources.

*2. Adequate Preparation*

Many respondents stressed that the success of their scheme owed much to adequate preparation by all levels in the social services department and the general practitioners before the scheme started. Lack of suitable preparation can be disastrous.

### 3. Choice of Social Worker

It is necessary to select social workers who, in addition to social work qualifications, have the necessary personal qualities and experience to have a flexible approach in their attitude to medical practice.

### 4. Communication

There was emphasis on the importance of regular meetings for the discussion of individual cases and general problems within the team — regularity being more important than the length of the meetings. Over one third of the respondents indicated that there had been an improvement in communication and understanding with the general practitioner and other members of the team.

About one third of the replies commented on the growth of knowledge and understanding of each other's roles and responsibilities as a result of working together.

### 5. Attitudes

It seemed that the difficult and less tangible area of attitudes is crucial to the success or failure of attachment and liaison schemes. Two comments illustrate this very well: "My replies should indicate that the practical issues have been quite secondary to the attitudinal issues." "The most important single factor was probably the desire of all concerned to make [the scheme] work, and therefore to work through the problems which did arise."

### Discussion

The response rate to the questionnare has been discussed earlier. It is, in view of our ignorance of the proportion of questionnaires sent to social service departments which actually reached social workers, impossible to provide an accurate estimate, but it falls within the range of 52 to 63 per cent, and is probably nearer the latter.

We use the term "attachment" to refer to those schemes where social workers see clients in general-practice premises, be they health centres, group practice premises, or traditional surgeries. When social workers relate to particular general practitioners and accept referrals from the practice, but do not actually see clients in the practice premises, they are described as participating in liaison schemes.

The replies to the first part of the questionnaire reveal that just over half the social service departments in Great Britain are involved in schemes of either type, two thirds of which had started since the end of 1973. Eighty per cent of the respondent social workers started to work in their schemes after that date, which appears to mark a watershed in the relationship between social work and general practice, following the implementation of the Seebohm report. Since the beginning of 1974 the number of attachment and liaison schemes has considerably increased.

Because of differing methods it is difficult to compare the results of this part of the questionnaire with the findings of the survey conducted in 1972 by Ratoff and colleagues. Their data were obtained from directors of social service departments and their enquiries remained outside the terms of the study. They discovered that although about 50 per cent of social service departments operated medical attachment schemes, they involved only a very small proportion of social workers (1.5 per cent of full-time equivalents), most of whom\worked in the hospital services with very few working in general practice.

We found that there is a higher proportion of schemes in the county councils than in the metropolitan boroughs (3:2), but many of the former are liaison arrangements, probably for geographical reasons, since long distances and scattered populations make attachment schemes difficult to administer.

Ratoff and his colleagues had found in their study that Greater London and the South-West had the largest number of social workers attached to general practice, whereas the North, Yorkshire and Wales had the smallest.

In our survey 60 per cent of the schemes were described as permanent, the remainder being experimental — a few for a limited period only, and the majority being subject to periodic review.

Of the 193 social workers who defined their categories, only six worked full time and six part time in general practice attachments, with no other social work commitment. Ninety-nine (45 per cent) spent part of their time in attachments, with their principal social work involvement elsewhere, and 82 (37 per cent) worked in liaison schemes.

Two thirds worked with groups of four or more doctors, either in health centres or general practice premises, suggesting that doctors practising in groups were more able to make social work help available to their patients than doctors practising alone or in smaller groups.

The answers to the section of the questionnaire concerned with the facilities available to the social worker in the practice premises revealed some disquieting deficiencies. In only 20 per cent of the schemes was there a room solely for the use of the social worker; 17 per cent of rooms used had no telephone, and only 21 per cent of social workers had secretarial help in the practice. Practice receptionists made appointments for clients in 35 per cent of the attachment schemes.

We consider that a personal interviewing room is as important to the attached social worker's task as the surgery is to the general practitioner's. We suggest that the following facilities are desirable for the effective operation of social work attachments, and should be negotiated at the initial planning meetings:

(1) Interview room.
(2) Telephone.
(3) Secretarial help.
(4) Filing and recording facilities.
(5) Receptionists' services.

Social workers in liaison schemes have more modest needs — the minimal requirements being access to a telephone, recording facilities, and the opportunity to discuss clients with doctors.

The replies to the section of the questionnaire on communication revealed that only six per cent of social workers recorded directly into the patient's notes, and that in no more than 20 per cent of cases were social reports inserted in the NHS records. The issue of confidentiality may be raised to account for these disappointing figures, but if shared care is to have meaning, it is necessary to share information in the interest of the patient. Equally disturbing is the revelation that in 30 per cent of replies there were no regular meetings between the social worker and the remainder of the practice staff, including the practitioners. Working under the same roof is not synonymous with working together.

It was gratifying to learn that the majority of social workers accepted referrals from the other members of the primary health care team and from the client directly, and that almost half were prepared to offer help to clients referred from any source in the community.

In an attempt to determine the patterns of work in general practice a list of 12 headings was included in the questionnaire (Section A, question 5 (ii)), and the respondents were asked to indicate in which problem areas they had received referrals. Seventy-five per cent had received requests for help in all but three groups; the least common being the provision of services for the deaf and the blind, and contact with the law, which tend to be the more specialized areas, and a number of social workers commented that referrals for the deaf and the blind were dealt with by specialist workers.

Forman and Fairbarn [1968], Cooper [1971] in his report of the Derby scheme, and Goldberg and Neill [1972] have described the range of social and psychological problems encountered by social workers in general practice attachments. Consideration of the replies to this section of the questionnaire, in the light of these accounts, suggests that a degree of uniformity of referral exists whenever social workers treat clients in the *milieu* of general practice.

From the results of Section B of the questionnaire, two of the three most frequently identified difficulties, that is, "lack of preliminary discussion between the social work agency (or social worker) and the practice team about the attachment" (problem four), and "absence of regular structured meetings between doctors and social workers to discuss clients' problems" (problem five), were rated as severe, and the third severe problem, "inadequate provision of opportunity for informal discussion about patients' problems" (problem six), is closely related in content to problem five.

The coincidence between the frequency and severity of problems four and five is highly significant and provides an opportunity to focus on the causes of potential failure of both attachment and liaison schemes, and perhaps to offer some suggestions for methods of prevention of such mishaps.

It is evident that without adequate preliminary discussion, liaison and attachment schemes are likely to founder on rocks which cannot be avoided by good intentions alone. A representative of social services management, the social worker likely to be involved in the scheme, and the general practitioner should participate in preliminary discussions in order to establish the basis of the collaborative relationship between the social workers and the general practitioners. It is suggested that discussions should include the following topics:

(1) The types of referrals most appropriate to the skills of a social worker in general practice.
(2) The quantity of social work time available to the doctors.
(3) Accommodation for the social worker.
(4) Access to medical records and type of recording.
(5) Secretarial help.
(6) Provision of a telephone.

Preliminary agreement about communication is essential for the success of the schemes. Time must be set aside for regular case meetings, in addition to informal discussions about mutual problems as they arise. There may be difficulties in communication in the early stages as a consequence of the different assumptions of each profession, and the different vocabularies used to describe similar problems — the social model may be unfamiliar to general practitioners and the medical model misunderstood or disliked by social workers.

The members of the General Practitioner and Social Worker Workshop believe that the questionnaire has served a useful purpose in discovering the amount of collaboration existing between social workers and general practitioners, and revealing some of the difficulties which have emerged from the attachment and liaison schemes.

## Acknowledgements

The authors thank all the social workers who returned the questionnaire, and the Research Foundation Board of the Royal College of General Practitioners for financial assistance.

## References

Association of Directors of Social Services (1975). "Directory of Local Authority Social Services Departments". ADSS, Newcastle.

Cooper, B. (1971). *Lancet* 1, 539–542.

Department of Health and Social Security (1975). "Health and Personal Social Services Statistics for England". HMSO, London.

Forman, J. A. S. and Fairbairn, E. M. (1968). "Social Casework in General Practice". Oxford University Press, London.

Goldberg, E. M. and Neill, J. E. (1972). "Social Work in General Practice". George Allen and Unwin, London.

Ratoff, L., Cooper, B. and Rockett, D. (1973). *British Medical Journal*, Suppl. 2, 51–53.

# HEALTH VISITORS AND SOCIAL WORKERS

ROSLYN H. CORNEY

## Summary

Relationships between social workers and health visitors are often difficult; the two professions often work in isolation from each other and have limited knowledge of each other's roles and training. In this study, 15 health visitors were interviewed regarding their referrals and contacts with local authority social workers and other social work agencies. Three of the health visitors were attached to a health centre which also had a social work attachment scheme in operation. The effects of the joint attachment scheme on the relationships between the two professions is discussed together with the findings of the study.

## Introduction

The health visitor is in contact with many of the more vulnerable sections of the community and is in a key position to detect and diagnose signs of stress in families with young children. A study of health visitors in Berkshire [1] found that although problems of physical ill health were still by far the major part of the health visitor's work, psychosocial problems were becoming increasingly more important. Attachment schemes to general practices has also contributed to this; attached health visitors usually cover a wider age group and a higher percentage of their visits are to families with special health or social problems specifically referred by doctors. [2, 3]

The general social worker deals with very similar sections of the population to the health visitor, i.e. families with children, the elderly, the physically and mentally handicapped. Her emphasis has been on the social and emotional problems of her clients varying from practical problems (e.g. finances, aids for the handicapped) to all sorts of relationship problems including mental illness and depression.

The roles of the health visitor and social worker thus overlap. One study estimated that 27.5 per cent of all matters referred to the medical social workers could have been managed entirely by the health visitor and 35.6 per cent dealt with partially by her. [4] It is therefore increasingly important

Reproduced, with permission, from the *Health Visitor* 53, 409−413, 1980.

that the two professions can collaborate together in the management of their cases to avoid omissions and duplication of work.

In this study, 15 health visitors were interviewed, all working under one nursing officer. The area covered was very diverse, including all types of housing and people of all social classes. Most of the health visitors covered mixed areas with rented, council and private housing but one health visitor covered a "high risk" area, a council housing estate where over 50 per cent of the families were single parents. Three of the health visitors were attached to a health centre with an attachment scheme of four part-time social workers. One of the areas of interest of this study was to find out whether the joint attachment scheme (of health visitors and social workers) enabled the two professions to work more closely together.

## Method

The health visitors were interviewed individually using a semi-structured questionnaire. This covered referrals and contacts with social workers in the social services department, in voluntary bodies and in other agencies such as hospitals or child guidance. Additional questions were asked about how the health visitors dealt with any social problems arising in their cases.

## Results

### 1. Referrals to Social Workers in the Local Authority

The health visitors were asked how many cases they had referred to the social workers in the past few months. They varied considerably in their referral rate to social workers in the local authority. Although the health visitor in the "high risk" area referred the most cases (about 12 a month) the numbers referred did not always relate to the type of area covered and the numbers of social problems presented. The three health visitors in the health centre also referred a substantial number of cases to the local authority social workers operating in the attachment scheme, approximately two to five cases a month each. The majority of the other health visitors made fewer referrals, approximately one case every two to three months, and two health visitors rarely referred a case.

The health visitors were also asked about the type of cases they had referred to the social workers in the past year and then given a checklist of problems and asked which ones they felt appropriate for referral. Recent referrals mostly consisted of families with multiple problems or severe practical or financial problems. They usually referred during a crisis or when the problems had become severe and chronic. Potential child abuse cases were also referred.

In addition to these types of cases, the health visitors attached to the health centre referred families with relationship and emotional problems, some of which had no accompanying material or financial problems. These cases included unsupported and depressed mothers and women with marital problems. The overall impression was that these health centre health visitors referred cases before they had either reached a state of acute crisis or had become chronic.

The health visitors outside the health centre rarely considered referring to social workers when patients had relationship or emotional problems only. With marital problems nearly all would suggest Marriage Guidance. With emotional problems or problems of minor or mental ill health, they would usually either contact the doctor involved or suggest that the client visits him. Many were uncertain about how much the social workers knew about depression and were wary of referring these cases directly. With other relationship problems the health visitors would sometimes refer to the social worker especially if other problems were present. One of the health visitors operating in a predominantly middle class area felt that she would rarely refer these problems to a social worker as her clients would prefer to manage their own problems. She felt that there was a stigma attached to seeing a social worker and that none of the problems in her families were so serious as to merit involving a social worker. Another health visitor had found similar problems: many of her clients had refused to see a social worker when she had suggested it.

Most of the health visitors considered that problems of bereavement, child care or social isolation were not appropriate for referral to social workers. They regarded dealing with these problems as part of their role. They encouraged their isolated mothers to attend play groups or toddlers groups which they often ran themselves. Some of the health visitors aimed to create new friendships between mothers by running a "matching service" whereby they introduced mothers who lived close to each other and who had babies of the same age. The health visitors would also not normally refer child care problems unless they were very severe or associated with other problems.

## 2. Contacts with Local Authority Social Workers

There was a similar variation among health visitors in the number of contacts made with social workers. Of those outside the health centre attachment, two rarely had any contact, six had monthly contact or less, and three had weekly contact. Most of these contacts were made over the telephone and many of the health visitors interviewed had never personally met any of the social workers in the area. The health visitor in the "high risk" area had almost daily contact with the social workers in the area. Social workers would often come into her office when in the area to discuss clients in common.

The three health centre health visitors also had a high degree of contact, usually several times a week. These contacts were informal, discussing patients over coffee or in each other's room. The health centre health visitors' discussions with the social workers often involved the doctor as well. The three professions discussed future handling of the case, who should be the key worker, how the problem should be dealt with, coordination of work and when to visit. The health centre health visitors also contacted the social workers for advice or information on matters such as welfare benefits and sometimes the social workers would ask them for advice. The health visitors would often discuss a case before referral so that mutual agreement could be reached about the appropriateness of social work intervention.

The health visitor covering the "high risk" area also discussed current problems and future case management with the social worker involved. She used the social workers as a source of information and would usually ring up the social services department before referring a case to see if it was appropriate. The other health visitors varied in the amount of discussion they had with the social workers. On the whole, there was very little sharing of information. The finer details of each other's involvement were not discussed. Most of the health visitors had never considered contacting the social workers for advice or information.

## 3. Helpfulness of Local Authority Social Workers

The health visitors were asked if they felt that the social workers had helped them in the management of their caseload. The health centre health visitors were all agreed on how much the presence of the social work attachment had helped them. The social workers were not only helpful with specific cases but they were able to share anxieties with them over certain cases, especially those of child neglect.

The health visitor covering the "high risk" area also found the social workers supportive and said that she "couldn't do without them". She felt that they helped most in areas such as legislation where she knew little.

Most of the health visitors operating outside the health centre attachment scheme had found the social workers helpful in the past. However, there were obvious difficulties in the relationships between the two professions. One health visitor felt that she could offer as much to her clients as a social worker could. Other health visitors felt that the local authority social workers did not attempt to involve them in their cases and often did not consult them before taking a major decision. They felt that the two professions often worked in isolation and in many cases were not aware of each other's involvement. Some of the health visitors thought that the social workers knew little about their training or work and consequently did not regard the health visitor's role in the case as being important.

## 4. Contacts with other Social Work Agencies

The majority of the health visitors had little contact with social work agencies other than the local authority. This includes psychiatric social workers, child guidance, the probation service and the NSPCC. Occasionally these agencies would ask for a report about the home situation from the health visitor concerned but she would receive little feedback from the agency in return. Only two of the health visitors had much contact with the NSPCC and one of these was the health visitor covering the "high risk" area.

The health visitors had most contact with medical social workers and the Deanery, a voluntary organization aiming to help single mothers. The medical social workers would refer cases to the health visitor as the mothers left hospital and they would also ask for reports. They seemed more aware of the health visitors' role than the other agencies.

## 5. The Overlap with Social Work

Thirteen out of the 15 health visitors interviewed regarded dealing with the social problems of their clients as part of their work and felt that they had to set aside enough time to deal with them. Often they considered these cases to be a priority. One health visitor regretted the amount of time spent on routine visits as this affected the time left to deal with the more difficult problems.

The health visitors were asked about the sort of work they did to help their clients with problems and they were read a list of agencies to find out if they had contacted them on their client's behalf. Most of the health visitors gave their clients advice on benefits or aids and also suggested to their clients the best agency to contact for their particular problem e.g. the housing department or the DHSS. Many suggested the Citizens' Advice Bureau for information when they weren't sure of it themselves. Most health visitors encouraged their clients to visit these agencies but occasionally they would do this for them. The health visitor in the "high risk" area would usually refer cases herself as she found that her clients' motivations were often lacking. With the physically handicapped, the health visitors nearly always contacted Specialist Services, a separate section in the local authority for the disabled. Generally, if the client's problems were simple, the health visitor would try to help without referring to a social worker.

With relationship and emotional problems, the health visitors usually tried to help by being supportive. Sometimes they would visit these clients very frequently, often several times a week. With marital problems, they helped by being understanding and sympathetic. Often they tried to get the wife to see her husband's point of view. Very few health visitors asked to see the husband or attempted to involve him. They were usually anxious that they would "get out of their depth". Generally they did not feel that they were trained in this way and would prefer to suggest Marriage Guidance.

With depression, the health visitor herself often tried to help. She would become someone the client could talk to or someone to be there when the client cried.|Health visitors would often encourage clients to ventilate their feelings. Normally, if the depression was severe or continued longer than expected, they would involve the doctor.

Most of the health visitors had contacted a large number of agencies on behalf of clients with problems. Most had contacted meals on wheels or the home help organizer to arrange these services for their clients. All had involved child minders, play groups and schools on behalf of their clients. Most health visitors had also involved voluntary organizations such as church groups or community associations. About half of the health visitors had contacted charities, housing agencies and particular societies for their clients. Alternatively they had given their clients information on other organizations, e.g. Gingerbread, and how to contact them.

Most of the health visitors interviewed thought that their role overlapped with that of the social worker, but did not regard this as a problem. They felt that each profession had its own priorities and that ideally they should complement each other. The social worker had few cases and could therefore visit more intensively when needed. Many saw the overlap as a safeguard. One of the health visitors in the health centre felt that by working closely with social workers, a safety net could be provided which no one could slip through. She felt it was essential that the relationship should be a close one for this to work effectively.

## Discussion

In the last few years, the number of health centres had increased, as well as the number of health visitor and social work attachments to general practice. [5, 6] Increasing emphasis has been placed on the team approach in policy documents such as the Havard Davis Committee Report. One of the main purposes of these attachments has been to enable doctors, nurses and social workers to work together and to tackle more effectively and efficiently the health and social problems brought to the general practice. However, putting people together in a group does not always make them function effectively as a team. [7]

In this study, the joint attachment scheme fostered close working relationships between the two professions. The health visitors were also very enthusiastic about it. Contacts were easy and informal and decisions about cases could be taken together, making misunderstandings less likely. Frequent meetings also helped the two professions to educate one another. The health visitors became more willing to refer cases needing sensitive handling once they got to know the social workers personally and became aware of their skills and abilities. Although most of the health visitors felt that there was some degree of overlap between their work and that of the social worker, they did not regard this as a problem. When cases were discussed, the two professionals involved could decide who would be the key worker and who would do certain tasks. The social workers reciprocated many of the health visitors' feelings: they felt that working closely with the health visitor made a great deal of difference to their work. [8]

Outside the health centre attachment, the local authority social workers and health visitors were not always aware of each other's involvement in a case, and decisions were often made without consulting the other disciplines involved. This was also the case with other social work agencies, the majority of health visitors having few contacts with social work agencies other than the local authority.

The health visitor is in the position not only of knowing the family and the home conditions of her clients (maybe over a long period of time), but she also has considerable knowledge of the community resources in the area. Nevertheless, she is rarely involved in decisions regarding treatment of a family by agencies such as Child Guidance, and receives little feedback from them.

The data collected from these interviews indicates that many health visitors spend a considerable part of their time dealing with the social problems of their clients and therefore perform many of the duties of social workers. They are not only supportive to both client and family but also give advice, information and contact many agencies on their clients' behalf. It is therefore very important that the two professions do not work in isolation from one another, as they then cannot support one another or work out a common plan of action. This may lead not only to repetition of work but also to the client receiving contradictory advice from the two or more agencies involved.

## Acknowledgements

This study was carried out as part of a research programme planned by the General Practice Research Unit at the Institute of Psychiatry, under the direction of Professor Michael Shepherd and with the support of the Department of Health and Social Security.

I would like to thank the 15 health visitors who participated in this study. I am particularly grateful to Mrs Cottingham for her help and advice.

## References

1. Clark, J. (1972). What do health visitors do? *Nursing Times* **68**, Occasional Papers, 117.
2. Ambler, M. *et al.* (1968). The attachment of local health authority staff to general practice: a study in three county boroughs with special reference to health visiting. *Medical Officer* **119**, 295.
3. Greater London Council. "The work of health visitors in London: a Department of Planning and Transportation Survey". Marris T. Research Report No. 12. GLC, London.
4. Forman, J. A. S. and Fairnbairn, E. M. (1968). "Social casework in general practice". Oxford University Press, London.
5. Watson, C. and Clarke, M. (1972). Attachment schemes and development of the health team. *Update* **4**, 489.
6. Gilchrest, I. C. *et al.* (1978). Social work in general practice. *Journal of the Royal College of General Practitioners* **28**, 675.
7. Beloff, J. S. and Willett, M. (1968). Yale studies in family health care — the health care team. *Journal of the American Medical Association* **205**, 663—669.
8. Bowen, B., Davis, Y. A., Rushton, A. and Winny, J. (1978). Adventure into health. *Update* **17**, 1512—1515.

# SECTION 3

# SOCIAL WORK INTERVENTION

# INTRODUCTION

Any discussion of the development of social workers within the setting of primary care cannot disregard the fact that at the present time there is considerable discussion about what precisely constitutes the role of the social worker. At the time of writing, an independent enquiry has just reported on this very question (Barclay 1982). Any temptation to consider the issue academic may be difficult to resist in the setting of the social service department — the sheer pressure of work coupled with a shared view of the relative importance of social work intervention understandably contributes to the feeling that questions about the necessity for and usefulness of social workers constitute a luxury, an indulgence which busy professionals cannot afford. However, the issue is far from academic in primary care. What it is social workers actually do becomes highly relevant for the general practitioner, anxious to refer appropriately, for the health visitor uncertain of the boundary delineating the end of health visiting competence and the beginning of social work, and the client, who may have conflicting views about the appropriateness of social work for his/her own problems.

Others have commented on the difficulty of making sense out of the many and varied definitions of social work that have been advanced [Reid and Shyne, 1969; Timms and Timms, 1977; Brewer and Lait, 1980]. Some definitions, such as that provided by the British Association of Social Work*, are couched in terms which are at once both ideologically provocative and professionally vacuous and which augur poorly for better collaboration between social work and medicine. Others, such as that of Herbert and his colleagues (page 179 below), are phrased in so general a manner as to make any deductions concerning what social workers might accordingly *do* very difficult to derive.

One way around this impasse is to take a very close look at what it is that social workers actually do. The deployment of social workers in general practice offers an opportunity to examine the extent and nature of their work in this setting and to compare and contrast it with the kind of work undertaken by social workers in the more orthodox situation of the social service department. This section, therefore, considers papers which are

---

* The special function of social work, and its inalienable element, is to protect and promote the interests of the individual client or clients and to ensure that social technological changes serve and do not enslave the individual as a person in his own right. (B.A.S.W., 1973.)

concerned with the issue of what social workers do. In our choice of such papers, we have been severely constrained by the fact that remarkably little in the way of thorough, well-researched and well-written papers concerning the tasks of the social worker in the primary care setting exist. There are, it is true, many anecdotal or highly individualistic accounts of particular primary care attachments [Dongray, 1958; Ratoff and Pearson, 1970; Graham and Sher, 1976] which testify to the possibilities inherent in such attachments. The papers included in this section attempt more than mere description, quantify their findings and reflect the very varied nature of the social worker's role thereby raising a number of intriguing questions concerning how best such a role might be developed and implemented in the light of the findings emerging from such research. They also focus on the type of work which can be carried out with patients with emotional and relationship problems as this is a major part of the attached social worker's task. The first paper compares the interventions of a group of attached social workers in primary care with social workers operating in a local authority team covering the same geographical area. Corney's paper is a companion one to that in Section 1 (pages 31 – 43) but the paper under discussion here concerns itself with analysing the social workers' activities.

The most striking finding is the difference between the social work service offered to clients in the two settings.

The local authority "intake" social workers tended to deal relatively briefly with their cases. Their main role, certainly in comparison with the attached social workers, was either that of "broker", finding the right agency to help their clients' problems, or that of "advocate", arguing before a statutory authority, such as a housing department or the DHSS, their clients' particular case. This brief service was offered to clients presenting with all manner of problems, including emotional, interpersonal and other forms of psychosocial difficulties.

The attached social workers, on the other hand, conducted many more interviews with their clients, kept their cases "open" very much longer and maintained contact with their clients after other agencies had been involved. It was not possible to attribute these differences in manner of working to differences in the sorts of problems presented by clients in the two schemes for the differences persisted when sub-groups of clients with similar problems were compared. Corney's suggestion that factors such as agency function and organization determine the type of social work actually carried out is difficult to contest and is certainly in agreement with views on this matter expressed by other commentators [Sainsbury, 1980; Timms and Timms, 1977; Warham, 1977; Parsloe and Stevenson, 1978; Howe, 1979].

While Corney's paper is an account of but one attachment scheme and how it compares with one intake team, its findings are comparable to those of a number of somewhat similar studies. Others have concentrated on the type of work undertaken by intake teams [Goldberg *et al.*, 1977; Parsloe and Stevenson, 1978] or on the effect on the sort of work done exercised by the setting-up of special intake teams [Boucher, 1976; Gostick, 1976; Jones, 1976]. The work undertaken by the general practice attachment team described by Corney is also in line with that reported by other attachment assessments in the literature [Collins, 1965; Forman and Fairbairn, 1968; Goldberg and Neill, 1972].

A more worrying difference between social work undertaken in the general practice attachment and that in the social services department, more worrying at any rate from the medical perspective, is the remarkable lack of contact that the intake social workers had with the medical services despite the fact that high proportions of their clients were elderly, disabled, physically or mentally ill. This sad state of affairs contrasted sharply with the attachment arrangement in which there appeared to be close collaboration between the doctors and the social workers. This finding only serves to underline the question raised elsewhere as to whether physically and mentally ill patients receive a better, more integrated service when their social worker is attached to general practice than when the social worker operates within a separate, independent social service department.

Another striking finding is the extent to which the continuity of care which is such a crucial feature of general practice as practised within the National Health Service rubs off as it were on to social workers working within it. The attached social workers were able to provide continuity to those clients who were in variable contact with the primary care services whereas the intake workers offered a different and more fragmented response. Once a case was closed by one social worker, it was re-opened by whosoever happened to be on intake duty. Yet, such consumer studies as have been carried out [McKay *et al.*, 1973; Sainsbury, 1975; Glampson and Goldberg, 1976; Corney, 1981] have indicated how much clients value the personal approach, how they want to have one particular social worker whom they can contact and whose name they know. If social workers do not or are unable to offer such a personalized and continuous service, then it could be argued that little of importance remains to distinguish them from the bureaucratic and impersonal qualities of the many other agencies contacted by their clients.

Of course social workers tend to reply to such findings that the remorselessness of the demand and the heaviness of the burden that they carry in the real world of the social service department, in contrast with the protected and elevated atmosphere of the general practice setting, makes it well-nigh impossible for such personal characteristics to be maintained. Yet Corney's paper challenges such an objection. The attached social workers had actually *higher* caseloads than their colleagues in the social service department; such differences in referral rate as existed were less significant when the numbers of clients actually interviewed were compared. Corney's point, namely that "referral rates and caseload size are often misleading as they are substantially affected by the social workers' speed at closing cases" merits particular attention for it does gently imply that the tendency for social workers to hide behind their imposing statistics when new modes of working are discussed needs to be questioned. Indeed what is one to make of a mode of working which means that social workers close cases after a very brief initial assessment only to spend large amounts of time reopening them within a relatively short period? This system of working almost certainly means that many of the clients who attend social service departments do not receive a thorough assessment of their problems. The social worker in such an arrangement resembles the medical specialist — offering limited contact, a specific intervention and a referral back to the agency or service from which the patient came. Yet the medical specialities are now under attack for such a piecemeal approach to patients' problems. It is somewhat ironic to find social workers, who are in general opposed to specialism and who endorse instead a wholistic approach to their clients' problems [Seebohm, 1968; B.A.S.W., 1973; Pincus and Minahan, 1973] — indeed they are even called the *personal* social services — actually operate in a manner whcih can be partial, fragmented and discontinuous. Other commentators have recognized this problem [Boucher, 1976; Gostick, 1976; Jones, 1976] and it is not surprising that alternatives to the intake approach have been suggested such as the patch system and others [Goldberg and Warburton, 1980; Hadley and McGrath, 1981].

The second paper included in this section describes a particular form of intervention, so-called "task-centred" social work. As has been pointed out [Timms and Timms, 1977], it might be said that all social work, by definition, is task-centred. The emergence of a particular term with which to describe such a general activity may well reflect the fact that it is in danger of being disregarded and neglected as social workers gravitate more and more to such theories and practices which are ennobled by prestigious-sounding names. In fact, so-called task-centred social work is used by only a very small number of social workers in practice [Parsloe and Stevenson, 1978], a finding which is less surprising given the fact, discussed in Corney's paper, that the great majority of social service clients are either interviewed for a relatively few times or become long-term supervisory cases. The essence of the task-centred approach, after all, is that the intervention should be based on a minimum number of interviews carried out over an agreed, limited yet reasonable time period. In attachment schemes in general practice, the conditions of social work are such as to suggest that the task-centred approach may be particularly suitable.

As described in some detail by Janet Butler and her colleagues, the task-centred approach clearly resembles and overlaps with the behavioural approaches endorsed by Martin Herbert and Brenda O'Driscoll in the third paper in this section. General practice would appear an appropriate setting for the implementation of such techniques given that clients are usually reasonably well motivated to participate in planned treatment programmes, particularly when these are endorsed by the general practitioner. The nature of many of the problems that present in general practice, including marital problems, behavioural problems in children and adolescents and difficulties in child-parent relationships, is of a kind for which behavioural methods of treatment are believed by their protagonists to be particularly well-suited. At the present time, experimental attachments of clinical psychologists and nurse therapists trained in behavioural therapy are being described and assessed [Broadhurst, 1977; Waters, 1981] and there has been a growing interest in and emphasis upon the use of behavioural approaches by social workers in preference to long-term supportive help [Fischer, 1978; Herbert, 1980; Hudson, 1978].

One of the most contentious aspects of social work practice concerns the issue of psychotherapy. Given the historical influence of psychiatry upon social work [Yelloly, 1980], the heavy emphasis on the notion of "casework" within social work itself [Hollis, 1964] and the tendency of some social workers to regard psychoanalysis and psychoanalytically derived approaches to the psychologically disturbed as the definitive therapeutic modality can be understood. After all, one short definition of casework reads: "An art in which knowledge of the science of human relations and skill in relationships are used to mobilise capacities in the individual and resources in the community appropriate for better adjustment between the client and all or any part of his total environment" [Biestek, 1957].

Psychoanalysis has been the theory which, more than any other in the realm of psychology, has laid claim to be the science of human relationships and in turning to psychology for help in meeting their expansive brief social workers understandably were drawn to analytic theory as a means to this end [Yelloly, 1980]. The fourth paper in this section considers the applicability of psychotherapy to the problems brought by clients to social workers. Clare's analysis critically assesses the appropriateness of such a treatment in the light of experience gained not merely in social work but in the wider area of psychiatry and medicine. While his paper does consider questions of efficacy (which in general are the concern of Section 4 of this book), the main thrust concerns the suitability of many of the clients of social workers for a therapeutic approach which even its most enthusiastic advocates appear to regard as an optimum therapy for patients much less disturbed, disabled and deprived.

In sharp contrast is the fifth paper by a practising social worker, Clare Creer. While the bulk of this paper reflects experience derived from the practice of social work in the management of the severely mentally ill in hospital and community psychiatry settings, the paper is included in this collection because, as Creer herself is at pains to point out, its implications for social work and general practice are immense. An important role for the social worker is that of offering support, help and information to the relatives of patients with acute and chronic ill-health. This paper describes the help which can be given to the relatives of patients diagnosed as suffering from schizophrenia. The Schizophrenia Fellowship survey, mentioned by Creer, revealed a dismal picture of professional neglect of these relatives despite the fact that for all practical purposes it is the relatives who more often than not constitute the only community that truly cares for such disabled and deprived patients. The neglect of such relatives is occasionally compounded by a tendency to blame them for the patients' illness, a tendency which is sometimes indulged in by social workers and doctors. Social workers too are often ignorant about the use of medication in conditions such as schizophrenia, are uncertain of the value of maintenance medication and unclear about the distinctions and the similarities between side-effects of such medication and symptoms of the original illness. Yet all of this merely emphasises the potential role for the social worker in ameliorating the lot of patient and relative by a combination of activities including education, reassurance, support and informed advice. While Creer's paper is inevitably concerned with one particular patient group, the implications for social work involvement with other groups, such as the mentally handicapped, the elderly mentally ill and the physically handicapped do not need to be spelled out.

These five papers then all concentrate on direct social work with clients. How much time should be spent on such activities and what might be the other functions of an attached social worker are just two of the many questions raised by such work. Some social workers may well regard "casework" as forming only part of their overall brief and may feel that much more time could usefully be spent on community, educational and group activities. One important advantage possessed by general practices is that they are usually sited in the centre of the area they serve. Thus, an attached social worker may well consider that an important part of his or her role is the development of the voluntary community services in the area. The social worker may encourage the setting up of good neighbour schemes, the visiting of the isolated elderly by individuals living in the same street, or the development of a community association. Such an association, in turn, may facilitate the provision of transport for the elderly or the handicapped to hospital or to outings. The social worker may also initiate or take part in the setting up of clubs for the mothers of young children or for parents of handicapped children or for the isolated elderly. Indeed, the social worker attached to a general practice health centre may well find it easier to set up groups, clubs or associations as there may well be space available for such meetings to be held. The sixth paper in this section is an account of the setting up and running of such a group, in this case a group for single parents. The first section of the paper outlines the social workers' views while the second recounts the impressions and assessments of the clients. Group work has for some time been considered as an alternative to individual treatment. While Hicks was doubtful of the advantages offered to social work by such an approach, he did emphasise, along with others, its potential for "giving people a constructive experience of membership in a group so that they may develop further as individuals and be better able to contribute to the life of the community" [Hicks, 1976]. Certainly, Rushton and Winny's impressionistic account does suggest that for patients who are isolated and who can benefit from the support of others, it can be a simple, economic and feasible innovation.

It is interesting to note once again discord between the social workers' expectations concerning their methods and those of their clients. The original aim of the social workers had been to run the group along psychotherapeutic lines with patients obtaining relief by discussing in some depth their problems and difficulties and learning a little about their "true" nature. The clients, however, did not see this to be the main function of such a group; indeed, some felt that the preoccupation with problems was depressing. The role in this study of the participating social workers as catalysts, encouraging by their energy, initiative and enthusiasm a client-based response may well prove a more significant role in the future, for some social workers at least, than more traditional roles laid down over the past three to four decades.

Nowhere in any of these papers is it suggested that the particular therapeutic approach is the prerogative of the social worker. Task-centred approaches are common to a variety of professional groups while behavioural approaches are currently being undertaken by doctors, nurses and psychologists and teachers in addition to social workers. As for psychotherapy and counselling, such interventions are so loosely defined as to entitle almost anyone using a non-physical procedure and a minimum of skill to argue that he is engaging in it. Perhaps only a social worker in practice can undertake Creer's practical and educational role although here again the health visitor and the community psychiatric nurse can and do play similar roles depending on their personal preferences, the availability or lack of social work personnel and the particular emphasis of the general practice or community programme. But the lack of a therapeutic approach exclusive to social work has not prevented social workers acquiring and applying a wide diversity of treatments, indeed it may well have contributed to such an eclecticism. Whether such an eclecticism is a positive virtue or actually contributes to the social worker's sense of professional instability is, however, a question we can only raise here. The other thorny question, namely whether any or all of such approaches are effective, is discussed in Section 4 of this collection.

## References

Biestek, F. (1957). "The Casework Relationship". George Allen & Unwin, London.
Boucher, R. (1976). The first 12 months of an intake team. *Social Work Today* 8, 12–13.
Brewer, C. and Lait, J. (1980). "Can Social Work Survive?" Temple Smith, London.
British Association of Social Workers. (1973). The Inalienable Element in Social Work. Discussion Paper No. 3. *Social Work Today* 4.
Broadhurst, A. (1977). What part does general practice play in community clinical psychology? *Bulletin of the British Psychological Society* 30, 305–309.
Collins, J. (1965). "Social Casework in a General Medical Practice". Pitmans Medical, London.
Corney, R. H. (1981). Client perspectives in a general practice attachment. *British Journal of Social Work* 11, 159–170.
Dongray, M. (1958). Social work in general practice. *British Medical Journal* ii, 1220.
Fischer, J. (1978). "Effective Casework Practice an Eclectic Approach". McGraw Hill, New York.
Forman, J. A. S. and Fairbairn, E. M. (1968). "Social Casework in General Practice". Oxford University Press, London.
Glampson, A. and Goldberg, E. M. (1976). Post Seebohm social services part 2 – the consumer's viewpoint. *Social Work Today* 8, 7–12.
Goldberg, E. M. and Neill, J. E. (1972). "Social Work in General Practice". George Allen & Unwin, London.
Goldberg, E. M., Warburton, R. W., McGuinness, B. and Rowlands, J. H. (1977). Towards accountability in social work: One year's intake to an area office. *British Journal of Social Work* 7, 257–283.
Goldberg, E. M. and Warburton, R. W. (1979). Ends and means in social work. *National Institute Social Services Library*, No. 35. George Allen & Unwin, London.
Gostick, C. (1976). The intake phenomenon. *Social Work Today* 8, 7–9.
Graham, H. and Sher, M. (1976). Social work and general medical practice: Personal accounts of a three year attachment. *British Journal of Social Work* 6, 233–249.

Hadley, R. and McGrath, M. (1981). Patch systems in social services departments: More than a passing fashion? *Social Work Service* 26, May, 13—19.

Herbert, M. and O'Driscoll, B. (1978). Behavioural Casework. A social work method for family settings. *Australian Child and Family Welfare*, No. 2, 14—25.

Hicks, D. (1976). "Primary Health Care: A Review". HMSO, London.

Hollis, F. (1964). "Social Casework: A Psychosocial Therapy". Random House, New York.

Howe, D. (1979). Agency function and social work principles. *British Journal of Social Work* 9, 29—47.

Hudson, B. L. (1978). Behavioural social work with schizophrenic patients in the community. *British Journal of Social Work* 8, 2, 159—170.

Jones, J. (1976). Intake structure in local authorities. *Social Work Today* 6, 710—713.

McKay, A., Goldberg, E. M. and Fruin, D. J. (1973). Consumers and a social services department. *Social Work Today* 4, 486—491.

Parsloe, P. and Stevenson, O. (1978). "Social Service Teams: The Practitioner's View". HMSO, London.

Pincus, A. and Minahan, A. (1973). "Social Work Practice: Model and Method". Peacock, Ithaca Illinois.

Ratoff, L. and Pearson, B. (1970). Social casework in general practice: An alternative approach. *British Medical Journal* 2, 475—477.

Reid, W. and Shyne, A. (1969). "Brief and Extended Casework". Columbia University Press.

Sainsbury, E. (1975). "Social Work With Families". Routledge and Kegan Paul, London.

Sainsbury, E. (1980). Client need, social work method and agency function: A research perspective. *Social Work Service* 23, 9—15.

Seebohm Report. (1968). "Report of the Committee on Local Authority and Allied Personal Social Services". HMSO, London.

Timms, N. and Timms, R. (1977). "Perspectives in Social Work". Routledge and Kegan Paul, London.

Warham, J. (1977). "The Organization Context of Social Work". Routledge and Kegan Paul, London.

Waters, H. M. (1981). Nurse Therapists in General Practice. *In* "The Misuse of Psychotropic Drugs". (Eds. R. Murray, H. Ghodse, C. Harris, D. Williams and P. Williams), p. 92. Gaskell Publications, Royal College of Psychiatrists, London.

Yelloly, M. A. (1980). "Social Work Theory and Psychoanalysis". Van Nostrand Reinhold, New York and London.

# SOCIAL WORKERS' INTERVENTIONS: A COMPARATIVE STUDY OF A LOCAL AUTHORITY INTAKE TEAM WITH A GENERAL PRACTICE ATTACHMENT SCHEME

ROSLYN H. CORNEY

## Introduction

Social work attachments to general practice have become increasingly common in recent years and now over 50% of boroughs have at least one scheme in operation. It has thus become increasingly more important to investigate the usefulness of placing social workers at the primary care level and to compare their work with that of the social workers in the local authority area teams. This study compares the activities of social workers in an intake team and an attachment scheme on referrals over a 3 month period.

## Previous Work

Several studies have investigated the activities of social workers in local authority and general practice attachment settings. Many attachment schemes have kept records on the types of referral and the activities of the social workers involved [Collins, 1965; Forman and Fairbairn, 1968; Goldberg and Neill, 1972; Corney and Briscoe, 1977]. The work of social services departments has also been monitored in several boroughs [Camden, 1975; Cheltenham, 1976; Kensington and Chelsea, 1975, Wiltshire, 1975] and a recent study has monitored the work resulting from one year's intake to an area office in Southampton [Goldberg et al., 1977]. However, because these studies have been carried out in a variety of locations, it has been difficult to compare the results as differences found could be due to the type of area covered.

In this study, information was collected on referrals to 4 part time social workers in an attachment scheme and 3 full time social workers in an intake team covering the same area over the same period of time. A previous paper compares the demographic details of the clients referred and the problems presented [Corney and Bowen, 1980]; this paper compares the work done by the social workers.

## Method

The 4 attachment social workers taking part in this study spent approximately two-thirds of their time on cases referred by 4 group practices. The social workers spent the remaining third of their time working for the local authority, 2 for the long term team and 2 for intake. The social workers dealt with all referrals from the Health Care team, including both short and long term work and on average had caseloads of approximately 40–50 cases each. All the social workers were experienced and generically trained.

The area office involved in this study had a long term team of six social workers and an intake team of 5 social workers (excluding the attachment social workers). The office covered an area that almost coincided geographically with the areas covered by the group practices and the patients registered with these practices were representative of the area. In order that similar numbers were referred to both schemes over the time period, only 3 out of 5 of the intake workers took part in the study. These social workers were the most experienced and all were qualified.

The intake team dealt with all referrals to the area, only care and supervision orders made by the Courts were referred directly to the long term team. The intake social workers spent regular days on duty and normally took on to their caseload all referrals that they opened whilst on duty. As the long term team had full caseloads at the time of the study, with a waiting list, this meant that in practice the intake workers rarely transferred any of their cases to the long term team and thus dealt with all short and long term work resulting from these referrals taken on duty. Their caseloads were variable and constantly changing but were on average 25–30 cases each.

The 7 social workers involved in the study completed three forms on all clients referred to them during a period of just over 3 months. This provided information on the client referred, reasons for referral and the social workers' assessment of the client's problems using a modified version of the Fitzgerald classification [Fitzgerald, 1978]. In order to increase reliability, a pilot study was run for 2 weeks before the main study started. The social workers were given detailed instructions on filling up the forms and guidelines were made on how to rate the severity of each problem. The social workers also practised on pen portraits and their recordings on the problem classification were compared. Any differences between social workers were discussed in order to increase reliability.

As the intake workers' casenotes were clear, concise and thorough, information regarding their interventions with each referral was collected by the author using their files, casenotes and correspondence. Any queries were followed up by asking the social worker concerned. Data were recorded on the work arising from the referrals from the data of first contact to the data of closure in the following 8 months after referral. Many cases were referred again after this period of time but information about these referrals and the work arising from them were not collected. The attachment social workers filled up the forms regarding their activities themselves.

## Results

During the 3 month period of data collection, 201 cases were referred, 119 to the 3 social workers in the intake team and the 82 remainder to the 4 part-time social workers in the attachment scheme. Only 1 case from the 119 intake referrals was transferred to a student in the long term team. In this instance, information was collected on contacts with both social workers involved.

When the information was collected on the social workers' activities, 8 months after the end of the study, 3 cases were still open to the intake social workers and 16 cases open to the attachment social workers. In these 19 cases, data were recorded on all the social workers' activities up to the date of collection.

## 1. Contacts with Clients

As can be seen from Table 1, the numbers and types of contacts made by the social workers in the 2 schemes were markedly different ($p < .01$). In nearly 30% of the intake cases the client was not seen by the social worker; contact was made either by phone or letter or with the referral agent only. In addition, only 25% of the intake clients were seen more than once compared with 65% of the attachment group. As 16 cases were still open to the attachment social workers at the time of data collection, it is likely that the figures given in Table 1 for attachment cases are underestimates of the final numbers of interviews carried out.

Information was also collected about all the telephone and letter contacts made with the clients. The attachment social workers not only contacted more of their clients by letter or telephone, but also made more of these types of contacts with them.

TABLE 1
Type and amount of contact with client

| No. of contacts | Intake group | | Attachment group | |
|---|---|---|---|---|
| | No. | % | No. | % |
| Contact with outside agency only | 16 | 13.5 | 8 | 9.8 |
| Phone or letter contact only* | 19 | 16.0 | 2 | 2.4 |
| 1 interview with client | 55 | 46.2 | 19 | 23.2 |
| 2 interviews | 11 | 9.2 | 16 | 19.5 |
| 3–5 interviews | 16 | 13.5 | 22 | 26.8 |
| 6–9 interviews | 0 | 0 | 6 | 7.3 |
| 10–14 interviews | 1 | 0.8 | 6 | 7.3 |
| 15–19 interviews | 1 | 0.8 | 3 | 3.7 |
| | 119 | 100 | 82 | 100 |

\* With client or friend/relative of client.

## 2. Length of Contact

In each case, the length of time was calculated between the date of referral and the date of the last contact with either the client or another agency concerning the client. The length of contact of the intake team was very short in the majority of cases; just over one third of their clients were dealt with during the day or referral and over 70% within a month of referral. In the attachment scheme, length of contact was much longer and was over 3 months in just less than 40% of the cases.

TABLE 2
Length of contact with client

| Length of contact | Intake group | | Attachment | |
|---|---|---|---|---|
| | No. | % | No. | % |
| One day or under | 42 | 35.3 | 12 | 14.6 |
| Under 1 week | 14 | 11.8 | 10 | 12.2 |
| 1 week to under 1 month | 30 | 25.2 | 10 | 12.2 |
| 1 month – under 3 months | 18 | 15.1 | 19 | 23.2 |
| 3 months – under 6 months | 5 | 4.2 | 12 | 14.6 |
| 6 months – under 1 year | 7 | 5.9 | 3 | 3.7 |
| Still open | 3 | 2.5 | 16 | 19.5 |
| | 119 | 100 | 82 | 100 |

The attachment social workers were also likely to leave their cases open well after their last contact with the client. Thus, if any problems arose during this period clients would be referred back to the social worker. In the intake team, cases were closed shortly after the last contact. Many of their cases were re-referred after closure, often with the same referral reason, and were often dealt with by another social worker.

## 3. Contacts According to Age and Problems of Client

In order to determine whether some of the differences between the 2 groups in terms of numbers of interviews undertaken were due to client differences, the numbers of social workers contacts made were investigated according to several categories of age of client (Table 3), their reason for referral (Table 4) and his major problem as assessed by the social worker.

Table 3 shows that the differences in social work contacts between the 2 schemes occurred in all age groups of clients. Large proportions of intake clients of all age groups were interviewed once or had no face to face contact. Similar differences were found when the 2 groups were compared according to each of their 23 reasons for referral (using the modified Fitzgerald classification). Table 4 groups the reasons for referral into 3 major categories for simplification. It can be seen that differences were particularly marked with clients referred for relationship and emotional problems (includes all types of relations problems, mental illness, bereavement, etc.).

TABLE 3
Number of interviews undertaken in both groups for four age groups of clients

| Age group | Number of interviews | | | | | | | |
| | Intake | | | | Attachment | | | |
| | 1 or less | | 2 or more | | 1 or less | | 2 or more | |
| | No. | %* | No. | % | No. | % | No. | % |
| Up to 20 | 15 | 12.6 | 3 | 2.5 | 1 | 1.2 | 6 | 7.3 |
| 20−44 | 26 | 21.8 | 12 | 10.1 | 11 | 13.4 | 25 | 30.5 |
| 45−64 | 12 | 10.1 | 4 | 3.4 | 5 | 6.1 | 10 | 12.2 |
| Over 65 | 36 | 30.3 | 9 | 7.6 | 11 | 13.4 | 12 | 14.6 |
| Age not known | 1 | 0.8 | 1 | 0.8 | 1 | 1.2 | 0 | 0.0 |
| | 90 | 75.6 | 29 | 24.4 | 29 | 35.3 | 53 | 64.6 |

* % of total intake group.

TABLE 4
Number of interviews for different reasons for referral

| Reason for referral | Number of interviews | | | | | | | |
| | Intake | | | | Attachment | | | |
| | 1 or less | | 2 or more | | 1 or less | | 2 or more | |
| | No. | % | No. | % | No. | % | No. | % |
| 1. Material/practical problems (including housing, financial) | 33 | 27.7 | 13 | 10.9 | 9 | 11.0 | 10 | 12.2 |
| 2. Relationship, emotional problem and mental ill-health* | 26 | 21.9 | 7 | 5.9 | 12 | 14.7 | 32 | 39.0 |
| 3. Problems associated with physical disability | 23 | 19.3 | 4 | 3.4 | 6 | 7.3 | 9 | 11.0 |
| 4. Other problems including fostering, adoption, educational problems | 8 | 6.7 | 5 | 4.2 | 2 | 2.4 | 2 | 2.4 |
| | 90 | 75.6 | 29 | 24.4 | 29 | 35.4 | 53 | 64.6 |

* Significant between intake and attachment groups at 1% level.

One fifth of intake cases and just less than one fifth of attachment cases were referred for very specific requests, for practical help, services and advocacy. Although these clients were more likely to be seen by the social workers fewer times than those referred for less specific problems, there were still differences between groups.

The social workers were also asked to make an assessment of the clients' problems using the same classification system and to choose the major problem. There were still large differences between the 2 groups in terms of numbers of interviews given to clients with the same problem as their major problem and this difference was significant for those with emotional or relationship problems as their major problem (P < .01).

## 4. Contacts with Other Agencies

Although the attachment social workers contacted more agencies on behalf of their clients, this was mainly due to their increased contacts with the surgery staff. Over 60% of cases were discussed with the doctor concerned (excluding discussion on referral) and nearly 20% with the health visitor. Intake social workers discussed fewer than 5% of referrals with doctors, even less with health visitors and had no contacts with district nurses.

TABLE 5
Type of contact with other agencies

| Type of contact | Intake | | Attachment | |
|---|---|---|---|---|
| | No. of cases* | % | No. of cases | % |
| For referral relinquishing own contact | 33 | 27.7 | 15 | 18.3 |
| For referral maintaining contact | 25 | 21.0 | 31 | 37.8 |
| For advice, discussion, etc. | 33 | 27.7 | 64 | 78.0 |
| Suggestion made to client relinquishing own contact | 14 | 11.7 | 3 | 3.6 |
| Suggestion made to client maintaining contact | 6 | 5.0 | 7 | 8.5 |

* This figure denotes the number of cases where one or more of this type of contact was made. The percentages do not add up to a 100% as the social worker can have several types of contacts with any one case.

Social workers in both groups were more likely to contact other agencies themselves rather than make suggestions to the clients to visit the agencies. The 2 groups referred many cases to housing, other social services sections and local authority departments, to the DHSS or voluntary agencies. However, the 2 groups differed as the intake social workers were more likely to relinquish their own contact after involving another agency whilst the attachment social workers maintained contact.

## 5. Reason for Closure

Usually the reason for closure was indicated clearly in the closing summary and presented no problems. Difficulties occurred when the social workers were unsure about whether they had helped the clients or not. A decision was made by the author to only use the category "unable to help" where the social worker felt she had given no help at all to the client, not even advice or information on where to go. This category was filled up for 12 intake cases and 2 attachment cases. Six of these 14 referrals were for housing problems and 2 for financial problems. The other 6 cases presented a variety of emotional and relationship problems.

A higher percentage of intake cases were closed because of referral to

TABLE 6
Reason for closure

| Reason for closure | Intake | | Attachment | |
|---|---|---|---|---|
| | No. | % | No. | % |
| Social worker or client withdrew — problem solved or alleviated | 41 | 35.3 | 39 | 59.1 |
| Social worker or client withdrew — social worker unable to help | 12 | 10.3 | 2 | 3.0 |
| Client refused to see social worker | 4 | 3.4 | 3 | 4.5 |
| Client withdrew during contact | 8 | 6.9 | 7 | 10.6 |
| Client referred on | 38 | 32.8 | 12 | 18.2 |
| Client died or admitted to hospital | 4 | 3.4 | 0 | 0 |
| No problems on investigation | 2 | 1.7 | 0 | 0 |
| Other social worker involved/or case transferred to another area | 7 | 6.1 | 3 | 4.5 |
| | 116 | 100 | 66 | 100 |

N.B.  3 cases were still opened to Intake, 16 cases to the Attachment Scheme.

other agencies. This accounts for some of the differences between the 2 groups in the percentage of cases closed because the social worker had alleviated or solved the clients' problem. However, a higher percentage of intake cases were closed because the social worker was unable to help.

Differences between groups were again greatest for clients with relationship and emotional problems as their major problem. In the intake group, only 28% of these cases were closed because the social worker felt she had personally helped in comparison with 70% of attachment cases.

## Discussion

The study showed clear differences in how the cases were handled by the 2 groups of social workers. Members of the community covered by these 2 schemes would therefore receive a very different service according to the agency to which they were referred. This was most marked for those with relationship and emotional problems.

What were the reasons for these differences between the social workers in the way that they worked? They could not be totally due to client differences as they still occurred when subgroups of clients were analysed separately.

The workloads of the 2 groups of social workers were also not sufficiently dissimilar to account for these differences in intervention. The attachment social workers had higher caseloads and the differences in referral rates during the study were not so great when the numbers of clients actually interviewed were compared (the manpower in the 2 groups being similar). In fact, referral rates and caseload size are often misleading as they are substantially affected by the social workers' speed at closing cases. The intake social workers closed their cases quickly reducing their caseload size but if the client returned after the case was closed, this was counted as a referral. The attachment social workers held their cases open longer, thus reducing their referral rate as subsequent contacts by the client were not counted as referrals.

It does seem likely that although client or workload differences may account for some of the differences in the type of intervention, other important factors such as agency function and organization account for much of the difference between the 2 schemes. Several writers have commented on the importance of these factors and the major effects they have on the social worker's roles, tasks and activities [Titmuss, 1954; Timms, 1964; Warham, 1977; Howe, 1979; Sainsbury, 1980].

Intake teams, in general, were originally developed as a means of coping with very high referral rates to the area. To protect the quality of social work with long term clients, a separate team of social workers dealt with all the new referrals to the area, only passing on a small proportion of these to the long term team when necessary. This encouraged short term work, the social workers dealing quickly with the presenting problem, closing the case shortly afterwards, so that they were free to apply themselves to the next load of referrals [Jones, 1976; Gostick, 1976; Boucher, 1976; McKitterick, 1980]. The policy of an intake team studied in Southampton was to deal with specific episodes as they arose and to encourage clients to return should the need arise [Goldberg et al., 1977]. In this study, 50% of the intake referrals were previously known to social services and many of the referrals during the study were re-referred again after that period. This suggests a similar policy to that in Southampton, social workers dealing with the problem presented, often by referring him to another agency and relinquishing their own contact, but reminding him that he can return if necessary.

This practice of dealing with the case quickly, often on the day of duty only, may also have been encouraged by the particular type of allocation system used in this intake team. Social workers normally took on themselves all cases that they opened whilst on duty eliminating the need for an allocation meeting. This may lead busy social workers either not to open cases seen on duty or to close them quickly, knowing that if the client did come back he would see the duty officer rather than themselves.

The attachment social workers handled the majority of their cases quite differently, they kept contact with their clients much longer and preferred to keep their cases open long after the last contact. Their rate of re-referral was much less, only 20% of their referrals were previously known to them or to the area team, although the scheme had been established for over 3 years. Although they also acted as "brokers" and "advocates" on behalf of their clients [the terms as used by Baker, 1976], similar to the intake workers, they were more likely to maintain contact with clients after involving other agencies. They conducted at least 3 interviews with 45% of their clients, suggesting that one way they tried to help their clients was by using their own therapeutic interventions. The attachment social workers also offered their clients more continuity, if another problem needed attention and the case was either still open or closed the clients would be referred back to the same social worker.

This style of working had developed even though the attachment social workers had a similar system to intake of allocating opened cases, each normally taking on the cases referred to them whilst on duty in one of the practices. In the attachment scheme, the social workers had to show they were a valuable addition to the medical team, they were dependent on the team for the majority of their referrals and reliant on them for the continued success of the scheme [Bowen *et al.*, 1978]. In addition, the referral agent often asked for a social work assessment (or more often expected it) and the majority of referrals were followed by a discussion of the cases. These factors would encourage the social worker to make a thorough assessment and to deal with the case personally until some favourable outcome had been reached.

The intake social workers, on the other hand, worked more in isolation from their referral agent. They were less dependent on them and probably felt less responsibility towards them. Moreover, the majority of these intake clients were self-referrals or referred by friends or relatives and studies of clients' views [Mayer and Timms, 1970; McKay *et al.*, 1973; Sainsbury, 1975; Glampson and Goldberg, 1976; Rees, 1978; Corney, 1981a; Corney 1981b] have indicated that the majority of clients had no clear expectations of how the social worker could help and would not necessarily expect much personal involvement. This, together with the other factors mentioned, plus the knowledge that little could be passed onto the long term team, may encourage the social workers to deal much more quickly with their cases.

The system of working developed in this intake team may mean that many of the clients' problems are missed. It may not always save the social worker's time. High proportions of intake cases were re-referred again, many more than once and often for the same problem. This takes up much of the duty officer's time whilst clients have to re-tell their story to another social worker. In addition, problems not dealt with during the initial referral may become more serious or chronic and less easy for the social worker to help in the long term.

The intake team in the social services department is thus in danger of becoming similar to services offered by many other agencies, the social workers taking on less individual responsibility for their clients and becoming less personally involved. Consumer studies indicate that this is not what the client wants. Clients appreciate warmth, sympathy and understanding, they like to be able to ask for one particular social worker and to know who they are going to see [Mayer and Timms, 1970; McKay *et al.*, 1973; Sainsbury, 1975; Glampson and Goldberg, 1976; Corney, 1981a; Corney, 1981b]. As others have commented the intake team which takes up a defensive role ends up protecting the agency more than serving community needs [Jones, 1974; Gostick, 1976].

## Acknowledgements

This study was carried out as part of a research programme planned by the General Practice Research Unit and the Institute of Psychiatry, under the direction of Professor Michael Shepherd and with the support of the DHSS.

I would like to thank the 7 social workers involved in this study: Mrs B. Bowen, Miss G. Clark, Mrs Y. Davis, Mr T. Jones, Jrs A. Rushton, Mrs J. Tombs and Mrs J. Winny. I am particularly grateful to Mr D. Wiggins and Mr D. Kirkman for their help on the initial stages of the study.

## References

Baker, R. (1976). The multirole practitioner in the generic orientation to social work practice. *British Journal of Social Work* 6.

Boucher, R. (1976). The first 12 months of an intake team. *Social Work Today* 8, 12–13.

Bowen, B., Davis, Y. A., Rushton, A. and Winny, J. (1978). Adventure into health. *Update* 6, 1512–1515.

Camden Social Services Department: Planning Unit. (1975). "Referrals to the Department – Area Summaries".

Collins, J. (1965). "Social Casework in a General Medical Practice". Pitman Medical, London.

Corney, R. H. (1981a). First time clients. *Community Care* April 9th, 1981, 21–23.

Corney, R. H. (1981b). Client perspectives in a general practice attachment. *British Journal of Social Work* 11, 159–170.

Corney, R. H. and Bowen, B. (1980). Referrals to social workers: a comparative study of a local authority intake team with a general practice attachment scheme. *Journal of the Royal College of General Practitioners* 30, 139–147.

Corney, R. H. and Briscoe, M. E. (1977). Social workers and their clients: a comparison between primary health care and Local Authority settings. *Journal of the Royal College of General Practitioners* 27, 295–301.

Fitzgerald, R. (1978). The classification and recording of social problems. *Social Science and Medicine* 12, 255–263.

Forman, J. A. S. and Fairbairn, E. M. (1968). "Social Casework in General Practice". Oxford University Press, London.

Glampson, A. and Goldberg, E. M. (1976). Post Seebohm social services part 2 – the consumer's viewpoint. *Social Work Today* 8, 7–12.

Goldberg, E. M. and Neill, J. E. (1972). "Social Work in General Practice". George Allen & Unwin, London.

Goldberg, W. M., Warburton, R. W., McGuines, B. and Rowlands, J. H. (1977). Towards accountability in social work: one year's intake to an area office. *British Journal of Social Work* 7, 257–283.

Gostick, C. (1976). The intake phenomenon. *Social Work Today* 8, 7–9.

Howe, D. (1979). Agency function and social work principles. *British Journal of Social Work* 9, 29–47.

Jones, J. (1974). The intake group as an alternative service delivery structure. *Health and Social Service Journal* 84, 672–675.

Jones, J. (1976). Intake structure in local authorities. *Social Work Today* 6, 710–713.

Kensington and Chelsea Social Services Department: Research Section. (1975). "Report on New Referrals to the Social Work Division Northern Area Office".

McKay, A., Goldberg, E. M. and Fruin, D. J. (1973). Consumers and a social services department. *Social Work Today* 4, 486–491.

McKitterick, B. (1980). A critique of the intake team system. *Social Work Service* No. 23, 20–23.

Mayer, J. E. and Timms, N. (1970). "The Client Speaks". Routledge and Kegan Paul, London.

Rees, S. (1978). "Face to Face". Edward Arnold, Southampton.

Sainsbury, E. (1975). "Social Work with Families". Routledge and Kegan Paul, London.

Sainsbury, E. (1980). Client need, social work method and agency function: a research perspective. *Social Work Service* No. 23, 9–15.

Timms, N. (1964). "Social Casework". Routledge and Kegan Paul, London.

Titmuss, R. M. (1954). The administrative setting of social service. *Case Conference* 1, No. 1.

Warham, J. (1977). "The Organization Context of Social Work". Routledge and Kegan Paul, London.

Wetton, K. (1976). The Cheltenham Intake Team: An evaluation. *Clearing House for Local Authority Social Services Research* No. 2. University of Birmingham.

Wiltshire Social Services Department: Research Unit. (1975). "Intake Referral Study".

# TASK-CENTRED CASEWORK WITH MARITAL PROBLEMS

JANET BUTLER, IRENE BOW and JANE GIBBONS

## Summary

The use of task-centred casework with people who have marital problems and have taken an overdose is described. The stages of task-centred work are illustrated and difficulties which were encountered are discussed. Task-centred casework is seen to be a feasible and helpful method of working with people with marital problems.

This paper uses part of the material gathered by the Southampton self-poisoning project in the years from 1975 to 1977 [Gibbons et al. [1] ). One of the aims of the project was to assess the effectiveness of social work intervention with people who have taken an overdose. During the year from April 1975 to March 1976, 539 people who had taken an overdose and had been seen in the casualty department of the Southampton General Hospital were included in the study. After baseline assessment by a research psychiatrist, the patients who were not in current contact with a social worker or psychiatrist and were not in need of immediate psychiatric care were allocated to the trial programme of task-centred casework. They were then randomly assigned to either the experimental or control group until there were 200 in each. The control group received the routine follow-up service: referral to a general practitioner, to psychiatric outpatients or to other services, usually the social services department. All those in the experimental group were offered a period of contact with one of two social workers, Irene Bow and Janet Butler. For our social work service we were using the task-centred casework model as set out by Reid and Epstein [2, 3].

Task-centred casework is a structured approach to the process of working with clients. The essential elements of the structuring are the use of a short time limit, the selection of a target problem from the problems presented, the use of tasks to work towards the alleviation of the target problem, and the negotiation between client and social worker on the time limit, target problem and tasks. This approach is being explored in British social work, and has been reported by Goldberg et al. [4], Collins [5] and Norton and Smith [6]; other literature indicates that there is a growing interest in using some elements of structuring in casework (Hutten [7]; Hudson [8] ).

Reprinted, with permission, from the *British Journal of Social Work* 8, 4, 393–409, 1978.

The American social work literature abounds with references to the development of various aspects of a more structured approach to social work intervention. The use of a contract is explored in Maluccio and Marlow [9], looked at more critically in Seabury [10], and examined in research by Rhodes [11]. Time limits and goals for work are discussed in Lang [12], Rosenberg [13], and Rapoport [14]. Pincus and Minahan [15] discuss a systematic approach to a very broad range of social work practice. They set out the need for outcome and method goals and for the use of a contract in social work and then look at the issuues involved in putting them into practice.

The work described in this paper is a more structured approach to marital problems than is found elsewhere in the British literature on marital work. Much of this literature originates from, or is strongly influenced by the Institute of Marital Studies and the Tavistock Clinic (Pincus [16], Bannister and Pincus [17], Guthrie and Mattinson [18], Dicks [19], and Monger [20]). The use of a time limit is explored by Guthrie and Mattinson, and Monger.

This paper raises some of the difficulties experienced in using task-centred casework with people with marital problems, and discusses ways of over-coming them. The method is explored through its five phases: the initial contact, the problem search, the task selection, the work on tasks, and termination. The method is illustrated by material obtained from 33 clients of the 100 referred to Janet Butler who were married, living with their spouse and who presented at the baseline psychiatric consultation with a problem in their marital relationship. The information obtained is drawn from social work records and follow-up research interviews. Half the cases were interviewed by independent research workers four months after their overdose; the other half were interviewed 18 months after it. A comparison of the outcome of experimental and control subjects with marital problems will be the subject of a separate paper. The majority of these 33 clients (24, 73%) reached the stage of working on defined tasks. Fifteen were couples working jointly at tasks, and in a further eight cases husband and wife were jointly involved in the problem search. In nine cases it was not possible to establish a contract to work on tasks; two refused all contact and seven did not get beyond the problem search stage.

### Initial Contact

Our initial contact with clients came within a few days of the overdose, if possible while they were still in hospital. After the overdose they were in a state of crisis. For some people the overdose itself was a response to a crisis, such as a threat to a marital relationship. For other people it represented a breaking point in their toleration of long drawn out problems. Also a crisis was often created by the overdose itself, when a couple would find themselves in a new situation which they did not know how to handle.

A social work service offered at this point of crisis provides an opportunity for clients to ventilate their feelings and to explore their problems. This was appreciated by some of the clients and reflected in comments which several made in the research interview. For example, a young man facing a break-up of his marriage said that the social worker was:

someone to talk to, ... could tell her how I felt, ... not being bottled up inside me any more was a relief.

An older women, Mrs L., facing a sudden announcement from her husband, who was overseas, that he wanted a divorce, said of the social worker:

when most depressed I could talk to her, get it off my chest, ... could not do this with family or close friends: an outsider was important.

If clients feel that the worker is not responsive to their feelings it is not possible to proceed to the next stage which is work on overcoming the problems. Responsiveness is not in itself a stimulus for change; for this the worker needs to develop systematic communication. Reid and Epstein [21] define as responsive communication those social worker communications which encourage self expression or help the client to feel accepted and understood. Systematic communications are defined as those which are designed to structure the process of the work, and focus it on problem-solving activities. Ideally the first interview should establish the worker as both a responsive person and one who can help the client to identify and solve problems in a systematic way. The idea of a systematic approach to the clients' situation can be introduced by explaining that the contact between worker and client will go through several stages: a problem search, the selection of a target problem and work on tasks. Other aspects of the structuring of the contact between worker and client which need to be introduced are the time limit, where the interviews will take place, and who is to be included in the interviews. It is often not possible to cover all these details in the first interview, and indeed even if this is possible it will be necessary to discuss the structure further in subsequent sessions.

An essential part of task-centred casework is the making of a systematic problem search. We found that it was usually not possible to do this in the one or two interviews advocated by Reid and Epstein [22]. The difficulties were the number of problems presented, the emotional state of some clients and the uncertainty experienced by them and also the necessity to involve the other partner in the work. A start was made on the problem search in the first interview, with clients expressing many of their feelings about their problems. The selection of a target problem and tasks should not occur until the problem search has been completed, but there were times when problem-solving activity had to be encouraged before the full problem search could be made. It is important to use the method flexibly, and at times the process of work cannot proceed in an orderly way. As Rapoport [23] says:

The primary need of the client is to experience in the first interview a considerable reduction in disabling tension and anxiety.

For some people this can be achieved by encouraging them to take immediate action to overcome some of the distress. This helps them to feel that they can master the confusion of the crisis. This happened in the first interview with Mrs A. which was obtained while she was still in hospital.

Mrs A. launched into what she felt was the main problem: not being able to talk to her husband about her feelings about Sam, her illegitimate son. She has low opinion of herself, feels she hurts people all the time, feels that she is hurting her husband by being depressed, and not able to tell him why. She was tearful throughout the interview; at the end I sat closer to her and reassured her that she could take her time, that there was no obligation to tell him. She agreed but wished she could. At this point she cheered up; I offered further help with talking over problems and arranged an appointment at home.

Records of interview two with Mrs A. begin:

Mrs A. told me she had been able to start talking to Mr A. after talking to me, and she had felt a lot of relief about this. Mr A. had been very understanding but said he felt that this was not the real matter; he wished he could believe it was.

Mrs A. had articulated some of her problems, and given vent to her despair. She had been encouraged to do something about the situation, and the social worker had tried to reduce the pressure she was under. As a result of this Mrs A. had been able to mobilize her inner resources to take action.

It was at times important to step in quickly with clients, to help them to examine their initial state of confusion. If there was too long an interval new ways of coping would have already been found, and the opportunity for social work intervention could be lost.

An impression gained in an initial interview can be considerably altered by events between the first and second interviews. It was possible to see Mr and Mrs C. before Mr C. was discharged from hospital; indeed, they both waited for some time for the social worker to appear on the ward. There were undoubtedly conflicts, but even though Mrs C. had grave doubts about the possibility of continuing their relationship, Mr C. seemed intent on trying to resolve some of their differences. It seemed that their relationship would survive and the worker was hopeful that they could make good use of a period of task-centred casework. This was discussed with them and the worker offered to see them individually two days later at home. She did see them individually, but in separate houses. Mr C. had left, having acknowledged that the relationship could not survive. However, because they had been seen before they had reached this resolution and while they were still in considerable distress, it was possible for both of them to accept help.

## Problem Search

Once initial contact with the client has been made, and any aspects of the client's situation which need immediate action have been explored, it is possible to move on to a systematic exploration of the problems. At the end of this exploration it should be possible to select the problem which will be the focus of work, the target problem. This should be the problem which the client most wants to work on, where there is hope of making effective changes, preferably those which can be brought about by the client's actions. Reid and Epstein [24] describe the process of target problem selection in the following way:

(1) The array of problems with which the client appears now to be concerned is elicited.

(2) The different problem or different aspects of the problems are defined in explicit behavioural terms.
(3) The problems are ranked into an order of priority according to where the major emphasis is placed by the client.
(4) The target problem is tentatively determined in collaboration with the client.
(5) The target problem is classified by the caseworker.

Many clients presented a large array of problems. Several had problems outside the marital area: relationship with children, loneliness, physical illness, housing and jobs. A systematic approach by the social worker is required to enable the client or client and spouse to examine their whole situation. It was important to explain that this was the beginning of the process whereby one area would be selected for more detailed discussion and planning of tasks. It can be a painful exploration, especially where a couple express, more openly than before, perceptions of their relationship. This was especially so with Mrs A., where the problem search continued until the fifth session, partly prolonged by Mr A.'s mother dying. The list of problems was:

(1) Mrs A. unable to relate warmly to the children.
(2) Mrs A. feeling Mr A. did not understand her feelings about Sam, and Mrs A. unable to talk to husband about these feelings.
(3) Mrs A. has low opinion of herself.
(4) Mr A. not as attentive to Mrs A. as she would like.

In the fourth session Mrs A. was able to express her uncertainty about her husband's caring. Though it pained Mrs A. to say this and Mr A. to hear it, it enabled them to realize that it was the marital problem that caused them the greatest pain. Hence they were able to select this as the target problem, which they described as follows:

Mrs A. feels Mr A. is unattentive; she feels she lacks interest in the house partly as a result of this. Mr A. is aware that he takes a lot for granted and that he always wants his own way in things, and is not as attentive as Mrs A. would like.

Mrs F. also presented with a long list of problems:

(1) Money: worry re rent arrears.
(2) Mr F. recently unemployed, anxiety that it might happen again causes stress.
(3) Mrs F. guilty re extra marital affair 12 years ago, just before son, who was killed, was born.
(4) Grief for loss of son five years ago.
(5) Mrs F. lack of sexual interest.
(6) Mr F. lack of sexual interest.
(7) Mr F. drinking.
(8) Mr and Mrs F. at loggerheads on a number of issues.
(9) Mrs F. gets tense and out of control with son Henry aged two and a half years.

This list was made over a period of four interviews, three with Mrs F. on her own and one with Mr F. In the fifth session, the first joint one, it was possible to go over these areas with both Mr and Mrs F. It was important to discover where they felt they most wanted help, particularly as Mrs F.

recalled with anxiety and hostility her previous experience of being helped. They decided that there were two areas in which there needed to be urgent changes. The first was the marital area and the other was the relationship between Mrs F. and her son. Hence two target problems were selected. This was rather ambitious, but it was just possible to keep the work going in both areas.

Indecision and uncertainty about what action to take are a part of crisis situations. This is especially so where the client's spouse has just left but has not decided whether their separation should be permanent. In this situation the problem for the client is this lack of certainty itself. There is no difficulty in establishing the priority of the problems. The client wants his or her partner back, and the aspects of the problem in "explicit behavioural terms" are obvious, the client is distraught. It may be the social worker who has to take steps to establish what the situation is with the departed partner. The situation may change rapidly, and the client may then have to face the certainty that his or her spouse will not return. Coming to terms with this kind of knowledge takes time, and it is only when this process has begun that the target problem can be defined. This was experienced with Mr E., who was eventually able to express his target problem in this way:

> Jane's left me, I feel so lost without her, I still think she may return, but I'm not sure how much I want her. I've got to get on without her. I depended on her too much, I want to try and get by by myself.

The process of acceptance had only just began but because he had been able to accept this much, Mr E. was able to move on to look at some tasks which would help him cope with this problem.

Many problems are difficult for the client to define exactly, especially where they relate to feelings of depression or anxiety, and helping the client to pinpoint the cause of these feelings can be a long process. It is a necessary process in that a hurried problem search may lead to the selection of an inappropriate target problem. Clients are often not able to put their problems into words clearly, and need to be helped to explore the dynamics of their situation before they are able to decide on their target problem. These difficulties, which are not examined by Reid and Epstein [25], need to be looked at further in the development of this method. Difficulties of this nature often arose where clients were undecided about whether or not to bring their marital relationship to an end. For some people the indecision became the target problem and the tasks were to consider the pros and cons of various alternatives.

Mrs D., a mature woman, had had an affair with her boss for 12 years; for the last two years her husband had known of this. She had made a decision to stay with her family but had felt overwhelmed by the pressures on her and took an overdose. She remained undecided when the worker met her and the first few interviews with this family (two with Mrs D., one with Mr D., one joint interview and one with the boyfriend) were an exploration of the situation, Mrs D. was helped to explore the problems honestly, encouraged to face the painfulness and to find a way to commit herself to a decision for the future. This exploration was the target for the first five sessions. It was perhaps a less well-defined target problem than Reid and Epstein [26] allow for, but nevertheless it was an important stage of work. Out of this exploration emerged a decision and a more definite target problem.

> Mrs D. was left with no feelings for Mr D., had resented marrying him from the start, and he had been very dependent upon her. She had disliked this. She and her boss have had a relationship for 12 years; both have decided to leave their spouses. Mrs D. is concerned about hurting her husband, fearing he would go to pieces.

From this problem definition, practical tasks evolved. The effect of this process is reflected in Mrs D.'s comments about the help she received, which she made in the follow-up research interview:

> Unbiased opinion, third party, disinterested, uninvolved. Helped immensely. Let me talk but guided me and helped me to bring it all out and relieve me. Helped me sort out my difficulties.

In order to work on marital problems it is essential for husband and wife to be able to come to some sort of agreement on the target problem, and to do this the social worker will need to help them listen to the other's perceptions and feelings. Mr H. was an extremely defensive man, so he could not listen to his wife's feelings. She was tired of the situation, and had given up trying to talk or listen. Six long sessions enabled Mr H. to be slightly less defensive and eventually a target problem emerged, which ended:

> Both feel they are out of touch with one another.

This was the nearest they could get to any common agreement. In order to accept this as a target problem it had also to be established that they wanted the situation to change and that they felt that changes were possible. It is important to establish with the clients that there is some real motivation for change in the problem area which they select. This can be difficult and involves helping clients to face painful situations.

In some marital situations the conclusion of the problem search must be that there are severe problems in the marital relationship, but no hope of any change. Mrs I. had an array of problems which included being fed up with her husband. It was quite impossible to engage Mr I. in any serious discussion of the relationship; the only problem that he could perceive was that at times she had deserted him. He was quite unprepared to accept any further discussion of the situation, and Mrs I. was reluctant to confront him about the difficulties. Hence in the review of problems by the social worker and Mrs I., the possibility of any work on the marital relationship was eliminated. In the process of doing this Mrs I. faced up to the limitations of her marital situation, but accepted that she had some responsibility for making other changes in her life.

With some clients the problem search ends with a decision not to pursue the work any further. This may be because either the client does not want to do anything about the problems, or they do not want the help of a social worker, or that there is nothing to be done about the problems. In some situations it may be advisable for the social worker to remain in contact with the client, even though there is nothing that can be done to alter the problems. This is especially so where people are experiencing acute distress and are wanting to continue a relationship with a social worker. This situation arose with two of the marital casework sample, but in both instances it was eventually possible to define tasks with clients which subsequently enabled them to alleviate their rather extreme problems.

The stage of selecting target problems is an extremely important one, for it clarifies the focus of work for client and worker. The definition of the target problem in the client's own words gives a good indication of what tasks should be selected in the next stage of the work. The process of target problem selection was at times longer than Reid and Epstein [27] indicated, prolonged by indecision or ambivalence in the clients, and at times by the complexity of the situation which clients faced.

## Task Selection

The task selection phase is a relatively short one. If the selection of the target problem has been done carefully the areas for change will have been defined. The tasks are specified actions which will help reduce the target problem. The exactness with which the behaviour is defined depends mainly on the social worker's assessment of the client's ability to translate tasks into action. For some clients a task such as: "to show feelings more" may be specific enough to trigger off attempts to be more expressive. For others it may be necessary to decide on a variety of ways in which they can show their feelings more. The social worker must work hard to get the client to select behaviour which the client feels will help. At times one can make suggestions, but these are less effective than the initially more long drawn out process of getting the client to think out his own tasks. The social worker's guidance is needed to help the client assess what effects the tasks will have and whether they are likely to be achieved. It is important that tasks should be realistic, for to set a task which is unlikely to be achieved is to produce yet more problems for the client.

Reid [28] has carried out an experiment in which he compares the outcome for two groups of clients. One group have the task set and with the social worker go through a task implementation sequence, which includes enhancing commitment to the task, planning the task implementation by spelling out exactly what to do, analysing obstacles which may arise, and practising the task. The other group have the task set but the worker does not go through this sequence. Reid found that the group with which a task implementation sequence was used made greater progress on the tasks, and slightly (though not significantly) greater progress on target problem reduction.

Task selection differs according to whether or not the work is being done with one client or with a couple. With an additional the process of task selection is relatively easy. Where the work is being done with a couple they must both agree on the tasks. Tasks are of two kinds: *shared or reciprocal.* With shared tasks husband and wife do the same thing, e.g. they may set aside time for talking or doing something together. Reciprocal tasks are tasks in which there is a bargaining process: "if you do that, I will do this". At times this process of bargaining can be used to encourage partners to make a change to which they are not very committed. Motivation can be increased if they know that their partner is also going to struggle to achieve something for them. However, it is preferable if each partner can identify for themselves the changes which they have to make.

Mr and Mrs J. were both able to identify their own shortcomings in the relationship, and they selected the following tasks:

To show feelings more.
(a) Mrs J. to try and show Mr J. when she is pleased and happy.
(b) Mr J. to look out for Mrs J.'s shows of pleasure.
(c) Mrs J. to pursue outside interests so she has more to talk about.
(d) Mr J. to be more demonstrative.
(e) Mrs J. to be more receptive.

The social worker's role in this process was to get Mr and Mrs J. to select some limited areas in which they could concentrate their efforts. The effect of this process was clearly felt by Mr J. who in the research interview talked about the social worker:

she was so easy to point out where I went wrong – she could listen to you. Talked to both of us, pointed out things. Easy to talk to, let me do the talking, felt more at ease after seeing her.

Tasks were usually set in the fourth to sixth interview. Even though work on some of the problems may have begun early in the contact, it was important to make an explicit agreement on the tasks. The tasks needed to be listed and agreed on by everybody involved. At times the changes that the tasks would lead to seemed small in comparison with the initial presentation of the problem. It is important that neither the client nor worker expects the total problem to disappear when these tasks are accomplished. The tasks should be seen to be small but necessary steps towards reducing the target problem, and clients must be prepared for some of the stress to continue. It was Mr H., with whom the struggle to select the target problem has been described, who was best to put into words how he experienced the process of task selection:

to get two people talking, myself and wife, it was difficult, but social worker brought about a formula for us to achieve something if we wanted or not as we desired.

The tasks which had been selected for him and his wife were:

To improve communications.
(a) to spent 10 minutes alone each evening talking about children.
(b) using hands to communicate feelings.
(c) to use more physical contact, with no expectation of intercourse.
(d) Mr H. to let Mrs H. out with no resentment.
(e) Mr H. to try and take Mrs H. out.
(f) Mrs H. to moderate her aggressive tone.
(g) to find things which give physical/sexual satisfaction to one another.
(h) to talk over and reach agreement on ways of handling son, Tom.

## Work on Tasks

Once tasks have been selected the focus of the subsequent work is ideally the progress that the client is able to make on the tasks. If the target problem and tasks have been clearly agreed this is usually possible. However, there are often other areas of concern which emerge, and decisions will have to be made as to whether or not it is necessary or helpful to pursue these other concerns. In many instances it is possible to devote most of the interview to issues related to the tasks and target problem. The interview begins with an exploration of how the client feels the work on the tasks is progressing, and how this is affecting the target problem. If the client begins with the successes, it may be that she is feeling more cheerful and optimistic or it may be a cover-up for failure and despondency. It is important to look at all the tasks, tempting though it may be for client and worker to avoid those that have not been achieved, or even attempted. It is in examining failures that further work can be done, and this may lead to modification of the tasks or to the target being changed. The examination of the failures must lead to attempts to understand the obstacles which have caused the failures. The obstacles may be of a practical or psychological nature and this can only be discovered by helping the client to explore why he feels that he has not been able to pursue the tasks selected. Often complex reactions are happening between husband and wife, and the worker can help them to understand these if they are causing obstacles. The obstacles will be perceived differently according to the theoretical orientation of the worker. Reid and Epstein [29] emphasize that they are not advocating the use of any particular theory of human behaviour, but they say that the task-centred method provides a framework within which workers with theoretical orientations from behaviourist to psycho-dynamic can work. We attempted to get clients to understand what they were communicating to one another by looking at the here and now causes and effects of behaviour and feelings.

Mrs A. had a recurrence of depression, and was feeling despondent. We looked together at various possible causes for this. The tasks seemed to have been tackled successfully and the only recent event was a kidney infection which had made her tired. She decided that this infection was the probable cause for the depression, and we looked at the effect it was having on the marital relationship. It was these effects that were causing Mrs A. to feel that relations were not improving. Mr and Mrs A. and the social worker decided that the problem was that she had not really been able to explain her feelings fully to her husband, and that this task needed to be pursued further.

An exploration of Mr and Mrs G.'s failure to achieve tasks led to additional tasks. The initial tasks were:

(a) Mr G. to listen to Mrs G.
(b) Mrs G. to wait until interesting TV programme has finished before trying to talk to Mr G.
(c) to talk over money between them.
(d) to show one another more affection.

The main reason for the difficulty with the tasks seemed to be that Mrs G. was not making her needs known clearly because she felt anxious about making demands of her husband. Hence she would bottle up her feelings until an explosion occurred. So we added to the task list:

(e) Mrs G. to be able to get angry with Mr G.
(f) Mr G. to hold on to his anger and allow Mrs G. to express herself.

In some instances there is a total and persistent failure to achieve tasks, in which case it is necessary to reassess the target problem. This may well lead to a decision to change the target problem, as occurred with Mr and Mrs K. They had decided that they must separate, but the tasks were never completed. Together client and worker looked at this, and decided that, bad though things were, neither could envisage separation. So they began to look at what they could do to improve their lives, and a redefined target problem and tasks were then tackled.

Tasks are usually worked on between interviews, but some can also be worked on more intensively within the interview. This is especially so where tasks are in the field of improving communications between husband and wife. The worker can help couples to listen to one another, help them to articulate their feelings and cope with the impact of bringing their feelings into the open, and a process for discussing contentious issues can be established with them. It is a time of helping couples to work out new ways of tackling their difficulties. Mrs A. said that the social worker helped her to:

talk to my husband. Shared feelings, began to know one another better.

Several couples recalled that the main impact of the work had been in this area of helping them to talk better to one another.

Some tasks are such that they must mainly be worked on with the social worker. This was especially so where there had been a separation, and the client was trying to come to terms with this. Mrs L., who faced the prospect of divorce reluctantly, was eventually able to select the following tasks:

to reorganize life.
(a) to get job.
(b) get new house.
(c) talk about feelings to social worker.

The process of work on the tasks can be upset by a further crisis. If it is related to the target problem it can be used to reassess the usefulness of the tasks. Mrs A. was able to predict a forthcoming stressful event which she felt could develop into a crisis. This led to an examination of ways in which she and her husband could approach the event and in this way new tasks were added to the list. Crisis in spheres other than the target problem may well have an impact on the target problem itself. Mr and Mrs M. had defined their target problem as being:

not being able to come to any decision about life's goals.

They were precipitated into looking in detail at one aspect of this by Mr M. being dismissed from work. The emergence of this new problem made it necessary for a new decision to be taken about what the tasks should be. Mr M. was also given help with the practical aspects of losing his job. Although not strictly selected as a target problem, it would have been inhuman not to help him in this area when he was faced with such a crisis. Other crises are such that the original target problem has to be abandoned and a new one formulated. Whether or not this should be done is determined by the client's capacity to contain the new crisis sufficiently so that he can continue to concentrate on the original target problem. With Mrs N. the original target problem had been the impact of her husband leaving her and also her inadequate housing. However, when her small child was admitted to hospital after swallowing aspiring, Mrs N. could not cope with the effects of this and the target problem had to be changed to:

> Mrs N. finding it impossible to care for children. Tim had been admitted to hospital after swallowing aspirin. Mrs N. felt undermined and frightened by this.

With many people the work on the task proceeds smoothly and success can generate further confidence and determination. Mr O. decided initially to tackle his unsatisfactory job situation. Through good fortune and persistence he eventually changed a situation where dismissal was imminent into one in which he gained promotion. His renewed confidence enabled him to decide to tackle an additional target problem, his estranged relationship with his wife.

## Termination and Time Limit

The structuring of the contact between social worker and client by the use of a time limit is an important aspect of task-centred casework. It is a feature of the method that is little developed in other casework methods. Reid and Epstein [30] give evidence that much work is brief in nature, and present theoretical and empirical evidence of the effectiveness of short term work. Once the case for brief work has been accepted, one is left with the problem of how to ensure its brevity. Reid and Epstein [31] propose that a time limit be applied to the duration of the contact between social worker and client. This, they say, enables the length of contact, in a situation where there are no natural end points, to be regulated. They also give other advantages: the time limit enforces a concentration of effort on achievable goals, leads to better use of the time available and stimulates social worker and client to greater effort. However, these effects can only be realized when time limits are clearly agreed between worker and client.

The process of establishing time limits was a difficult one. When tasks involve coming to terms with a separation, it is hard for either social worker or client to predict how long this process will take, or for there to be any clear-cut point when the process is near enough completed. As the work progresses with any client it becomes easier to predict when there will have been progress towards alleviating the target problem and hence when termination could occur. We discovered that the setting of the time limit could not be done on a once and for all basis. The idea of a time-limited contact was introduced where possible in the first interview, but more definite plans could not be made until the task-setting phase; it was easier then to ask the clients how long they felt they would need help with these tasks. Replies were often vague, and it was usually the worker's decision as to how many weeks or sessions there should be. Often an approximate date would be fixed for the contact to end, and as work progressed clients would be reminded of this and a more definite date for termination would be made. Occasionally a future event can be selected as a time around which to arrange termination. With one person this was the family's proposed move away from the area. Another couple chose to end contact shortly after an impending sterilization. With most people a time limit of three months from the overdose was selected. This was frequently clearly recalled by clients. Fifteen of the 21 people with whom casework was completed, and who were subsequently interviewed, recalled the time limit. On the whole the clients felt that the length of time they were in contact with the social worker was about right. Only two of the 21 followed up said it was too short, and one of these had had 33 weeks of contact. Three said the contact was too long, 14 said it was about right.

Early on in the social worker's contact with Mr E. she had noted:

> I spelt out fairly carefully the limits of the contact as I suspected there could be all kinds of problems because of his dependency.

In the final session with him he reported that he felt the time limit was a "good idea, can't depend on someone all my life". Others expressed more mixed feelings. Mrs G. in her last session with the social worker said:

> Don't like the idea [contact with the worker ending] in some ways; however, I know we have got to do this on our own, we can't be dependent on you and I want to be able to do it on our own. After all, you have not been here all the time but I know I've stored things up until you've come but we have now been talking more on our own.

The planning of the termination right from the start helps the process of coming to terms with it. As the time limit became more firmly established it was possible to talk about what would be the effect of the ending of contact with the social worker. The anxieties were fewer than expected, but where there were anxieties it was possible to find ways of helping clients to cope with them. Mrs A. expressed considerable anxiety. She felt that the sessions had helped her to express herself more and cope with her anxiety. Mr and Mrs A. were encouraged to think of ways in which they could cope with the anxiety about termination. They reconfirmed their need to focus on the tasks. In her follow-up interview Mrs A. said:

> I felt very apprehensive about the ending of social work contact but pleased that it did have a definite end because I was becoming quite dependent. If it had gone on much longer I think I would have wanted social work help for ever.

Mr O. did not discuss his anxiety about termination. However with him, as with several other clients, the weekly interviews became fortnightly toward the end of contact. When discussing the time limit in the research interview, 18 months after his overdose, he reported:

O.K. now, but felt worried about it during the three months of social work contact. Wondered what I would do when it came to an end, but it worked out well. Felt particularly anxious at the time that visits were cut from weekly to two weekly, but this helped me cope on my own.

The final interview was an excellent time for reviewing progress and giving encouragement to clients. At the time of the final interviews the worker's estimate of task achievement by the clients was:

| | |
|---|---|
| Tasks completely achieved | 1 |
| Tasks substantially achieved | 10 |
| Tasks partially achieved | 10 |
| Tasks minimally achieved | 3 |

Hence for all but three clients it was possible to identify and praise some definite areas of improvement. As part of the final assessment the worker would help clients identify further areas of work and usually they confirmed an intention to continue the work on tasks.

With five of the 24 people the time limit was extended beyond three months. With three people this was because their anxiety and inability to cope with the problems was such that a longer supportive relationship with a social worker was necessary. With two other people a planned extension to a time limit was made because they experienced a crisis towards the end of the three months. In both these instances the length of the extension was planned with the client. With two people termination came before the planned end point. Hence with 17 of the 24 with whom a period of task-centred casework was completed it was possible to plan and keep to a time limit. The average length of contact was 14.4 weeks. Excluding the cases where there was an extension to the time limit the average length of contact was 10.8 weeks with a range from four to 14 weeks.

## Conclusion

Task-centred casework provides a method the structure of which has been useful in helping a small group of people to cope with problems in their marital relations. It has not been possible to help everyone or to adhere to the task-centred method all the time. Nevertheless it has been a useful and popular service for these people. At times the structure was not adhered to through lack of practice of the practitioner, at other times this was because of the nature of the client's situation. The method seems easier to apply in situations where the presenting problems are fewer in number and where the client is in a secure situation from the point of view of relationships and accommodation, and where the client is a relatively stable person. However, there were instances where, in spite of such difficulties, it was possible to use the method, wholly or in part, and it seems a useful and economical way of trying to structure the contact with clients with a marital problem.

## Acknowledgements

The self-poisoning project was under the overall direction of Professor J. L. Gibbons. The psychiatric staff were Dr John Elliott and Dr Peter Urwin. The research interviews were done by Mrs G. Glastonbury, Mrs Coral Foster and Mrs Jackie Powell. The funds for the project came from the Department of Health and Social Security and the Wessex Regional Health Authority. We are grateful for all their contributions.

## References

1. Gibbons, J. S., Butler, J., Urwin, P. and Gibbons, J. L. (1978). Evaluation of a social work service for self-poisoning patienrs, *British Journal of Psychiatry* 133, 111–118.
2. Reid, W. J. and Epstein, L. (1972). "Task-centred Casework". Columbia University Press.
3. Reid, W. J. and Epstein, L. (1977). "Task-centred Practice". Columbia University Press.
4. Goldberg, E. M., Walker, D. and Robinson, J. (1977). Exploring the task-centred method, *Social Work Today* 9, no. 2.
5. Collins, J. (1977). A contractual approach to social work intervention, *Social Work Today* 8, No. 18.
6. Norton, P. and Smith, D. M. (1974). Thoughts on short-term casework, *In* "Families and Groups at Work" (Ed. D. M. Smith). Bookstall Publications.
7. Hutten, J. M. (1977). "Short-term Contracts in Social Work". Routledge and Kegan Paul.
8. Hudson, B. (1975). An inadequate personaligy, *Social Work Today* 6, No. 16.
9. Maluccio, A. N. and Marlow, W. D. (1974). The case for the contract, *Social Work* 19, No. 1.
10. Seabury, B. A. (1976). The contract: uses, abuses and limitations, *Social Work* 21, No. 1.
11. Rhodes, D. L. (1977). Contract negotiations in the initial stage of casework service, *Social Service Review* 51, No. 1.
12. Lang, J. (1974). Planned short-term treatment in a family agency, *Social Casework* 55, No. 6.
13. Rosenberg, B. N. (1975). Planned short-term treatment in development crises, *Social Casework* 56, No. 4.
14. Rapoport, L. (1970). Crisis intervention as a mode of treatment, *In* "Theories of Social Casework" (Eds R. E. Roberts and R. H. Nee). The University of Chicago Press.
15. Pincus, A. and Minahan, A. (1973). "Social Work Practice: Model and Method". Itasca, Illinois, Peacock.
16. Pincus, L. (1962). "The Marital Relationship as a Focus for Casework". Institute of Marital Studies. The Tavistock Institute of Human Relations.
17. Bannister, K. and Pincus, L. (1965). "Shared Phantasy in Marital Problems". Institute of Marital Studies. The Tavistock Institute of Human Relations.
18 Guthrie, L. and Mattinson, J. (1971). "Brief Casework with a Marital Problem". Institute of Marital Studies. The Tavistock Institute of Human Relations.
19. Dicks, H. V. (1967). "Marital Tensions". Tavistock Institute.
20. Monger, M. (1971). "Husband, Wife and Caseworker". Butterworth.
21. Reid, W. J. and Epstein, L. (1972). "Task-centred Casework". Columbia University Press.

22. Reid, W. J. and Epstein, L. (1972). "Task-centred Casework". Columbia University Press.
23. Rapoport, L. (1970). Crisis intervention as a mode of treatment, *In* "Theories of Social Casework" (Eds. R. E. Roberts and R. H. Nee), p. 288. The University of Chicago Press.
24. Reid, W. J. and Epstein, L. (1972). "Task-centred Casework". Columbia University Press.
25. Reid, W. J. and Epstein, L. (1972). "Task-centred Casework". Columbia University Press.
26. Reid, W. J. and Epstein, L. (1972). "Task-centred Casework". Columbia University Press.
27. Reid, W. J. and Epstein, L. (1972). "Task-centred Casework". Columbia University Press.
28. Reid, W. J. (1975). A test of a task-centred approach, *Social Work* **20**, No. 1.
29. Reid, W. J. and Epstein, L. (1972). "Task-centred Casework". Columbia University Press.
30. Reid, W. J. and Epstein, L. (1972). "Task-centred Casework". Columbia University Press.
31. Reid, W. J. and Epstein, L. (1972). "Task-centred Casework". Columbia University Press.

# A SOCIAL WORK METHOD FOR FAMILY SETTINGS

MARTIN HERBERT and BRENDA O'DRISCOLL

## Introduction

Contemporary behaviour modification (or therapy) seems to offer what is both a useful theoretical and practical approach to the treatment of a very wide range of childhood and adolescent disorders [Gelfand and Hartmann, 1975; Herbert, 1975]. We intend in this paper to describe this relatively new method of assessment and treatment of problem behaviour as it applies in family settings, and examine its relevance to social work practice. In doing this we shall consider briefly the nature of the social work task. After a discussion of the theoretical basis of behaviour therapy we shall attempt to demonstrate how the methods themselves can be applied in the social work setting giving examples from our casework in the Child Treatment Research Unit (CTRU) at the School of Social Work, Leicester University. Some of the traditional objections to a behavioural approach will be discussed and the ethical considerations examined. We conclude, on the basis of evidence accumulated on 117 families [Herbert, 1978] in a Unit staffed mainly by social workers that an adaptation of behaviour modification (which we call behavioural casework) can be used by trained social workers to alleviate many of the problems of childhood and adolescence. Although this is a casework method it is firmly grounded, as we hope to demonstrate in sound community work principles.

## Definitions

Definitions of the social work tasks have been debated extensively over the years but the central theme running through most ideas, no matter which school of thought, involves a genuine, humanely motivated attempt to assist people to cope with the troubles and crises of everyday life in a way which does not diminish their work or dignity as human beings.

## Value Base

The value base of social work existed long before there was any systematic attempt to introduce borrowed knowledge from the social sciences to

Reprinted, with permission, from the *Australian Child and Family Welfare* 2, 14–25, 1978.

implement these values, however as knowledge in the fields of social science increases it is important that social workers are aware of new technologies in order that they may evaluate them in terms of their usefulness in furthering these values. The case-worker requires a knowledge of a range of perspectives so that in individual situations she may choose the most helpful and appropriate method — the "informed eclecticism" to which so many social work theorists aspire. Doubtless many social workers have been put off from even a preliminary exploration of behaviour modification because they find the laboratory-based language of behaviourists alien and because the methods (especially when described out of context) evoke images of "clockwork orange" machinations such as aversive conditioning, psycho-surgery and brainwashing. The very words "behaviour modification" sound sinister and dehumanizing.

## Back Handed

It is perhaps a back-handed compliment to the effectiveness of behaviour moditication, that its many critics pay particular attention to its ethical implications. It may be that some critics become anxious about this kind of intervention because they suspect that it really works. Others are contemptuous of the changes brought about by behaviour modification because of their alleged superficiality. Behaviourism is said to be sterile because it fails to get at the "real" person, assuming him to be a passive bundle of stimulus-response connections; the behavioural analysis is unfeeling, deterministic, and futile. Other commentators warn that behaviour modification is downright dangerous because its practitioners are out to "control" human behaviour. Therapies are not always quite how they are seen by the uninitiated. Caricatures of theoretical models and practical procedures are set up as "straw men" for the critics (often poorly briefed) to knock over. Psychoanalysis has suffered the same fate, often at the hands of behavioural zealots, so it is rough justice that the latter should now be on the receiving end. There is, in any event, a case to answer [see: Stolz et al., 1975].

## First Point

The first point that has to be made is that social learning theory which informs so much modern behavioural practice is not the crude fundamentalist behaviourism of history and popular stereotype [see: Bandura, 1969; Herbert, 1974]. The second point is that whereas the medical model provides a reasonably unambiguous ethical rationale for treatment by a criterion of "health" and "pathology", behaviour modifiers construe abnormality as being on a continuum (i.e. not essentially different) from normal behaviour. This means that they face ethical decisions with which the medical model has not been confronted. As Leung [1975] explains, if problem behaviour is considered to be learned, the therapists are involved in making, or at least concurring with, a value or social judgement of what is abnormal and of what other behaviour would be preferable. This inevitably leads to the question: "to whom is the behaviour undesirable and is it really in need of change?"

## Produce Change

Of course, all caseworkers are in the business of trying to produce change, no matter what their orientation. But one of the dimensions along which therapies differ is that of direction/indirection. Behaviour modification is highly directive — although that statement requires a good deal of qualifying as we shall see from our description of behavioural casework.

The possibilities of client-choice, a democratic negotiation of treatment objectives and the opportunity for introspective discussion (especially in self-management work) are increasingly allowed for in current practice. Tharp and Wetzel, [1969] note that far from assuming an authoritative posture and considering the art of therapy as a secret cult, behaviour modification is more willing to rally the support of non-professionals like parents, housewives, siblings and peers, than most others.

## Unfeeling and Mechanistic?

What of the accusations of behaviour modification being unfeeling and mechanistic? Whatever their failings, behavioural theorists have a great respect for empirical research. And research studies have frequently shown that certain core qualities of sympathy, friendliness and sensitivity on the part of the therapist enhande the effect of any sort of treatment, although alone they have no significant effect [Truax, 1966]. Shapiro's review [1975] of the literature of psychotherapy research suggests that the findings do not justify, and may indeed make untenable, the view that social relationships have no place in the modification of psychological disturbances. He states that the client-centred therapeutic conditions of empathy, warmth and genuineness [Truax and Garkhuff, 1967] may serve as a useful adjunct to behaviour modification. Two studies have found that the level of the Truax conditions offered by interviewers does effect their efficacy as behaviour modifiers [Vitalo, 1970; Mickelson and Stevic, 1971]. An interesting use of relationship to foster behavioural change is also reported by Persons [1966].

## Article of Faith

Bandura [1969] notes that it is an article of faith for many that "relationship" factors are the primary agents of behavioural change, and consequently that the specific methods employed are of secondary importance. As he puts it, "this view — which is somewhat analogous to replying on 'bedside manner' rather than on specific therapeutic interventions in the alleviation of physical disorders — can be seriously questioned".

## Behavioural Approach

In using a behavioural approach as a casework method we accept the importance of a caring and accepting relationship with the client. We also accept Younghusband's injunction [Younghusband, 1967] that in order to demonstrate one's caring effectively one should be skilled and knowledgeable enough to select the method of treatment most relevant to the client's needs. When using a behavioural approach we find we can work effectively on the basis of a friendly but business-like relationship with the client. A highly charged relationship is not a desideratum for therapy and in any event would exclude the majority of social work clients from treatment. Relationship, when elevated to a mystique, seems to assume, with some degree of arrogance, that the social worker should be one of the most significant figures in her client's life. In behavioural casework no such intense relationship is required. It is only necessary for the client to have enough trust and confidence in the social worker to accept treatment in the first place. A closer relationship may then develop as treatment progresses and the client hopefully sees evidence that the social worker is offering a genuinely helpful way of dealing with his problems.

## Role of Insight

The role of insight in therapeutic outcomes is another point of contention between behaviour modifiers and their critics. Bandura [1969] reanalyses the psychodynamic interpretive insight-giving process as an instance of social influence or brainwashing rather than genuine self-understanding and revelation. He contends that patients in the emotive ethos of this kind of therapeutic relationship are highly amenable\to (sometimes unwitting) persuasion and conditioning. As he sees it, suggestive probing and selective reinforcement of client's verbal reports lead to a self-validating interview in which the patient imperceptibly but increasingly replaces his own opinions and ideas about himself with the therapist's views and interpretations. Truax [1966] has shown that Carl Rogers selectively but subtly reinforced certain classes of desirable behaviours and that the "unconditional positive regard" which should be accorded to the client was *by no means unconditional.* There are many instances of successful therapies without insight being invoked and examples where insight having apparently been obtained has had little effect on behaviour. It can be argued that insight is a consequence rather than an agent of beneficial change. Cautela [1965] has suggested that changes in verbalizations during psychotherapy, commonly called "insight" frequently *follow* rather than precede behavioural changes. As relief of tension and difficulties proceed, insight as to their causation may develop.

## Fair Comment

Yelloly [1972] makes what seems a fair comment on this vexed question, and one which provides a guideline in CTRU practice:

> ... awareness may operate in a number of ways. The sheer provision of accurate information may correct a false and erroneous belief and bring about considerable change in behaviour; prejudice, for instance, may be diminished by new information which challenges the prejudiced belief. And in human beings (preeminently capable of rational and purposive action) comprehension of a situation, knowledge of cause and effect sequences, and of one's own behaviour and its consequences, may have a dramatic effect on manifest behaviour. Thus

to ignore the role of insight is just as mistaken as to restrict attention wholly to it. It would seem that the relative neglect of insight by behaviour therapists until recently has occurred partly in reaction to the over-emphasis on it in traditional psychotherapy, and partly because of their pre-occupation with directly observable behaviour, particularly in laboratory studies of animals. As Bandura notes, the potential of symbolic factors for therapeutic change has not been fully exploited.

Over recent years methods such as family therapy, crisis intervention, task centred casework, contract work and systems theory have all been incorporated into casework practice.

These are all ways of approaching particular problems and can be adapted for use with whichever theoretical model one adheres to, whether it be sociological, psychodynamic or behavioural. Behavioural psychologists have "rediscovered" in the last two decades, some ideas, discussed in the 1920s, which suggest that many forms of childhood psychopathology can be conceptualized as maladaptive or inappropriate responses that have been acquired through learning [Jones, 1924].

## Genetic Disposition

The importance of genetic predispositions and biological differences is recognised but the focus is on learned behaviour. It is based on the concept of a functional relationship with the environment in which changes in individual behaviour produce changes in the environment and vice versa.

The behaviour of any child tends to be highly specific to the persons, places and situations in which he finds himself involved [Mischel, 1968]. Assessment techniques designed to identify and gauge generalized attributes (e.g. deep-seated personality traits) in children have poor predictive value.

## Assumption

Likewise, with treatment based on the assumption of generalized effects, the evidence [see: Herbert, 1978] suggests that successful treatment of a child's problems in the home does not necessarily resolve his problems at school, or vice versa. Prediction (for assessment) is best from observation of behaviour in one situation to behaviour in similar situations. In order to get a good intellectual grasp of what a child is doing and why, it is necessary to have highly detailed and specific information (based on specially designed "sharp focus" interviews and direct observation) about the child's behaviour in his various life situations. The so-called behavioural assessment method and the ecological interview [Herbert, 1978] are aids in obtaining the kind of evidence on which rigorous assessment (and thereby sound casework) is based. The prerequisite of any successful treatment is careful and accurate assessment of the "problem" to be treated. This is especially vital when the essence of treatment will be in some way to change the relationship of the client with his environment. It is achieved by the careful collection and recording of data by the client or in the case of a young child those in direct contact with him and direct observation by the social worker of the actual behaviours in the client's natural environment. From this information a behavioural analysis of the antecedent and consequent events surrounding behaviour is made. One of the clearest accounts of the assessment of problem behaviour and planning of its treatment is provided by Derek Jehu [Jehu *et al.*, 1972]. He describes in detail the various stages before treatment is attempted: the identification and specification of the patient's problems and the conditions controlling them; the ascertainment of the available resources; the selection and specification of therapeutic goals, and finally, the planning of the treatment programme. Stress is laid on monitoring the assessment and treatment process throughout the contact with the client.

Many of the processes of change that take place in the various psycho-therapies are somewhat mysterious and invisible to the patient or client. (And one might add that *all* therapies are like this for very young children.) At the CTRU it is policy to explain to the children (and allow them to be privy to) all the proceedings in working out a treatment programme. The social worker acts as an advocate for the child, in the sense of representing his point of view.

## Focus on Overt Problems

Behavioural casework tends to focus on the child's overt problems, attempting to remedy them by direct intervention. The social worker attends, particularly, to contemporary events — the here and now — rather than delving far back (as a major preoccupation) into the history of the child. This strategy of concentrating on specific and observable behaviours arises not from the naive belief that no aspect of a child's problem behaviour is determined by unobserved or unobservable factors (past or present), but from a conviction that a significant part of it is controlled by events — antecedent and consequent — that can be observed, measured and modified. As a tactic it also has a particular appeal to parents who are struggling with current events and who cannot see the relevance of an obsession with historicism. They know as well as any behaviour theorist that the social environment has a crucial role in shaping and maintaining human behaviour. What they often misunderstand is the precise working of the contingencies, their timing, their paradoxical effects and their potency. When their con-tingencies of reward and punishment — so often inconsistent or illtimed — don't work, they tend to show a certain inflexibility. Behaviourists, by recognising at last, interior cognitive events [see: Kanfer and Karoly, 1972] are losing some of *their* rigidity. Thus contemporary behaviour modification belatedly makes room for such concepts as self-control, self-observation, observational learning, and cognitive mediation.

The behavioural casework approach [Herbert, 1978] takes as its frame-work for therapeutic change, the available literature on learning and normal development. Much of our casework with parents involves what would be more appropriately called "counselling". The transmission of information about "normal" child development is often as important as suggestions about ways of dealing with difficult behaviour. It is assumed that parent education is one of our primary aims and it is hypothesised that the rearing of children is itself a skill. Other casework methods — clarification of problems, support-giving, sympathetic listening and acceptance — are utilized as appropriate. The central proposition is that many behaviour problems of childhood are essentially developmental problems which are exacerbated in faulty social learning interactions.

## Techniques

The behavioural casework techniques developed at the CTRU appear to offer particular advantages for social work practice in areas where the traditional approaches have been found deficient. For example, it can be used with the less educated and non-verbal clients and those displaying anti-social behaviour who may lack the social skills necessary for achieving more appropriate behaviour. Also by emphasizing or focusing on observable behaviour and limiting itself to the reduction of maladaptive behaviour and the encouragement of adaptive choices it respects the integrity of the client; because its principles can be clearly and simply explained it minimizes any mystification about treatment methods and objectives to the client's advantage. It is during the initial interview with both parents and child that an account is given (with down-to-earth examples) of the theoretical rationale and practical policies of the CTRU, pointing out how problem behaviour, like normal behaviour, can be acquired through failures or anomalies of learning and how individual differences (e.g. temperament) in children can affect and be affected by the environment. Such problems, it is suggested, can be alleviated by specific methods based on theories of learning.

## Stressed

The "commonsense" and familiar aspects of child management are stressed. It is emphasized that if a behavioural treatment is felt to be appropriate then this is likely to involve altering the consequences of the child's problem behaviour. Parents are asked whether they would be prepared to change *their* present responses to such behaviours, and, indeed to initiate actions — provided that they are not required to do anything contrary to their values as parents. They are warned that a good deal of time and effort could be required from them. The point is stressed that we are not there as "experts" to take over the burden of the child's problem from the parents but that it will be a cooperative venture with a major part of the "therapeutic" responsibilities rightfully in their hands.

## Permeated

The traditional view of "psychopathology" is so permeated by the medical or disease model that it places sole emphasis on the therapeutic role of the professional "expert". This is associated with the belief that therapeutic activities must only be engaged in by very highly trained professionals (from one or two favoured disciplines), to the exclusion of other people in the patient's immediate environment, whose involvement in the helping enterprise is viewed as only peripheral. The so-called dyadic model obtains: the expert "treats the patient" usually in the clinic setting. This is a situation far removed from the child's experience of life and occupying a miniscule proportion of it. Frequently, the therapist is unable to see parent-child (or teacher-child) interactions in their natural settings, and indeed, he may not even observe directly, in the artificiality of his consulting room, the problem behaviours for which the child was referred. Much of his information is hearsay and there can be a startling discrepancy between what parents say the child (and they themselves) are doing and what actually happens.

## Anchored

By contrast the behavioural casework approach is anchored in the natural environment; it seeks to utilize the powerful influence of those people in the community closest to the client; it uses to the full the good-will and therapeutic potential of those involved in close everyday contact. The triadic model, as it is called, is crucial to our work. Indeed, there is growing evidence that effective assessment and treatment of many childhood disorders (particularly "acting-out" problems) requires observation and intervention in the natural environment of the child [Tharp and Wetzel, 1969]. Furthermore, the systematic and successful involvement of parents, and particularly mothers, in the psychological treatment of children has increased considerably [O'Dell, 1974; Patterson *et al.*, 1975].

## Sharing with Parents

We believe it is important to share our thinking and information with the parents. In doing this we indicate to them, at an early stage, that there could be disagreement over treatment objectives (reservations on their part or the part of the CTRU) about behaviours to be changed (the so-called "target behaviours" of children and parents). Parents are invited to the case-conference which occurs after some two weeks of assessment (the baseline period) so as to debate and finalise the plan of treatment, and to draw up a contract. Once the case-conference has arrived at a formulation of the problem (a set of hypotheses about the controlling factors in the situation) a plan is made with the parents for the intervention, which *they* initiate with a good deal of practical and moral support from the social worker.

## No Set Formula

There is no set formula; there is a wide choice of methods but their implementation and back-up require sensitivity, ingenuity and creative casework skills. The tendency at many diagnostic conferences is to "distance" the problems, leaving them relatively undefined or in the "soft focus" of global terminology [Herbert, 1978]. This leads directly to *premature* "free-associations" about case and effect. To discuss causal factors before the "to-be-explained" phenomenon is carefully specified and precisely described and measured is to reverse scientific method, a perfectly human tendency.

After all, it is much more interesting to try to solve fascinating "why" and "how" riddles in connection with behaviour problems, then to wrestle with the more mundane "what" questions. Traditionally, the "case history" has taken a vertical form, an attempt to relate present troubles to past experience so as to see how they have evolved. Such a retrospective look at past events is often of interest but there is nothing that can be done to change history.

## Tends to Distance

It also tends to distance the problems. Social learning theorists attempt to conceptualize the "why" or "how" question and its answers in a more horizontal way, viewing the client as part of a complex network of inter-acting social systems any aspect of which may have bearing on his present troubles. Thus in attempting to reach some kind of assessment and plan a programme of treatment the unit of attention is far more broadly conceived; the focus of help is on a family unit rather than an individual child.

## Extensively Researched

Perhaps the most extensively researched of the behavioural techniques is systematic desensitization developed by Wolpe [1973] and based on positive counter conditioning. In its classic form this method of treatment involves teaching the client relaxation and then gradually taking him through a hierarchy of anxiety-provoking images gradually approaching the full phobic situation. At each stage in the hierarchy the client is encouraged to use relaxation to complete with any fear reaction until eventually the phobia is overcome. In some cases the hierarchy is experienced *in vivo* rather than in imagination. Although systematic desensitization has been used mainly in the treatment of phobias the underlying principles are very relevant to good social work interviewing technique. Fischer and Gochros [1975] suggest that if social workers are warm, sympathetic and concerned about clients' problems and optimistic about their solution and give an impression of reliability and competence then their clients are likely to react with feelings or confidence and increased self-esteem which will help counter anxiety, guilt or self-devaluation.

## Treatment Processes

The following case illustrates an adaption of systematic desensitization. Mark N. was referred to the CTRU suffering from severe encopresis. He was seven years old and had been soiling from birth. Assessment revealed that Mark had a history of severe constipation which had caused him considerable pain on defeacation and had required hospitalisation and the administration of enemas when he was three years old. These experiences had left Mark with a fear of defaecation and he soiled because he tried to ignore the signals which told him he needed to use the toilet, a process which he associated with fear and pain. Mark's fears were allayed by discussion and reassurance and by using an operant programme to reward Mark for successive approximations of the desired behaviour e.g. first changing his own clothes, standing near the toilet and eventually sitting on it. In a matter of weeks his anxieties gradually diminished to the point that he could use the toilet fearlessly and appropriately thus solving the soiling problem.

## Modeling

Modeling, a treatment developed from discoveries about observational learning [Bandura and Walters, 1963] is a procedure social workers often use without associating it with behaviour modification. Clients are frequently paired with a social worker who, it is felt, may provide a suitable model of masculine or feminine behaviour especially when no such appropriate models exist in the client's own environment. This informal use of modeling can be effective but more systematic use of such procedures as role-playing could be very valuable in teaching clients social skills in such areas as assertive training [Wolpe, 1973].

## Difficult to Cope

Jenny was a quiet, shy woman in her late twenties who found it difficult to cope with her bright, forceful four-year-old daughter and was also experiencing feelings of frustration and anger about her unsatisfactory marital relationship, feelings which she had not dared to communicate openly to her husband. Assessment revealed that Jenny had almost no self-confidence and a very poor self-image mainly due to past negative life experiences. Jenny was well aware of the reasons for her self-deprecation and self-doubts but this insight did not seem to affect her behaviour. We began an informal programme involving role-playing situations in which she felt unable to assert herself. By modeling appropriate reactions and using relaxation to allay her anxiety we were able to teach her to be more assertive — behaviour which reduced her feelings of helplessness and frustration and gave her confidence to make a realistic appraisal of her marriage and exert more control over her life.

## Assertive Training

Assertive training has also been successfully used in the treatment of impulsive and self-defeating aggressive behaviour — commonly the defensive reaction of a person who does not have sufficient skill or confidence to assert himself in a more appropriate way [Herbert, 1975]. The use of groups in assertive training and social skills training has also been found to be successful in dealing with timid and withdrawn clients [Fischer and Gochros, 1975].

## Operant Conditioning

Treatment methods based on operant conditioning are those which attempt to control the outcome of certain behaviours through the use of positive or negative reinforcers. A social worker using operant methods can analyse a family system and find out how the various members reinforce undesired behaviour in some members and intentionally or unintentionally ignore or punish desired behaviour. It is then possible to make alterations in such dysfunctional systems by planning with the family to systematically rearrange the consequences of behaviour so that all members of the family receive social reinforcement for desired behaviours.

## Conduct Disorders

Conduct disorders in children can also be effectively dealt with by using these methods. Gary was six and a half years old at referral and was described as a very unloveable child. He constantly screamed and shouted abuse at his parents and had violent temper tantrums when he would indulge in physical aggression, hitting and punching people and furniture and screaming at the top of his voice until he got his own way. He was also persistently defiant and disobedient and seemed to enjoy provoking confrontations with his parents. Observation and assessment confirmed that Gary was indeed showing all these behaviours but also revealed that they were being heavily reinforced by attention from his parents and by the fact that the shouting and temper tantrums usually resulted in Gary getting his own way and were therefore highly functional for him.

## Not surprising

Not surprisingly, against this background, family relationships were very strained and Gary was so unpopular that on the rare occasions when he did behave appropriately it went unnoticed und unattended to, which meant he was only getting attention for anti-social behaviour. By instituting an extinction programme to deal with the shouting and temper tantrums which involved removing Gary from the room as soon as he started to shout, a procedure known as "Time Out from Positive Reinforcement" and designed to eliminate the possibility of him receiving reinforcing attention for anti-social behaviour and also insisting that he complied with the original request on his return, we were able to eliminate these outbursts almost entirely. At the same time great emphasis was placed on rewarding Gary for pro-social behaviour with tokens which he could then exchange for a privilege (such as staying up late) or a treat (such as a favourite play activity with his parents).

This programme was designed to improve their relationship with Gary by providing opportunities for mutually reinforcing activities. By the end of the programme Gary was much happier, showing much more pro-social behaviour and getting on a good deal better with his parents.

This case illustrates how by changing behaviour one can also affect attitudes, and our experiences in the CTRU is that by modifying children's more difficult behaviour they become more rewarding to their parents, and mothers who have been at the stage of rejecting and even abusing their difficult children find they can see more positive sides to the child and start to enjoy the experience of being a parent.

## Use of Extinction

The use of extinction procedures which has just been illustrated involved the removal of all reinforcers. Simply ignoring problem behaviour can also have this effect and is a very straightforward procedure for the social worker to institute. An example of this, coupled with contingency management, is illustrated in the next case. Suzy was a nine-year-old spastic girl, the only child of rather anxious and overprotective parents. They were very concerned at her difficult behaviour during meal times when, although perfectly able to feed herself, she would refuse to eat unless fed, would throw food and utensils on the floor and often refuse food entirely. Assessment revealed that at school lunches the child showed none of these behaviours. Nor were they displayed at home when she ate informally in front of the television in the evening. Her problem behaviour was specific to family lunch at weekends and holidays, the only occasions when the whole family sat down together at the table. It appeared that this setting was providing Suzy with an audience to which she gladly reacted. In order to combat this her parents were instructed to ignore any "naughty" behaviour and only to speak to Suzy when she was eating properly. They were not to feed her or coax her and any food refused was to be removed without comment. Between meals snacks were forbidden and the dining room table was rearranged so that Suzy's parents were not directly looking at her. In order to help them ignore her, which they found very difficult at first, they were told to talk to each other, in order to take their minds off Suzy. Within three weekends Suzy was eating normally and has continued to do so. Her parents also used behavioural principles in encouraging self help skills and have themselves become less over-protective.

The use of response-cost procedures is another method of treatment used in behaviour modification. With this, a penalty is invoked for failure to complete a desired response. This may involve the forfeiture of rewards currently available — as for example, when failure to complete homework results in the loss of television privileges.

## Hyperactive Boy

A hyperactive boy, Darren, was extremely disruptive and noisy. He made life miserable for his older brothers and sisters, whilst they read or watched television, by constantly interrupting them — making loud humming and wailing noises and also banging things. An extension of the range of rewards for therapeutic interventions is enshrined in the Premack principle or "Granny's Rule" — where a preferred behaviour is made contingent on correctly performing a nonpreferred behaviour. This principle worked well with Darren. A bottle or marbles representing his pocket money plus a bonus was placed on the mantelpiece. Each transgression "cost" a marble (or penny). As always, sanctions were balanced by rewards. Punishment alone tells a child what he cannot do, not what he is expected to do. He was required to play quietly for set periods — timed with a kitchen timer, and if he did this successfully he was rewarded by tokens. These tokens could then be exchanged for treats — for example, he could loudly blow his sister's trombone for five minutes: something he had always wanted to do and something he found a great incentive.

Two other treatment methods developed from operant conditioning theory are aversive conditioning and the use of token economies. Both of these methods present ethical problems for the social worker and other therapists. It is difficult to justify the use of aversive conditioning in any but the most extreme cases, as for example, with self mutilating children and adults where the damage or pain inflicted by the treatment is considerably less than the situation it is designed to cure.

## Grave Reservations

The authors do have grave reservations about the use of token economies and behavioural methods involving sanctions in closed institutions and with "captive" clients such as psychiatric and delinquent cases. The most sensitive and worrying moral dilemma is the use of behavioural methods to deal with the rebellious and nonconformist behaviour of youths in penal institutions. Stolz *et al.* [1975], rightly observe that the probation officer/social worker with behaviour modification skills is often placed in the invidious position of assisting in the management of inmates whose rebelliousness and antagonism to authority are catalysts for conflict within the institution. Because of this, distinctions among many possible functions — as caseworker, manager, and rehabilitator — can become blurred and her allegiance confused. Although the professional may quite accurately perceive her role as benefiting the individual, she may at the same time appear to have the institution, rather than the youthful offender, as her primary client. The authors comment that often the goal of effective behaviour modification in penal institutions is the preservation of the institution's authoritarian control. Although some institutional behaviour modification programmes are designed to educate the inmates and benefit them in other ways, other programmes are directed towards making the offenders less troublesome and easier to manage, thus adjusting the inmates to the needs of the institution. The effectiveness of behavioural techniques as applied to non-voluntary individuals is in any event doubtful as the kinds of behaviours necessary for survival in a closed institution are very different from those necessary in the outside world. And if behaviour is not functional (useful and rewarding) to the individual in the natural environment (when the artificial reinforcers are removed) the behaviour will extinguish as it is not receiving natural social reinforcement. This is the old problem of poor generalization of rehabilitation carried out in closed institutions [Herbert, 1978]. Behaviour modification in such settings could be much more usefully employed in the teaching of social skills. Social skills training is an area where social workers could be very important as therapists and models in shaping behaviour.

## Recent Developments

Some of the most interesting recent developments in behaviour modification have been in the area of self control procedures. These are designed to give the subject a more effective means of manipulating the eliciting, reinforcing and discriminate stimuli which affect his behaviour. The caseworker's role is first to carefully examine the antecedents and consequences of a piece of behaviour over which the subject wishes to have more control and to then suggest ways in which these events may be altered. They may be altered by either physical or cognitive changes in order that the subject may achieve a greater degree of control over his behaviour. Sue (to give one example) was heavily overweight and was anxious to control her eating behaviour. She was asked to carefully record everything she ate or drank and the time at which it was consumed over a two week period. From this data it became evident that her overeating was restricted to certain types of food and occurred only during the latter part of the day. Further investigation revealed that the sorts of food Sue ate to excess were packets of sweets, cakes and biscuits which she usually bought at a local shop on her way home from work. She admitted that she felt very guilty about overeating and bought these sorts of foods because they were easy to conceal from her flat mates. Sue never overate in company, only when she was alone.

## Self Control

A self control programme was designed in order to help Sue resist the temptation to overeat. She was instructed to take a different route home so as to avoid the shop she usually called at; and if she was to be alone in the flat, was told to change immediately from her day clothes into a housecoat to help discourage her from popping out to the shops later in the evening. Her flat mates agreed to help by not bringing any forbidden cakes or sweets into the flat when Sue was around and they also made an effort to ensure that she was not left alone in the evenings. Sue was allowed to reward herself for sticking to her diet by having a favourite cake or sweet at the end of each "successful" evening. When tempted to cheat she was told to visualise an unpleasant and humiliating scene where a group of boys made rude and teasing remarks about her size — a hazard which she would do anything to avoid.

## Fast Procedure

This last procedure, known as covert sensitization was developed by Cautela [1967] and involves teaching a subject to obtain a clear visual image of an aversive situation or experience and to conjure up this image when trying to avoid temptation. This method has been used successfully with alcoholics who have been trained to imagine a scene where, when they reached for a glass of beer or wine the alcohol changed into a revolting liquid which caused them to vomit violently and resulted in public humiliation. This image helps them to resist temptation.

## Main Aim

The main aim of the social worker using behavioural methods is to give her client the necessary skills and understanding so that in the future he will be able to apply the principles himself. In the CTRU we have found that an excellent way of achieving this is to let those parents who have successfully modified their own and their children's behaviour meet with and teach other families who are starting treatment. This is done through a weekly self-help parents group [Herbert and Iwaniec, 1977a; Herbert and Iwaniec, 1977b] at which value issues are debated and new techniques and ideas discussed.

## Inappropriate

There are, of course, occasions when behavioural casework is deemed inappropriate. Henry, aged 10 years was referred to the CTRU by his housemother with the following complaints: he taunted other children; was abusive to residential staff; and ate noisily. In addition, he was so un-controlled when out of the Home that the guide who escorted him to the school bus had been obliged to use a restrainer to stop Henry running off and across busy roads. Henry was also reported to have severe temper tantrums about three times a week and he was said to be highly disruptive, often upsetting the whole household by banging on the floor and by shouting obscenities at some members of staff.

A comprehensive assessment of this child helped to identify several possible factors that seemed to indicate real obstacles to any possible approaches to treatment. As regards biological deficits, it was clear that Henry was very considerably handicapped by intellectual retardation; bearing this in mind and the related poor social development, it seemed that some of the specific complaints suggested that perhaps staff were setting too high expectations for Henry's capacity (e.g. his unpredictability in traffic). He was also found to have a genetically determined clinical syndrome which made more under-standable his reported clumsiness, hyperactivity, as well as deficient social and intellectual development. As regards the antisocial behaviour problems, the initial assessment identified several factors which were of relevance. It was clear that such problems occurred only with some staff members. His houseparents were able to control Henry. It seemed that three members of staff had real difficulties in dealing with him, and it appeared that they helped to reinforce the bad behaviour by the very considerable attention they paid to its. His housemother noted that by ignoring his swearing and so on, she very rarely found that it caused her any problem.

## Hyperactive Behaviour

It was also apparent that any hyperactive behaviour and difficulties arising out of the child's poor social skills were exacerbated by the rather restrictive regime. For example, when the Unit-therapist had tea at the Home as part of assessment, it emerged that the children were not usually allowed to talk at the table. Secondly, all the children were ready, washed and in night-clothes by 6 p.m. each evening, and as the tables were set for the next day's breakfast, the children had little space in which to play. Finally, it was apparent from the comments of staff that no one was able to think of positive characteristics in the child; the emphasis was almost wholly on his bad points.

Rather than attempt to set up any specific treatment plan, the caseworker emphasised the child's very real handicaps, arising out of his intellectual, physical and social retardation. Secondly, a considerable correspondence ensued which stressed the advantages of planned social casework designed to facilitate the child's rehabilitation with relatives who lived some considerable distance away from the Midlands.

## Psychodynamic

Many theorists and practitioners of a psychodynamic persuasion question the appropriateness of a behavioural approach because they believe that therapy for a particular problem must direct itself to the "root cause" of the problem. According to this view, disorders of psychological origin should be treated by some form of psychotherapy. They regard as symptoms (the outward and visible signs of underlying disorder) what the behaviourally orientated therapists might take as the focus of treatment. It is often argued that a failure to deal with the underlying problems (e.g. intrapsychic conflicts) leads to "symptom substitution". Just how one defines operationally such a construct is never made clear. Without measurable indices of "substitution" — a clearcut way of specifying the links, symbolic or otherwise, between symptoms — the criticism is impossible to prove *or* disprove. Studies [e.g. Baker, 1969] designed (inter alia) to investigate whether *other* problems appear when behavioural programmes have successfully removed symptoms (such as enuresis — a problem which is amenable to treatment by bell and pad administered by social workers) do not indicate that such an eventuality occurs. The belief in symptom substitution ignores the fact that physicians from time immemorial have applied themselves diligently to symptom relief and removal in both functional and organic ailments. In the absence of empirical evidence to support the idea of symptom substitution but with plentiful evidence for the successful treatment of "symptoms" or (as the behaviourists would prefer) alleviation of problems, we suggest that symptom relief is a legitimate goal in any therapeutic intervention. After all, in most cases it is exactly this for which the client is asking. Indeed, Baker [1969] found, as we have at the CTRU [Herbert, 1978] that children treated behaviourally, often show improvements in areas that had not been specific targets of the behaviour therapy. It may be that serious problem behaviour blocks the child from engaging in behaviour that might be a source for him of positive reinforcement from his parents and peers, the absence of which hinder his socialization and development of a repertoire of prosocial behaviours. The answer to fears about symptom-substitution is to avoid metaphors such as "underlying" and "deep-seated" causes, and rather to carry out rigorous and comprehensive assessment into *all* the contributory causal factors which have a bearing on the planning of successful casework interventions. The "safety net" is to engage in thorough and systematic follow-ups after the intervention is terminated.

## Micawber Syndrome

In the authors' opinion, a reliance on "psychotherapy" (especially if it is the vaguely conceived relationship therapy indulged in by some inexperienced caseworkers) rather than carefully planned specific measures, gives rise to the "Micawber syndrome". "If I develop a good relationship with a child and keep seeing him, some benign change is bound to turn up." It seldom does in the conduct disorders so commonly a matter of concern to social workers, not even "spontaneous remission" is on the side of the serious conduct disorders.

Hollis [1964] has criticised behaviour therapy on the grounds that "it means the abandonment of our present highly valued principle of giving priority to enhancing the client's control over his own treatment". This seems to us to be a very naive argument which fails to take into account the fact that the use of any intervention strategy is an attempt to control some-one else's behaviour and we suggest that behaviour therapy's openness about this goal is an advantage to the client. He then at least has the choice to refuse to become involved if he does not wish to change — a choice which is likely to be more obscured if the therapy is based on the worker's inter-pretation of hidden motives and desires of which the client himself is unaware.

## Morality of Behaviour Control

The idea that controlling behaviour is in itself somehow immoral ignores the reality that:

> All behaviour is inevitably controlled and the operation of psychological laws cannot be suspended by romantic conceptions of human behaviour anymore than an indignant rejection of the laws of gravity can stop people falling. [Bandura, 1969]

From the social worker's point of view the issue to be decided with any kind of treatment is not whether behaviour is to be controlled but where the controlling forces lie and to what extent she should intervene or encourage others to intervene in their operation. The moral issues of whether to intervene and if so what the aim of intervention should be can only be answered with reference to the individual worker's value base and that of her profession. In proposing that behaviour therapy be used as one of the social work methods we would emphasize that its usefulness in a particular situ-ation must be carefully evaluated with reference to the cultural, social and economic factors which may also be contributing to the "problem". Behaviour modification *does* have a "human face"; and it might be argued (to take but one example) that the approach described in this paper returns dignity to demoralized parents and provides increased choices for restricted and unhappy children.

Another genuine and understandable concern about behaviour modification is the one of bribery. Contingency contracting, for example, has been said to foster a manipulative, exchange orientation to social interaction, and token economies, an emphasis on materialistic evaluation of human efforts. The most comprehensive answers to these criticisms are provided by O'Leary, Paulos and Devine [1972] and, as with other value issues which pervade these criticisms and counter-arguments, the reader must form his own conclusions.

### Ethical

From the ethical point of view we feel that some of the values implicit in the use of behaviour therapy are a safeguard rather than a threat to clients' integrity. Its insistence on monitoring of methods and results for evaluation, and its requirement that a knowledge base, empirically substantiated, be used as a reference point from which any treatment method starts, gives clients an opportunity to question and check a worker's competence and reliability which the more interpretive approaches to therapy do not.

The resistance of behaviour therapy to labels such as "mentally ill" or "abnormal behaviour" removes the possibility that such labels will become self-fulfilling prophecies setting up a chain of responses that reinforce expected patterns of dysfunctional behaviour.

### Classical Example

A classic example of this last situation can be seen in the case of Robert a ten-year-old boy labelled "autistic". His parents were told that to expect anything other than bizarre and aggressive behaviour from an "autistic" child was being unrealistic and as a result for years they made no attempt to check or prevent his more anti-social behaviour.

### Successfully Treated

This child was successfully treated using a behavioural programme which assessed his "autistic" behaviour in the same way as any other behaviour would be assessed. By changing certain antecedent and consequent events the social worker was able to reduce his "irrational aggression" (which in behavioural terms could be quite rationally explained by looking at the reinforcement it was receiving) and similar anti-social behaviours so that he was able to start mixing socially and begin to develop the potential he did have without the label getting in the way.

### Behaviour Therapy

The emphasis in behaviour therapy of an open and honest relationship with no hidden agendas or secret labels and the way in which the value of an intervention is judged in terms of whether stated objectives are achieved means that clients avoid the possibility of being labelled inadequate or manipulative if they fail to share the worker's "insight" into their "real" problem.

## Relationship

In behavioural casework the casework relationship consists of one person with a problem working with another person who has both special skills and an interest in helping people and although this relationship should be warm and friendly it should not be a replacement for relationships in the client's or social worker's environment.

In conclusion we would suggest that the behavioural methods outlined in this paper are a potentially valuable tool which social workers seeking to increase their practice skills should study and select in appropriate cases. They offer a very effective and relatively quick way of changing certain maladaptive behaviours and of teaching adaptive ones and can only improve the range of help social workers already seek to offer to their clients.

## Bibliography

Baker, B. L. (1969). Symptom treatment and symptom substitution in enuresis. *Abnormal Psychology* 74, 1, 42–49.

Bandura, A. (1969). "Principles of Behaviour Modification". Holt, Rinehart and Winston, New York.

Bandura, A. and Walters, R. H. (1963). "Social Learning and Personality Development". Holt, Rinehart and Winston, New York.

Cautela, J. R. (1965). Desensitization and insight. *Behaviour Research and Therapy* 3, 59–64.

Cautela, J. R. (1967). Covert sensitization. *Psychological Record* 20, 459–468.

Fischer, J. and Gochros, H. L. (1975). "Planned Behaviour Change: Behaviour Modification in Social Work". Collier Macmillan, London.

Gelfand, D. M. and Hartmann, D. P. (1968). Behaviour therapy and children: a review and evaluation of research methodology. *Psychological Bulletin* 69, 204–215.

Gelfand, D. M. and Hartmann, D. P. (1975). "Child Behaviour: Analysis and Therapy". Pergamon Press, Oxford.

Herbert, M. (1974). "Emotional Problems of Development in Children". Academic Press, London.

Herbert, M. (1975). "Problems of Childhood: A Guide for All Concerned". Pan Books, London.

Herbert, M. (1978). "Conduct Disorders of Childhood and Adolescence: A Behavioural Approach to Assessment and Treatment". John Wiley, Chichester.

Herbert, M. and Iwaniec, D. (1977a). "The Formation of a Parents Group for Training in, and Discussion of, Child-Management Procedures". Child Treatment Research Unit, Leicester.

Herbert, M. and Iwaniec, D. (1977b). Children who are difficult to love. *New Society* 40, 759, 111–112.

Herbert, M. and Iwaniec, D. (1979). Managing children's behavioural problems. *Social Work Today* 10, no. 33, 12–14.

Hollis, F. (1964). "Social Casework: A Psycho-social Therapy". Random House, New York.

Jehu, D. *et al.* (1972). "Behaviour Modification in Social Work". Wiley, London.

Jones, M. C. (1924). The elimination of children's fear. *Journal of Counseling Psychology* 7, 383–390.

Kanfer, F. H. and Karoly, P. (1972). Self-control: a behaviouristic excursion into the lion's den. *Behavior Therapy* 3, 398–416.

Leung, F. L. (1975). The ethics and scope of behaviour modification. *Bulletin of the British Psychological Society* 28, 376–379.

Mickelson, D. J. and Stevic, R. R. (1971). Differential effects of facilitative and non-facilitative behavioural consellors. *Journal of Counselling Psychology* 18, 314–319.

Mischel, W. (1968). "Personality and Assessment". Wiley, New York.

O'Dell, S. (1974). Training parents in behaviour modification: a review. *Psychological Bulletin* 81, 7, 418–433.

O'Leary, K. D., Poulos, R. W. and Devine, V. T. (1972). Tangible reinforcers: bonuses or bribes? *Journal of Consulting and Clinical Psychology* 38, 1–8.

Patterson, G. R. *et al.* (1975). "A Social Learning Approach to Family Intervention: Vol. 1, Families with aggressive children". Castalix Publishing Co., Eugene.

Persons, R. W. (1966). Psychological and behavioural change in delinquents following psychotherapy. *Journal of Clinical Psychology* 22, 337–340.

Shapiro, D. A. (1975). Some implications of psychotherapy research for clinical psychology. *British Journal of Medical Psychology* 48, 199–206.

Stolz, S. B., Wienckowski, L. A. and Brown, B. S. (1975). Behaviour modification: a perspective on critical issues. *American Psychologist*, November, 1027.

Tharp, R. G. and Wetzel, R. J. (1969). "Behaviour Modification in the Natural Environment. Academic Press, New York.

Truax, C. B. (1966). Reinforcement and non-reinforcement in Rogerian psychotherapy. *Journal of Abnormal Psychology* 71, 1–9.

Truax, C. B. and Carkhuff, R. R. (1976). "Toward Effective Counselling and Psychotherapy". Aldine, Chicago.

Vitalo, R. L. (1970). Effects of facilitative interpersonal functioning in a conditioning paradigm. *Journal of Counselling Psychology* 17, 141–144.

Wolpe, J. (1973). "The Practice of Behaviour Therapy". 2nd ed. Pergamon Press, New York.

Yelloly, M. (1972). Insight, *In* "Behaviour Modification in Social Work" (Eds D. Jehu *et al.*). Wiley, London.

Younghusband, E. (1967). "Social Work and Social Values". Allen & Unwin, London.

# CASEWORK, PSYCHOTHERAPY AND SOCIAL WORK

## A. W. CLARE

## Introduction

Most social workers refer to their work as "casework" [Parsloe and Stevenson, 1978] but the diversity of meanings attached to this term has tended to limit its usefulness in clarifying what it is that social workers actually do with, to and for their clients. Historically, the term "casework" was the name given to a case-by-case approach or individualized social work activity directed at a particular situation and undertaken in a particular spirit [Timms and Timms, 1977]. Gradually, however, ideas of "therapy" infiltrated this approach so that eventually virtually everything done by the social worker had to be justified in terms of its contribution to or part of treatment. Yelloly [1980] has documented the growth of the influence of psychoanalysis on social work, first in the United States, and later, in the 1950s, in Britain. At the present time, "casework", as a concept in social work, bears much the same relationship to psychoanalysis as the concept of psychotherapy in psychiatry does; that is to say, it is respectable in so far as it can demonstrate its links with analysis and it is open to allegations of superficiality in so far as it cannot. Because of the over-riding importance given to the development of insight or self-awareness as a treatment mdality in the classic psychodynamically-derived psychotherapies, there has been a tendency in social work and in medicine to regard insight-based approaches as profound, revealing and, reconstructive. In contrast, as Reid and Shyne have pointed out [Reid and Shyne, 1969], therapies which involve a different approach are labelled with a more pallid group of adjectives — "supportive", "modifying", "restorative" — and are regarded as less significant, more modest and, in the final analysis, less effective.

While there is a sizeable literature developing which questions such a dichotomy and the assumptions derived from it, the idea that profound, analytic exploration involving a suitably trained therapist and a willing client constitutes the optimum therapeutic situation lingers on. In so far as this approach is not preferred by social workers and others involved in interpersonal professional work it seems to be more because of the complexity of analysis than anything to do with the question of its efficacy. The responses to a recent British inquiry into field social workers' professional viewpoints make interesting reading in this regard. While none of the social workers surveyed believed that casework consisted solely of solving problems by forming a therapeutic relationship with the client and exploring feelings and changing attitudes within it, many stated or implied that casework, in contra-distinction to undertaking practical interventions, involved "in-depth work" of a time-consuming nature. As a direct consequence of this association of casework with time-consuming and profound exploration, many felt that it was an inappropriate approach in the busy setting of a local authority office [Parsloe and Stevenson, 1978].

There is more than a suggestion here that social workers, like many general practitioners, while interested in and alive to the possibilities of developing interviewing skills and using psychological methods to bring about social change, are somewhat intimidated by the assumption, held most notably by specialized psychotherapists, that somewhere at the heart of every psychotherapy lies a dynamic conceptualization [Wolff, 1973]. Such a view has been hotly contested within general practice by Madden [1979] who asks:

> if analytically-based psychotherapy is as vital at the general practice and community level as those, such as Balint, have suggested [Balint, 1957] how has it come about that it is almost unobtainable at the expert level, and then only after intensive screening of the potential case as suitable for treatment.

Balint's insistence on the importance of analytic conceptualizations for analytically derived psychotherapy in general practice is echoed by the comments of analysts addressing social workers during the 1950s. John Bowlby was in no doubt of the need for social workers to familiarize themselves with the principles of psychoanalytic theory, declaring that "unless a social worker has a good understanding of unconscious motivation she will be powerless to deal with many an unmarried mother, many a home which is in danger of breaking up, and many a case of conflict between parent and child" [Bowlby, 1951]. Later, at a conference of the Association of Psychiatric Social Workers at Leicester in 1956, another psychoanalyst, Dr John Sutherland, then Director of the Tavistock Clinic, laid considerable emphasis on the similarities between dynamic psychotherapy and counselling in that both, apparently, utilized a knowledge of the dynamic unconscious. Sutherland also argued for a greater acquisition of therapeutic skill on the part of the social worker, such a skill being clearly identified with some form of psychoanalytically-derived, psychotherapeutic training. It is one of the ironies of the present attack on social work that psychiatrists, who were so responsible for the promulgation of psychoanalytic ideas in social work in the 1950s, should now criticize contemporary social workers for an undue reliance on supposedly outmoded notions of mental functioning [Brewer and Lait, 1980].

At the present time, while the case for a retention of dynamic psychotherapy is argued hotly by the Group for the Advancement of Psychodynamics and Psychotherapy in Social Work [Bleech, 1981; Hornby, 1973; Yelloly, 1980], there is some evidence that its appeal and influence may be waning. Texts such as Hollis's psychoanalytic text "Casework: A Psychosocial Approach" still figure prominently on reading lists supplied by the main social work departments of training but enquiries made to the departments of social work at Oxford, Bristol, Leicester, East Anglia, Sheffield and the London School of Economics revealed that at none of these was a specific course on psychoanalytic theory or practice provided. One lecturer at East Anglia believed that there had been "a long and steady assault on the use of these (analytic) theories in social work training" and that many teachers were no longer convinced that Freudian-based psychologies had very much to offer social workers [Howe, 1982]. This contrasts with Parsloe's personal recollection of training at the social work department at the L.S.E. in 1958 when "almost the only theory about human development to which we were exposed was psychoanalytic theory" [Parsloe, 1982]. Parsloe's own reservations about the usefulness of psychoanalysis, and she speaks as a social worker who has undergone a personal analysis, concern the *techniques* of analysis. She regards psychoanalytic *theory* with more favour and wonders whether the pendulum against intra-psychic exploration may have swung too far and that now "we are about to experience a comeback of psychoanalytic theory". Butrym [1981], senior lecturer in social work at the L.S.E., likewise regards psychodynamic theory as important to social workers, and she echoes Yelloly's emphasis in defining casework as a distinctive approach to human problems in which the two essential characteristics are its psycho-social focus and its "emphasis on the importance of the relationship between the social worker and his or her client" [Butrym, 1981]. However, she does have a somewhat inclusive notion of dynamic psychology which she defines as incorporating "any type of psychological knowledge or insight which is concerned with the processes occurring in the mind — both conscious and unconscious" and encompassing in addition to classical Freudian psycho-analytic theory "its various derivatives regardless of how far some of these may have departed from the original". But Butrym shares Parsloe's doubts concerning the applicability of psychoanalytic *techniques* in social work, regarding them as inappropriate and even harmful. Social work must make use of dynamic psychology as it would of medicine, law or sociology "but it must avoid at all costs becoming a pseudo-psychotherapy".

In practice, social work, like psychiatry, works with a very broad idea of psychotherapy and one which is very different from the relatively circum-scribed, technically complex procedure for the analysis of serious intra-psychic disturbance which is psychoanalysis. Social work theorists and practitioners make use of such different and differing perspectives as systems theory [Forder, 1976], behavioural techniques [Hudson, 1978; McAuley and McAuley, 1980], non-directive counselling [Baldock and Prior, 1981] and transactional analysis [Pitman, 1982]. The growth of these and other therapeutic approaches, including task-centred case-work, is but one factor contributing to the lively debate concerning the precise skills and training necessary for social workers to undertake psychological inter-ventions and to bring these to a successful conclusion.

## The Necessary Skills

While psychodynamic theory apparently is of value to social workers, psycho-dynamic techniques are not. Yet it is not entirely clear, as a consequence of such a distinction, quite what are the therapeutically vital ingredients of casework and counselling and whether these are related in any way to psychodynamic theory. There does appear to be a consensus developing which appears to regard many of the central tenets of classical psycho-analytical *theory* as dispensible from the point of view of therapy. An example of this view is contained in the introduction of a recent book on psychotherapy by a respected, analytically-trained psychiatrist [Storr, 1979]. In it, he expresses the opinion that the psychoanalytical schools will soon disappear as discrete entities. The labels Jungian, Freudian, and Kleinian, he declares: "will become less and less important as research discloses the common factors which lead to a successful outcome in psychotherapy".

Of course this opens up the possibility that the "common factors" so revealed may have nothing to do with such psychodynamic constructs as transference analysis, the dynamic unconscious or the development of insight. Yet Storr goes on to argue that personal analysis "will continue to be an important part of training for those who wish to specialize in psycho-therapy". While this may appear reasonable it is not entirely clear why it necessarily need be true. The argument, it is important to point out, is not about the therapeutic aspects of the doctor-patient relationship or the social worker-client relationship for these can be believed in without the necessity of subscribing to elaborate analytical formulations. Rather it concerns those elements that are of therapeutic importance in these relationships.

In the light of recent research into the efficacy of various types of psycho-therapy, it seems reasonable to ask what forms seem particularly indicated for workers in the primary care setting? Putting the question another way, and in an historical setting, was Freud right when he pugnaciously declared in his celebrated address in Budapest in 1918:

> It is very probable too that the large-scale application of our therapy will compel us to alloy the pure gold of analysis freely with the copper of direct suggestion; and hypnotic suggestion too might find a place in it again, as it has in the treat-ment of the war neuroses. But whatever form this psychotherapy for the people may take, whatever the elements out of which it is compounded, its most effective and most important ingredients will assuredly remain those borrowed from strict and untendentious psychoanalysis. [Freud, 1918]

As Hogan, the latest of a long line of reviewers in this area, points out, psychotherapy "for the people" remains an amorphous and a vaguely defined process with wide variations in therapy and technique [Hogan, 1979]. Its shadowy definition, as we have seen, is similar to that of "case-work". The earliest use of the word "psychotherapy" was by J. C. Reil in 1803 in an article entitled "Rhapsodies in the Application of Psychic Methods in the Treatment of Mental Disturbances" [Veith, 1958]. The distinction between psychoanalytic and other forms of psychotherapy appears to rest on the importance attributed by the former to the develop-ment of a regressive transference neurosis and the techniques of inter-pretation. In contrast, the definition of psychotherapy lays much stress on the more general relief of suffering through psychological means [Frank, 1978], provided by a trained professional [Strupp, 1978], and the establishment in a deliberate fashion of a relationship [Wolberg, 1977] involving the use of words [Storr, 1979]. As the elements gradually come together, a composite definition takes shape:

> ... the informed and planful application of techniques derived from established psychological principles, by persons qualified through training and experience to understand these principles and to apply these techniques with the intention of assisting individuals to modify such personal characteristics as feeling, values, attitudes and behaviours which are judged by the therapist to be maladaptive. [Metzolff and Kornreich, 1970]

Wolberg [1977] attempted with some success to group the psychotherapies into those which provide support, guidance, advice and reassurance, those which attempt to teach the individual new behavioural patterns, and those which attempt to dismantle and rebuild a new personality (Table 1).

TABLE 1
Types of psychotherapy

| Supportive | Re-educative | Reconstructive |
|---|---|---|
| Guidance | Behaviour therapy | Freudian analysis |
| Milieu therapy | Cognitive learning | Kleinian |
| OT | Client-centred | Ego analysis |
| Music therapy | Casework | Neo-Freudian |
| Reassurance | Interviewing | Individual psychology |
| Persuasion | Group | Analytical psychology |
| Pressure | Family | Reichian analysis |
| Confession | Conjoint marital | Dynamic-cultural |
| Ventilation | Mysticism | Existential |

If this model is accepted with all its shortcomings, then the question that must be asked is whether there is any evidence that the so-called reconstructive therapies are in fact superior to those approaches which have more modest aims. In recent years, there have been a number of attempts, some quite ingenious in terms of design, to answer this question and their results must be of considerable interest to those, such as GPs and social workers, whose everyday professional activities involves them in the manipulation of psychological and other interpersonal variables to bring about relief and change.

Perhaps the most celebrated, and certainly one of the most quoted psychoanalytic studies is the Menninger Foundation's Psychotherapy Project which involved the intensive longitudinal study of 42 cases and which was expressly designed "to explore changes brought about in patients by psychoanalytically-oriented psychotherapies and psychoanalysis" [Menninger Foundation, 1972]. The 42 patients underwent "treatment designed within the framework of psychoanalytic theory ranging from supportive psychotherapy to psychoanalysis". Psychoanalysis was defined in this study as:

> a technique employed by a neutral analyst resulting in the development of a regressive transference neurosis. The ultimate resolution of this neurosis is achieved by techniques of interpretation alone.

On the basis of the results obtained with the 42 patients studied (there was no non-treatment group for comparison), the authors of the report concluded that for patients with "high Ego Strength, high Motivation, high Anxiety Tolerance and high Quality of Interpersonal Relationships, psychoanalysis is the treatment of choice". "Ego Strength" was defined in this study as a combination of the degree of integration, stability and flexibility of the personality, the degree to which relationships with others are "adaptive, deep and gratifying of normal instinctual needs" and the degree to which the individual's disturbance is manifested by symptoms. Stripped of the psychoanalytical language, the conclusions are that psychoanalysis is useful for moderately healthy, well-motivated, socially functioning and reasonably personable individuals. Plainly it is not for the sick. Nor is it for those chronically incapacitated individuals who constitute a disproportionate amount of the burden of demand placed on social workers and general practitioners [Cooper, 1972; Corney and Bowen, 1980]. Those patients with low Ego Strength, low Motivation, low Anxiety Tolerance and an impairment of Interpersonal Relationships, did not appear to benefit from psychoanalytical intervention.

A second classic study is the Penn Psychotherapy Project [Luborsky *et al.*, 1980]. In this study, a total of 73 patients were treated in "psychoanalytically oriented psychotherapy", the average number of treatment sessions devoted to each patient being 44. The study was designed to establish prognostic indicators and involved 35 neurotic, 18 personality disordered, 20 mixed neurotic and 3 "latent" psychotic patients, together with one case of situational maladjustment and one psychophysiologic disorder. The bulk of the patients was made-up of young, single, college-educated white women. The outcome, when assessed by the therapists, showed that 65% had made a good or moderate improvement, a figure which fell to 56% when the assessment of outcome was made by clinical observers. These might appear impressive figures but there is room for caution. An even more rigorous study in Britain, assessing time limited, psychoanalytically-based therapy produced less impressive figures [Malan *et al.*, 1973a] and one's doubts are further strengthened by the fact that the Tavistock group had earlier drawn attention to the suggestion from the literature that improvement of a symptomatic kind is the rule rather than the exception in *untreated* neurotic patients [Malan *et al.*, 1968]. In a 2–8 year follow-up of 45 patients assessed but not treated at the Tavistock, 23 (51%) were found to be at least symptomatically improved, of whom 9 were regarded as being symptomatically recovered. Only one patient, however, was regarded as dynamically recovered. The rather "soft" nature of the distinction between "symptomatic" and "dynamic" improvement or recovery may be illustrated by one of the examples provided by the authors. One patient, "symptomatically" recovered but "dynamically" doubtful, was a 33 year old man who originally attended for impotence, doubts about his masculinity, difficulties relating to women and related anxieties. At follow-up, 4½ years later, he was married, potent and happy with his wife. However, the doubts about his dynamic recovery were due to the fact that in the follow-up interview he expressed two slips of the tongue, revealed that on the rare occasions during sexual foreplay that his wife made a remark in some way out of keeping his penis "would go down just like that", and he occasionally found himself unable to urinate in a public lavatory when other men were present!

Another evaluation of psychoanalysis as treatment, this time compared with non-analytic therapy, is provided by Malan in his review of what he terms "the outcome problem" in psychotherapy research [Malan, 1973b]. Malan distilled five studies from a very much larger number on grounds of methodological soundness, presence of controls, a reasonable period of follow-up and appropriate assessment. Two studies were of peptic ulcer, two were of ulcerative colitis and one was of arthritis. All five gave a positive results but the methods of treatment represented a complete spectrum. One study employed 3—4 years of psychoanalysis, whereas another used a didactic approach. Two used a range of group approaches designed to bring out and help patients ventilate unexpressed feelings while the fifth employed a similar range of dynamic individual therapies from brief psychoanalytical methods to full-scale analysis. Malan restricted his comments to the fact that "dynamic therapies seem to have been more or less validated for psychosomatic conditions and for no other conditions whatsoever". From the vantage-point of primary care and social work, in which psychosomatic conditions are not uncommon, one is, however, struck by the fact that a fairly straight-forward psychotherapeutic intervention consisting of the active avoidance of interpretations and the training of the individual patient to think of something pleasant and avoid worrying was every bit as effective as 3—4 years of time-consuming and expensive analysis.

One final example of psychoanalysis, in brief form, compared with other forms of treatment, and one which raises considerable doubt about the specific efficacy of such revered analytic interventions as interpretation and transference analysis, is that of Sloan and his colleagues in Philadelphia [Sloan *et al.*, 1975]. In this study, 94 patients presenting at a psychiatric out-patients department and diagnosed as suffering from moderately severe neurotic disturbances or personality disorders, were randomly assigned to one of three groups. One group was treated by experienced psychoanalytically-trained psychotherapists. Another group was treated by experienced behaviour therapists while the third group received no formal treatment other than the initial "in-depth" assessment interview common to all groups, and a monthly telephone call reassuring them that they had not been forgotten and would be assigned to treatment as soon as possible. The three groups were assessed at four months, twelve months and two years. At four months, all three groups had improved significantly with respect to so-called "target" symptoms. Both treatment groups improved significantly more than those on the waiting list but there was no significant difference in the amount of symptomatic improvement, social adjustment and work ability between the psychotherapy and the behaviour therapy groups. The one and two year follow-up assessments supported the view that those who had shown most improvement at four months continued to do well.

The results of this study, as Marmor pointed out in the introduction to the report, offer little comfort to those adherents

of either group (psychoanalytically-derived psychotherapy and behaviour therapy)
who are involved in passionately proclaiming the inherent superiority of this
particular brand of therapy over all others.

But the study does provide results of interest and possibly comfort to
professionals working in the community with scarece time and resources for
it appeared to show that such differences as exist between therapies may be
more a matter of degree than substance and, more important, that the
therapist's style and certain personal characteristics might be of greater
therapeutic significance than the elaborate nature of his theory and his
technique. Behaviour therapists, for instance, in the Philadelphia study
tended to be more directive, more concerned with symptoms, less concerned
with childhood memories and, despite their reputation for coldness and lack
of clinical involvement, warmer and more active therapists. Tape-recorded
interviews showed that they made as many interpretative statements as did
the psychotherapists. Given the similarities between the two approaches in
practice, it is not clear from the study whether the behaviourists and the
psychotherapists did use fundamentally different approaches to reach the
same therapeutic conclusions or whether the effectiveness of their treatment
was due to factors common to both schools. But the patients themselves
were in less doubt. Those who had improved, attributed their improvement
less to the theoretical framework within which they had been treated and
more to the personality, enthusiasm and involvement of the therapists by
whom they had been treated.

Evidence too began to accumulate questioning the assumed superiority of
the more involved and intricate therapies over the simpler ones. One study
compared various therapeutic approaches, psychotherapy versus group
psychotherapy, time-limited versus time-unlimited, client-centred versus
traditional and so on [Luborsky et al., 1975]. Only studies of reasonable
quality were chosen and these were graded on various criteria. More than
100 studies were included and the authors concluded that different forms of
psychotherapy do not make significant differences in the proportion of
patients who improve at the end of psychotherapy. Most patients who do go
through any form of psychotherapy gain benefit from it. Of 33 studies
comparing psychotherapy with no therapy at all, 20 favoured therapy, 13
indicated no difference and none concluded that no therapy was better than
some form of therapy. The authors explain the lack of difference in effectiveness among major therapies as a result of the major common elements
operative in each (especially the personality of the therapist) and the
difficulty of a particular therapy appearing more effective when all appear to
have significant effectiveness.

But perhaps the most remarkable review of research on psychotherapy is
the "meta-analysis" conducted by Mary Lee Smith and Gene Glass at the
University of Colorado. Meta-analysis is "the statistical analysis of a large
collection of analysis results from individual studies for the purpose of integrating the findings" [Glass, 1976]. Such an analysis is in contradistinction
to casual, narrative discussions of research studies which generally suffer
from significant methodological difficulties. Smith and Glass inspected more
than 1000 studies, retained 500 as appropriate and fully analysed the results

of 375 controlled investigations. To be selected, a study had to have at least one treatment group compared with an untreated group or a different therapy group. The definition of psychotherapy used was that of Meltzoff and Kornfeich quoted earlier and studies in which the treatment was labelled "counselling" but whose methods fitted this definition were included. Drug therapies, occupational therapy, hypnotherapy, marathon therapy and peer counselling were excluded as were sensitivity training, milieu therapy, consciousness raising and psychodrama groups.

The most important feature of any outcome study is the magnitude of effect or "effect size" and was calculated by Smith and Glass as the mean difference between the treated and control subjects divided by the standard deviation of the control group. Thus an effect size of +1 indicates that a person at the mean of the control group would be expected to rise to the 84th percentile of the control group after treatment. The effect size was calculated on any outcome variable that the researchers chose to measure. The effect sizes of the various studies became the dependent variable in the meta-analysis while the independent variables were 16 features of the study described or measured as follows:

(1) Type of therapy (10 types in all — see Table 2)
(2) Duration of therapy (in hours)
(3) Group or individual
(4) Experience of therapist (in years)
(5) Status of clients (neurotic or psychotic)
(6) Age of clients
(7) IQ of clients
(8) Source of subjects (outpatients, inpatients etc.)
(9) Therapists' training (psychiatry, psychology, education etc.)
(10) Social and ethnic similarities between therapists and clients
(11) Type of outcome measured used (symptom or behavioural change etc.)
(12) Follow-up period (no. of months after therapy ended that outcome assessed)
(13) Reactivity of outcome measure
(14) Date of publication of study
(15) Form of publication (paper, thesis, report etc.)
(16) Internal validity of the research design.

Two points deserve particular mention. The first is that the symptoms which appeared to respond best were anxiety and depression whereas attempts to change attitudes tended to founder. The most striking finding was that the average treated client is better off than 83% of those untreated with respect to fear, anxiety and self-esteem. The second finding is that there is not a great deal to choose between the various therapies. The average effect size for the 10 therapies is shown in Table 2. Psychodynamic is described as "Freudian-like", that is to say dynamically based, and achieves an average effect size of approximately .6 of a standard deviation. Studies of Adlerian therapy show an average of .7 while eclectic therapies, that is verbal, cognitive, non-behavioural therapies, a mean effect size of about .5 of a standard deviation. Although the number of controlled evaluations of

TABLE 2
Effects of ten types of therapy on any outcome measure

| Therapy | Av. effect size | No. of effect sizes | S.E. of mean effect size | Mdn. treated person's percentile status in control group |
|---|---|---|---|---|
| Psychodynamic | .59 | 96 | .05 | 72 |
| Adlerian | .71 | 16 | .19 | 76 |
| Eclectic | .48 | 70 | .07 | 68 |
| TA | .58 | 25 | .19 | 72 |
| Rational | .77 | 35 | .13 | 78 |
| Gestalt | .26 | 8 | .09 | 60 |
| Client-centred | .63 | 94 | .08 | 74 |
| Systematic desensitisation | .91 | 223 | .05 | 82 |
| Implosion | .64 | 45 | .09 | 74 |
| Behav. Modific. | .76 | 132 | .06 | 78 |

(From, Smith and Glass, 1977, with permission.)

Berne's transactional analysis was rather small, it gave a respectable average size of .6, the same as dynamic therapy. Albert Ellis's rational-emotive therapy, with a mean effect size of nearly .8, finished second in the top ten. Gestalt therapy did poorly. Rogerian encounter therapy performed creditably. The average of over 200 effect size measures from approximately 100 studies of systematic desensitisation was .9, the largest average effect size of all the therapies. More recently, Andrews and Harvey re-examined this data and eliminated from consideration all studies save those involving patients with neurotic symptoms, phobias and emotional-somatic conditions [Andrews and Harvey, 1981]. The results of 81 controlled trials were integrated statistically using the meta-analytic technique. Their findings provide further evidence of the overall efficacy of psychotherapy — the condition of the typical patient being better than 77% of untreated controls measured at the same time. The behavioural therapies appeared significantly effective as did what they termed "psychodynamic verbal" therapies.

While Andrews and Harvey made a number of modifications to the analysis to ensure that patients with at least a moderate degree of disturbance were included, doubt still remains. There is evidence that patient selection for psychotherapy is quite restrictive and this is particularly true of studies of therapeutic effectiveness. The abortive Maudsley-Tavistock study of psychotherapy is a case in point. This was a carefully designed trial in which it was agreed that the aim should be to include only those patients "who appeared to be highly suitable for the particular form of psychotherapy to be used" [Candy et al., 1972]. Selection of patients took place in three stages. First, psychiatrists working within a reasonable distance of the two centres referred patients who appeared to them to fulfil particular criteria for psychotherapy (Table 3). In all, 113 patients were referred. Of these, 23 failed to return the Screening Questionnaire (which asked for details of the individual's difficulties, family circumstances and history, sexual experience, and occupation). Ninety patients were left. However, on the basis of the Tavistock psychotherapists' assessments of the questionnaire responses, only

TABLE 3
Maudsley-Tavistock psychotherapy study selection criteria

| | |
|---|---|
| 1. | No evidence of serious physical or psychotic illness |
| 2. | No serious drug addiction, sexual deviation or sociopathic disorder |
| 3. | Discernible and lasting problems in interpersonal relationships |
| 4. | No evidence suggesting need for hospital admission |
| 5. | Average intelligence — at least |
| 6. | No previous formal psychotherapy |
| 7. | Active motivation for treatment |
| 8. | Willingness to participate in research |
| 9. | Age between 18 and 45 |
| 10. | Willing for a relative to be seen |

27 of the 90 were accepted to pass on to the third stage of selection. Each of the 27 were given an interview with one of the four Tavistock participants, an interview which lasted at least one and a half hours and which was tape-recorded. The Tavistock participants then met and discussed each case and agreed to accept 8! These 8 represented 9% of those individuals who had completed the screening questionnaire and 7% of those patients identified as likely candidates for psychotherapy by the referring psychiatrists. It may well be that the research studies reviewed by Glass did not employ such stringent selection criteria. There is supportive evidence, however, of the remarkable degree of selectivity exercised by psychoanalysts [Gedo, 1979; Malcolm, 1981].

The message which emerges from such evaluative studies of the efficacy of psychoanalytic therapy as have been performed is that, in general, patients so treated are relatively healthy and socially intact, (in contrast with the bulk of the clientele of social workers), and that accordingly it is not in the main a suitable treatment for the socially dysfunctioning and the mentally ill. At the other end of the spectrum, however, results questioning the value of theoretical and technical knowledge, the need for technical skills and the importance of the diagnostic function have tended to receive less attention. Yet there is a sizeable literature testifying to the effective use of minimally trained paraprofessionals and lay individuals in psychotherapy [Hogan, 1979]. One of the most intriguing studies is the "Pilot Project in Training Mental Health Counsellors" undertaken by Margaret Rioch and her colleagues under sponsorship from the U.S. National Institute of Mental Health [Rioch *et al.*, 1965]. This project investigated the results of a two-year programme to train eight college-educated housewives to provide psychiatric help with only a minimum of supervision. This programme was evaluated from a number of perspectives, ranging from outside observer ratings, staff observation of the progress of the trainee's patients, supervisor ratings and the impressions of the trainees, as well as objective tests. The results were uniformly positive. For example, four senior psychotherapists judged the trainee's performance to be comparable to that of more highly trained therapists and 61% of the patients were reported to be improved. A similarly positive picture of the effectiveness of minimally trained personnel emerges from a number of studies provoked by Rioch's work

[Carkhuff and Truax, 1965; Poser, 1966; Durlak, 1971]. Indeed, Durlak's review, in Hogan's view "probably the most incisive analysis of the literature available" [Hogan, 1979], found 13 studies comparing the effectiveness of non-professionals with professionals, in 6 of which the lay individuals had achieved significantly superior results and equivalent results in the remaining 7.

## Summary

In the light of the overall psychotherapy literature, it is difficult to avoid the conclusion that personal qualities and interpersonal skills constitute the basic ingredients of the therapeutic relationship rather than specific techniques or training in particular psychological theories. The central issue raised by the research results but to date neglected concerns the actual elements in psychotherapy which constitute the actual effective factors. It is certainly true that virtually all theorists and clinicians from Rogerians to Freudians, agree on the importance of such factors as empathy and involvement. There is less agreement about but much interest in other interpersonal skills such as confrontation ability, persuasive potency and the ability to focus on patients' coping mechanisms. But perhaps the most important conclusion for those such as social workers, health visitors, GPs and other working in the setting of the community and primary care is that of Schofield [Schofield, 1964] who argued that effective psychotherapy may consist largely of friendship in that the necessary qualities are very similar to those one looks for in a good friend. In the light of the available evidence, it is difficult to contest Hogan's summary of the current state of play vis-à-vis the effective elements in psychotherapy, a summary which, if accurate, has enormous implications not merely for the practice but also of the training of those involved in the detection and management of those with psychosocial problems:

> The importance of theoretical and technical knowledge for effective psycho-
> therapy, while often believed to be crucial, has received virtually no attention in
> the empirical literature. The effectiveness of paraprofessionals, however, suggests
> that traditional conceptual knowledge may be less important than previously
> believed. [Hogan, 1979]

## References

Andrews, G. and Harvey, R. (1981). Does psychotherapy benefit neurotic patients? *Archives of General Psychiatry* 38, 1203–1208.

Association of Phychiatric Social Workers. (1956). "The Boundaries of Casework". Conference, Leicester.

Baldock, J. and Prior, D. (1981). Social workers talking to clients: A study of verbal behaviour. *British Journal of Social Work* 11, 1, 19–38.

Balint, M. (1957). "The Doctor, the Patient and the Illness". Pitman Medical, London.

Blech, G. (1981). How to prevent 'burn out' of social workers. *In* "Supervision and Tea Team Support". (Ed. S. Martel). Family Service Units, Bedford Square Press, London.

Bowlby, J. (1951). "Maternal Care and Mental Health". Monograph Series No. 2. WHO, Geneva.

Brewer, C. and Lait, J. (1980). "Can Social Work Survive?" Maurice Temple-Smith, London.

Bulletin of the Menninger Clinic. (1972). "Psychotherapy and Psychoanalysis: Final Report of the Menninger Foundation's Psychotherapy Research Project". Vol. 36, Nos. 1–2.

Butrym, E. (1981). The role of feeling. *Social Work Today* 13, 11, 6–9.

Candy, J., Balfour, F. H. G., Cawley, R. H., Hildebrand, H. P., Malan, D. H., Marks, I. M. and Wilson, J. (1972). A feasibility study for a controlled trial of formal psychotherapy. *Psychological Medicine* 2, 345–362.

Carkhuff, R. R. and Truax, C. B. (1965). Lay mental health counselling: The effects of lay group counselling. *Journal of Consulting Psychology* 29, 426–431.

Cooper, B. (1972). Clinical and social aspects of chronic neurosis. *In* "Psychosocial Disorders in General Practice" (Eds. P. Williams and A. Clare), pp. 57–63. Academic Press, London.

Corney, R. H. and Bowen, B. A. (1980). Referrals to social workers: A comparative study of a local authority intake team with a general practice attachment scheme. *Journal of the Royal College of General Practitioners* 30, 139–147.

Durlak, J. A. (1971). The use of nonprofessionals as therapeutic agents: research, issues and implications. Ph.D. Dissertation, Vanderbilt University. *Dissertation Abstracts International*, V. 32B, 2999–3000.

Forder, A. (1976). Social work and social theory. *British Journal of Social Work* 6, 1, 23–42.

Frank, J. D. (1978). General psychotherapy: The restriction of morale. "American Handbook of Psychiatry" (Ed. S. Arieti), 2nd Edition, Ch. 7, 117–132. Basic Books, New York.

Freud, S. (1918). Turnings in the ways of psychoanalytic therapy. "Paper delivered to the International Psychoanalytical Congress", Budapest, 1918.

Gedo, J. E. (1979). A psychoanalyst reports at mid-career. *American Journal of Psychiatry* 136, 5, 646–649.

Glass, G. V. (1976). Primary, secondary and meta-analysis of research. *Educational Researcher* 5, 3–8.

Hogan, D. B. (1979). "The Regulation of Psychotherapists". Vol. 1. Ballinger, Mass.

Hollis, F. (1964). "Casework: A Psychosocial Therapy". Random House: New York.

Hornby, S. (1973). "The Place of Psychotherapy in Social Work". Group for the Advancement of Psychodynamics and Psychotherapy in Social Work, London.

Howe, D. (1982). Personal Communication.

Hudson, B. L. (1978). Behavioural social work with schizophrenic patients in the community. *British Journal of Social Work* 8, 2, 159–170.

Luborsky, L., Singer, B. and Luborsky, L. (1975). Comparative studies of psychotherapies: Is it true that "Everyone has won and all must have prizes?" *Archives of General Psychiatry* 32, 995–1008.

Luborsky, L., Mintz, J., Auerbach, A., Christoph, P., Bachrach, H., Todd, T., Johnson, M., Cohen, M. and O'Brien, C. P. (1980). Predicting the outcome of psychotherapy. *Archives of General Psychiatry* 37, 471–481.

Madden, T. A. (1979). The doctors, the patients and their care: Balint reassessed. *Psychological Medicine* 9, 5–8.

Malan, D. H. (1973a). The outcome problem in psychotherapy research. *Archives of General Psychiatry* 29, 719–729.

Malan, D. H. (1973b). Therapeutic factors in analytically-oriented brief psychotherapy. *In* "Support, Innovation and Autonomy" (Ed. R. H. Gosling). Tavistock, London.

Malan, D. H., Bacal, H. A., Heath, E. S. and Balfour, F. H. G. (1968). A study of psychodynamic changes in untreated neurotic patients. I. Improvements that are questionable on dynamic criteria. *British Journal of Psychiatry* 114, 525–551.

Malcolm, J. (1981). "Psychoanalysis: The Impossible Profession". Picador, London.

McAuley, R. and McAuley, P. (1980). The effectiveness of behaviour therapy with families. *British Journal of Social Work* 10, 1, 43–54.

Meltzoff, J. and Kornreich, M. (1970). "Research in Psychotherapy", pp. 3–5. Atherton, New York.

Parsloe, P. (1982). Personal Communication.

Parsloe, P. and Stevenson, O. (1978). "Social Service Teams: The Practitioners' View". DHSS HMSO, London.

Pitman, E. (1982). Transactional analysis: an introduction to its theory and practice. *British Journal of Social Work* 12, 1, 47–63.

Poser, E. G. (1966). The effect of therapists' training on group therapeutic outcome. *Journal of Consulting Psychology* 30, 283–289.

Reid, W. J. and Shyne, A. W. (1969). "Brief and Extended Casework". Columbia University Press, New York and London.

Rioch, M. J., Elkes, C. and Flint, A. A. (1965). "Pilot Project in Training Mental Health Counsellors". U.S. Department of Health, Education and Welfare, Washington D.C.

Schofield, W. (1964). "Psychotherapy: The Purchase of Friendship". Engle Wood Cliffs, New Jersey, Prentice-Hall.

Sloan, R. B., Stables, F. R., Cristol, A. H., Yorkston, N. J. and Whipple, K. (1975). "Psychotherapy Versus Behaviour Therapy". Harvard University Press, Boston.

Smith, M. L. and Glass, G. V. (1977). Meta-analysis of psychotherapy outcome studies. *American Psychologist* 32, 752–760.

Storr, A. (1979). "The Art of Psychotherapy". Secke and Warburg, and Heinemann, London.

Strupp, H. H. (1978). Psychotherapy research and practice: an overview. *In* "Handbook of Psychotherapy and Behaviour Change", Chapter I. (Eds S. L. Garfield and A. E. Bergin), 2nd Edition. Wiley, New York.

Timms, N. and Timms, R. (1977), "Perspectives in Social Work". Routledge and Kegan Paul, London.

Veith, I. (1958). Glimpses into the history of psychotherapy. *In* "Progress in Psychotherapy: Techniques of Psychotherapy", Vol. 3, 1–19 (Eds J. H. Masserman and J. L. Moreno). Grune and Stratton, New York.

Wolberg, L. R. (1977). "The Technique of Psychotherapy", 3rd Edition, Vol. 1. Grune and Stratton, New York.

Wolff, H. H. (1973). The place of psychotherapy in the district psychiatric services. *In* "Policy For Action" (Eds R. Cawley and R. McLachlan). Nuffield Provincial Hospital Hospitals Trust and Oxford University Press.

Yelloly, M. (1980). "Social Work Theory and Psychoanalysis". Van Nostrand, Reinhold & Co., Amsterdam.

# SOCIAL WORK WITH PATIENTS AND THEIR FAMILIES

## CLARE CREER

Given the growing recognition of the importance of family influences upon the development and course of schizophrenia, interest has inevitably focused on how social work intervention might be directed towards helping the relatives of the patient suffering from schizophrenia who are supporting the patient (to whatever extent) in living outside hospital. Many patients suffering from chronic schizophrenia who would at one time have been kept in hospital indefinitely are now living outside. Yet at present the community medical and social facilities to cater for the needs of such chronically disabled patients are far from being provided on the scale required. Frequently it is the relative or relatives of a patient who in effect take on the role of the primary agent of community care, with all the responsibilities that entails.

In such cases the social worker's task could be interpreted as one of offering support to the relatives to help them in supporting the patient. Many patients suffering from chronic schizophrenia become totally cut off from their families, and this can seriously reduce the patient's chances of making any kind of life for himself outside a hospital setting. The social worker would therefore be concerned to find ways of reducing tensions between the patient and his family so as to avoid any total severing of relations between them. Some of the ways this might be achieved will be considered below.

Apart from the family setting, the other major environmental influence upon the patient is the extent and quality of support offered to him by agencies outside the home. Whatever these agencies may offer in the way of sheltered employment, financial help, medical advice, or social activities may make an important contribution to shaping the framework of the patient's daily life outside hospital. This paper will therefore also examine the ways in which the various services can be used to support the patient living in the community.

Most of the material which will be used to illustrate the arguments put forward comes from the survey published in 1974 in the report "Schizophrenia at Home" [Creer and Wing, 1974]. This survey was carried out

Reprinted, with permission, from "Schizophrenia. Towards a New Synthesis" (Ed. J. K. Wing), pp. 233–251. Academic Press, London, 1978.

between March and December 1973. Eighty interviews were conducted with relatives of patients suffering from schizophrenia. Fifty of these interviews were undertaken with relatives who were members of the Schizophrenia Fellowship — a charitable fellowship aiming to promote the welfare of patients and their relatives. The value of talking to these relatives lay in the fact that they tended to be an articulate and thoughtful group. One potential disadvantage is that being a highly self-selected group they were unrepresentative. To attempt to counteract any bias in the results a parallel survey was undertaken of a randomly selected group of relatives (all residing in one defined area of inner-suburban London). If anything, this group was unrepresentative in the other direction, i.e. the relatives presented fewer problems than average because the patients were all in touch with services in an area where medical and social work standards were high. The national picture seems likely to fall somewhere between these two levels. The aim of the interview was to find out more about how the patients functioned at home, how they usually behaved, and what their daily lives were like. Relatives were encouraged to talk about the problems they were currently encountering which were connected with the illness, and also to describe their experiences with the various services available to the patient and to them. It was hoped to build up a picture of where services were inadequate and of how they could be improved.

While many accounts have been written of the problems and symptoms of sufferers from chronic schizophrenia, this study looked specifically at the problems as seen through the eyes of the relatives. As such it is perhaps of special interest to social workers who are concerned with helping relatives with their difficulties in coping with patients at home. Since much current concern in the social work profession centres around the need to evaluate the service we provide, the relatives' accounts of their experiences with services and their ideas about possible improvements are also particularly pertinent.

This paper will consider whether social work intervention can be used to modify the effects of both family and outside agencies upon the patient's daily life and the course of his illness. An attempt will be made to suggest how supportive influences in the environment could be maximized and damaging ones reduced. The family life of the patient will be looked at first, and the effects of outside help examined in a subsequent section. The problems described by relatives interviewed in the 1974 survey fell into three groups. The first of these concerned the patient's actual behaviour when it caused distress or disturbance to his family. The second group of difficulties arose around the relative's own reactions to the patient's illness. The third area where problems arose was in damage done in relatives' relationships with neighbours, friends, and the wider community brought about by the patient's illness. Each of these three areas of potential problems will be looked at, and then some suggestions offered as to how social workers may be able to intervene constructively.

## Problems which Patients' Behaviour Could Cause in the Home and how Relatives Coped

Relatives describe two major problems: one is that patients can be withdrawn and lead almost completely solitary lives even though living under the same roof as their family, the other is that some patients are excessively active or behave in a socially embarrassing way.

Patients who behave violently, aggressively, or in an embarrassing way which draws public attention to the fact that they are ill present obvious difficulties for their families, but social withdrawal is far more widespread. It is a sadly accepted fact of everyday life for many of those who live with a schizophrenic patient. A patient's withdrawal from outside contact can lead to a considerable amount of suffering for his family. Most people expect social relationships to be rewarding. Many relatives who care for a patient and have perhaps stood by him loyally over years of illness feel hurt at how little the patient seems to return their caring. The commonest way in which a patient's withdrawal seems to manifest itself, is in difficulties in mixing with other people. One mother said to her son, "He just can't bear *people* — even to be in the same room as another person." This comment sums up the way many patients feel. Some patients cannot tolerate the physical presence of others for long even if no demands are being made upon them to talk or be sociable. As one mother said, "You just can't understand it. Here's someone you've known all these years and you've always got on well with, and suddenly he can't even stand being in the same room with you." Another mother described how her son would grab his cigarettes and make a dash for his room whenever the doorbell rang, so afraid was he of having to see or speak to a visitor.

Other patients like to be with other people as long as they do not have to interact with them directly. One such patient, for instance, enjoyed going to family parties as long as he could sit slightly apart and was not expected to speak to anyone. Another had said he liked to go and visit his aunt. His aunt was surprised to hear this as during these visits he would just sit in a chair and say nothing.

Many relatives refer to the patient's lack of conversation as a problem. If the patient is married and lives with husband or wife, the spouse will usually expect quite a lot of conversation and companionship from the patient. If a relative lives alone with the patient, the relative might want to spend some time chatting and generally enjoying the patient's company. One elderly lady who lived alone in a damp basement flat with her niece (the patient), said wistfully that she would have been glad of a chat in the evenings when her niece came back from the Day Centre. This lady could not get out much because of her arthritis. She was obviously rather lonely, but she said that each evening on her return from the psychiatric day centre, her niece would eat the meal she had ready for her in silence, and then go at once to her room.

Apart from a natural desire for some social contact, relatives also feel distress on another level. It is very hard to live with somebody who appears to be unhappy and yet to feel that all one's attempts to share the burden of the unhappiness are rejected. Often relatives want to be of some use by listening to the patient, learning what is troubling him, talking things over, or somehow conveying their concern and affection. The patient, however, may prefer to remain silent. The elderly aunt mentioned above was baffled by her niece's silence. "If only she'd unburden herself and tell me what's on her mind, I'm sure she'd be better. I can't make out if she's unhappy or what."

Another way in which a patient's withdrawal from the outside world can manifest itself is in a lack of desire to occupy himself in any way during the day. Many patients spend periods (and sometimes quite long periods) of the day doing nothing at all, simply sitting in a chair or lying on the bed staring vacantly into space. One mother described how, "in the evenings you go into the sitting-room and it's in darkness. You turn on the light, and there he is, just sitting there staring in front of him." Other patients, whilst not doing absolutely nothing in this way, spend a lot of time in rather pointless repetitive activities, such as brewing endless cups of tea, or chain smoking for hours at a time.

Relatives are often unsure what to do about helping a patient to fill the long series of empty hours stretching between breakfast and bedtime. Some feel the patient's inactivity might be self-protective and that he needs his periods of doing nothing in order to keep from relapsing. One patient, a young man, had told his mother he had to lie on his bed for several hours in the evening because he was "all fizzing up inside". This young man was less handicapped than many in that he was able to communicate so well why he behaved as he did. This enabled his mother to understand and not feel unduly anxious about the hours he spent on his bed. Also in this case the young man worked during the day and his mother appreciated that this imposed a strain on him and felt he needed his times of inactivity in order to compose himself and "recharge his batteries".

Sometimes relatives fear that allowing the patient to spend too many hours in complete inactivity might lead to increasing withdrawal. Some encourage the patient to take up some hobby or interest. Often however, it is an aspect of a patient's withdrawal from life that he has little interest in any outside activity. When a patient does attempt some task, he may be clumsy and slow in movement. One mother said she sometimes asked her daughter to vacuum the floor. The daughter would take ages over it, vacuuming a tiny square of floor at a time, and stopping every now and again in a "fixed" sort of posture. Some patients neglect their appearance and personal hygiene, and this can create problems in the home. Some relatives find ways of dealing with this. One mother said she had found that if she asked her son directly to change into clean clothes he got angry and refused. However if she simply left a clean set of clothes hanging over a chair in his room, he would sometimes put them on.

It may be because meal-times are such social occasions that many patients behave oddly over meals. Some will not eat with other people but will take their meals off to the bedroom and eat alone. Others are suspicious about food, sniffing it dubiously, or sometimes hurting relatives' feelings by refusing to touch a carefully prepared dinner. Many patients exist for long periods on extremely odd diets and relatives worry about the effect on the patient's health.

Although problems of these kinds constitute the majority recounted by relatives, there are also numerous instances when patients' behaviour draws unwelcome and embarrassing attention to the patient and his family. Some patients suffer from bouts of restlessness when they rush around the house in a frenzy of pointless activity or pace up and down a room for an hour or more at a time. Sometimes a patient will do this at night and keep his relatives awake. Things are even worse if a patient's periods of restlessness take some noisier form, such as playing the same pop record over and over again very loudly at midnight. When neighbours are disturbed by such activity a whole new set of difficulties is created. Some relatives manage to persuade the patient to conceal such behaviour to some extent. The elderly aunt mentioned earlier, who was so puzzled and disappointed at her niece's lack of conversation, described how she had dealt with one problem of this kind. Her niece had a habit of pacing up and down in front of the house for an hour or so at a time. As the niece's appearance was rather odd anyway and she tended to mutter to herself, she was attracting a lot of attention from neighbours and people passing in the street. Fortunately the aunt had been able to persuade her niece to do her pacing "round the back where people can't see". This simple expedient had helped to ease tensions which were beginning to arise with neighbours and relieved the aunt of much embarrassment and anxiety.

Probably through their general lack of interest in and comprehension of the outside world many patients do not realize that their behaviour is off-putting and disturbing to other people. Odd behaviour is very handicapping socially, and although some patients have no desire for social contact anyway, there are others who actively seek it. These patients frequently suffer because they still wish to interact with others but do not have the social skills to do so. One young patient's parents described how he would "collar" any friend of his brother's who happened to call at the house, and would talk at the unfortunate friend non-stop until somebody in the family saw what was happening and came to the rescue. Other relatives described how patients would try to join in a conversation, but would somehow manage to make a remark so odd and out-of-tune with the general discussion that a dreadful silence would fall. The wife of a patient said regretfully and with some bitterness that, "we never get invited anywhere more than once".

Relatives describe numerous other ways that a patient's behaviour causes embarrassment in front of other people. A patient might sit in strange postures, make bizarre gestures or wierd grimaces. Some would talk or laugh to themselves from time to time, perhaps in response to voices which only they can hear. In some instances, relatives succeed in getting patients to control such behaviour in public. One mother said that if her son started to mutter to himself when outsiders were present, a quick and quiet reminder from her was almost always sufficient to make him stop, or else he would leave the room and go somewhere on his own until he had finished. Perhaps this mother's success came partly from her calm but firm attitude to his problem. She did not make a fuss or show undue concern about her son's muttering, but she did make it quite clear to him that it was something he should do in private and not in front of other people. Of course relatives are not always so successful, particularly if a patient is highly disturbed or strongly preoccupied with delusional ideas.

Some patients express ideas of a delusional nature from time to time, perhaps saying that people are plotting against them or following them, or that their food is being poisoned. Relatives often feel in a quandary about how to respond to these remarks. If they express disbelief they fear the patient might feel more isolated than ever and might even decide they are in league with his persecutors. But they feel it would be wrong to agree with the patient and perhaps reinforce his belief in his unreal world. One patient, a middle-aged married lady, was relating how she had poured away several pints of milk recently, believing them to be poisoned. Her husband, who seemed very warm and tolerant towards her, but also deeply puzzled by her illness, became anxious when she spoke about this incident. He tried, rather nervously, to make a joke about it, saying, "Wasn't that a silly thing to do Annie? Fancy wasting all that milk. I don't know." But his wife became somewhat irritated at this, saying, "Well what would you do if a voice told you the milk was poisoned? I mean if you heard an actual voice?" Her husband, trying to appease her now, said, "Yes, I know it didn't seem silly at the time, but you know now it was the illness, don't you?" His wife however remained doubtful, replying, "I don't know. I still don't see how a voice can be an illness."

Sometimes a patient's delusional ideas involve his relatives. One young husband described how during her last relapse his wife had struggled with him on the very public walkway of the block of council flats where they lived, shouting out that he was trying to kill her. He now felt extremely embarrassed with the neighbours as he was sure they believed he ill-treated his wife. When a patient holds the belief that a relative is hostile towards him, he can become threatening or even violent. One mother said that she frequently reminded herself that however frightened she might feel of her son, "He is really much more frightened than I am." Several relatives feel as she did, that it is the patient's inner terror that makes him strike out at those he sees as his persecutors. In other instances relatives think they can trace the reason for an outbreak of violence back to some recent frustration the patient has suffered, such as an unsuccessful attempt to join in some social activity. Nevertheless, however understanding relatives might be, violence or threats of it can make life impossible in the household. An atmosphere of tension in the family tends to remain if an incident of violence has ever occurred, even if this was a long time ago. Relatives do not forget such incidents, but are particularly nervous of a recurrence if the previous violence has come "out of the blue" and without any warning. One father recounted how he had been taking his son somewhere in the car. There had been no sign of anything amiss, and nothing had happened to upset his son that day. But when the father turned round to reverse, his son suddenly punched him hard, breaking his nose. Because there had been no apparent reason for this sudden outbreak of violence the patient's parents felt it could happen again at any time and that they were powerless to prevent it.

Few relatives report problems arising out of the patient's sexual behaviour. Most patients showed a complete lack of interest in sex (a fact which causes problems when the patient is married). Most relatives say they would welcome any indication of normal sexuality from the patient.

To complete this discussion of problems associated with patients' behaviour, a word should be said about patients who suffer from depression or suicidal ideas. Some patients have periods when they become morose, sometimes weepy, and feel that life is not worth living. Depression sometimes seems to be associated with the patient's realizing that a brother or sister, perhaps younger than himself, is being more successful at work or in social life than he. Talk of suicide and attempts at suicide are sometimes associated with depression. This is not always so however, and suicide attempts can occur without prior warning, even when the patient appears to be quite cheerful. Once again the unpredictability of the patient's actions makes it difficult for his relatives to know what to expect and how to prevent him from harming himself.

## Problems for Relatives Connected with their own Reactions to the Patient's Illness

Some relatives feel drained and exhausted by caring for the patient. This anxiety arises most often when patients are unpredictable in their moods and actions. Relatives speak of being "constantly on a knife-edge", "living on your nerves", or "living on the edge of a volcano". The elderly mother of a patient described how she lay in bed in the morning listening for her son — if she heard him stamping and swearing about his room her heart would sink as she knew it would be "one of his bad days". Very often relatives keep some terrible past incident in their minds, the recurrence of which is a constant dread. One young man's sister told how her brother was once eating a meal with the family. Nothing was amiss, nothing out-of-the-ordinary had happened, and he appeared to be in quite a cheerful frame of mind. At some point he left the room, and after a while somebody realized he had been gone a long time and went to look for him. He was found to have taken an overdose and had to be rushed into hospital. Several relatives said that the strain and tension of living with someone who is so unpredictable, and whose moods can change so suddenly, is hard to imagine for anyone who has not experienced it.

As well as the anxiety they suffer, many relatives feel guilty about the patient's illness. Parents, in particular tend to feel they are to blame in some way. Such feelings are exacerbated when doctors or social workers imply that they are at fault and have caused the illness.

Guilt can give rise to depression, which is a reaction relatives mention frequently. Depression also results from exhaustion and a feeling of pointlessness. Elderly relatives are particularly susceptible to this. They find that they have all the strains and demands on their time which might be associated with bringing up a small child. It is worse if they can see no end in view; the patient will never be independent or able to look after himself. None of the rewards from watching young children grow and develop are available. There is also the worry of knowing they are getting on in years and that the patient may not be able to cope if they fall ill or die.

In some cases, the depression relatives feel is closely akin to mourning. Many feel a permanent sense of grief because the person they had known no longer seems to exist. If the patient occasionally still shows glimmerings of his former personality, this often keeps hope alive in the relatives that he might somehow eventually be cured. Such hope can raise expectations too high. Some relatives say, paradoxically, that it is only once they have given up hope and decided the patient will never improve, that life seems to become more bearable.

Another reaction some relatives mention is anger. They say they have to "blow up" from time to time to relieve their feelings. On the other hand, many patients are terrified of any show of anger (even though they themselves might shout and be aggressive at times) so that relatives feel forced to contain their irritation as best they can. On a deeper level, many relatives feel an intolerable sense of frustration because nothing they do seems to help.

Some relatives do come to terms with their feelings about the illness, and the effect it has had on their lives, particularly when they have worked out ways to manage their problems, as the result of years of trial-and-error and a great deal of patience.

### The Effects of Schizophrenia on Families' Relations with the Wider Community

In some cases families are divided because of their experience of schizophrenia. For example, one or two members might be prepared to stick by the patient but get no support from other relatives. Similarly, neighbours and friends vary in their reactions. In fact a common difficulty for relatives lies in the attitudes towards mental illness which are currently prevalent in our society. One husband in his forties, whose wife had only recently become ill, said, "When our friends heard about my wife's breakdown they seemed to look on it as some kind of catastrophe — they seemed to take the attitude that she'd never be right again — never be able to go out again or anything."

The effect on relatives' social life can be devastating. Relatives might feel unable to invite people to their homes because they fear they might be shocked or embarrassed by the patient's behaviour. Equally the relatives can be prevented from going out because the patient does not like being left alone for long. One mother spoke of the problems which arose with new social contacts. Sooner or later the conversation always turned to, "And do you have any children ... Oh yes, and what does your son do?" "Mention mental illness," she said, "and an awful hush descends on the whole room." One mother had found least upset was caused in these circumstances by saying, "My son suffers from depression", as people seemed to find this a more socially acceptable condition than schizophrenia.

### In What Ways can Social Work with the Families be of Help?

Quite a number of relatives, when asked, can remember with gratitude a particular doctor, nurse, or social worker who has been of great help at some stage, or some occasion when a specific service agency has given prompt and appropriate aid. This indicates that the potential exists for much useful help to be given. The uniform application of such knowledge as we have at present, could make a substantial difference to many families' problems.

How can the professional helper best apply what knowledge we currently have, in order to mobilize the supportive potential within a family? The first step is to assess what the relatives see as the main problems in living with the patient. In order to do this, it will be necessary to get as full a picture as possible of what the patient is like at home, how he usually behaves, how his daily routine goes, how handicapped he is, and in what areas. As the relatives bring up specific problems, the social worker can find out how they have been dealing with them, and whether their methods have met with any success. If the patient is behaving in ways which the relatives find unmanageable, the social worker can try to devise with them some more effective methods of handling this difficult behaviour. Such discussion must of necessity be very much a two-way process since the extent of our knowledge of the management of schizophrenia is as yet limited. Very often relatives who have coped with a patient for many years, have learned a great deal by trial-and-error about how to cope with a variety of problems. The knowledge they have built up can offer many ideas and guidelines about ways of coping with difficult behaviour which the social worker may usefully be able to pass on to other families facing similar problems.

When considering general principles about how to deal most constructively with a patient's behaviour, two basic guidelines need to be borne in mind. The first is that if a patient is not stimulated enough, he may become excessively withdrawn. The classic example of the effect of totally inadequate stimulation is the very withdrawn and institutionalized patient seen in the worst of the back wards of the old style mental hospitals. The second principle to remember is that if a patient is overstimulated he may relapse with a predominance of florid symptoms, showing evidence for example, of hallucinations, delusions, over activity or even violence. Applying these two basic principles to the patient living with his family the aim would be to encourage the development of an environment within which the level of stimulation is optimum for that particular patient.

The relatives of a patient who tends to withdraw from the outside world can learn through experience that they should encourage him not to withdraw to excess. They might insist on the patient doing some small household task each day, even though supervising him in this might cost a lot in time and effort. Relatives who have coped with the illness for many years have often reached an agreement with the patient on how much he is expected to do, in other words they reach an understanding of how much stimulation is beneficial to him. The brother of a patient said that at one time he had frequently lost his temper with his sister because she did nothing around the house, and he would return from work each evening to find the place untidy and dirty. Now he no longer got angry about this because he had reached the conclusion that it was no use expecting her to do very much. However, instead, he insisted that she should always have the potatoes peeled ready for him to cook for their supper when he got home from work. He knew she would not remember this unless he left the potatoes out on the table each morning where she would notice them. He always left out the correct number as he knew it would be beyond her to work this out. He also told her not to worry about putting in the salt as he had found she was unable to judge this, and "would put in half the packet if I asked her to do it". Like many relatives, this brother had adjusted the demands he made of the patient to a realistic level. Whilst he put some pressure on her to do more than she would choose if left to herself, he had come to appreciate her limitations, as was shown in his understanding of the need to remind her daily in an indirect way of what he expected her to do.

On the other hand, too much emotional pressure upon the patient by his family can produce overstimulation. The same is true if relatives do not make it clear to the patient what is expected, or if they make confusing or complicated demands of him. The socially embarrassing type of behaviour is probably best controlled by a firm, but emotionally neutral, approach. One mother had had problems in the past when her son had broken windows and furniture. She now made it quite clear to him that he would have to go straight to hospital if such behaviour occurred again. She said her son knew she meant it and had therefore made the effort to control himself. This mother was tolerant of many of her son's odd habits but firm about anything which was actively antisocial. She had come to feel quite confident of her ability to cope. Her son, perhaps because of her confidence, seemed to have found a certain security within the framework of the expectations she laid down so unambiguously.

It is perhaps because changes in his environment can overstimulate the patient that too many changes occurring all at once have been shown to be a factor contributing to relapse. Such changes do not necessarily have to be distressing. A birth in the family, a marriage, or moving house, are as much possible precipitators of relapse as are death or illness in the family or the loss of a job. Social workers can assist families by advising them to try and plan such events so that too many do not occur all at once. When this is unavoidable, the family can at least be warned of the likely effects on the patient, and it may be possible to devise ways of offering the patient extra support during a temporarily stressful period.

Besides discussing ideas with relatives about how to manage difficult behaviour and what action to take to reduce the likelihood of relapse, social workers could also help by talking to relatives about the way they are feeling and how they are reacting to the patient's illness. Often relatives may not have had the opportunity to talk in this way, and it can be a relief to them. If they are, for example, becoming overwhelmed by feelings of grief or guilt, then talking about this can help them to work through and eventually cope with such feelings. However social workers need to remember that relatives are not always ready and willing to discuss such matters. Many will have mixed feelings about talking to a social worker, and these may have to be talked through first before the relatives are ready to trust the worker enough to discuss fully their feelings and anxieties concerning the patient. Some relatives for instance, may feel they are betraying the patient or talking behind his back if they tell the worker about problems they are having with him. Some may have a vague fear that the worker represents authority, and may admit the patient to hospital if they complain too much about him. One patient's sister said during interview, "I don't like saying anything about him, I feel like I'm betraying him. After all, blood is thicker than water. I wouldn't like them to say he had to go back into hospital." Alternatively, relatives may have grown so used to feeling depressed or anxious, that they are now scarcely aware of it; they may have ceased to expect life to be any different, and it may not occur to them to bring up as problems matters which other people would certainly regard as such. For reasons like this, relatives will often tend to be reticent and uncomplaining, so it is useful if the social worker has some idea in mind of what the relatives feelings and problems are likely to be. The worker is then much more likely to pick up allusions to problems which may actually be having a serious effect, but which the relative may only mention vaguely as a matter of small importance.

The skills required to help relatives to talk about and cope with their feelings, are the same ones used by social workers in dealing with people in distress in all kinds of contexts, not just in the field of mental illness. It is therefore disturbing to hear so many relatives say they have had experience of social workers who lacked understanding of their feelings. Many felt social workers had dismissed them as over-anxious, or "just a fussing mother". It is important for those who have contact with the relatives to remember that they have much about which to be anxious. It is questionable whether any-body can reasonably be expected to retain an appearance of balanced calm whilst living under the kinds of stresses some relatives face, often over very long periods. Bearing this in mind, it should be possible for social workers to use their traditional skills to some effect in helping relatives to become aware of, and thus to begin to cope with, any disabling reactions they may experience in response to the patient's problems.

The third way in which attempts can be made to modify the patient's family environment, is by helping to reduce the effects of the isolation or even ostracism which some relatives suffer within the wider community because of the patient's socially unacceptable handicaps. This is an area where it can be difficult to effect any change, since it has to do with the widespread and deeply seated unfavourable attitudes towards mental illness held by many people in the community. The most feasible way to approach the problem seems to be by introducing relatives to such selfhelp groups as the National Schizophrenia Fellowship, 29 Victoria Road, Surbiton, Surrey, where they can gain support and companionship from other relatives who can understand their problems from their own first-hand experience. Such a group can also do much towards educating the public towards a more under-standing attitude to mental illness.

### The Co-ordination of Services as a Means of Improving the Patient's Day-to-day Environment

If efforts can be made to obtain the maximum possible help from all the various services, this can make a marked difference to the pattern of a patient's daily life. Some relatives who have had years of experience of the illness have built up a substantial knowledge of the services available in their

locality, and of how to make use of them. It is unfortunate that it seems to
take a long time to reach this stage and that chance often seems to play a
large part in the extent of relatives' awareness of the use of services. Many
relatives make their initial approach for help to the general practitioner or to
the local Social Services office. Some relatives have had the experience of
being told by their family doctor to go and see a social worker, and by the
social worker that the doctor was the only person that could help them.
Some relatives feel that Social Services seem to operate a purely crisis-
oriented service, observing that in a crisis, when the patient becomes highly
disturbed, and a compulsory admission to hospital needs to be arranged at
once, Social Services often give prompt and efficient service. But this
frequently proves to be the end of the matter, and no further contact is
offered. Similarly relatives complain that in the initial stages of the illness,
before the patient has become so ill as to constitute a danger to himself or
others, little interest is shown in the problem. In fact, many relatives who
have approached the Social Services office with worries at this stage of the
illness, have the impression that they are regarded as "over-anxious" and
their accounts of their difficulties seem to be briskly dismissed.

Given the harsh reality of the present scarcity of resources in the Social
Services field, it seems important to look at what social workers could
theoretically do if they had the time, the knowledge, and the resources.
Some will have both the desire and the opportunity to devote time to
supportive and preventive work with psychiatric patients living in the
community. (Those who occupy posts attached to psychiatric hospitals may
have more opportunity for this than others.) This chapter has already looked
at ways in which social workers can offer advice and guidance to families in
the day-to-day management of the illness. The other kind of help the social
worker can give is to ensure that the patient and his family are in touch
with all the requisite services. When dealing with numerous other types of
problem, social workers generally regard it as part of their role to co-ordinate
whatever services are appropriate to a client's need. This aspect of the social
worker's task is particularly vital in dealing with the patient suffering from
schizophrenia and living in the community. In many areas of the country the
services which do exist are thin on the ground. Nevertheless relatives are
sometimes not in touch even with those which are available in their locality.

To begin with medical services, one of the most valuable assets to any
patient and his family is a sympathetic general practitioner. Such a GP can
be helpful in giving the initial diagnosis and in explaining the meaning of it
to the relatives. He can also convey this information to the patient if he feels
the patient is sufficiently rational to be able to make sense of it and if he
thinks the information will have a positive rather than a negative effect upon
the patient's state of mind. Many relatives wait for long periods before
receiving any clear statement about diagnosis. Some eventually learn the
diagnosis by indirect means, such as by seeing it written by the family doctor
on the patient's Sickness Certificate. A sympathetic doctor can also be of
help in sorting out problems which arise with a patient's medication. One
patient's sister described how worried she had been because her brother had
refused to go to the surgery for his three-weekly injection. She had phoned

the doctor, who had been most cooperative. He called to the house and told the patient he had wondered why he had not come in for his injection. He had not mentioned that the sister had rung him, as the sister had felt the patient would have been angry with her. The doctor talked with the patient about the way he was feeling, and discussed with him various odd ideas which were preoccupying and disturbing him at the time. He then persuaded the patient to have his injection.

Not all doctors are as understanding or as approachable as this. Many relatives have doubts and fears about a patient's medication, but feel their doctor is too busy to be approached. Relatives often receive no explanation about the medication the patient is receiving, nor any indication of how important it is that he takes it regularly. One husband who clearly did not realize the importance of his wife taking her medication regularly said, "I leave all that to her. I would not know if she remembers to take it or not. I have enough to do without thinking about her tablets as well." This husband certainly did have "enough to do" as his wife had "spells" lasting for a few days every four weeks or so, when she seemed incapable of doing anything, and would just sit in a chair, and would not wash or eat. Then the husband had to take time from work to care for her and their four small children. Yet nobody had looked into the possibility that these "spells" were linked to the patient's not taking her medication. Nobody had suggested to the husband that this could be the case.

Some relatives worry whether a patient will "get addicted" to his tablets, and have anxieties about the effects of long-term medication. Here an opportunity for discussion with a sympathetic GP is helpful. Relatives also need to have some information about possible side-effects. Some have not been told about such unexpected side-effects as the patient's eyes rolling involuntarily upwards. In such cases they do not know whether the phenomenon is a side-effect, another symptom associated with schizophrenia, or an indication of something physically wrong with the patient. If relatives are nervous about approaching the family doctor but have some medical problem they wish to discuss, the social worker can intervene by approaching the doctor on their behalf. Often social workers are themselves unsure of the value and effects of medication and in any case they are not qualified as the doctor is to give relatives information of this kind. When a patient is in hospital more could be done to ensure that relatives have the opportunity to discuss their anxieties with a doctor there. Again many find hospital doctors unapproachable or unwilling to include them in plans made for the patient's treatment.

Very often it makes a great contribution towards easing family tensions if arrangements can be made for the patient to spend part of the day out of the home. If there is a Psychiatric Day Centre, Rehabilitation Centre or any form of sheltered employment available in the vicinity this can be of considerable help. Such services increase the amount of stimulation present in the patient's daily routine by providing several hours of occupation each day. At the same time these services can reduce undesirable overstimulation by reducing the amount of time spent each day by the patient in contact with his family. This is particularly valuable if the relatives are inclined to place emotional pressure upon him or have rather high expectations of his behaviour. Also, by providing a break for relatives, day-care services can make it more possible for them to offer the right kind of support to the patient during the part of the day that they do have the care of him.

In some cases it is the fact that relatives are unable to have a break that makes life intolerable. It would help relatives in this position if any ways could be found of giving them temporary relief, either by arranging a short period of care for the patient while they could have a holiday, or perhaps by encouraging the patient to attend a social club (if there is one locally catering to the needs of psychiatric patients) so that the relatives could have the occasional "evening off". In some cases however, more radical measures are necessary. Many patients would do better, and their families would be enabled to offer much greater support, if the patient could be accommodated somewhere other than in the household with the relatives. Again we are faced with the problem of scarcity of resources. The provision of long-term forms of sheltered accommodation is extremely inadequate to the need. Even if a hostel place is found for a patient, many patients prefer to remain with relatives, or may exhibit behaviour too difficult to be acceptable within a hostel. The patient often ends up by returning to the relatives, and while the relatives may accept this as inevitable, they often wish things could be otherwise.

One area where relatives often mention problems is that of finance. Here help is theoretically available uniformly throughout the country in the form of various types of benefit but obtaining the financial assistance to which the patient is entitled often seems to be a formidable task, and problems are common. A major problem is that the scheme of sickness and unemployment benefits is designed to cater for people who live at a permanent address and are either temporarily out of work or are sick, but still capable of obtaining a certificate to prove sickness from their GP and of sending this in to the appropriate office. Patients suffering from schizophrenia often move about a good deal, take jobs they are too ill to manage, and then give them up after a few days or weeks. The patient is then not eligible for unemployment pay because he has left the job of his own accord. However, he is no longer eligible for sick pay either, without going through the whole process of application again, since he has been in employment. He could claim Supplementary Benefit, but arranging this quickly is notoriously difficult. If he has no permanent address it is even harder. Patients often take one look at the queue in their local Supplementary Benefits office, or at all the questioning and form-filling which is required, and give up. Many relatives take over this side of things completely. Some patients go every week to the employment exchange and sign on to obtain unemployment pay, but many find this weekly encounter with officialdom too much. Many relatives struggle through the system so many times on the patient's behalf that they know how to work it. Even so, there can be sudden unexpected disruption just when relatives think that the finances, at least, have been sorted out. One mother whose son has been on sick benefit for some time suddenly received a notice for him to attend for DHSS medical examination. He did so, was pronounced fit for work, and his benefit instantly stopped.

Fortunately, in this case a sympathetic GP stepped in and sorted matters out. This patient was fortunate in having relatives to fight for him and a GP to support them.

Many relatives say how difficult it is to get some form of benefit started for the patient; if initial arrangements are made, however, then the benefit comes through automatically without any further effort on the patient's part. This applies as long as the patient's circumstances do not change, for example as long as he does not move, or suddenly take a job and then drop it again. Where patients have relatives who lack the ability to cope with official-dom, or where patients are no longer in touch with their families, it seems highly possible that they will not get the benefits to which they are entitled. Patients who become destitute are of course at risk of becoming dragged down by a whole host of secondary problems.

This paper has examined some of the ways in which existing services are functioning from the relatives' point of view. Relatives' descriptions of their experiences with services produce a picture of an extremely patchy system of services over the country. Most relatives can recall one or two occasions when they have received excellent service from one particular source. But they recount far more instances when services had been unhelpful. The hope-ful part of the picture is that on the occasions when the right kind of help is offered to families at the right time, it makes an invaluable contribution to their ability to cope with the patient at that point. Looking towards the future with this in mind, it is possible to see how services which at present scarcely exist could be of enormous help to families. Even taking the present situation and assuming no new services can be provided and no expansion of present ones is likely, much could still be done to obtain a better and more consistent standard of care from those which exist already. It is here suggested that social workers, community nurses, and doctors should see it as part of their role to seek out and obtain the maximum benefit from all existing services. These services should be used in any feasible way to modify the routine of a patient's daily life so as to alleviate the pressures on the patient and his family, and to support their strengths in any way possible.

### Reference

Creer, C. and Wing, J. K. (1974). "Schizophrenia at Home". London National Schizophrenia Fellowship.

# GROUP WORK WITH SINGLE PARENTS – A SINGLE AND SEPARATED PARENTS' GROUP

ANDRÉE RUSHTON and JENNIFER WINNY

Two social workers attached to a health centre organised a group for single and separated parents with problems, as an addition to medication and individual treatment available. This paper covers the selection, aims and structure of the group and examines the content of the meetings. It concludes that this is a viable method for alleviating the social isolation and anxiety of lone parents beyond their participation in groups.

The established forms of treatment for depressed and isolated parents are the prescription of drugs and the use of social casework techniques. The single and separated parents' group referred to in this paper was run in a health centre by two social workers who wished to explore an additional treatment model for this patient group.

The health centre is serviced by nine doctors divided into three practices, in South Norwood, in the London Borough of Croydon. This is an area of mixed population and housing. although it does have a high proportion of small owner occupied houses.

There is a team of four social workers attached to the health centre and employed by the General Practice Research Unit of the Institute of Psychiatry. Research is being carried out by the GPRU to evaluate the attachment and the ways various groups of patients can be helped in such a setting. The social work unit has been in existence for several years and until now has provided a casework service to a wide range of clients and an opportunity for working with the health centre team.

Two of us became particularly interested in group work as an alternative to the traditional medical and social work models of intervention and because of the opportunity to carry this out in a unique setting. The health centre offered excellent facilities and was generally acceptable to the public, which brings its wide range of social problems to the doctor.

We decided to run a group for single and separated parents having looked first at which sectors in society were lacking support, and secondly at those groups of patients who were making heavy demands on health centre staff. The Finer Report [1] highlights both the practical and emotional problems

Reprinted, with permission, from the *Health and Social Service Journal, October 27/28, Centre Eight Papers*, 1978.

facing these parents. Supplementary benefit is now the main source of income of one half of fatherless families, other than widows' families, and of one third of all one parent families. This figure has risen markedly in recent years [2]. Housing problems closely rival money problems as a source of hardship and distress [3]. There are also disadvantages in the field of employment for the single parent, who is usually a woman; although the sole wage-earner, she is probably in a less skilled job and being paid less than a man. There are also the problems of arranging for child care in working hours [4]. Single parents have to cope with social isolation and loneliness in addition to practical problems. They often feel outsiders in the circle of friends shared during marriage and perceive themselves as the subject of gossip and disapproval [5].

We had found that many of the referrals made to us in the past by the health centre staff related to single or separated parents. They were often referred because of depression, anxiety or worry about their children's behaviour.

## Aims

We used the social group work model described by Klein [6] as a basis for planning the group. In "Effective group work", he outlines stages of group development, emphasising that the values and style of the leaders must allow the group to develop some autonomy and a sense of identity. Our approach is also comparable to the reciprocal model of social group work developed by Schwartz [7]. This model aims to create a mutual aid system which group members use to alleviate personal problems and common difficulties via their relationships with one another. The tasks of the group are set by members, not by the leaders beforehand.

As leaders we aimed, therefore, to help the members establish some common ground. By introducing topics, encouraging the participation of silent members and intervening when the focus of work was being evaded, we hoped to facilitate the emergence of an open and honest atmosphere with group members making personal statements rather than generalising. We set similar demands on ourselves, in terms of sharing our feelings and making an honest response to the group process.

## Selection

We approached the health centre doctors, health visitors and district nurses for names of single parents they considered suitable for the group. We needed to remind them several times, but finally received twenty-one names. Although we had hoped to include men in the group, none was referred. We visited all the women referred before the first session to tell them about the group and ascertain whether they wanted to come. We also wanted to give them an opportunity to get to know at least one of the leaders before the group sessions started.

We saw several West Indian women but none became regular attenders. It was difficult to convey to them the purpose of the group or explain who we were. Either they said they could not talk in a group or they did not think it would be helpful. They seemed overawed by the health centre setting.

The women who did attend the group were mostly lower middle class, were separated and had previously been accustomed to a reasonable standard of living.

## Structure

We originally planned one evening session a week at the health centre lasting one-and-a-half to two hours for eight to ten weeks. We wanted the group to decide exactly when the sessions should finish.

The health centre is conveniently situated and the room we used was a spacious and pleasant one. We were able to provide tea and coffee which created a relaxed atmosphere at the beginning of each meeting. Two volunteers cared for the children in an adjoining room as we knew many of the group members would have difficulty arranging for a babysitter.

Nine women attended the first meeting. Everyone we expected came, except for one mother who had not been sure she could come because of unusual working hours. This was a surprising and very encouraging start, but numbers fell in the weeks that followed and attendance varied between four and seven. The group decided after two or three meetings to bring in new members and a steady core of seven emerged with one or two attending infrequently. These seven, having established trust and liking for each other decided to exclude any more new members. Most members had to miss at least one week either through sickness or holiday but we always wrote to those who had been absent saying that we had missed them and hoping they could attend the following week.

## Content

During the course of the nine meetings, characterised by a very fluent interchange of thoughts and feelings, several key issues were identified. Not surprisingly, as most of the members were separated rather than single parents, the breakdown of marriage was the first common ground explored. Feelings of hurt, rejection, anger and puzzlement were revealed very quickly. Most of the husbands had left their wives for other women and the one group member to whom this had happened very recently was treated with sympathy and concern by the others. Another seemed to overwhelm the group with her bitterness but was willing to accept that others felt less strongly than she did. After several sessions we challenged the group to look beyond absent husbands and instead talk more about themselves and what they wanted. In a roundabout fashion this worked.

It was apparent from the beginning that many of the group members were keen to attend and needed to talk about themselves to others who had had similar experiences. Little was said about the children at first and we were surprised at the appearance of very personal revelations. Sometimes these took the form of a lengthy confession; one session was almost entirely devoted to a member's account of how she gave up heroin. The others were willing to identify with this, seeing some connection between hard drugs and their own reliance on prescription drugs.

As the sessions progressed, more of the group members began to identify their emotional and, in some cases, their sexual needs. Confidence grew as they began to know each other better, but we noticed that the larger meetings with seven or eight members were more superficial although none the less relaxed and friendly. Later sessions were interrupted by the presence of some of the children.

Apart from discussing themselves, their husbands and marriages, group members talked a lot about their children in the later meetings, about money, housing and their isolation from what they regarded as normal: nuclear family life with two parents at home. Most of their children were under five and the group's concern centred on childhood illness, the finding of baby-sitters and unsatisfactory arrangements for their husbands to visit. What could be said to disappointed children about a father who failed to arrive for a promised outing? How often should children see their father and should they be allowed to stay overnight with a father who is living with another woman? How can it be explained to a child that his father has lost interest in him? Should another man be found who can be a substitute father? All the group members were agreed that they would only consider a serious relationship with a man who would like and want their children too. No easy answers were supplied to all the questions, but there was some relief by comparing notes.

We were strongly and often sadly aware of how little confidence the group members retained after separation from their husbands. However, they were determined to compensate to their children for the vital loss of a father. Although they often felt angry with the children and tired of them and wanted an adult social life, the children came first. One member referred to her son and daughters as: "the light of my life and the apple of my eye".

Money was constantly in short supply. Some women survived on maintenance payments from their husbands, some of the low payments made by social security. When feeling depressed, they would talk about how lack of money trapped them, how they made do with few clothes and toys, few outings, and budget recipes.

Housing was less of a problem for the separated than for the single women. Most of those who were separated had been able to stay in their homes after the marriage broke down. Two of the single women, however, were rehoused by the council during the course of the group. We talked about tenants' rights, homeless families' accommodation and the uncertainty of events during the process of being rehoused by the council.

During the later meetings, interest turned to how members could meet outside the group. Some of the many suggestions were rather fanciful — to hire a minibus and drive to the coast, for example. But others — like visiting each other, sharing child care, or going out for a low cost evening together — were more possible. The group was sobered by the thought of how little money there was to spend but everyone joined in these discussions.

Generally, the mood of these meetings was relaxed and open, sometimes sad or angry. Some members participated more than others, but all were interested in what was going on. Those who held back from contributing perhaps felt frustrated that the group was failing to meet their needs, but as we told one member who admitted to this, she had a choice and had to take some responsibility for her part in the life of the group if it was to mean something to her.

## Group Development

One way of examining the growth of the group is via aspects of internal structure and mood. We have chosen three pairs of polar opposites as follows:

(1) Group power/powerlessness;
(2) intimacy/superficiality;
(3) unity/disunity.

These were chosen not because of any objective value but because they are useful in looking both at group interaction and the behaviour of individual members. They are derived from Kelly's personal construct theory, specifically the notion of construct dimensions [8]. This states that we perceive themes, moods and concepts in terms of opposites or positions along the continuum in between opposites.

### 1. Group Power/Powerlessness

A measure of the maturity of a group is the extent to which it moves towards experiencing its power constructively [9]. The danger is leaders emphasise this too early is that individuals will be frightened into silence or anxious chatter. To avoid this we opened the first meeting with the suggestion of a simple communications execise and were surprised, but tolerant, when the idea was rejected unanimously. Everyone preferred to talk naturally and in making this decision the group established a pattern of relative independence that later events bore out.

Three or four of the meetings were dominated by one or another group member as described above. Yet none of these women made a bid for leadership, seeking only to establish a position as a group member. The natural leader of the group emerged after several sessions, a quietly spoken woman who led the move to exchange names and addresses and who held a group meeting in her own home during the week we were both away on holiday. Unassuming, but consistently supportive, she was the informal group organiser, although her initial shyness never hinted at her capabilities.

Later sessions with us were dominated by the presence of several of the children who refused to behave according to plan and remain in an adjacent playroom with the volunteers. Perhaps it was our mistake to encourage this mingling but we were afraid of losing members should we suggest that crying children be ignored. We also felt this was an issue for the group members to tackle. With the children in the room, a more superficial, disrupted atmosphere prevailed. The members were embarrassed when their children cried, perhaps unwilling to seem hard by leaving them and so invariably resolved the conflict by surrendering their own freedom. Their central goal, which was to develop relationships among themselves, was diverted but not overwhelmed by the children.

These points illustrate that the group had found and was using its own power as a small group. The members never challenged our plan of weekly meetings in the early evenings and we were ready for discussion to run over time, which it usually did. Initially we contracted for ten sessions and found this number was quite sufficient for the development of a friendly and supportive atmosphere. Before the ten weeks were over, group members had already started meeting in each other's homes or going out together. As we withdrew, they made the spontaneous decision to continue to do this, exceeding our expectations considerably. It was really this development that led us towards thinking of the group as relatively powerful. The challenge to us came in the members' assertion of social goals over our original therapeutic goal.

Interestingly enough, although these women discovered their power and value as a social support group, the fact that the group was located in the health centre was in some ways incidental. Accessibility was important and so were the physical surroundings, because they were comfortable and familiar. The nature of the health centre was only referred to occasionally, however, when someone wished to complain about medical treatment. Our impression, never made explicit, was that the group members were generally satisfied with the health services they received, or pehaps had not thought how they might be improved. They saw themselves as a group of women and mothers rather than a patients' group.

## 2. Intimacy/Superficiality

The development of the group progressed from the establishment of trust among members to their testing of the limits of the group and negotiating for roles within it. A sense of security was apparent after membership stabilised. The members were eventually able to move towards their chosen goal of finding companionship with others in similar circumstances [10].

They were hesitant and sometimes ambivalent about achieving this goal. There was a pattern of people constantly approaching and avoiding each other. In only one meeting with four members present did we feel real closeness and "get in deeper" as one woman put it. It was she who observed during that meeting that she could not talk to women as easily as men. However, when asked what she wanted to say to us, as a group of women, she used the opportunity very well, to admit her loneliness and sexual needs. Another woman followed her lead and none of the other group meetings was as intimate as this one. Although valuable in the promotion of a group identity they were larger, more lively and more superficial. When feeling strong, group members would explore their reliance on one another through such questions as: "Can I ring you up if my baby is sick and I need some help?" or, "Will you come out with me for the evening?" or, "Will you come round for coffee in the morning?" In this way, the members were approaching each other and we noticed they saw each other outside the group increasingly as the weeks passed.

However, when feeling discouraged, the group would retreat and members avoid each other within the meeting. They would take flight and launch into repetitious accounts of how ill treated they were. It was initially valuable for them to express their hurt and sadness but after a while they began to use it as a way of avoiding the growth of self-awareness and their relationships with each other in the present. Eventually one of us confronted the group with this repetition and it was acknowledged that it was time to forget the past for a while and concentrate on the present. For the members the main issue became the formation of friendships within the group.

### 3. Unity/Disunity

The biggest early problem for the group as we saw it was the gulf between the majority of separated, women. This was immediately apparent in the way the separated women, who were older, more articulate and more obviously unhappy, dominated group discussion. The single members were relatively silent, younger and much less experienced. As leaders we championed the single women each week for four sessions, encouraging discussion about the gulf we saw.

Finally the group was able to deal with this when one young confident woman, a new member, led the way for the other single women to establish themselves as group members. She achieved this through talking about herself and the others followed her. For the moment, the gulf was bridged, but it widened in later meetings. We concluded that the age range of 19 to 35 and the range of experience was too great to allow for a truly homogeneous group. Perhaps the tension created by fragmentation increased understanding on either side, but we decided as we watched the single women drop away that the experience of marriage and separation was the most important common factor within this group and that parenthood was secondary.

### Conclusion

Our original plan to run a therapeutic group for single and separated parents was successfully challenged by the members themselves who needed social relationships more than therapy. The core of seven members comprised highly motivated articulate women from a lower middle class background. Their main problem was loneliness and their goal within the group was to make friends with others who had been through similar experiences.

When the sessions led by us ended, the group decided to continue by taking turns to meet in each other's houses. We count this as a measure of the achievement of the group. It removed the edge from the social isolation of its members and arrested the decline of confidence experienced as a single or separated parent.

Our experience raise certain questions which need resolution before running further groups. Clearly the ages and experiences of members are important to the success of a group and the decision about how homogenous or how varied group membership should be needs careful thought. Our experience suggests that for any group similar to the one described, a relatively great degree of homogeneity is necessary. One possibility for the future is to run a discussion or social group for young single parents, perhaps in collaboration with health visitors.

## References

1. Report of the Committee on One Parent Families. (1974). Chairman, The Hon. Sir Morris Finer, Comnd 5629. HMSO, July 1974.
2. Report of the Committee on One Parent Families. (1974). Chairman, The Hon. Sir Morris Finer, Comnd 5629. Vol. 1, p. 247. HMSO, July 1974.
3. Report of the Committee on One Parent Families. (1974). Chairman, The Hon. Sir Morris Finer, Comnd 5629. Vol. 2, p. 357. HMSO, July 1974.
4. Report of the Committee on One Parent Families. (1974). Chairman, The Hon. Sir Morris Finer, Comnd 5629. Vol. 1, p. 426. HMSO, July 1974.
5. Report of the Committee on One Parent Families. (1974). Chairman, The Hon. Sir Morris Finer, Comnd 5629. Vol. 1, p. 427. HMSO, July 1974.
6. Klein, Alan F. (1972). "Effective Groupwork". Association Press, New York.
7. Specht, H. and Vickery, A. (Eds) (1977). "Integrating Social Work Methods". Chapter eight, p. 145. George Allen & Unwin.
8. Kelly, George A.(1955). "A Theory of Personality", p. 106. W.W. Norton & Co. Ltd. New York.
9. Klein, Alan F. (1972). "Effective Groupwork", p. 111. Association Press, New York.
10. Klein, Alan F. (1972). "Effective Groupwork", p. 134 *et seq.* Association Press, New York.

# GROUP WORK WITH SINGLE PARENTS – THE CONSUMER'S VIEWPOINT: PARTICIPANTS' IMPRESSIONS

## ROSLYN H. CORNEY

This paper is based on interviews with everyone who attended the group at least once. It concentrates on the members' feelings about joining the group, their previous group experiences, whether or not they found it helpful, how it could have been improved and their impressions of the leaders. It discusses questions raised by members about the group composition and the necessity of having leaders.

Shortly after the last meeting of the group, a letter was sent by the group leaders to all clients who attended the group at least once. They were asked to give their opinions about the group so as to help the group leaders in future planning of similar groups. I was introduced as a research worker at the health centre who would be pleased to visit them at home and an appointment was made. The letter stressed that the interview with me was confidential and that no information would be linked to any one individual.

Of the 21 women referred, 13 attended the group at least once. I interviewed 12 of these attenders approximately two weeks after the last meeting. The only girl I did not see had only attended once. She had left home suddenly and I could not trace her new address.

I used a set number of open ended questions in the interview. At the beginning, I stressed my independence from the group leaders and told the clients that their criticisms would be welcome as they were valuable for future planning.

## Attendance

Of the 13 attenders, four attended only once and two others attended for approximately half the sessions and then stopped coming. The remaining seven were regular attenders; six started at the first session of the group, one started half way through the sessions.

Reprinted, with permission, from the *Health and Social Service Journal* October 27/28, Centre Eight Papers, 1978.

## Feelings about Joining the Group

Most of the participants saw the group as a chance of meeting others in the same position as themselves, two of them hoped that they would make friends through the process. These feelings contrasted markedly with those of the social workers, whose initial aim was to provide a therapeutic group.

Two of the 12 interviewed had negative feelings towards the group, both doubting that it would help. Of these two, one became a regular attender and one dropped out after the first session. Only one of the participants before joining viewed the group as a therapeutic venture. She believed that group therapy would help her with her difficulties and was attending another group at the local day hospital.

## Previous Experiences with Groups

Seven of the 12 participants had thought of joining Gingerbread in the past. Four of these had been to Gingerbread meetings, but none had attended recently. Of these four, only one had made a friend through Gingerbread. All had found it difficult to join in the activities and had gone only a few times.

Half of the women felt nervous about going to the group for the first time. One of the women interviewed felt that it was very important that the group leaders visited them all beforehand. It was only by knowing that at least one face would be familiar that she had enough courage to go to the first meeting of the group.

## Helpfulness of the Group

Of the nine women who attended the group more than once, six women found it helpful. It was interesting to note that all of these six women were either separated or divorced, the other three women were unmarried mothers.

The six women had found that it had helped to hear that others had similar problems and to be able to share theirs with others. Some found the discussions helpful and to hear other people's points of view. One girl who had been separated recently said that the group had helped her in making some decisions. These women did not feel, however, that attending the group had helped with any particular problem or had changed them in any way.

The six women were unanimous about the most major contribution of the group. Through it they had been able to make new friendships with mothers in the same position as themselves. Most stressed that before the group they had not known others in a similar position; they had friends who were married, but found that they could not talk to them about their problems. When they first separated, it was possible to talk to their married friends, but all felt that they had been given a time limit in which their unhappiness was accepted by their friends. After this they had to put on a brave face or risk losing their friends. Thus, many felt they had no one with whom they could be open about their feelings.

The women also felt keenly that nobody really understood what it felt like to be separated and divorced with young children unless one had been through it personally and this was why these new friendships were so important. Several spontaneously mentioned the different stages one had to go through after being separated and they felt they could support one another through these stages. When asked about who had helped them most, all six felt the group had helped them most in recent times and that they had found it easiest to talk within the group.

Of those it had not helped were:

(1) those who attended only once, and
(2) a few who attended several meetings.

The first group included four girls, three of whom were interviewed. Of the three interviewed, one was divorced, the other two unmarried. The divorcee differed from the others in that she was enthusiastic about the group and felt that they seemed "quite a nice crowd" with children in a similar position to herself. She would have liked to have gone again but found it impossible having no permanent place to live, as well as a full time job.

The two other girls in this group were unmarried and both under 22 (a few years younger than most of the others). One girl was reluctant to go in the first place. She did not find it helped to talk about problems to others and usually kept things to herself. On being questioned further it became obvious that both these girls had felt outsiders in the group. Before they had gone they had assumed that the other group members would be unmarried like themselves, as this is what they considered "single" meant. They also did not find that they had the same problems as the others, problems such as arranging access, feelings of anger towards the husband, etc. In fact, one of the girls felt unable to join into the conversation as her ex-boyfriend was married with a family and she felt very guilty about this in the group situation.

Of the second category, two had attended a few of the meetings at the beginning and then stopped coming. A third was a regular attender but had only started going to the meetings half way through the session.

All three of these girls were unmarried and all felt their problems were different from the others. None of them felt the group had helped her very much. One of these girls had recently been discharged from the local psychiatric hospital and had recently been a heroin addict. She had normally found it helpful to talk, but had felt that the group hadn't understood her problems or difficulties. Additionally, she felt that their problems were minor in comparison. This seemed very familiar to me as it was exactly what the other members of the group (the separated) had been saying about their married friends. Both the two other girls did not find talking helped very much either within the group or outside it. The regular attender found it very difficult to talk within the group but had continued going as it was "something to do in the evenings". She was the only regular attender who was thinking of discontinuing meetings as she had applied to evening classes instead.

## Changes to be Made

I asked all those interviewed whether the group should have been run differently or changed in any way. Many of the group spontaneously mentioned the problems of including both unmarried and separated women in the same group. Those that were separated and divorced varied on whether they felt two groups should have run instead of one and some felt that as the two groups had different problems it would be best to separate them. Others felt that it was healthy to have a mixture and to hear other people's problems and points of view. The unmarried women were mostly agreed, however, that it would have been better if they had been a separate group.

Age was also mentioned by several of the younger unmarried women and by the oldest member of the group (mid 30s). Both felt that the age range was too great and that it would have been better if all the group members had been more similar in age.

The women varied on whether they thought it would have been better to include men or not. The group was originally intended for both sexes, but no male referrals were made. Four of the women felt it would have been interesting to include men to hear their side of the story. One of these four women saw the inclusion of men as helpful in a practical sense as well. They would be able to swop jobs around the house. Other women had more mixed feelings about the inclusion of men, foreseeing certain difficulties. One felt that the common group feeling might have been threatened if men were included. She felt the discussion would become more light hearted in nature and that some women would sympathise more with the men and offer to do the washing for them, etc, thus alienating the other women. She found this had happened at the Gingerbread coffee parties. Two others felt that the inclusion of men would have inhibited the frank discussions that they had had and that the women would put on "more of a show" if men were around.

Most participants emphasised that they considered that the social side of the group was the most important and all the regular attenders of the group except one had welcomed the change in the group towards this. Indeed, five of the nine group participants (those attending more than once) thought that there had been too much concentration on problems and that this had become rather depressing. They had found that the group became much more optimistic once they were meeting in each other's homes, without the social workers. One woman felt that they were more relaxed now they were on their own. One of these five women, however, felt that it had been important to talk about their problems at first, as it had been a good way for them to get to know each other and had promoted a feeling of a common bond between them.

## The Group Leaders

All the nine attenders had felt that the two social workers had handled the group well. They had suggested topics of discussion and had filled up silences when necessary, keeping the conversation going, but they had not intervened too much. The attenders had found them helpful and easy to talk to. The attenders did vary, however, on whether they considered that the group leaders should have been "single" parents as well. One woman felt this quite strongly, feeling that it would have been better if they had been through it themselves or if they had been married with children. Four others felt that it would have been possibly more helpful if the group leaders had lived through the experience themselves. However, four of the attenders did not feel it really mattered as long as the group leaders were sympathetic and tried to understand. Two of these four in fact felt it was better to have "outsiders" as they had a more balanced view of the situation.

All the attenders felt that at least one social worker was needed at the beginning of the group. Two of the nine women felt that the group could have been led successfully with only one social worker. The participants felt that the social workers were necessary to start the group, to suggest topics of discussion but most of all to give them "a prod" at the beginning; otherwise, the group might not have continued. On the whole they felt the length of social work involvement was about right (nine sessions in all) and that they could now manage on their own. Two of the regular attenders suggested that they would like the social workers to come back for a session from time to time.

### Contacts between Group Members

Six of the members had met outside the group setting. All of these, except one, were new friendships made by meeting within the group. These new friendships were very apparent even while I was interviewing. Often one woman would leave a message with another telling me when they would be in to see me. On one occasion, one member of the group called while I was interviewing another. The women valued these friendships highly, they had also exchanged phone numbers and knew they could count on one of the others to give help if they needed it suddenly. One woman had already done this. In addition three of the women had been to a Gingerbread party together and several had decided that they would go out together in the future. They were also considering setting up a babysitting club.

Only one of the regular attenders of the group had not seen any of the members outside it. She was the one regular attender who had not found the group helpful and she told me in the interview that she hadn't wished to make friends of the others. She was also the only regular attender who had regretted the transition of the group to its more social nature.

The other six non-regular attenders had not met any of the others outside the group.

### Future Running of the Group

At the time of the interviews, all the regular attenders except the one mentioned above were committed to carrying on with the group. They had, however, found difficulties in meeting in each other's homes as the group size was large without volunteers to look after the children. The children's presence also prevented discussions on certain topics and discussions within the group as a whole. Instead, the group split up into smaller groups.

Later on, we learnt from informal contacts with group members that the group as a whole only met for three sessions after my interview. Instead they began to meet for coffee occasionally, to babysit for each other or to go out for the evening in twos and threes. One of the group members gave a party to which she invited all the others, another was given help in decorating her flat. A year later, six of the women are still in contact and feel able to turn to each other for companionship and help.

Ten of the 12 attenders said that they would be willing to join another group in the future. The mother who had been separated very recently felt that she would like to help others in the way in which she had been helped by the group. Two of the members felt that they would like to be involved in organising a group in the future.

The two attenders who did not feel they would join another group were both women who had not attended regularly. One had been reluctant to join from the start.

## Discussion

The main purpose of the study was to obtain the clients' impressions of the group and the clients were interviewed shortly after the last formal meeting of the group, so that these impressions were still clear in the clients' memories. No separate evaluation of the effects of the group on the clients was undertaken except by asking the clients how helpful they had found it.

The group had short-term effects as well as the long-term effect of making friends within it. The regular members had received emotional support from each other and it had reduced their sense of isolation. All the regular participants had found that the group had helped them most in recent times, more so than friends or professionals. This was because they were all in a similar position and thus could really understand how the others felt. Many would have preferred the group leaders to be single parents. Other studies (Mayer and Timms) have shown that clients often assume that only persons who have had a similar experience to themselves could possibly comprehend what it was like and prefer social workers of the same age, marital status and sex as themselves.

One of the major questions raised by the study is whether the composition of the group should have been different. One of the principles for composing a group is that there should be a certain amount of homogeneity within the group members [1]. The group leaders had attempted to do this by selecting single parents. They did not anticipate any difference between those who were unmarried with those who were separated or divorced. However, all the "outsiders" and the majority dropped out. This indicates that perhaps the two groups should have been separated; the unmarried mothers were also much younger than the other group and generally less vocal. One of the group members felt that those who had dropped out in the course of the meetings had done so because they found it difficult to talk. If the unmarried group had been more vocal, stressing their difficulties as well, the conversations may have eventually centred around problems common to both groups, such as loneliness and problems with the children rather than those problems related to deserted wives.

It might have been more useful to limit the age range of people referred to the under 25s, or to aim for a group over this age. It is difficult to judge whether the inclusion of men would have presented the difficulties voiced by some of the members, only future experience can tell this, and then each group depends so much on the characteristics of the individuals themselves.

One of the most interesting findings in this study was that the aims of the group leaders for the group were different from those of the group participants. The social workers' main aim, at least initially, who to provide a psychotherapeutic group, while the majority of participants were pleased when the group changed to being more social in nature and half found that the preoccupation with problems had become depressing. Many previous studies have stated that members of the working class do not fully understand psychotherapeutic process and a study of clients' impressions of casework [2] found that many of the clients interviewed were dissatisfied with the "insight-orientated" approach of some of the social workers. The clients in Mayer's study had been surprised and puzzled by the social worker's lack of active partidipation, by the emphasis on talk and exploring the past. The findings in this study are similar; the clients did not wish to concentrate on difficulties in the past or on problems for more than a few sessions and possibly did not fully understand the reasons why the social workers were bringing up these topics.

### Were the Social Workers Necessary?

As the attenders felt that the most important benefits gained from the group were the friendships they made, this raises the question of whether it was necessary for the social workers to be involved to such an extent. Was it also necessary for the social workers to emphasise the problems of the "single" parent, which many of the participants found depressing? On the other hand, the attenders' responses implied that the social workers handled the group skilfully and were primarily responsible for keeping the group going at the beginning. The emphasis on problems may also have firmly cemented the friendships that were being made (as one participant pointed out), each realising that the others needed her friendship and help as much as she did. The practice of writing to all those who were absent for one meeting, encouraging them to come again, was also helpful and the participants had continued to do this themselves for the few informal group sessions but phoned instead of writing. These could be some of the reasons why their attempts at meeting people at Gingerbread had failed. Perhaps everyone put on a brave face and no single person was responsible for encouraging the new attenders to come again.

It does seem necessary to have one organiser or group leader with either some group experience or with some knowledge of group processes (preferably both), who feels committed to making the group a success. Ideally, in the future, one or two of the original group members may organise a group themselves (perhaps under the guidance of one of the social workers) and in this way the leader would be a single parent as well as the members.

## References

1. McCullough, M. K. and Ely, P. J. (1968). "Social Work with Groups". Routledge and Kegan Paul, London.
2. Mayer, J. E. and Timms, N. (1970). "The Client Speaks". Routledge and Kegan Paul, London.

# SECTION 4

# EVALUATION OF SOCIAL WORK

# INTRODUCTION

The issue of the effectiveness of social work, long-standing and contentious as it undoubtedly is [Mullen and Dumpson, 1972; Timms and Timms, 1977; Brewer and Lait, 1980; Fischer, 1976], acquires an even greater urgency and pointedness in the setting of primary care. Deploying social workers alongside general practitioners is a strategy which assumes not merely that social workers have something unique to offer, a response over and above that provided by other members of the team such as health visitors and practice nurses. It assumes that whatever it is that social workers do is effective.

Not every general practitioner is convinced that social workers do offer any particular skill [Ratoff *et al.*, 1974]. Nor does every GP who welcomes the active participation of social workers in primary care automatically assume that the social worker has some definitive role to play [Harwin *et al.*, 1970]. Many see the addition of a pair of hands, any pair of hands, as welcome in an area in which time is scarce and the demand appears insatiable. Social workers, health visitors, nurses, receptionists even are all welcomed by general practitioners without any clear demarcation being made between the different groups in terms of their abilities, skills or knowledge.

However, there are those, such as the Department of Health and the various social service departments, who are particularly concerned about the question of effectiveness. There are many competing demands being placed on social work at the present time — problems of child abuse, the elderly, the physically and mentally handicapped, the chronic psychiatric patient — so that any impetus for further elaboration of stretched social work resources requires a well-documented argument. While elsewhere in this book, and in the available literature, there is extensive data supporting the feasibility and the advantages of locating social workers alongside general practitioners [McCulloch and Brown, 1970; Goldberg and Neill, 1972; Thompson, 1977; Jenkins, 1978] there is, in comparison, a striking lack of research data concerning the effectiveness of social work in this setting.

Admittedly there are difficulties in mounting such research. Doubts are expressed concerning the applicability to social work research of the model of the clinical trial so favoured within medical and basic science research [Timms and Timms, 1977]. In such a model there are five crucial requirements: a reliable and valid measurement of conditions before and after the social intervention or "treatment"; random assignment of different interventions or "treatments" to an experimental and control group that are similar in all relevant respects; measurement of the amount of the "treatment" in question; establishment of criteria of success; and fifthly some means of connecting outcome to the intervention or interventions involved.

Now such conditions pose particular problems for social work research. Data collection and recording in social work has been the subject of a number of criticisms; the Seebohm Report pointed out that failure to record and analyse what happens in social work practice "indicates a careless attitude towards human welfare" [Seebohm, 1968] while Fitzgerald's review of recording procedures used by local authority social services departments revealed "major inadequacies" in the methods being used [Fitzgerald, 1978]. The need for and availability of standardized and structured measures of social disability, dysfunction and maladjustment is discussed elsewhere [Clare and Cairns, 1978; Fitzgerald, 1978] but it is worth emphasizing at this point the fact that without a more emphatic move in this general direction it is very difficult to envisage a situation in which questions concerning the usefulness and effectiveness of social work interventions can ever be clarified.

There are problems, too, in comparing experimental and control groups. The influences, whether specific or non-specific, which go under the heading of social work intervention do not affect an individual who is isolated from all other influences. As has been pointed out, by Orford and Edwards in their comparative study of treatment and advice in married couples with drinking problems, treatment can be seen as an element added to or interacting with a continuously evolving field of what might be termed "natural influences". Indeed, treatment may be quite puny in its powers in comparison to the sum of these background forces [Orford and Edwards, 1977].

Measurement of the amount of a social work intervention is bedevilled by problems, only one of which concerns the amount of involvement, skills and commitment of the social worker in carrying out the intervention under discussion and trials of social work have been criticized because of the vaguely defined objectives of treatment [Goldberg, 1970].

Such problems occur to a greater or lesser extent in the studies presented in this section. However, this fact hardly justifies what has been termed "a rather wholesale gloom" which allegedly settles on social workers when they look at the results of social work evaluative research in general [Timms and Timms, 1977]. It is true that the majority of research ventures which have employed control groups have consistently failed to produce evidence of the positive effects of social work treatment [Fischer, 1973, 1976; Segal, 1972; Wood, 1978]. Many social work theorists and practitioners, faced with such results, have tended to criticize the studies on methodological grounds, indicating that the outcome measures used were relatively insensitive, that the follow-up assessments were undertaken too soon after treatment or too late, or that the actual interventions undertaken were unclear, old-fashioned, inadequate or unrelated to the needs of the client [Goldberg, 1970; Fischer, 1976].

In addition, however, a disproportionate number of these studies concentrated on work with children, especially juvenile delinquents, and many dealt with low income clients rather than across the social class spectrum. Many of the clients included in these studies had not actually sought out social work help and might well have been lacking in motivation [Goldberg, 1970]. It is, therefore, quite possible that these groups of clients are not especially susceptible to social work intervention and that better results might have been achieved with other, more suitable clients.

The studies in this section evaluate the effects of social work on patients with minor psychiatric disorders. The first paper, that by J. S. Gibbons and her colleagues at the University of Southampton, describes a study of 539 self-poisoners admitted to casualty. Of these, 200 were referred to a control group, receiving routine care and attention, while another 200 were referred to a social worker. The remaining 139 patients were not included in the study either because they had a formal psychiatric disorder necessitating immediate treatment, were already in contact with a social worker or psychiatrist, or were considered to be an immediate suicidal risk. Ninety per cent of the experimental group received some social work help of a task-centred nature and limited in time to up to three months. (Further details of the treament involved are included in the paper by Gibbons and her colleagues included in Section 3). The two groups were assessed on follow-up on a number of clinical, social and behavioural criteria. However, the disappointing main finding was that those who received help from a social worker were as likely to make further suicidal attempts as the controls – approximately 14% of both groups being readmitted into hospital for this reason. However, although there was no difference in clinical scores, measured four months after entry into the study, the clients differed according to their social scores and how they viewed the help provided. Clients receiving the social work service showed more improvement in their social scores than did the controls. They also considered that they had been given more help following their self-poisoning, especially with regard to improving their relationships and leading a more satisfactory social life.

These benefits of treatment notwithstanding, it is difficult to contest the judgement that this study "failed in is most important task", namely the prevention or reduction of further episodes of self-poisoning [Brewer and Lait, 1980]. However, we open this section with the study not because it is a failure but because it illustrates that a control trial can be designed and carried out using appropriate measures without doing damage to the nature and integrity of the social work ethos. Yet even in this well-designed study there were problems of method. Differences in outcome between the experimental and control groups could have occurred yet being obscured by the fact that the control group did receive treatment elsewhere – more of the control group did have contact with the psychiatric and social services. Against this, however, is the fact that the study was set up to establish the effectiveness of a special social work service in comparison with the "normal" service, which ordinarily would include psychiatric and social services contact. Overall the study did not support the usefulness of task-centred intervention (although evidence of social improvement was obtained) and the special social work facility was discontinued after the study ended.

The results of the treatment trial undertaken by Weissman and her colleagues are broadly similar. Although the methods used by the social workers differed from those in the Southampton study, the main effect was the same, social intervention bringing about additional social but not clinical improvement. The design of this study was much more complex however as the patients' medication was also controlled. The women were first given an antidepressant for 4–6 weeks on entry to the study and those who responded to this drug were then accepted for a study of the effect of maintenance therapy. Here they were randomly assigned to eight months of antidepressant, placebo or no pill treatment, with or without psychiatric social work. Results for 106 women who completed the trial without relapse suggested that the antidepressant therapy did indeed reduce relapse and prevent symptom recurrence while the social work intervention appeared to enhance the quality of the adjustment achieved with drug treatment.

Whereas the social workers in the Southampton study undertook task-centred case-work, the social workers in the American study performed what the authors term "psychotherapy". The similarity between such psycho-therapy and what might be termed orthodox social work in Britain has already been commented upon [Williams and Clare, 1979a]. The psycho-therapy was "supportive", emphasized the "here and now", was oriented around the patient's current problems and interpersonal relations and was geared to providing the patients with assistance in the modification of maladaptive behaviour. More important, the therapy was non-dynamic; no attempt was made to uncover so-called unconscious material, modify infantile drives or induce a regressive transference.

There is difficulty and ambiguity regarding the delineation of what it is that social workers actually did in these two studies. There is some confusion too with regard to the definition of social adjustment employed in the Weissman study in that the instrument used in the evaluation of such adjust-ment, namely the Social Adjustment Schedule, is heavily contaminated with psychological features and factors and is almost as much a measure of psychological health as it is of social adjustment. The two studies of the efficacy of social work intervention undertaken at the General Practice Research Unit included here avoided this problem by using an instrument, the Social Maladjustment Schedule, specially devised so as to focus particularly on social as distinct from psychological functioning (See Section 4, page 285). The papers concern a study of patients with chronic neurotic disorders, problems of particular concern in the general practice setting. This study was part of the evaluation of an experimental service which included psychiatrists and social workers rather than just social work treatment alone. The control subjects, i.e. those not in receipt of the experimental service, were recruited from a number of different general practices; fortunately, they were found to be similar initially to the experimental group in respect of their demographic features, physical health and psychiatric status.

It is interesting to note that the most dramatic difference between the experimental and the control groups occurred in relation to the social scores. What is particularly interesting in this study is the conclusion that the benefits of the experimental service may well have been an effect mediated through the interaction between psychiatrist, social worker, general practitioner and client rather than one exercised by the social worker alone. Again, this study illustrates a number of methods whereby the thorny question of efficacy might be addressed including the use of psychotropic drug prescribing levels as a measure of outcome, the distinction between psychiatric and social functioning and the attention paid to confounding variables, such as the amount of contact with other agencies which clients in the two groups had.

The fourth paper, by Michael Shepherd and his colleagues, describes in more detail the social worker's involvement and activities. She participated in the management of two-thirds of the patients, either alone or together with a psychiatrist. The social worker was, in most cases, the key worker for the psychiatrist's role tended to be limited to a further interview for the purpose of reassessment. However, it is worth noting that a number of patients did not actually see the social worker. Some refused contact, others had problems not considered amenable to social interventions, others had conditions which re-mitted before referral, while still others were regarded as suitable for continued supervision by the general practitioner. Much of the social work that was carried out involved dealing with the patient's practical problems and difficult-ies. Contacts with other agencies were made in about one-third of the cases.

Clinical outcome proved to be unrelated to the social worker's activities. Those who received short-term intervention were more likely to improve than those receiving episodic or continuous social work support but this result cannot be taken as indicating that short-term social work intervention is more effective than a longer-term variety. As designed, the study permitted the social worker to discontinue treatment as soon as her patient improved — by definition, therefore, clients who did not respond or who actually deteriorated were more likely to have been in longer contact.

One must be careful too in interpreting the finding that no significant difference in outcome could be identified between those who saw the social worker and those in the experimental group who did not. The majority of those who did see the social worker were specially selected as in need of her help, were more clinically disturbed and, accordingly, less likely to improve. An additional factor, affecting outcome in clients in the control group, is the possibility that the setting-up of a service involving a social work attachment may well have a beneficial effect on the treatment of *all* the patients in the practice as the GP may be made more aware of and sensitive to his patients' social problems and their effect on ill-health. Certainly, the doctors working in this particular arrangement claimed that the presence of social workers had increased their awareness of social problems generally, and in relation to specific patients, the increased knowledge and fuller understanding of the social situation derived from the social workers allowed them to provide more comprehensive care [Williams and Clare, 1979b].

The fifth paper in this section describes the application of social work in the case of women attending general practitioners with acute depression. Patients were referred from a health centre and a single-handed practice and were randomly allocated to an experimental group receiving the attentions of a social worker or a control group receiving routine orthodox general practice management. After six months, the patients were reassessed clinically and socially and with regard to psychotropic drug consumption and attendance frequency at the general practice.

This study is of particular interest in that in addition to examining the effectiveness of social work with regard to a relatively specific problem group commonly found in primary care, that of depressed women, it explored the possibility that different patterns of depressive ill-health might manifest different rates of response to intervention. Such indeed was the case; patients assessed initially as "acute-on-chronic", that is to say women depressed for some time but showing a recent intensification of symptoms, actually benefited from the additional help of the social worker whereas acutely ill women did not show such a positive response. The "acute-on-chronic" women showing the most beneficial response were those with major relationship difficulties involving a spouse or boyfriend. This study also highlights the importance of client motivation and the availability or lack of an intimate confidante to whom the depressed woman could turn.

The results of this study, taken together with the other studies discussed in this section, strongly suggest that social work may be efficacious in those patients who have been depressed for some time or who have accompanying major social problems. Practical assistance provided in a sympathetic yet realistic fashion may be of most help in patients with psycho-social problems. To date, it is difficult to be more specific about the particular aspect of a social worker's intervention which is the effective factor for none of these studies attempted to break down the social worker's approach into anything more than fairly general descriptive categories. That it is possible to demarcate the various social work activities with more precision has been demonstrated [Raynes *et al.*, 1982] but, to date, there has been no evaluative study published which has embodied such a detailed approach.

Another approach to the assessment of social work is to ask the recipients for their views. Consumer studies do not measure effectiveness as such. Nonetheless, they are useful indicators particularly when it is possible to compare the client perspectives with those of the social workers themselves. Through such comparative studies we can explore the clients' views of the components of the social work task and obtain some appreciation of the degree to which the client is aware of what precisely the social worker is trying to accomplish. The last paper in this section describes such a study. Fifty clients were asked their views of the help received from social workers in an attachment scheme and their responses were then compared to the assessments of the social workers themselves.

The results were in many ways strikingly similar to those obtained in consumer studies of social work carried out in other settings. Clients do appear unclear about what it is that social workers actually do [McKay *et al.*, 1973; Reith, 1975; Sainsbury, 1975]. While clients are often referred for emotional or relationship problems, only a small proportion of them (10% of them in Corney's study) expect to participate in discussion of such problems. The great majority of clients expect more in the way of practical and material assistance. There are differences too in the way in which clients and social workers comprehend the problems presented. Clients tend to blame others or their social situation or physical ill-health for their predicament whereas social workers tend to locate the source of the trouble in the client and the client's relationship with others. It is true that many social workers appear aware of such discrepancies yet it is far from clear the extent to which it is possible to reconcile such different positions. Corney's study does suggest that when clients and social workers do share a common understanding of the probable causes of the problem, that is to say when clients see themselves as partially or even completely responsible for their problems, the clients are more likely to consider that they have been helped by social work intervention.

There are differences too in the way that social work is seen. Social workers believe they use "casework" techniques to a far greater extent than appears the case to their clients. It may well be that if clients do not see themselves at fault they are less likely to be aware of their social workers' often painstaking efforts to persuade them to alter their ways. Social workers also appear more optimistic than their clients, consistently believing that they have helped more clients with more problems than their clients do.

It is interesting to note that only 10% of the clients who saw attached social workers in Corney's study had considered going to the local authority social services with their problems. Indeed, only one in three believed before referral that their problems were appropriate for social work help. There was, however, a reassuringly high level of satisfaction with the service and enthusiasm for the attachment arrangement.

Such consumer assessments serve to caution social workers against assuming that social work assessments can be taken as reliable estimates of clients' feelings. Often there is a fundamental clash in perspective between client and social worker [Mayer and Timms, 1970; Beck and Jones, 1974; Rees, 1978] and this clash needs to be considered carefully by practising social workers. Otherwise, much of their professional effort and their particular techniques, time consuming, exploratory, encouraging of insight and emphasising reflection and self-scrutiny as they often are, may count for naught if the client has little understanding of what is actually happening and little sympathy with the underlying theoretical and practical therapeutic assumptions.

It remains to be seen, of course, whether client satisfaction is related in the long-term to outcome. Indeed, it is a feature of the enclosed studies that each raises almost as many questions as it attempts to answer (often a feature of a good research project). Indeed, one of the reasons that they have been chosen, additional to the fact that they demonstrate what can be done, is that they are not over-inclusive in their scope, over-ambitious in the questions they choose to examine nor over-confidant in the claims they make concerning their findings. Rather they illustrate what can be done in the area of primary care social work and it does appear that this setting offers research possibilities which not only have implications for the development and clarification of social work in this particular setting but of social work in general.

## References

Beck, H. and Jones, M. (1974). A new look at the clientele and services of family agencies. *Social Casework* **53**, 589–599.

Brewer, C. and Lait, J. (1980). "Can Social Work Survive?" Temple Smith, London.

Clare, A.W. and Cairns, V.E. (1978). Design, development and use of a standardised instrument to assess social maladjustment and dysfunction in community studies. *Psychological Medicine* **8**, 589–604.

Fischer, J. (1973). Is casework effective? A review. *Social Work* 8, 5—20.
Fischer, J. (1976). "The Effectiveness of Social Casework". Charles C. Thomas, Springfield, Illinois.
Fitzgerald, R. (1978). The classification and recording of "Social Problems". *Social Science and Medicine* 12, 255—263.
Goldberg, E. M. (1970). Measurement in casework. *In* "Research and Social Work, Monograph No. 4". B.A.S.W. Publications.
Goldberg, E. M. and Neill, J. E. (1972). "Social Work in General Practice". George Allen & Unwin, London.
Harwin, B. G., Eastwood, M. R., Cooper, B. and Goldberg, D. P. (1970). Prospects for social work in general practice. *Lancet* 2, 559—561.
Jenkins, M. E. (1978). "The Attachment of Social Workers to GP Practices". Research Section, Mid Glamorgan County Council.
Mayer, J. E. and Timms, N. (1970). "The Client Speaks". Routledge and Kegan Paul, London.
McCulloch, J. W. and Brown, M. J. (1970). Social work in general medical practice. *Medical Social Work* 22, 9, 300—303.
McKay, A., Goldberg, E. M. and Fruin, D. J. (1973). Consumers and a social services department. *Social Work Today* 4, 486—491.
Mullen, E. J. and Dumpson, J. R. (1972). "Evaluation of Social Intervention". Jossey-Bass, San Francisco.
Orford, J. and Edwards, G. (1977). "Alcoholism: A Comparison of Treatment and Advice with a Study of the Influence of Marriage". Maudsley Monograph No. 26. Oxford University Press, Oxford.
Ratoff, L., Rose, A. and Smith, C. (1974). Social workers and GPs: problems of working together. *Social Work Today* 5, 16, 497—500.
Raynes, N. V., Winny, J. and Mulgrew, K. (1982). What do social workers do: A method for classifying social workers' activities. *British Journal of Social Work* (In press).
Rees, S. (1978). "Face to Face". Edward Arnold, Southampton.
Reith, D. (1975). I wonder if you can help me? *Social Work Today* 6, 66—69.
Sainsbury, E. (1975). "Social Work with Families". Routledge and Kegan Paul, London.
Seebohm Report. (1968). "Report of the Committee on Local Authority and Allied Personal Social Services". HMSO, London.
Segal, S. P. (1972). Research on the outcome of social work therapeutic interventions: A review of the literature. *Journal of Health and Social Behaviour* 13, 3—17.
Thompson, K. (1977). Social workers have helped in care in general practice. *Update* 14, 1401—1405.
Timms, N. and Timms, R. (1977). "Perspectives in Social Work". Routledge and Kegan Paul, London.
Williams, P. and Clare, A. (1979a). "Psychosocial Disorders in General Practice", p. 258. Academic Press, London and New York.
Williams, P. and Clare, A. (1979b). Social workers in primary health care: The General Practitioner's viewpoint. *Journal of the Royal College of General Practitioners* 29, 554—558.
Wood, K. M. (1978). Casework effectiveness: A new look at the research evidence. *Social Work* 23, 437—458.

# EVALUATION OF A SOCIAL WORK SERVICE FOR SELF-POISONING PATIENTS

J. S. GIBBONS, J. BUTLER, P. URWIN and J. L. GIBBONS

## Summary

Four hundred patients aged at least 17 who came to Casualty in one year after deliberately poisoning themselves were randomly assigned between an Experimental social work service (task-centred casework) and a Control (Routine) follow-up service. 139 patients were excluded from the trial, most of whom were already in continuing psychiatric treatment. After one year there was no difference in the proportions of E and C patients who repeated self-poisoning (about 14 per cent), but significantly more of the excluded group had repeated (36 per cent). A random half of the trial patients were re-interviewed four months after admission. Both E and C groups had improved to a significant extent on measures of depressed mood and of social problems. E patients showed more change in social problems and were more satisfied with the service they had received.

## Introduction

Deliberate self-poisoning has increased so markedly over the past two decades that in young women it is now the commonest cause of emergency admission to a medical ward, and it has been predicted that by 1984, if the trend continues, adults who have poisoned themselves will fill all the emergency beds [Jones, 1977]. Although in each year only 1–2 per cent of patients kill themselves following the original attempt, this is a very high suicide rate compared to that of the general population [Ettlinger, 1975]. The rate of non-fatal repetition is also high, about 20 per cent repeating their attempt within a year. Since little is known about the reasons for the rise in self-poisoning, it is difficult to plan programmes for primary prevention, but secondary prevention – prompt intervention after the event to prevent a repetition of it – is an important aim in view of the high repetition rate. The literature on secondary prevention is conflicting. Table 1 gives brief details of six studies carried out in different parts of the world since 1971, three of which report positive findings. However, the only study using a random

Reprinted, with permission, from the *British Journal of Psychiatry* **133**, 111–118, 1978.

TABLE 1
Outcome of secondary prevention of parasuicide

| Author | Date | Intervention | Follow-up | Positive outcome: Repetition | Other criteria | Experimental design |
|--------|------|--------------|-----------|------------|-------|--------------|
| Greer and Bagley | 1971 | Psychiatric treatment | 1—2 years | Yes | — | No |
| Kennedy | 1972 | Poisons treatment centre | 1 year | Yes | — | No |
| Chowdhury et al. | 1973 | Intensive after-care | 6 months | No | Yes | Yes |
| Ettlinger | 1975 | Systematic assessment, etc. | 1 year | No | No | No |
| Oast and Zitrin | 1975 | Social work | — | Half sample refused service | No | No |
| Ternansen and Bywater | 1975 | Intensive after-care | 3 months | Yes | Yes | No |

allocation design [Chowdhury *et al.*, 1973] found no difference in the repetition rate of parasuicides who had received intensive after-care, including 24-hour availability, compared to that of a control group having routine follow-up. The present study was designed as an experimental trial of the feasability and effectiveness of a specially designed social work service for cases of deliberate self poisoning.

## Nature of the Experimental Service

Although all "attempted suicides" are officially required to be assessed by a psychiatrist before leaving hospital, only a minority suffer from a major psychiatric illness. The act is more usually an impulsive answer to an unbearable social situation, often involving other key people and persistent social and relationship difficulties. Psychiatric treatment is not necessarily the most appropriate way of responding to this complex of problems, and the structure of psychiatric services may make them least accessible to people with the severest social problems. For these reasons it was decided that the experimental service should be a social work one, crisis-oriented, explicitly time-limited and directed wherever possible at the patient in the context of his close relationships and in his home rather than the hospital.

The method used, task-centred casework [Rcid and Epstein, 1972] is based on an explicit contract of limited work which both social worker and client agree to undertake during a defined time-period (up to a maximum of three months in this trial). This social work method is considered suitable for problems of personal relationships; social transitions — losses and changes which impose the necessity of finding new roles; problems in social relations generally; problems of role performance, as a worker, parent, etc; emotional distress interfering with coping ability; problems with officials and organizations; and of inadequate resources. Difficulties in all these areas were thought to be common in the lives of self-poisoning patients, although it was recognized that some of their problems, such as alcoholism, were less likely to respond to the task-centred approach. The method involves four stages of work:

(1) The range of problems the client perceives in the life areas listed above is explored in order to locate a *target*, the problem perceived as most salient by the client and which he is most motivated to reduce.
(2) The goal of treatment is then defined in terms of one or more specific *tasks*, formulated collaboratively by client and worker. Agreement is reached about the time needed to complete the tasks.
(3) The social worker's job is then to help the client complete the tasks.
(4) At termination there is a formal *evaluation* when client and worker discuss what has been achieved and identify further tasks to be undertaken by the client alone.

This social work service was provided by two qualified and experienced social workers who were employed in the Department of Psychiatry.

## Methods

Patients attending the Accident and Emergency Department of Southampton General Hospital from April 1975 to March 1976 after deliberate self-poisoning (defined as the deliberate taking of a pharmacologically active substance in more than the prescribed dose or the usual consumption), who were aged 17 or over and came from a defined geographical area, were assessed for inclusion in the trial. Altogether 539 patients were assessed; while 14 per cent of eligible patients were not assessed for a variety of reasons: refused, failed to contact, too ill, in police custody. The 87 missing patients included more men and fewer people admitted to a medical ward.

One of two research psychiatrists interviewed every patient as soon as possible on full recover of consciousness and obtained demographic, clinical and social information, using structured instruments. After all assessment procedures were completed, the psychiatrist decided whether a patient was eligible for the trial. Patients were excluded if they had a formal psychiatric illness requiring immediate psychiatric treatment (34 cases, 6 per cent of the sample); if they were judged, from scores on a predetermined scale, to be an immediate suicide risk (9 cases, 2 per cent of the sample); or if, though otherwise suitable, they were in continuing treatment with a psychiatrist or social worker whom they had seen within two weeks (18 per cent of the sample). On one or other of these grounds 139 patients were excluded from the trial. The remaining patients were randomly allocated to Experimental or Control groups until there were 200 in each. E patients were directly referred to one of the special social workers, who tried to make immediate contact. C patients received the routine service: referral back to a GP (54 per cent); psychiatric referral (33 per cent) and other referral (13 per cent). The trial therefore, was not comparing a treated with an untreated group, but the E service differed in being systematic, explicitly time-limited, immediately available and offered in the patient's home.

E and C groups did not differ significantly on any baseline measures. As described, 139 patients were excluded from the trial as needing, or already in, some other form of treatment. This "T" group differed significantly from the rest both clinically and socially. They included more men and more from social class V. They had had more previous psychiatric treatment and admissions for parasuicide. In relation to the index attempt they scored significantly higher on measures of intent to die and on a standard predictive scale [Buglass, 1974] were shown as more likely to repeat their attempt.

### Follow Up

Table II summarizes our outcome criteria and sources of information. To check on repeated admissions for self-poisoning during the year after the index admission medical records of the two general hospitals serving the area (Southampton General and the Royal Hampshire County; Winchester) were

TABLE 2
Criteria of outcome and sources of information

| Criterion | Period of follow-up | Source of data |
|---|---|---|
| Repetition of self-poisoning | 1 year | GP and hospital records |
| Use of psychiatric and social services | 1 year | GP, hospital, social service and probation records |
| Change in depressive mood | 4 months (18 months) | Scores on Beck Depression Inventory |
| Change in social problems | 4 months (18 months) | Interview |
| Satisfaction with service | 4 months (18 months) | Interview |

monitored. A search was made of general practitioner records, including those of patients who had moved, and any mention of a repeated admission was checked from the hospital concerned. The records of the three psychiatric hospitals serving the area were monitored, and GP records were used to obtain data on psychiatric treatment during the following year. The records of Hampshire Social Service and Probation Departments were examined.

Information about changes in depressive mood and social problems was obtained by re-interviewing patients. A randomly chosen half of E and C groups were re-interviewed four months after the index attempt. The remainder are being re-interviewed 18 months after it, but these data of longer-term social outcome are not yet available. The follow-up interviews were carried out by three experienced interviewers after a short training period. The interviewers had had no connection with the Project and did not know what treatment patients had received. Out of 200 patients 159 were successfully re-interviewed, 78 per cent of the C sample and 81 per cent of the E sample. Forty-one could not be re-interviewed. Three were too ill, 14 refused, 24 had moved out of the region and/or could not be traced. There were no differences in age and sex distribution between the interviewed sample and the missing cases.

## Results

### Service Input

Nearly 90 per cent of E cases had some social work help immediately after their overdose, and in two-thirds of the cases the contact lasted for twelve weeks or less. The mean number of interviews per case (including interviews with collaterals) was 10. Twenty-two cases (11 per cent) had to be re-opened after closing at the prearranged time limit, and 34 cases (17 per cent) had to be referred on to another agency when the case was finally closed. The mean number of significant other people contacted per case was 1.55, and the mean number of social or medical agencies contacted on the client's behalf was 2.65 per case.

Table 3 shows the number of E, C and T cases who were in contact with psychiatric or social agencies during the 12 months after the index self-poisoning. Significantly more T cases were in contact with psychiatric and social services ($P < .001$). C cases had significantly more contact with psychiatric services than did E cases ($P < .02$).

TABLE 3
Contact with psychiatric and social services in year following index self-poisoning

|  | *E* <br> *N = 200* | *C* <br> *N = 200* | *T* <br> *N = 139* |
|---|---|---|---|
| Psychiatric services | 44 (22%) | 65 (38%) | 115 (83%) |
| Social services department | 34 (17%) | 47 (23%) | 63 (45%) |
| Probation | 13 (6%) | 10 (5%) | 21 (10%) |

### Satisfaction with Service

Compared with C patients who had the routine after-care service, E patients reported themselves at the four months follow-up as having had significantly more help following their self-poisoning. Forty-eight per cent of E cases, compared with 15 per cent of C cases, said they had had "a lot" of help. In particular, E cases reported themselves as having had more help with improving their relationships with some significant other person ($P < .05$) and with leading a more satisfying social life ($P < .01$). Of those who had received any service, half the E patients but only 17 per cent of the C patients were "very satisfied" with the service received.

## Repetition of Self-Poisoning

Repetition can be measured in four ways. 1. Readmission for self-poisoning to a medical ward or to Casualty at the same hospital as the original attempt. 2. Documented readmission for self-poisoning at any hospital. 3. Repetition of self-poisoning known to general practitioners including cases not taken to hospital. 4. All repetitions reported by patients in interview, whether or not they led to medical attention. Since we carried out a systematic survey of general practitioners' records we were able to compare the results obtained by the first three methods. If "readmission to the same hospital" is taken, 95 cases repeated self-poisoning in the 12 months following the index attempt. Eleven cases are added if "documented hospital readmission" is taken. Thirteen more cases are added if all self-poisonings recorded by a general practitioner are counted. We decided to use method 2, since our primary concern, from the public health point of view, was with the strain on hospital services imposed by repeaters.

There was no significant difference in repetition of self-poisoning in the 12 months following the index attempt between Experimental and Control cases (13.5 per cent *vs.* 14.5 per cent). In the T group 50 patients (36 per cent) repeated self-poisoning, a significantly greater number (P < .001).

It was likely that the increased repetition rate of the T group could be explained by its containing a preponderance of high risk patients. This was tested by means of the scale developed by Buglass *et al.* [1974] to predict the risk of repetition of parasuicide. The scale contains six items: previous parasuicide; previous in-patient and out-patient psychiatric treatment; not living with relatives; problem in the use of alcohol; diagnosis of sociopathy. Risk category is computed by adding one point for each item positively scored. Overall, the scale performed approximately as well in Southampton as in Edinburgh in predicting repetition. If 0 were taken as the cut-off point, one-third of the total cases could be ignored at a cost of missing 5 per cent of the repeaters. Table 4 shows that the Experimental service did not perform significantly better than the routine service for any risk category. However, patients in the T group continued to repeat significantly more even when their higher level of risk was controlled for.

TABLE 4
Repetition of self-poisoning, by predicted risk of repetition (Buglass scale)

| Buglass score | *E* N = 200 | *C* N = 200 | *T\** N = 136 | *All* N = 536 | *Edinburgh sample* N = 907 |
|---|---|---|---|---|---|
| | | | *% Repeating* | | |
| 0 | 6 | 6 | 0 | 5 | 5 |
| 1 | 12 | 16 | 18 | 15 | 9 |
| 2 | 19 | 25 | 43 | 27 | 16 |
| 3 | 36 | 15 | 59 | 36 | 27 |
| 4 | 40 | 20 | 43 | 38 | 37 |
| 5–6 | 25 | 60 | 67 | 57 | 48 |

\* Buglass score not known for 3 T cases.

*Change in Depressive Mood*

After they had recovered consciousness, the self-poisoning patients were asked to complete a self-rating depression inventory [Beck, 1961]. A randomly selected 50 per cent of the E and C cases were followed up four months later and the depression inventory was repeated. 74 E patients and 72 C patients (73 per cent of the follow-up sample) completed ratings on both occasions. The missing patients did not show any significant difference in age, sex or mean depression score at time of self-poisoning.

Elsewhere, the relationship of scores on the Beck Depression Inventory to PSE ratings of psychiatric illness in the present sample is shown. Scores on the BDI are correlated with measures of intent to die [Silver *et al.*, 1971], and have been shown to correlate well with psychiatrists' ratings of the severity of illness in about two-thirds of a group of depressed patients; in the remaining cases agreement was poor [Bailey and Coppen, 1976]. A high score on the BDI is therefore not always equivalent to a clinical diagnosis of depressive illness, but it can be regarded as an indicator of depressed mood [Metcalfe and Goldman, 1965]. Table 5 shows that the mean BDI scores of both E and C groups had fallen to a highly significant extent four months after the index self-poisoning. There was no difference between E and C groups in the amount of change shown.

TABLE 5
Mean Score on Beck depression inventory at time of self-poisoning (T.1) and after four months (T.2)

|  | E<br>N = 74 | C<br>N = 72 |
|---|---|---|
| Time 1 | 17.61 | 19.63 |
| Time 2 | 11.15 | 13.49 |
| Difference | −6.46 | −6.14 |
| t = | 6.05* | 4.84* |

* $P < .001$

*Change in Social Problems*

A semi-structured questionnaire was developed and tested during the pilot stage to gather information about patients' perceived social problems. Structured information was gathered about the nature and extent of the problems experienced by patients in various life areas. The problem areas were those which the method of social work offered to the E group (task-centred casework) had most chance of influencing, according to the literature. After detailed questioning, patients were asked to rate the severity of the difficulties they mentioned under each heading on a scale ranging from 0 (no problem) to 4 (very considerable problem).

During the pilot stage a reliability study was carried out on 20 patients who were independently assessed by the two male psychiatrists doing the baseline interviews. Reliability was 90 per cent or better on all but two of the problem areas investigated. The exceptions were questions relating to perceived problems in the domestic roles of housewife and parent, where reliability was reduced to 70 per cent. The women follow-up interviewers obtained more information under these headings, so that measures of change were also unreliable. In its final version, therefore, the social problem questionnaire provided information on five areas of social life — personal relations, social transitions, social relations, emotional distress interfering with coping, and material resources — each rated on a scale of perceived seriousness by patients at the time of self-poisoning and four months later.

Table 6 shows how patients' views of their overall social circumstances changed in the period following self-poisoning. Although the social problems of both E and C groups had improved, the improvement was significantly greater for E patients.

TABLE 6
Improvement in social problems four months after self-poisoning

|   | Improved | Not improved | Total |
|---|---|---|---|
| E | 70 | 11 | 81 |
| C | 53 | 23 | 76* |

$$\chi^2 = 6.43; df\ 1; P < 1.02.$$

* 2 C cases not known.

## Discussion

In considering the results of the trial, questions must be asked about how far they can be applied to the treatment of self-poisoners in general. Our original aim was to exclude from the trial only those self-poisoners whom it would have been unethical to include, because of their urgent need for some other form of treatment. In fact, only 43 cases (8 per cent) would have been excluded on these grounds. However, the trial sample was less representative than we had planned for two reasons. First, because of the difficulty of contacting the total population of casualty attenders for baseline assessment, 87 cases were not interviewed. The interviewed sample of 539, though representative of the total in terms of age distribution and marital status, included more women. Secondly, an unexpectedly high proportion of the interviewed sample had to be excluded on administrative grounds: they were already in continuing treatment with someone else whom they had seen within two weeks. The 139 excluded cases turned out to be an unexpectedly homogeneous group in terms of their high degree of psychiatric and social disability. The trial sample of 400, therefore, represents relatively lower-risk self-poisoners, living in more stable conditions and with relatively less personal and social pathology. The psychiatric and social services appear to be highly successful in selecting the most disturbed and disadvantaged people for treatment. However, being in continuing active treatment at the time of self-poisoning is shown in this study to be an unfavourable prognostic characteristic [cf. Hankoff, 1976].

The second point to consider in assessing the results is our choice of outcome criteria. Repetition of self-poisoning is an objective criterion, relatively easy to establish in a reliable way. Trying to assess change in people's subjective morale and immediate social circumstances is a more difficult undertaking. In gathering information about patients' psychiatric and social status we obtained standardized clinical and social data which will be reported elsewhere. However, in assessing change, we were interested in penetrating as far as we could into the subjects' views of their own social situations, rather than imposing meanings on their experiences from our vantage point. We have therefore been prepared to use as data patients' own statements of how they assess their problems, together with changes in their statements, both over time and resulting from treatment. Since self-poisoning is a willed act carried out by a person as a result of his own view of his social situation at that time, we believed that his own estimation of improvement had more meaning than a value judgement by an outside observer.

These limitations and assumptions borne in mind, the results of this study are consistent with those of Chowdhury *et al.* [1973] in suggesting that preventive intervention after self-poisoning has no effect on repetition. The studies of Greer and Bagley [1971] and Kennedy [1972], both of whom suggested that psychiatric assessment or treatment had a positive effect, did not use an experimental design. Our findings do not support the view that psychiatric treatment reduces repetition (in fact the opposite could be argued). The Canadian trial reporting reduction in repetition after three months follow-up is of interest in its methods of intervention: "mental health workers" followed up the experimental group very intensively but for a short period — daily in week 1, every two days in week 2, twice in weeks 3 and 4, thereafter declining. However, methodological problems make the findings hard to evaluate [Ternansen and Bywater, 1975].

Our Experimental social work service had no advantage over the Control (routine) service in preventing repetition. However, it was rated as more satisfactory and helpful by its consumers. After four months, E patients also showed more improvement in social problems than did C patients. At present our conclusions must be that we do not know how to prevent people from repeating self-poisoning, but that a planned social work service using a task-centred approach is more acceptable to patients and can reduce some of their most pressing difficulties in a relatively economical way.

## Acknowledgements

Thanks are due to Mrs I. Bow, who with Miss J. Butler, provided the social work service, Dr J. Elliott who interviewed patients after self-poisoning, Mrs C. Foster, Mrs G. Glastonbury and Mrs J. Powell who carried out follow-up interviews. The study was supported by the Department of Health and Social Security, and the Wessex Regional Health Authority.

# References

Bailey, J. and Coppen, A. (1976). A comparison between the Hamilton Rating Scale and the Beck Inventory in the measurement of depression. *British Journal of Psychiatry* **128**, 486—489.

Beck, A. T., Ward, C. H. and Mendelson, M. (1961). An Inventory for measuring depression. *Archives of General Psychiatry* **4**, 561—571.

Buglass, D. and Horton, J. (1974). A scale for predicting subsequent suicidal behaviour. *British Journal of Psychiatry* **124**, 573—578.

Chowdhury, N. L., Hicks, R. C. and Kreitman, N. (1973). Evaluation of an aftercare service for parasuicide (attempted suicide) patients. *Social Psychiatry* **8**, 67—81.

Ettlinger, R. (1975). Evaluation of suicide-prevention after attempted suicide. *Acta Psychiatrica Scandinavica*, Supplement 260.

Greer, S. and Bagley, C. (1971). Effect of psychiatric intervention in attempted suicide: a controlled study. *British Medical Journal* **i**, 310—312.

Hankoff, L. D. (1976). Categories of attempted suicide: a longitudinal study. *American Journal of Public Health* **66**, 558—563.

Jones, D. I. R. (1977). Self-poisoning with drugs: the past 20 years in Sheffield. *British Medical Journal* **i**, 28—29.

Kennedy, P. (1972). Efficacy of a regional poisoning treatment centre in preventing further suicidal behaviour. *British Medical Journal* **iv**, 255—257.

Metcalfe, M. and Goldman, E. (1965). Validation of an inventory for measuring depression. *British Journal of Psychiatry* **111**, 240—242.

Oast, S. P. and Zitrin, A. (1975). A public health approach to suicide prevention. *American Journal of Public Health* **65**, 144—147.

Reid, W. and Epstein, L. (1972). "Task-Centered Casework". Columbia University Press.

Silver, M. A., Bohnert, M., Beck, A. T. and Marcus, D. (1971). Relation of depression of attempted suicide and seriousness of intent. *Archives of General Psychiatry* **25**, 573—576.

Ternansen, P. E. and Bywater, C. (1975). S.A.F.E.R.: A follow-up service for attempted suicide in Vancouver. *Canadian Psychiatric Association Journal* **20**, 29—34.

# TREATMENT EFFECTS ON THE SOCIAL ADJUSTMENT OF DEPRESSED PATIENTS

MYRNA M. WEISSMAN, GERALD L. KLERMAN, EUGENE S. PAYKEL,
BRIGITTE PRUSOFF and BARBARA HANSON

The effects of maintenance treatment on social adjustment are examined in depressed outpatients randomly assigned to eight months of amitriptyline hydrochloride, a placebo, or no pill, with or without psychotherapy, using a 2 x 3 factorial design.

Results for the 106 patients who completed the trial show a significant main effect for psychotherapy apparent only after six to eight months' treatment. Psychotherapy improved overall adjustment, work performance, and communication, and reduced friction and anxious rumination. There was no effect on the patients' social adjustment for amitriptyline and there were no drug/psychotherapy interactions.

The results support the value of weekly maintenance psychotherapy in recovering depressives. Since amitriptyline has been shown to reduce relapse and prevent symptom return, and psychotherapy was shown to enhance adjustment, there is evidence for combined treatments.

Although the efficacy of antidepressants in the treatment of acute depression has been established, many questions remain. Among these, two have special importance for long-term treatment of depression. Does the initial advantage of symptom reduction by drugs have any long-term effects on the patient's social adjustment? Does the addition of psychotherapy to drug produce any further benefit?

Frank [1], some time ago, emphasized the distinction between symptom relief and social effectiveness and showed that psychotherapy was largely effective on the latter. Over the last 15 years this point of view has received considerable, but not unanimous acceptance. Although theoretical opinion, clinical observations, and debate about procedures exist, the value of continuing psychotherapy, with or without drugs, in depressed patients is largely untested. Psychotherapeutic studies, in the past, may have included patients with depressive symptoms, but systematic study of psychotherapy in a homogeneous sample of depressives is still lacking. Problems in designing

Reprinted, with permission, from the *Archives of General Psychiatry, Vol. 30, June,* 771–778, 1974.

such research have included disagreement about the type of psychotherapy, its interactions with drugs, and what psychotherapy is supposed to do.

In 1968, a controlled outpatient trial of amitriptyline hydrochloride and psychotherapy in the maintenance treatment of depressed women, using a 2 x 3 factorial design, was initiated in two clinics. Multiple outcome measures, including the traditional ones of clinical relapse and symptom status, were employed. Social adjustment was also assessed because, in agreement with the work of Frank, it was felt that this would be a necessary outcome measure in a prophylactic trial. This concept became more meaningful when findings showed that the social morbidity of depression was high and had a definite effect on work and family life [2].

The relapse rate and the patient symptom status under the various maintenance treatments will be described elsewhere (G. L. Klerman *et al.* and E. S. Paykel *et al.*, unpublished data) [3]. Results indicate that maintenance amitriptyline is effective in reducing relapse and preventing the return of symptoms. This report will describe the social adjustment of recovered depressed outpatients who completed, without relapse, the eight months of maintenance amitriptyline, placebo, or no pill, with or without psychotherapy. The specific questions raised are: (1) Does maintenance pharmacotherapy or psychotherapy enhance the social adjustment of recovered depressed patients? (2) How long does it take for effects to become apparent? (3) Does psychotherapy contribute to the improvement of specific social disturbances? (4) Does the combination of the two treatments have a negative or positive interaction?

## Methods

### Subjects

Subjects for this study were 150 moderately depressed women between the ages of 25 and 60 years, who responded to four to six weeks of preliminary treatment with amitriptyline. Criteria for entrance into preliminary treatment was a definitive depression of at least two weeks' duration and of sufficient intensity to reach a total score rating of 7 or more on the Raskin Depression Scale (range 3 to 15) [4]. Patients were excluded if the depression appeared secondary to another predominant syndrome, such as schizophrenia. Also excluded were alcoholics, drug addicts, patients with subnormal intelligence or serious physical illnesses, patients receiving ongoing psychotherapy, or patients who had failed to respond to an adequate course of tricyclic antidepressants in the last six months. Patients who met the initial criteria were treated with amitriptyline hydrochloride on a flexible dosage ranging between 100 to 200 mg daily, most as outpatients. The criterion for inclusion into the maintenance trial was an improvement of at least 50% on the Raskin Depression Scale at the end of four to six weeks.

The study was a collaborative one that took place at two centers (the Connecticut Mental Health Center—Yale Medical School, and Boston State Hospital—Tufts Medical School), with 78 patients participating in the Connecticut clinic and 72 in the Boston clinic.

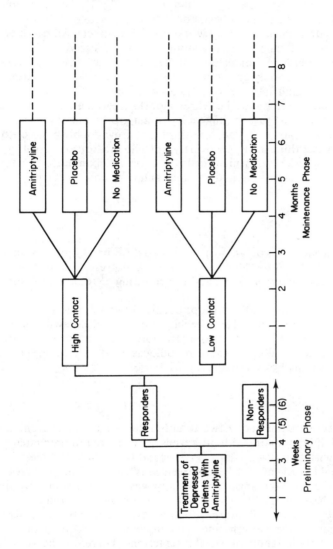

**Fig. 1** Design of study.

## Design

Following the four to six weeks preliminary treatment phase, responders entered the maintenance study, which took the form of a 2 x 3 balanced factorial design, stratified further by the two clinics (Fig. 1). On a randomized basis, one half of the patients began once-to-twice weekly individual psychotherapy with psychiatric social workers (high contact). All patients also saw the initial treating psychiatrist monthly in brief interviews for assessments and prescribing. For the second half of the patients these brief interviews comprised the only continuing contact (low contact). All patients continued to receive amitriptyline for a transitional phase of two more months. At this point, after a total of three months treatment, patients were further randomized as to drug. Within each contact group, one third of the patients continued on amitriptyline, one third withdrew double-blind onto the placebo, and one third withdrew overtly onto no medication. Treatment then continued in these six treatment cells for a further six months to a total of nine months (eight months in maintenance and one month in acute treatment).

## Drug Treatment

Maintenance treatment was on an outpatient basis. Amitriptyline was on a flexible dose range of 100 to 150 mg daily. Taking of prescribed medication was monitored both by direct report and the counting of returned tablets, and found to be adequate.

Randomization into medication groups occurred two months after the start of maintenance treatment. The placebo group was withdrawn double-blind by administering identical half-strength tablets for one month before switching to the placebo. Withdrawal to no pill was overt by cutting the number of tablets in half over the one-month period.

## Psychotherapy (High Contact)

Psychotherapy consisted of one or two weekly interviews with a psychiatric social worker. A minimum of one hour a week was devoted to individual psychotherapy with the patient alone. The second hour could include further individual treatment or other interventions, such as family or group treatment with the same therapist. The therapy was primarily supportive in nature with emphasis on the "here and now", and oriented around the patients' current problems and interpersonal relations. Patients were assisted in identifying maladaptive patterns and attaining better levels of adaptive response, particularly in family or social interactions. Therefore, no attempt was made to uncover unconscious material, modify infantile drives, or induce a strongly regressive transference.

There were five therapists, two at the Connecticut clinic and three at Boston. Care was taken in the selection of therapists to include persons who were judged to be skilled on criteria of considerable importance to outcome, such as experience, warmth, and empathy [5, 6]. A separate study of the process of the psychotherapy, including patient attendance and the content and quality of the sessions was undertaken, which assisted in documenting the treatment and in enhancing comparability of goals between therapists [7].

## Assessment of Social Adjustment

Social adjustment was assessed at the end of the one month short-term treatment (which was the beginning of maintenance treatment) and after two, four, and eight months maintenance treatment. Assessment ratings were carried out during a 1- to 1½-hour semistructured interview with the patient, by two Bachelor Degree-level research assistants not involved in the treatment. Ratings were made on the Social Adjustment Scale (SAS) [8, 9], a modification of the Structured and Scaled Interview to Assess Maladjustment (SSIAM) by Gurland *et al.* [10]. The format of the scale, training of raters, scoring, reliability, and validity have been described elsewhere [8]. It contained 48 rating items that assessed the patients' instrumental performance, interpersonal relations, and satisfactions in five major roles (work, social and leisure activities, extended family, marriage, parental), as well as individual rater global evaluations of the five roles and an overall rater evaluation. All items were rated on a 5-point scale with defined anchor points. Rater global evaluations were made on a 7-point scale. In each case, the time period of the rating was the two months immediately preceding the interview.

In order to simplify the data representation, individual items will not be reported. Three types of scores were used: six scales derived from a factor analysis of total item pool, the mean of all 48 items, and the clinical raters' global evaluation. The individual items making up each factor scale are described in Table 1 and the derivation of these factors has been described elsewhere [9]. Work performance contained items reflecting instrumental performance in the work situation. The remaining factors cut across social roles. Anxious rumination contained a number of items denoting subjective feelings of distress, overconcern, and dissatisfaction. The other four factors described specific patterns of disturbed interpersonal relations. Interpersonal friction referred to a pattern of overt friction and arguments, extending across all role areas. Inhibited communication involved reticence in communication with marital and extended family and friends. Submissive dependency described a pattern of undue dependency and submissive behavior, particularly with respect to the spouse. Family attachment was a pattern of diminished social interaction and withdrawal into the extended family.

## Data Analysis

The study was analyzed by a three-way analysis of covariance in accordance with the factorial design (2 contact groups x 3 medication groups x 2 hospitals). The covariate in each case was the initial rating of the particular scale or other scores used as dependent variables in the analysis. Special nonorthogonal contrasts were used to test medication differences, as these were the contrasts originally specified in the design of the experiment.

TABLE 1
Description of the social adjustment factors

| Factor | Item | Role | Loading |
|---|---|---|---|
| Work performance | Impaired performance | Work | .81 |
| | Time lost | Work | .71 |
| | Disinterest | Work | .64 |
| | Feelings of inadequacy | Work | .54 |
| | Guilt | Family unit | .53 |
| Interpersonal | Friction | Social and leasure | .78 |
| | Friction | Extended family | .76 |
| | Friction | Work | .69 |
| | Resentment | Family unit | .66 |
| | Friction | Marital | .56 |
| | Friction | Parental | .56 |
| | Resentment | Extended family | .54 |
| | Hypersensitive behavior | Social and leisure | .46 |
| Inhibited com- munication | Reticence | Extended family | .73 |
| | Reticence | Social and leisure | .62 |
| | Impaired communication | Parental | .58 |
| | Domineering behavior | Marital | .52 |
| | Diminished contact with friends | Social and leisure | .48 |
| | Withdrawal | Extended family | .47 |
| | Reticence | Marital | .46 |
| Submissive dependency | Dependency | Marital | .81 |
| | Submissiveness | Marital | .65 |
| | Guilt | Extended family | .58 |
| Family attachment | Family attachment | Extended family | .68 |
| | Diminished social interactions | Social and leisure | .60 |
| | Sexual problems | Marital | .56 |
| Anxious rumination | Worry | Family unit | .59 |
| | Worry | Extended family | .58 |
| | Lack of affection | Parental | .53 |
| | Boredom | Social and leisure | .52 |
| | Disinterest in sex | Marital | .51 |
| | Social discomfort | Social and leisure | .50 |
| | Lack of involvement | Parental | .49 |

A separate analysis was carried out for month 4, which was two months after drug randomization, and for month 8, which was the termination of the study.

## Results

### Characteristics of the Sample

Patients were all women, predominantly in their 30s (mean age 39), white (83.3%), Catholic (55.3%), married (60.0%), and from working and lower-middle class backgrounds [11]. The modal patient was a married housewife with children. Over half (59.0%) had experienced one or more previous depressive illnesses. Patients were predominantly neurotic depressives: 87% received a diagnosis of depressive neurosis and 13% a diagnosis of affective psychosis [International Classification of Disease, 1968]. There were no apparent differences in a variety of sociodemographic characteristics between the patients completing the study and those who relapsed.

## Completion Rates

One hundred fifty patients completed at least two months of maintenance treatment and were not replaced in the study. Of this total, 44 patients dropped out of the study between the second and eighth month (33 because of clinical relapse and 11 because of noncooperation), leaving a total of 106 patients who completed, without relapse, the one month short-term treatment and the eight months maintenance treatment. These 106 patients can be considered the treatment successes in terms of symptomatic improvement and absence of relapse. By completing the trial, they experienced the full effects of the treatment. Therefore, their social adjustment status deserves special attention. The analysis of this report will be on these 106 patients.

## Results at Four Months of Maintenance Treatment

The results of the covariance analysis following drug randomization are presented in Table 2. The effects of the three factors, drug, contact, and hospital, as well as their interactions, were examined, as shown on the top half of the table. The criterion measures were the previously described social adjustment variables. All significances were adjusted by one covariate that, in each case, was the same social adjustment rating at the beginning of the maintenance treatment. The adjusted means of the three drug groups and the significances of these contrasts are presented in the bottom half of the table. The adjusted means of contact groups are presented also. The significances are, of course, the same in both portions of the table.

Table 2 shows that there were no significant treament or hospital interactions and virtually no treatment effects on social adjustment after four months.

There were a few differences between the amitriptyline and the placebo group and these are of interest because the double-blind nature of the treatment makes them less sensitive to bias. There was a trend for patients receiving amitriptyline to be less impaired on all variables, and differences reached statistical significance on two. The patients receiving the drug had less interpersonal friction and were rated as overall less impaired. There was only one significant difference between the placebo and no pill groups, which indicated that the taking of a pill was not having a specific effect, further supporting the relationship of the drug and placebo differences to a specific pharmacologic effect. It was interesting to note the tendency for patients on the placebo, as contrasted with no pill, to be rated as more impaired.

## Results at Eight Months of Maintenance Treatment

Table 3 presents the same analysis described except that social adjustment is measured at eight months, the termination of the maintenance trial. The

## TABLE 2
### Three-way analysis of covariance after four months treatment (N = 106)

*Summary of F-values*

| Social adjustment | Contact A 1 df | Drug B 2 df | Hospital C 1 df | Interactions AB 2 df | AC 1 df | BC 2 df | ABC 2 df |
|---|---|---|---|---|---|---|---|
| Dimensions of adjustment | | | | | | | |
| Work performance | 0.05 | 0.78 | 3.92 | 0.12 | 0.01 | 3.04 | 0.25 |
| Interpersonal friction | 0.43 | 2.19 | 3.84 | 0.27 | 0.01 | 2.34 | 0.23 |
| Inhibited communication | 2.49 | 0.64 | 0.07 | 1.18 | 0.14 | 1.51 | 0.79 |
| Submissive dependency | 0.32 | 2.00 | 0.55 | 2.15 | 4.80* | 2.77 | 1.01 |
| Family attachment | 0.04 | 0.94 | 0.66 | 0.28 | 0.80 | 1.07 | 2.36 |
| Anxious rumination | 0.10 | 0.84 | 0.25 | 0.06 | 1.13 | 0.99 | 0.25 |
| Mean of all social adjustment items | 1.08 | 1.98 | 1.29 | 0.89 | 0.32 | 2.21 | 0.37 |
| Overall global evaluation | 3.69 | 3.10 | 3.17 | 0.43 | 2.48 | 2.97 | 0.09 |

*Adjusted means† and significances of individual contrasts*

| Social adjustment | Contact Low | High | F-value | Medication Amitriptyline | Placebo | No pill | Amitriptyline vs Placebo, F-value | Placebo vs No pill, F-value |
|---|---|---|---|---|---|---|---|---|
| Dimensions of adjustment | | | | | | | | |
| Work performance | 1.65 | 1.68 | 0.05 | 1.57 | 1.73 | 1.73 | 1.18 | 0.00 |
| Interpersonal friction | 1.86 | 1.80 | 0.43 | 1.74 | 1.96 | 1.79 | 3.97* | 2.29 |
| Inhibited communication | 2.46 | 2.25 | 2.49 | 2.26 | 2.43 | 2.37 | 1.24 | 0.12 |
| Submissive dependency | 1.62 | 1.56 | 0.32 | 1.47 | 1.75 | 1.56 | 3.85 | 1.58 |
| Family attachment | 2.05 | 2.08 | 0.04 | 2.08 | 2.18 | 1.94 | 0.28 | 1.86 |
| Anxious rumination | 1.69 | 1.66 | 0.10 | 1.60 | 1.73 | 1.70 | 1.54 | 0.08 |
| Mean of all social adjustment items | 1.99 | 1.91 | 1.08 | 1.88 | 2.05 | 1.93 | 3.80 | 1.63 |
| Overall global evaluation | 3.65 | 3.29 | 3.69 | 3.33 | 3.79 | 3.28 | 4.12* | 4.94* |

* P < .05.   † Means are adjusted for initial level of the items.

## TABLE 3
### Three-way analysis of covariance after eight months treatment (N = 106)

#### Summary of F-values

| Social adjustment | Contact A 1 df | Drug B 2 df | Hospital C 1 df | Interactions AB 2 df | AC 1 df | BC 2 df | ABC 2 df |
|---|---|---|---|---|---|---|---|
| Dimensions of adjustment | | | | | | | |
| Work performance | 5.96* | 1.34 | 8.98† | 5.33† | 0.70 | 0.56 | 0.81 |
| Interpersonal friction | 7.70† | 0.58 | 2.05 | 0.39 | 0.05 | 1.45 | 0.28 |
| Inhibited communication | 4.93* | 0.27 | 0.10 | 0.48 | 0.00 | 2.94 | 1.13 |
| Submissive dependency | 0.50 | 0.31 | 0.35 | 1.28 | 4.07* | 4.40* | 0.21 |
| Family attachment | 0.79 | 0.32 | 0.13 | 0.01 | 1.41 | 0.62 | 1.18 |
| Anxious rumination | 4.97* | 0.79 | 0.01 | 0.02 | 0.15 | 2.83 | 0.23 |
| Mean of all social adjustment items | 7.16† | 0.63 | 1.40 | 0.16 | 0.03 | 1.86 | 0.43 |
| Overall global evaluation | 4.95* | 1.07 | 0.45 | 0.31 | 1.90 | 0.81 | 0.27 |

#### Adjusted means‡ and significances of individual contrasts

| Social adjustment | Contact Low | High | F-value | Medication Amitriptyline | Placebo | No pill | Amitriptyline vs Placebo, F-value | Placebo vs No pill, F-value |
|---|---|---|---|---|---|---|---|---|
| Dimensions of adjustment | | | | | | | | |
| Work performance | 1.76 | 1.50 | 5.96* | 1.52 | 1.66 | 1.70 | 1.65 | 0.08 |
| Interpersonal friction | 1.86 | 1.60 | 7.70† | 1.70 | 1.80 | 1.69 | 0.84 | 0.86 |
| Inhibited communication | 2.33 | 2.09 | 4.93* | 2.19 | 2.17 | 2.26 | 0.00 | 0.41 |
| Submissive dependency | 1.60 | 1.51 | 0.50 | 1.59 | 1.48 | 1.58 | 0.47 | 0.45 |
| Family attachment | 2.05 | 1.91 | 0.79 | 2.01 | 2.03 | 1.88 | 0.03 | 0.59 |
| Anxious rumination | 1.70 | 1.53 | 4.97* | 1.56 | 1.67 | 1.62 | 1.58 | 0.31 |
| Mean of all social adjustment items | 1.95 | 1.78 | 7.16† | 1.83 | 1.91 | 1.86 | 1.25 | 0.39 |
| Overall global evaluation | 3.39 | 2.93 | 4.95* | 3.06 | 3.36 | 3.06 | 1.70 | 1.42 |

* $P < .05$.  † $P < .01$.  ‡ Means are adjusted for initial level of the items.

hospital treatment interactions are minor — one hospital contact and one hospital drug interaction. There is one contact drug interaction on work performance and this could not be interpreted: the patients on the placebo and on psychotherapy had the best work performance, while those on the placebo and low contact were the most impaired. Table 3 shows that there are no drug treatment effects at eight months, indicating that drugs do not have an effect on the patients' social adjustment.

However, differences between the high and the low contact groups were numerous. Patients receiving high contact, as contrasted with low contact, showed significantly less impaired work performance, less interpersonal friction, better communication, and less anxious rumination. The mean of the 48 individual variables reflected the differences between groups, as did the raters' overall evaluation of the patients. These findings indicated that high contact significantly improved the patients' social adjustment. Figure 2 illustrates the percent of improvement in the contact groups, using as an

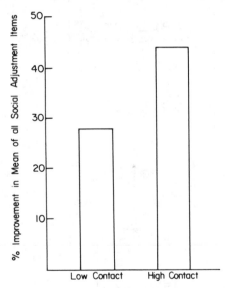

**Fig. 2**   Improvement in social adjustment in two contact groups over eight months.

index the mean of all social adjustment items during eight months. It shows that the percent of improvement in social adjustment was substantially greater in high contact (44%) as contrasted with 28% in low contact. We are aware that selective attrition is a potential bias in an analysis that only includes completers. To exclude this possibility, we have done several analyses that compared the completers and early terminators by treatment group on base line characteristics and on symptom and social adjustment variables at entrance, prior to, and at the point of relapse. Preliminary results of these analyses indicate that no selective attrition occurred that might have confounded results. These analyses and related ones will be presented in a separate publication.

## Comment

The social adjustment of recovering depressed women, treated initially with antidepressants, is enhanced by the addition of weekly supportive psychotherapy. These beneficial effects, however, take some time to develop. They are not apparent after two to four months of treatment, but are after six to eight months, indicating that psychotherapy should not be short-term. The effects are seen in the improved work performance, reduced interpersonal friction, freer communication, reduced anxiety, and in overall adjustment. Maintenance amitriptyline, either alone or with psychotherapy, does not afford these advantages.

### Design

Before discussing the findings, it is important to place the research methodology of this study in perspective. This was not an ideal design to test psychotherapy. Many features of the design bias against an effect so that the fact that a psychotherapy effect was found may be an underestimate of its magnitude. For example, the introduction of psychotherapy after the short-term symptomatic treatment may have delayed the effects of psychotherapy since recovering patients are usually less interested in treatment. Also, patients were initially treated with medication without psychotherapy and were clear drug responders. They attributed their improvement to the medication and often did not feel an immediate need for psychotherapy, which was a supplemental approach.

Similarly, at the initiation of psychotherapy, therapists may have been careful about undoing the patients' recent symptomatic recovery and, therefore, proceeded cautiously. The introduction of psychotherapy meant the introduction of a new therapist in addition to the psychiatrist who prescribed the medication, and it took time for a new therapeutic alliance to form. These factors may be one explanation for the delayed effect of psychotherapy. Future research should be directed at demonstrating the use of psychotherapy in the short-term as well as maintenance treatment phase.

In regard to the sample studied, the patients were all women who showed symptomatic improvement on medication. None was under 25 years of age and most were diagnosed as neurotic depressives. It is this group, the young female neurotic depressives, that is the most frequent attenders of out-patient-clinics. However, more heterogeneous samples, including men and bipolar manic depressives, are required for further generalizability.

### Assessment of Social Adjustment

The importance of suitable outcome criteria for psychotherapy studies has been repeatedly stressed [12]. Frank [1], as noted previously, emphasized the distinction between symptom comfort and social effectiveness and showed that group psychotherapy effects were predominantly on the latter. This distinction has since been made by others [12–20]. These findings underscore the need for appropriate outcome criteria for psychotherapy.

Had symptomatic improvement, relapse rate, or hospitalization been the sole outcome measures, or if treatment had been shorter, we would not have demonstrated a psychotherapy effect. Social adjustment appears to be an appropriate outcome measure.

Attention should be paid, however, to the social adjustment assessment used, which was a rather judgment based on what the patient told the interviewer. The lack of independently validated behavior measures, such as a relative rating, may have influenced ratings. For example, psychotherapy, unlike drug treatment, could not be blinded. Even though raters were independent of treatment, the raters' preconceptions about psychotherapy could possibly have colored the ratings. Alternatively, patients receiving psychotherapy may have felt more comfortable with the raters and, therefore, appeared better adjusted as assessment interviews. The fact that psychotherapy effects were not consistent, either at both time periods or on all variables, however, argues against this possible influence.

Two ways of reducing bias might be through the use of patient self-report rather than interviewer ratings, and through independent relative ratings. At the time this study began, there were no patient self-report scales that adequately covered the areas of social adjustment. However, The Katz Adjustment Scale, which is an excellent and widely used relative rating, was available [21]. We seriously considered incorporating this relative rating. While it would have been possible to interview spouses of married patients, selection of reliable informants for older, unmarried patients may have created problems. Informants who are not in close daily contact with subjects often lack access to detailed information on intimate aspects of the patient's life. This might also apply to the nonperceptive or hostile spouse. In addition, we found our patients reluctant to have their spouses interviewed. We chose the alternative of obtaining information from the subject alone, giving careful attention to interviewing technique and training of raters [22]. None of the techniques alone (patient self-report, relative, or patient interviews) is ideal. If this study were replicated, independent assessments of the patients' adjustment through relative interviews using the Katz Adjustment Scale, and possibly a patient self-report as well, should be incorporated.

### Psychotherapy: Characteristics, Specificity, Timing Interactions

There are innumerable clinical reports describing the benefits of various psychological treatments for depression [13, 23–26]. However, controlled psychotherapy or social work studies of mixed patient groups are less enthusiastic in their findings, [27–30] and the absence of published controlled trials of psychotherapy in a homogeneous sample of depressed patients is noteworthy [29]. The beneficial effects of psychotherapy represent the most important finding in this study. In view of these effects and the absence of similar studies, the nature of the psychotherapy will be described in further detail.

*Characteristics*    Psychotherapy consisted of supportive contacts on a weekly basis over eight months, beginning after the acute depressive episode had subsided with medication. The therapists were trained psychiatric social workers with sufficient experience and personal qualifications to insure the quality of treatment. Up to two hours a week was allowed for treatment. In practice, patient attendance was excellent, but patients rarely came more than once a week [31]. Most psychotherapy was with the patient alone, although a wide range of interventions selectively occurred, such as home visits, family, and group therapy.

Therapy primarily emphasized the "here and now", rather than reflective discussions of uncovering of early childhood material. Therapists took a reassuring, helpful, and active stance, rather than assuming a neutral position. Separately collected data on what patients discussed indicated that descriptive accounts of practical problems, such as employment, housing, finances, and close interpersonal relations, usually spouse and children, comprised most of the discussion [32]. Early experiences, reflective consideration of antecedents, or sexual problems were rarely discussed.

This form of psychotherapy seemed most appropriate to the treatment of these recovering depressed women [33], who were predominantly from the working and lower classes, and had a number of practical problems that concerned them and may have contributed to the development of the depression. Whether therapeutic interest in more dynamic issues and in early experiences would be more characteristic of upper-class women and whether such uncovering would, in fact, result in further patient improvement cannot be answered by this research. A comparison of the topics discussed and the reflective quality of interviews between patients from the lower- and upper-social classes in this sample revealed no differences [34]. The approach described is consistent with supportive treatment given by mental health personnel. It is quite likely that similar treatment might be given by other professionals and paraprofessionals other than social workers, if they are carefully selected.

Interestingly, these patients did not fit many of the sociodemographic criteria considered important for good outcome with psychotherapy, namely, higher education and social class, psychological mindedness, and high motivation for psychotherapy [34]. On the other hand, the pressence of short-term depression has been one of the clinical criteria considered to be a predictor of positive psychotherapy outcome [29]. It is possible that sociodemographic features are less important predictors of outcome for depressed patients if supportive psychotherapy is geared to their current problems.

*Specificity of Psychotherapy*    The effect of psychotherapy was specific to the patient's social adjustment. As reported, maintenance psychotherapy did not prevent relapse and was not the target of symptoms. Neither did it exacerbate symptoms, as has been suggested by clinicians. On the other hand, maintenance pharmacotherapy did not enhance social adjustment.

In considering the specific effects of psychotherapy on social adjustment and their importance, it should be noted that, at the point psychotherapy began, patients were only mildly symptomatic and had achieved at least 50% relief of symptoms with amitriptyline hydrochloride. However, data from previous research indicated that a residual of social impairments remained despite symptomatic recovery, indicating that symptoms and social recovery did not entirely parallel one another [2].

In a comparison study of the first 40 depressed women entering maintenance treatment and a matched normal control sample, we found that depressed women were considerably more socially impaired than normals at the height of illness and that the remission of social impairment was considerably slower than that of symptoms. The most rapid decrease of social impairments occurred in the first two months. There was slower improvement in the next two months, following which, to a total of eight months, the average course was relatively static. At the end of eight months, these relatively symptom-free patients, who had not relapsed during the eight months, were still more socially impaired than the normal controls. The patients' impairment was evident in increased interpersonal friction and impaired communication, and was reflected in work performance, relations with friends, and in their marriages. The conclusion of this study was that the depressed patients were likely to be socially impaired even though free of depressive symptoms, and to remain with these impairments despite a successful course of pharmacotherapy. This observation has often been made by others working with depressives who are being treated with pharmacotherapy [14]. This patient-normal comparison raised an important question, which has now been partially answered, about the value of psychological intervention in reducing the social impairments.

The current findings in an enlarged sample support the value of psychotherapy in this regard. These improvements found in patients receiving psychotherapy were mainly in the areas that were noted to be abnormal in the recovered depressive, namely, the maintenance of harmonious interpersonal relations.

*Timing of Psychotherapy Benefits*    The effects of psychotherapy in this study were delayed and took at least six to eight months to develop. This finding is consistent with the recent speculations of Kubie [15], who noted the difficulties of estimating the appropriate timing of the outcome of any slow process of maturation, such as education and all the psychological therapies. It is also consistent with the work of Hogarty and his group [35]. While Hogarty demonstrated the importance of long-term psychotherapy in a study of maintenance rehabilitative treatment of schizophrenics, a positive psychotherapy effect took one year to develop. The negative psychotherapy findings in previously reported studies may be related to inadequate timing of follow-up.

*Combining Psychotherapy and Drugs*    The design of this study enabled the testing of interactions between drugs and psychotherapy and found none. The effects were largely independent, operating on different outcome measures. Drugs did not have a negative effect on psychotherapy and psychotherapy did not have an adverse effect on the symptom reduction achieved by drugs. This finding is contrary to clinical speculations about combined treatments. There was a slight deterioration in social functioning at the point that patients were withdrawn from amitriptyline, probably due to an association with slight symptomatic worsening.

It should be noted that only those who had completed the eight months of treatment were the subjects for this analysis. There were no psychotherapy effects for patients who were terminated from the study due to relapse. Therefore, psychotherapy effects depend on patients remaining symptomatically well. On the other hand, we know that drugs help to prevent relapse [3] and to maintain patients in a symptomatically well state. The results was a kind of synergistic effect of the two treatments (drug and psychotherapy) that did not produce any formal interactions, since the treatments effected different areas at different times. This observation is a strong argument for combined treatments.

## Conclusions

This study supports the value of weekly maintenance psychotherapy over a period of six to eight months in enhancing the social adjustment of recovering depressed female outpatients. Psychotherapy is not an alternative to antidepressant treatment and does not prevent relapse or the recurrence of symptoms. Alternately, maintenance amitriptyline has no effect on social adjustment and is no better or worse than a placebo or no pill. A study of these patients following termination from treatment is now underway, which will provide data on any enduring effects of treatment. This information is necessary before any conclusions about long-term preventive effects can be drawn. Further research in enlarged populations, using different timing and types of therapy would be of value and some of this research has been carried out by Covi and his associates in Baltimore [36] and by Friedman and his associates in Philadelphia [37].

## Acknowledgements

This study was supported by Public Health Service grants MH 13738, MH 15650, and MH 17728, from the Psychopharmacology Research Branch of the National Institute of Mental Health, Department of Health, Education and Welfare.

Alberto DiMascio, PhD, directed the Boston State Hospital study. Clinical care was provided in Boston by Abram Chipman, PhD, David Haskell, MD, Eva Deykin, MS, and Shirley Jacobson, MS, and in New Haven by the late Mason de la Vergne, MD, Clive Tonks, MD, Ruth Bullock, MSW, Effie Geanakoplos, MSW. Social adjustment ratings were done in Boston by Jean Fasman and Margaret Zwilling, and in Hew Haven by Catherine Roby and Risé Siegel. Data analyses were carried out by Janis Tanner.

Marck, Sharp and Dohme supplied the special tablets of amitriptyline hydrochloride and the placebo.

## Nonproprietary Name and Trademark of Drug

Amitriptyline hydrochloride — *Elavil Hydrochloride.*

## References

1. Frank, J. D. (1961). "Persuasion and Healing". Baltimore, Johns Hopkins Press.
2. Weissman, M. M. and Paykel, E. S. (1974). "The Depressed Woman: A study of Social Relationships". Chicago, University of Chicago Press. (In press)
3. Klerman, G. L. *et al.* (1974). Treatment of depression by drugs and psychotherapy. *Am. J. Psychiatry* **131**, 186–191.
4. Raskin, A. *et al.* (1969). Replication of factors of psychopathology in interview, ward behavior and self report ratings of hospitalized depressives. *J. Nerv. Ment. Dis.* **148**, 87–98.
5. Cartwright, R. D. (1966). A comparison of the response to psychoanalytic and client-centered psychotherapy. *In* "Methods of Research in Psychotherapy" (Eds L. A. Gottschalk, A. H. Auerbach). Appleton-Century Crofts Inc., New York.
6. Traux, C. B. and Carkhuff, R. F. (1967). "Towards Effective Counseling and Psychotherapy, Training and Practice". Aldine Press, Chicago.
7. Weissman, M. M., Prusoff, B. A. and Paykel, E. S. (1972). Checklist quantification of a psychological therapy: Pilot studies of reliability and utility. *J. Nerv. Ment. Dis.* **154**, 125–136.
8. Weissman, M. M. *et al.* (1971). The social role performance of depressed women: Comparisons with a normal group. *Am. J. Orthopsychiatry* **41**, 391–405.
9. Paykel, E. S. *et al.* (1971). Dimensions of social adjustment in depressed women. *J. Nerv. Ment. Dis.* **152**, 158–172.
10. Gurland, B. J. *et al.* (1972). The structured and scaled interview to assess maladjustment (SSIAM); Description, rationale, and development. *Arch. Gen. Psychiatry* **27**, 259–264.
11. Hollingshead, A. (1957). "Two Factor Index of Social Position". Copyrighted, mimeographed, Yale University, New Haven, Conn.
12. Fiske, D. W. *et al.* (1970). Planning of research on effectiveness of psychotherapy. *Arch. Gen. Psychiatry* **22**, 22–32.
13. Levine S. (1965). Some suggestions for treating the depressed patients. *Psychoanal. Quart.* **34**, 37–65.
14. Park, L. C. and Imboden, J. B. (1970). Clinical and heuristic value of clinical drug research. *J. Nerv. Ment. Dis.* **151**, 322–340.
15. Kubie, L. S. (1973). The process of evaluation of therapy in psychiatry. *Gen. Psychiatry* **28**, 880–884.
16. Goldman, R. K. and Mendelsohn, G. A. (1969). Psychotherapeutic change and social adjustment. A report of a national survey of psychotherapists. *J. Abnorm. Soc. Psychol.* **74**, 164–172, 1969.
17. Malan, D. H. *et al.* (1968). A study of psychodynamic changes in untreated neurotic patients. *Br. J. Psychiatry* **114**, 525–551.
18. Strupp, H. H. and Bergin, A. E. (1969). Some empirical and conceptual bases for coordinated research in psychotherapy; A critical review of issues, trends, and evidence. *Int. J. Psychiatry* **7**, 18–90.
19. Cawley, R. (1971). The evaluation of psychotherapy. *Psychol. Med.* **1**, 101–103.
20. Murriel, S. A. (1970). Intra-family variables and psychotherapy outcome research. *Psychother. Theory Res. Practice* **7**, 19–21.
21. Katz, M. M. and Lyerly, S. B. (1963). Methods of measuring adjustment and social behavior in the community: Rationale, description, discriminative validity and scale development. *Psychol. Rep.* **13**, 503–535.

22. Spitzer, R. L. and Endicott, J. E. (1973). The value of the interview for the evaluation of psychotherapy. *In* "Psychopathology: Contributions in the Biological, Behavioral and Social Sciences" (Eds M. Hammer *et al.*). John Wiley and Sons Inc, New York.

23. Jacobson, E. (1954). Transference problems in the psychoanalytic treatment of severely depressive patients. *J. Am. Psychoanal. Assoc.* 2, 595–606.

24. Cohen, M. B. *et al.* (1954). An intensive study of 12 cases of manic depressive psychoses. *Psychiatry* 17, 103–137.

25. Bonime, W. (1966). The psychocynamics of neurotic depression. *In* "American Handbook of Psychiatry", vol. 3 (Ed S. Arieti). Basic Books Inc. Publisher, New York.

26. Spiegel, R. (1960). Communications in the psychoanalysis of depressives. *In* Psychoanalysis and Human Values", pp. 209–220. Grune and Stratton Inc., New York.

27. Segal, S. P. (1972). Research on the outcome of social work therapeutic interventions: A review of the literature. *J. Health Soc. Behav.* 13, 3–17.

28. Fisher, J. (1973). Is casework effective? A review. *Soc. Work*, pp. 5–20. January 1973.

29. Luborsky, L. *et al.* (1971). Factors influencing the outcome of psychotherapy: A review of quantitative research. *Psychol. Bull.* 75, 145–185.

30. Uhlenhuth, E. H., Lipman, R. A. and Covi, L. (1969). Combined pharmacotherapy and psychotherapy. *J. Nerv. Ment. Dis.* 1, 52–64.

31. Deykin, E. Y., Weissman, M. M. and Tanner, J. Participation of depressed women in psychotherapy. *J. Nerv. Ment. Dis.*, to be published.

32. Weissman, M. M. and Klerman, G. L. (1973). Psychotherapy with depressed women: An empirical study of content themes and reflection. *Br. J. Psychiatry* 123, 55–61.

33. Deykin, E. Y., Weissman, M. M. and Klerman, G. L. (1971). Treatment of depressed women: Therapeutic issue with hospitalized patients and outpatients. *Br. J. Soc. Work* 1, 277–291.

34. Weissman, M. M., Geanakoplos, E. and Prusoff, B. A. (1973). Social class and attrition in depressed outpatients. *Soc. Casework* 54, 162–170.

35. Hogarty, G. E., Goldberg, S. C. and the Collaborative Study Group (1973). Drugs and sociotherapy in the aftercare of schizophrenic patients. *Arch. Gen. Psychiatry* 28, 56–64.

36. Covi, L., Lipman, R. and Derogatis, L. R. (1973). Drugs and group therapy in depressive disorders. Read before the Annual Meeting of the American Psychiatric Association. Honolulu, May 1973.

37. Friedman, A. S. *et al.* (1972). Drugs and family therapy in treatment of depression. Read before the Annual Meeting of the ACNP, San Juan, Puerto Rico, December 1972.

# MENTAL HEALTH CARE IN THE COMMUNITY:
# AN EVALUATIVE STUDY

B. COOPER, B. G. HARWIN, C. DEPLA and MICHAEL SHEPHERD

## Synopsis

A study was designed to assess the therapeutic value of attaching a social worker to a metropolitan group practice in the management of chronic neurotic illness. The psychiatric and social status of a group of patients before treatment and after one year was compared with the status of a control group treated more conventionally over the same period. The results indicate that the experimental service conferred some benefit on the patient population.

Minor mental disorders are common in the general population and impose a heavy burden on medical services [Watts *et al.*, 1964; Shepherd *et al.*, 1966]. Studies under the National Health Service have shown that each year only one in 20 such cases are referred to psychiatrists [Kaeser and Cooper, 1971]. The dimensions of the problem thus place it well beyond the scope of specialist services, and render the provision of effective treatment and management by the primary care team an important public health issue [WHO, 1973].

Broadly speaking, three modes of treatment are open to the primary care team in dealing with mental illness: the pharmacological, the psychological, and those procedures aimed at modifying the patient's environment. While pharmacotherapy remains a medical prerogative, both psychological and social methods may be shared with other professions. Social casework, for example, overlaps extensively with psychotherapy and medical counselling. Intervention in family problems may require collaboration between doctors, community nurses, and social workers.

The immediate background of the present experiment was a study of chronic neurotic illness, which revealed an interaction between the patient's clinical symptoms and their social adaptation [Cooper, 1972a, 1972b]. This finding suggested that improvement in social adjustment might lead to a corresponding reduction in clinical severity. One way to test the hypothesis was to examine the effects of social worker intervention on a sample of patients with chronic neurotic illness.

Reprinted, with permission, from *Psychological Medicine*, Vol. 5, No. 4, pp. 372–380, November 1975.

Over the past 20 years, a number of studies have been published of collaboration between general practitioners and social workers [Collins, 1965; Forman and Fairbairn, 1968; Goldberg and Neill, 1973]. These reports have consistently advocated the development of closer liaison; several have emphasized that much of social work in this setting is concerned with psychosocial problems, which can be better dealt with by general practitioner and social worker together than by either singly. So far, however, there has been a dearth of evaluative studies.

## Method

### Establishment of an Experimental Service

The nucleus of the present study was the attachment of a social worker to a metropolitan group practice, with a broad remit to help the practice team deal with patients' psychosocial problems. The practice in question had at the time four partners, a part-time assistant, two practice nurses, several receptionists, two attached district nurses, and two attached health visitors providing medical and nursing care for a registered population of about 13,000.

Since teamwork is the essence of good community care, it would be misguided to try to evaluate the work of any single member of the team in isolation. In the present instance, the social worker not only collaborated with the doctors and health visitors; she also received consultative backing from two psychiatrists in the research group, and to some extent worked in harness with them. For each patient referred to the experimental service there was thus a choice of four principal methods of care and disposal, singly or in combination:

(1) recommendations to the practitioner most directly concerned;
(2) referral to the local psychiatric or social services;
(3) social support within the experimental service;
(4) consultation with one of the research team psychiatrists.

Thus, while the emphasis was placed on social supportive care, the approach was kept as flexible as possible. This flexibility was considered vital, since there are few guide-lines as to which types of psychosocial problems are best dealt with by which professional workers. All medication for patients referred to the experimental service was prescribed by the general practitioners, exactly as for their other patients. No direct link existed with local psychiatric services; hence patients in need of hospital care had to be referred through the normal channels.

Regular fortnightly meetings attended by the practitioners, the health visitors, the social worker, and one or other of the two research psychiatrists were held in the practice to discuss both new referrals and the process of old cases. By arrangement with the practitioners, the research psychiatrists were given the use of a consulting room during one evening surgery each week, to interview patients selected for the trial.

## Evaluation of Experimental Service

Once the experimental service had been established, the evaluative study had to be superimposed on it. This called for systematic assessment of the psychiatric and social status of a selected patient sample, first at the point when they came into the trial and again after one year; changes in their condition during this time then had to be compared with those in a control group of similar cases treated more conventionally.

*Selection of Cases for Treatment*    Cases referred to the experimental service covered a wide diagnostic spectrum; for the evaluative study, however, a relatively homogeneous sample had to be selected. In planning the project, we decided to take patients with chronic neurotic illness, since their care devolves on general medical services for the most part and seldom involves statutory work.

*Chronicity* was defined operationally as the presence of continuous symptoms and/or dependence on psychotropic drugs for at least 12 months; *neurotic illness* as any clinically-diagnosed, non-psychotic mental disorder corresponding to categories 300–309 of the Eighth Revision of the *I.C.D.* [WHO, 1967, 1969].

In the event, the great majority of patients thus selected were suffering from morbid anxiety or depression, or both; in short, they were typical of the bulk of psychiatric cases in general practice [Shepherd *et al.*, 1966; Goldberg and Blackwell, 1970]. A few patients were diagnosed, mainly from their medical histories, as having endogenous rather than reactive depressions; hence they were technically cases of psychosis according to the *I.C.D.* They did not, however, manifest florid psychotic symptoms, or present special problems of management.

*Control Group*    Even were the present climate of opinion in this field favourable to randomized controlled trials, the care of a control group of patients drawn from the same practice could not have remained unaffected by the presence of the experimental service. We decided, therefore, that control patients should be drawn from other local practices with no access to this type of facility. Since no two practices are exactly alike, either in patient-population or in the doctors' professional habits, we tried to eliminate possible bias by drawing the control cases from eight practices with widely differing features. One doctor in each practice kept a special record of his patients' attendances during one month and these records constituted the sampling frame. For various reasons, the collection of control patients had begun about 18 months before that of the experimental group; there was, however, no reason to believe that the treatment of prognosis for this type of illness had changed in the interim. More important was the inevitable difference in sampling procedure as between experimental and control groups. Though confirmation depended in each instance on a standardized psychiatric interview (see below), the experimental cases had been put forward in the hope that expert help might be given, whereas the control patients were selected from lists prepared by their own doctors purely for research.

*Mode of Assessment: Initial Psychiatric Assessment*    Both experimental and control patients were examined by the research psychiatrists to confirm that they were suffering from chronic neurotic illness as operationally defined. First, each patient was discussed with his doctor and his case-notes were reviewed. Apparently suitable patients were then interviewed by one or other of the research psychiatrists using a standardized interview technique [Goldberg *et al.*, 1970]. Any patients not confirmed as chronic cases were discarded from the study at this point, though many of those excluded from the formal evaluation were still treated in the experimental service. The standardized interview provides the basis for a series of ratings of clinical phenomena which are reliable when made by trained psychiatrists. It does *not* necessarily improve the reliability of psychiatric diagnosis: a point to be borne in mind in considering the findings.

*Mode of Assessment: Initial Social Assessment*    The patients' social adjustment and functioning were assessed independently by means of a standardized interview which generates a series of simple 3- and 4-point rating-scales [Cooper, 1972a]. This instrument is reliable in the sense that it shows a high level of agreement between trained interviewers when used in a joing-interview situation. The ratings can be grouped on either of two main axes: one covers a range of social circumstances such as housing conditions, occupation, income and finances, etc.; the other moves from the more objective to the more subjective aspects of social adaptation, grouped under the three principal headings of material conditions, social management, and social role-satisfaction.

   The social interview was normally carried out in the patients' home and, unless the patient was living alone, in the presence of another member of the household, by a social research worker who took no subsequent part in the patient's care and management.

*Mode of Assessment: Measurement of Clinical and Social Changes*    The ratings derived from the standardized psychiatric interview can be combined to give a total weighted score which, for non-psychotic patients at least, provides a useful index of clinical severity [Goldberg *et al.*, 1970]. As the ratings are reliable, change in scores over time can be employed as a measure of clinical change. For this purpose, experimental and control patients were interviewed both at the outset of the trial and again after one year. In those cases where one of the research psychiatrists had played a part in the patient's care and management during the follow-up year, he did not interview the patient at follow-up. The social interview was also repeated after one year, to give a corresponding measure of change in social adjustment.

## Results

### Patient-Response and Follow-up Rate

The patients' response to the experimental service was generally favourable. Of 301 patients referred to the service, either by their doctors or by the health visitors, 82.1% attended for the initial clinical interview. Agreement to a home interview, also required for inclusion in the trial, was given by 82.2% of patients confirmed at interview as suffering from chronic neurotic illnesses.

The selection of control patients differed in that only those thought to have chronic neurotic illness were approached in the first instance. A total of 86.8% attended for interview, while 92.0% of patients confirmed as chronic cases then consented to home interview. The overall response rate was thus similar for the two groups, despite the differing conditions under which they were recruited. The most obvious source of bias in both groups was failure to secure a number of home interviews because the patient's spouse would not cooperate: as a result, marital problems were probably under-represented among both experimental and control patients.

Of the experimental patients 86.8% and of the controls 84.3% were successfully followed-up and reinterviewed after one year.

## Comparability of the Groups

*Demographic Characteristics*   Since neither randomization nor individual matching of the groups had been feasible, the establishment of their comparability in demographics as well as medical terms was crucial. The main demographic features are summarized in Table 1.

The two groups thus proved broadly similar on their demographic profiles. The main differences comprised a relative excess of 60–65 years olds and of social classes I and II among the controls and a small excess of retired persons and of social classes IV and V patients in the experimental group. The possible effects of these differences on outcome are considered below.

TABLE 1
Summary of demographic characteristics of experimental and control groups

|  | *Experimental group (n = 92)* | *Control group (n = 97)* | *Test of significance $(\chi^2)$* |
|---|---|---|---|
| Proportion of: |  |  |  |
| Males | 26.1 | 22.7 | 0.14 NS |
| Single persons | 19.6 | 15.5 | 3.40 NS |
| Married persons | 65.2 | 58.7 |  |
| In gainful employment | 54.3 | 54.7 | 3.41 NS |
| Social classes: |  |  |  |
| I and II | 15.2 | 24.7 |  |
| III | 66.3 | 61.9 | 4.08 NS |
| IV and V | 18.5 | 13.4 |  |
| Mean: |  |  | *t test* |
| Age (yr) | 42.1 | 45.5 | 1.67 NS |
| Persons in household (no.) | 3.1 | 3.1 | 0.29 NS |
| Children (no.) | 1.5 | 1.5 | 0.14 NS |

*Physical and Psychiatric Status*    The physical health of the two groups at outset was closely similar, as judged by the ratings given by the two research psychiatrists, using a simple 4-point rating-scale. The findings are summarized in Table 2.

TABLE 2
Physical health and ratings of experimental and control groups

| Physical health | Experimental group (n = 92) (%) | Control group (n = 97) (%) |
|---|---|---|
| Good | 57.6 | 54.6 |
| Minor ill-health only | 31.5 | 33.0 |
| Moderate or severe ill-health | 10.9 | 12.4 |
| Total | 100.0 | 100.0 |

The clinical psychiatric ratings made at interview likewise suggest a close similarity between the groups. The point is illustrated in Fig. 1 by means of profiles of the mean item scores.

This correspondence between the groups extends less closely to the distribution of *I.C.D.* diagnoses. The distribution of diagnoses at follow-up (more reliable than the initial diagnoses, because based on more information) is set out in Table 3.

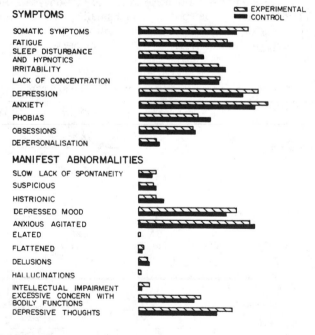

Fig. 1    Initial mean psychiatric scores.

TABLE 3
Diagnostic distribution of experimental and control groups at follow-up

| Diagnosis | Experimental group (n = 92) (%) | Control group (n = 97) (%) |
|---|---|---|
| Neurosis | | |
|   Anxiety | 21.8 | 29.9 |
|   Depressive | 53.3 | 45.4 |
|   Other | 10.8 | 4.1 |
| Personality disorder | 5.4 | 6.2 |
| Endogenous depression | 2.2 | 11.3 |
| Other | 6.5 | 3.1 |
|   Total | 100.0 | 100.0 |

These findings are of doubtful significance because of the unreliability of diagnosis, especially for affective disorders. Analysis of the data for individual psychiatrists[1] showed disparities unlikely to have been due to real differences among the patients; examination of the clinical profiles confirmed that the differences lay in the psychiatrists' diagnosis rather than in the patients' symptoms. Nevertheless, the possibility of a bias in outcome due to diagnostic differences had to be considered.

*Treatment Provided during Follow-up Period*   Comparison between the groups was based, not on the simple model:

Experimental service vs. no treatment

but on the more complex model:

Experimental service + existing services
vs.
existing services alone

Patients in both groups received medication from their own doctors as usual and could be referred to specialist agencies in the normal way. In the event, only 5.4% of the experimental patients were referred to psychiatric services during the year, compared with 15.5% of the control patients. Similarly, only 30.0% of experimental patients were in touch with any outside social agency as against 40.0% of the controls.

These findings suggest that patients and practitioners alike came to rely on the experimental service as a partial alternative to specialist agencies. Any bias due to outside treatment would thus have tended to work against, rather than in favour of, the experimental hypothesis.

Comparison of general practitioner treatment for the two groups was confined to their prescribing of psychotropic drugs. Data summarized in Table 4 indicated that the experimental group had received less medication

1 Because of a change in the research team, three psychiatrists took part in the clinical interviewing and rating.

TABLE 4

Mean duration of prescribing of psychotropic drugs by general practitioners
during follow-up year

| Psychotropic drug | Experimental group (n = 92) (months) | Control group (n = 97) (months) |
|---|---|---|
| Sedatives and minor transquilizers | 6.8 | 8.0 |
| Antidepressants | 3.5 | 4.9 |
| Major tranquillizers (neutroleptics) | 0.5 | 1.5 |
| All psychotropic drugs | 7.5 | 9.0 |

of this kind than the control group. Clearly, the accuracy of these findings
depended on the doctors' consistency in recording prescriptions.

The medical records provided no reliable guide to the frequency with
which psychotherapy, counselling, or simple explanation and reassurance
had been provided by individual doctors. Since none of those taking part in
the study was specially interested in psychotherapy or had had postgraduate
psychiatric training, it seems improbable that such factors could have biased
the findings.

## Change in Clinical and Social Status

The overall changes in psychiatric state and social adjustment during the
follow-up period are indicated in Table 5. It shows that, while the initial

TABLE 5

Change in psychiatric and social adjustment ratings in follow-up year:
experimental and control groups

| | Experimental group (n = 92) | Control group (n = 97) | Test of significance |
|---|---|---|---|
| Psychiatric mean score: | | | |
| Initially | 26.9 | 26.1 | |
| At follow-up | 16.6 | 19.7 | |
| Change in score: | | | |
| Mean | −10.3 | −6.4 | t = 2.68 |
| SD | 10.2 | 9.9 | P < 0.01 |
| Social adjustment mean score: | | | |
| Initially | 15.4 | 15.3 | |
| At follow-up | 12.1 | 15.1 | |
| Change in score: | | | |
| Mean | −3.3 | −0.2 | t = 4.79 |
| SD | 5.0 | 3.7 | P < 0.001 |

It shows that, while the initial clinical and social scores of the two groups
were closely similar, those of the experimental group fell significantly more
during the follow-up year. Clinical scores dropped for patients in both

groups, though less markedly for the controls. Social scores fell appreciably only for the experimental group, control patients showing little apparent change in social adaptation during the year.

Change in the mean psychiatric scores correspond to change in the patients' clinical condition. At follow-up, 38.0% of the experimental group had been taken off psychotropic drugs, as against only 24.7% of the controls ($\chi^2$ = 4.53; d.f. = 1; P < 0.05). Similarly, 59.8% of the experimental group were still judged to need medical care and supervision, compared with 77.3% of controls ($\chi^2$ = 7.60; d.f. = 1; P < 0.01).

When the social scores were examined more closely, the experimental patients were found to have improved more than the controls in all main areas of social functioning. The point is illustrated by Table 6, which shows the distribution of scores for material conditions, social management, and social role-satisfaction.

TABLE 6
Change of ratings for three principal aspects of social adjustment:
experimental and control groups

|  | *Experimental group* *(n = 92)* | *Control group* *(n = 97)* | *Test of significance* |
|---|---|---|---|
| Material conditions mean score: |  |  |  |
| Initially | 4.5 | 5.0 |  |
| At follow-up | 4.1 | 5.1 |  |
| Change in score: |  |  |  |
| Mean | −0.4 | +0.1 | *t* = 1.97 |
| SD | 1.5 | 1.8 | P < 0.05 |
| Social management mean score: |  |  |  |
| Initially | 5.9 | 5.5 |  |
| At follow-up | 4.5 | 5.5 |  |
| Change in score: |  |  |  |
| Mean | −1.4 | 0.0 | *t* = 4.71 |
| SD | 2.1 | 1.9 | P < 0.001 |
| Social role-satisfaction mean score: |  |  |  |
| Initially | 5.0 | 4.7 |  |
| At follow-up | 3.5 | 4.4 |  |
| Change in score: |  |  |  |
| Mean | −1.5 | −0.3 | *t* = 3.42 |
| SD | 2.8 | 2.3 | P < 0.01 |

Changes in the various mean scores were found to be intercorrelated. The association between psychiatric mean score and overall social score is demonstrated for the experimental group in Fig. 2, in which the relative change for each patient has been plotted in the form of a scatter-diagram. The visual impression that psychiatric score tended to fall with social score was confirmed by product-moment correlation ($r$ = +0.36).

The changes of score on three principal aspects of social adjustment, summarized in Table 6, were also intercorrelated — that is to say, patients who showed the greatest improvement in ratings of material condition

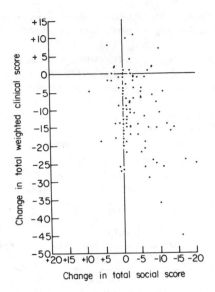

**Fig. 2**    Relationship between change in total clinical and social scores-experimental group.

tended to improve most on the social management and role-satisfaction ratings.[2]

### Relation of Outcome to Demographic and Clinical Factors

Because the two groups were imperfectly matched, it was necessary to examine for any possible effect of their differing composition on their relative outcome, as measured by change in clinical and social ratings. When this was done, small differences of outcome were found in relation to age-group, marital status, social class, and psychiatric diagnosis, though in all instances the trend towards greater improvement for the experimental group was maintained.[3] Standardizations of the two groups for each in turn

2  For the experimental group, product–moment correlations were as follows:
material conditions and social management, $r = +0.16$
material conditions and role-satisfaction,  $r = +0.24$
social management and role-satisfaction,  $r = +0.57$

3  The difference between the standardized means was calculated as follows:

$$\bar{X}_1 - \bar{X}_2 = \epsilon w_j(\bar{x}_{1j} - \bar{x}_{2j})$$

where $w_j = \dfrac{t_j}{\epsilon t_j}$

and    $t_j = \dfrac{n_{1j}n_{2j}}{n_{1j}+n_{2j}}$

$n_{1j}$ = number of observations in the jth group of the experimental group.
$n_{2j}$ = number of observations in the jth group of the control group.
$w_j$ are the standardized weights.
$\bar{X}_1 - \bar{X}_2$ is the difference the standardized means.

of these related variables had no effect on either the direction or the significance level of the differences in outcome.

With the small numbers involved, a detailed analysis of the relation between outcome and different types or intensities of treatment within the experimental group was not feasible. One simple way of dividing the sample was in relation to the professional workers most concerned with each patient's care. Of the 92 patients in the experimental group 52.2% had been dealt with mainly by the social worker; 14.1% by the social worker and psychiatrist together; 16.3% mainly by the psychiatrists; and 17.4% were referred back to the general practitioner with recommendations, the latter group usually because the patient did not want any more specific help. The mean ratings of change for these groups were as shown in Table 7.

TABLE 7

Change of psychiatric and social adjustment ratings for experimental group by professional workers involved

| *Rater* | *Change in psychiatric score* | *Change in overall social score* |
|---|---|---|
| Social worker alone | −10.9 | −3.5 |
| Psychiatrist alone | − 9.7 | −4.1 |
| Social worker and psychiatrist | −12.5 | −1.8 |
| GP (with or without health visitor) | − 7.1 | −2.8 |
| All cases | −10.3 | −3.3 |

It seems, therefore, that even those patients who were referred back to the general practitioner after only one or two initial contacts fared better on the whole than the patients in the control group. This finding suggests that the therapeutic effect of the experimental service was not confined to the work of any single member of the team but was to some extent the result of a group interaction.

## Discussion

There have been very few controlled attempts to evaluate medicosocial intervention in the community and none to have demonstrated benefit, however small, to so notoriously resistant a group of patients as those suffering from chronic neurotic disorders [Segal, 1972; Fischer, 1973; Goldberg, 1973]. For these reasons alone the results of this investigation carry some general implications which extend beyond the findings themselves, limited as they are by the length of follow-up. Perhaps the most significant conclusion is the demonstration that evaluative research in the mental health field can be carried out in an extramural setting. Despite the many practical difficulties encountered, it is essential to establish the feasibility of such work if the functioning of health services is to be monitored effectively.

To obtain definitive results, it will be necessary to mount trials based on the principles of random sampling or, failing that, on individually matched groups. At present the climate of opinion militates against the prosecution of randomized, controlled trials in this sphere but clearly they must be mounted in due course. Meanwhile, from the standpoint of medical administration Matthew has commented aptly:

> Controlled trials of medical treatments with random allocation of subjects to experimental and control groups were accepted into clinical research at about the same time as the NHS was launched. There is now extensive experience of their use ... Although the dangers of departing from the scientific rigour of these methods has often been demonstrated, it seems fully justifiable to explore their use in the many practical situations where trials cannot be carried out blind and other imperfections may have to be accepted, provided that the results are interpreted with great care [Matthew, 1971].

This study has touched marginally on the question of the psychiatrist's contribution to the primary care team. With the spread of health centres and large group practices, there is bound to be a growing participation in primary health care by both psychiatrists and psychiatric nurses. There are strong arguments in favour of such a development, in which the primary care team would come to be regarded more and more as the keystone of community psychiatry [WHO, 1973]. It must be recognized, however, that there are many siren voices trying to lure psychiatrists into a multiplicity of service commitments, sometimes at the danger of neglecting the most seriously ill patients. What is most urgently needed is a determined effort to evaluate the role of the psychiatrist in a number of different professional environments, so as to make maximum use of his specialized knowledge within the limits of the available manpower resources.

### Acknowledgements

This study formed part of a programme of research into problems of community health care, supported by the Department of Health and Social Security, and by one of us (B.C.) by the Mental Health Research Fund. We are grateful to the former Medical Officer of Health for Croydon, Dr S. L. Wright, for his support of the project and to the Director of Social Services for Croydon, Mr H. N. Grindrod, who subsequently continued this support. Part of the work of interviewing was carried out by Mrs R. Fitzgerald, Dr M. R. Eastwood and Mrs V. Howard. We are greatly indebted to Mr F. Gattoni for help and advice with the statistical analysis and to the following general practitioners for their cooperation: Drs J. B. and June Armstrong, P. Boffa, J. Booth, G. Clementson, W. Dolman, T. Duffy, J. Fletcher, C. Gifford, S. Hamilton, M. Rapoport, S. Rowell, and B. Todd.

### References

Collins, J. (1965). "Social Casework in a General Medical Practice". Pitman, London.
Cooper, B. (1972a). Clinical and social aspects of chronic neurosis. *Proceedings of the Royal Society of Medicine* **65**, 509–512.

Cooper, B. (1972b). Social correlates of psychiatric illness in the community. *In* "Approaches to Action" (Ed. G. McLachlan), pp. 65–70. Oxford University Press for Nuffield Provincial Hospital Trust, London.

Fischer, J. (1973). Is casework effective? a review. *Social Work* 1, 5–20.

Forman, J. A. S. and Fairbairn, E. M. (1968). "Social Casework in General Practice". Oxford University Press, London.

Goldberg, E. M. (1973). Service for the family. *In* "Roots of Evaluation" (Eds J. K. Wing and H. Häfner), pp. 281–296. Oxford University Press for the Nuffield Provincial Hospitals Trust, London.

Goldberg, D. P. and Blackwell, B. (1970). Psychiatric illness in general practice. A detailed study using a new method of case identification. *British Medical Journal* 2, 439–443.

Goldberg, D. P., Cooper, B., Eastwood, M. R., Kedward, H. B. and Shepherd, M. (1970). A standardized psychiatric interview for use in community surveys. *British Journal of Preventive and Social Medicine* 24, 18–23.

Goldberg, E. M. and Neill, J. E. (1973). "Social Work in General Practice". Allen and Unwin, London.

Kaeser, A. C. and Cooper, B. (1971). The psychiatric patient, the general practitioner, and the outpatient clinic: an operational study and a review. *Psychological Medicine* 1, 312–325.

Matthew, G. K. (1971). Measuring need and evaluating services. *In* "Portfolio for Health (Ed. G. McLachlan), p. 27. Oxford University Press, London.

Segal, S. P. (1972). Research on the outcome of social work therapeutic interventions: a review of the literature. *Journal of Health and Social Behavior* 13, 3–17.

Shepherd, M., Cooper, B., Brown, A. C. and Kalton, G. W. (1966). "Psychiatric Illness in General Practice". Oxford University Press, London.

Watts, C. A. H., Cawte, E. C. and Kuenssberg, E. V. (1964). Survey of mental illness in general practice. *British Medical Journal* 2, 1351–1359.

World Health Organization (1967 and 1969). Injuries and causes of death. *In* "Manual of the International Statistical Classification of Diseases". 8th revision vol. 2. World Health Organization, Geneva.

World Health Organization (1973). "Psychiatry and Primary Medical Care". World Health Organization, Regional Office for Europe, Copenhagen.

# SOCIAL WORK AND THE PRIMARY CARE OF MENTAL DISORDER

MICHAEL SHEPHERD, B. G. HARWIN, C. DEPLA and VICTORIA CAIRNS

## Synopsis

An account is given of the role of an attached social worker to a primary care team in the management of chronic neurotic illness in the community. The medico-social implications of the findings are discussed.

## Introduction

A previous communication has reported the method and principal findings of a study designed to evaluate the therapeutic role of a social worker attached to a metropolitan general practice in the management of chronic neurotic illness (Cooper *et al.*, 1975]. The psychiatric and social status of 2 matched groups of patients, one attending the practice with a social worker attachment and the other attending neighbouring practices without this facility, were ascertained independently at the beginning and end of a 12-month period, using standardized interview techniques. A comparison between the outcome of the groups indicated some benefit to patients who had received the experimental service. Although both groups showed a reduction in psychiatric symptoms during the follow-up year, the fall was much more pronounced in the experimental group. At follow-up, 38.0% of the experimental group had been taken off psychotropic drugs, compared with 24.7% of the controls. Continuing medical care and supervision were deemed necessary for 59.8% of the experimental patients, compared with 77.3% of the controls. Similarly, the experimental patients were found to have improved in all main areas of social functioning, whereas the controls showed very little change in this respect at the end of 12 months. Changes in the psychiatric and social-adjustment scores for the 2 groups were positively correlated.

These findings suggested that social worker intervention has a therapeutic effect on chronic neurotic illness, at least in some cases, and hence that it is realistic in this context to speak of social treatment. Such a general conclusion, however, provides insufficient guidance for the planning and development of effective treatment services. Much more information is

Reprinted, with permission, from *Psychological Medicine* 9, 661–669, 1979.

required as to the types of neurotic disorder which respond to this form of
sociotherapy, the precise nature of the intervention made by the social
worker, and the extent to which it depends on the special skills of this
professional group, as distinct from those shared with psychiatrists, general
practitioners, health visitors and other professionals. The purpose of this
paper is to explore these issues in more detail, with particular reference to
the role of social work.

### Method and Material

The design of the experimental study has been described in the earlier
report. The social worker (C.D.) was attached to a metropolitan group
practice with 4 principals, several paramedical workers and a list-population
of about 13 000. Patients were selected for the study (*a*) from among those
referred to the experimental service by the practice doctors and health
visitors (in all, some 300 patients were referred in the first 18 months);
(*b*) by means of a systematic screening of the clinical notes for consulting
patients. To qualify for inclusion, patients had to meet the criteria for
"chronic neurosis". Chronicity was defined operationally as persistence of
psychiatric symptoms, and/or continued prescribing of psychotropic medication, for at least 12 months prior to interview. Neurotic illness was taken to
include all conditions listed in categories 300–309 of the International
Classification of Diseases, 8th Revision [WHO, 1967]. Cases of depressive
illness without definite psychotic symptoms were included under this
definition.

The initial clinical and social assessments were made independently of one
another, by means of interviews carried out by psychiatrists and social
research workers, respectively. Patients meeting the operational criteria were
discussed individually, in the course of regular fortnightly meetings held in
the practice. Those thought suitable for social work were then referred
accordingly to the practice social worker, who made contact with each
patient either at his next attendance or by means of a home visit.[1] Patients
deemed unsuitable for this form of intervention were retained in the
experimental group and followed up for one year, in the same way as those
who received social worker support.

Evaluation of a medical or social service facility is intrinsically more
complex than that of a specific therapy, since the units of "treatment"
cannot be quantified in the same way, and the services offered by different
treatment centres cannot be safely compared with one another. As a first
step towards overcoming this major difficulty, we grouped the services
received by patients in the experimental group on 3 axes:

(1) According to professional workers and services involved (social worker,
    general practitioner, psychiatrist, etc.);
(2) According to the content of social worker intervention, categorized in
    3 broad subgroups:

1 Examples of case-material are provided in the Appendix.

(*a*) "Practical" functions (assistance with financial, housing, legal and other problems); (*b*) "Casework" functions (encouragement, counselling, and discussion of emotional problems); (*c*) a combination of these 2 functions;
(3) According to the frequency and pattern of social worker contacts, categorized in 3 broad subgroups: (*a*) short-term; (*b*) episodic; (*c*) continuous throughout follow-up year.

At the end of one year, clinical and social reassessments were made, using the same techniques as for the initial assessments. The social worker took no part in these assessments. She did, however, keep detailed records of all contacts made with patients and relatives, including telephone calls, as well as of all contacts with medical and social services, courts, housing authorities, schools, etc., made on behalf of her clients.

## Results

Complete information, including psychiatric and social reassessment at follow-up, was obtained for 92 patients in the experimental group (representing 86.8% of all those included). The group was characterized by an excess of females (73.9%), of married persons (65.2%) and of persons in the Registrar General's social class III (66.3%). The latter features reflected the composition of the patient-population, but the proportion of female patients in the experimental group greatly exceeded that among consulting patients as a whole. Unexpectedly, the proportion of elderly patients was relatively small: the mean age of the group was 42.1 years, and only 10 patients were over 60.

### Professional Care within the Experimental Service

Table 1 summarizes the professional contacts made with this patient sample during the course of the experiment. It appears that the social worker, alone or together with a psychiatrist, was involved in the care and management of two-thirds of the patients.

In view of the nature of the conditions in which the study was conducted, it becomes manifestly important to know something about this four-fold allocation of the patients. The decision to refer a patient to the social worker

TABLE 1
Professional contacts made with patient sample

| Patients seen by | No. patients | % |
|---|---|---|
| GP + social worker | 48 | 52.2 |
| GP + social worker + unit psychiatrist | 13 | 14.1 |
| GP + unit psychiatrist | 16 | 17.4 |
| GP only | 15 | 16.3 |
| Total | 92 | 100.0 |

did not exclude continued care by the general practitioner; it did, however, rule out referral to hospital care or to the unit psychiatrist and it implied acceptance of the recommendation by the patient. The social worker was therefore charged with the management of about two-thirds of the patients, working alone with three-quarters of them and jointly with the research psychiatrist with the remainder. In only a minority of cases, however, did the psychiatrist undertake treatment with the collaboration of the social worker; in the remainder his role was limited to a further interview for the purpose of reassessment. Of the 14 patients who were referred to hospital for psychiatric treatment, only 3 required admission.

Of the 16 patients seen by the research psychiatrist alone, 7 refused to see the social worker, preferring to remain under medical care. In another 3 cases the problem was not regarded as amenable to social intervention, and in a further 6 cases the condition had remitted before referral to the social worker could be undertaken. In no more than 8 cases, it may be noted, was formal treatment undertaken by the unit psychiatrist or, on his recommendation, by a hospital psychiatric department.

Most of the patients (12 out of 15) who saw neither the social worker nor the research psychiatrist during the follow-up period were regarded as suitable for continued supervision by their general practitioners. Two were under the care of the practice health visitor and one was referred by the practitioner to a psychiatric outpatient department.

### Selection for Social Worker Referral

A systematic attempt was made to identify clinical and social features associated with the decision to refer to the social worker. For this purpose, a number of comparisons involving demographic, psychiatric and social variables were made between the 61 patients given social worker help (Group A) and the 31 who received no such help (Group B). In the event, only two significant differences could be established. First, Group A contained a much smaller proportion of married patients than Group B: 52.5% as against 90.3%. This difference could not be explained by the relative age-distributions. Of 29 unmarried patients in Group A, 16 were single, 7 widowed and 6 "other" or divorced.

Secondly, the Group A patients had been assessed at the initial psychiatric interview as more severely disturbed on average than the Group B patients: 52.4% of the former group, compared with only 25.8% of the latter, were rated as having severe or moderately severe psychiatric disturbances.

The initial social assessment was carried out by means of a social-interview schedule which is designed to tap information in 3 broad areas of social adjustment: namely, material living conditions, social competence and social role-satisfaction [Clare and Cairns, 1978]. Comparison on all items of the social schedule revealed no significant differences between Groups A and B apart from a relative excess of *mild* marital difficulties in Group B. The proportion of severe marital problems was closely similar for the 2 groups (Table 2).

In summary, it appeared that those patients referred to the social worker

TABLE 2
Marital adjustment

| Score for marital adjustment (married subjects only) | All patients referred to social worker (Group A) | | Patients not referred to social worker (Group B) | |
|---|---|---|---|---|
| | *No.* | *%* | *No.* | *%* |
| 0 (good) | 4 | 12.5 | 14 | 50.0 |
| 1 (mild problem) | 15 | 46.9 | 3 | 10.7 |
| 2 (moderate problem) | 8 | 25.0 | 7 | 25.0 |
| 3 (severe problem) | 5 | 15.6 | 4 | 14.3 |
| Total | 32 | 100.0 | 28 | 100.0 |

$P < 0.01$

had, in general, more severe psychiatric disturbances than the experimental group as a whole and, to that extent, could not be regarded as presenting purely social of "psycho-social" problems.

## The Activities of the Social Worker

During the 12 months covered by the study the mean number of personal contacts made by the social worker with the patient population was 6.6; with relatives and household members it was 1.6, and with friends 0.6. Her mean number of telephone contacts with patients was 2.1, with friends and household members 0.2.

Table 3 summarizes the work carried out by the social worker in relation to other agencies. Contacts with other agencies were made in no more than

TABLE 3
Number of other agencies contacted through social workers

| No. services | No. patients and type of service | | | | | | | |
|---|---|---|---|---|---|---|---|---|
| | Medical services | | Social services | | Voluntary services | | Other | |
| | *No.* | *%* | *No.* | *%* | *No.* | *%* | *No.* | *%* |
| None | 43 | 70.5 | 46 | 75.4 | 49 | 80.3 | 43 | 70.5 |
| 1 service | 12 | 19.7 | 11 | 18.0 | 12 | 19.7 | 11 | 18.0 |
| 2 services | 4 | 6.6 | 4 | 6.6 | 0 | 0.0 | 5 | 8.2 |
| 3 services | 2 | 3.3 | 0 | 0.0 | 0 | 0.0 | 2 | 3.3 |
| Total | 61 | 100.0 | 61 | 100.0 | 61 | 100.0 | 61 | 100.0 |

about one third of all the cases. Tables 4 and 5 show the work-pattern and the measures taken by the social worker.

In nearly two-thirds of this sample the social worker's contribution was restricted to helping the patient and his or her family in dealing with practical problems and difficulties, a function for which social workers are

TABLE 4
Work-pattern of social worker

| Work pattern | Cases | | Mean no. of social work contacts |
| | No. | % | |
|---|---|---|---|
| Short term | 20 | 33.9 | 2.7 |
| Episodic | 14 | 23.7 | 3.2 |
| Continuous | 25 | 42.4 | 12.1 |
| Not known | 2 | – | – |
| Total | 61 | 100.0 | |

TABLE 5
Measures taken by social worker

| Measures taken | Cases | | Mean no. of social work contacts |
| | No. | % | |
|---|---|---|---|
| Practical work | 38 | 63.3 | 5.6 |
| Case work | 14 | 23.3 | 6.8 |
| Practical and case work | 8 | 13.3 | 11.8 |
| Not known | 1 | – | – |
| Total | 61 | 100.0 | |

TABLE 6
Pattern of social work contacts

| Initial mean area score on social activities* | Single | Intermittent | Continuous |
|---|---|---|---|
| 3–10 | 13 | 8 | 4 |
| 13–27 | 7 | 6 | 21 |
| | | | P < 0.01 |

* The overall scores in the subsections were found by summing the scores found on those individual items making up the subsection. A higher score indicates a larger number of problems in that subsection.

TABLE 7
Social work action taken

| Initial overall mean satisfaction score* | Practical | Casework | Casework + practical |
|---|---|---|---|
| 2–10 | 25 | 11 | 2 |
| 12–30 | 13 | 3 | 6 |
| | | | P < 0.05 |

* See note to Table 6.

specially trained and in which their skill do not overlap to any large extent with those of the psychiatrist. In the remaining one-third she exercised what may be regarded as a quasi-psychotherapeutic function, though here also practical help and support were given in a proportion of cases.

Table 6 shows that the social worker worked for longer on those patients with more problems in the area of social activities. Within no other social area or domain was there a significant change in the length of time she spent on the clients.

The social worker did more casework with those patients who expressed themselves as more satisfied, as shown in Table 7. Within no other social area or domain was there a significant change in the action taken.

The attitude of patients to the social worker was recorded by her as "cooperative in three-quarters of the cases; fewer than 10% were deemed "uncooperative", the remaining fifth being characterized as "accepting"?

## Clinical and Social Outcome in Relation to Social Work

Clinical outcome, graded on a 4-point scale as "recovered", "improved", "no change" or "worse", proved to be unrelated to the social worker's activities, to the number of her contacts with patients and other significant figures, or to the patient's expressed attitude to intervention. There was, however, an association between "improvement" and "short-term" intervention, reflecting the lesser degree of clinical severity among these patients (Table 8).

TABLE 8
Nature of social work contacts

| Clinical outcome | Short-term | Episodic | Continuous |
|---|---|---|---|
| Recovered | 6 | 4 | 4 |
| Improved | 13 | 3 | 6 |
| No change or worse | 1 | 7 | 15 |
| | | $P < 0.01$ | |

There was no association between changes in the overall social score and the action taken by the social worker, nor between these changes and the nature of her contacts. There was also no significant difference between the changes in social score for those who saw and those who did not see the social worker, as shown in Table 9.

## Discussion

The data emerging from this study lead to a number of conclusions:

(1) The underlying premise that the clinical concept of chronic neurotic illness includes a significant social component was supported by the assessment that social worker intervention was appropriate in two-thirds of cases so diagnosed. In a small proportion of the remainder the social

TABLE 9
Number of patients

| Change in social score | Group A | | Group B | |
|---|---|---|---|---|
| | No. | % | No. | % |
| −20 to −6 | 18 | 29.5 | 8 | 25.8 |
| −5 to −1 | 23 | 37.7 | 13 | 41.9 |
| No change | 7 | 11.4 | 8 | 25.8 |
| Worse | 13 | 21.3 | 2 | 6.4 |
| Total | 61 | 100.0 | 31 | 100.0 |

worker's services were not invoked because of the continued involvement of the psychiatrist, either at his suggestion or at the request of the patient. For the most part, however, the reason for non-involvement of the social worker was either an unexpected remission or a refusal to accept the social worker or the assessment team's decision that the general practitioner was able to provide all the service required.

(2) In respect of their demographic, socio-economic and clinical character-istics, the only significant differences between the patients who were and were not referred to the social worker were that the former group (a) contained many more "not married" individuals, (b) was rated clinically as more severely disturbed and (c) enjoyed a less satisfactory marital adjustment.

(3) The detailed analysis of outcome in relation to both initial medico-social status and the subsequent social and medical action taken revealed no clear-cut differences and no overall trends except for (a) a better prognosis enjoyed by patients with only a single episode of illness and (b) an overall improvement in rated marital adjustment.

(4) An analysis of the social worker's workload shows that more than two-thirds of her time was devoted to "practical activities". "Casework" alone accounted for no more than a quarter of her time and was employed in fewer than half the cases with whom continuous contact was maintained. The nature and quantity of her activities were seemingly unrelated to outcome.

At first sight such findings appear to provide disappointing support for the original attribution of the more favourable outcome of these 92 patients compared with their controls to social worker intervention. The relatively small differences of outcome between the 2 subgroups in this study, however, must take account of the greater degree of clinical disturbance exhibited by the patients referred to the social worker. Further, about half these patients were unmarried and the marital relationship was the one sphere in which clear-cut improvement was associated with social intervention. It would seem, therefore, important, in view of the relatively small-scale nature of the investigation, to place the results in wider perspective if their implications are to be explored.

A much-quoted paragraph from the influential Report of the Committee on Local Authority and Allied Personal Social Services [the Seebohm Report, 1968] reads as follows:

> We regard teamwork between general practitioners and the social services as vital. It is one of our main objectives and the likelihood of promoting it is a test we would like to see applied to our proposals for a social service department. During the next decade there will be a thousand health centres and group practices that could provide a proper base for joint working, and we wish we could recommend the attachment of a social worker to each of these.

Ten years later we are confronted with a partial realization of this objective. Though the precise number of attachment-schemes is impossible to ascertain, it probably now runs into many hundreds whose nature and quality differ widely. A small number of these projects have been conducted within a research framework, at least to the extent of recording descriptive statistics [Goldberg and Neill, 1972], but the great majority are empirical endeavours, and it is difficult to quarrel with the conclusion reached by Hicks in his searching survey of the field:

> Those who have direct experience of collaborating with social workers in general practice are generally enthusiastic about the place of casework social workers in the primary team. But we need to be careful not to be carried away by an ideology based on impressions. Careful evaluation of what the social worker does, and the resulting benefits, are essential ... Models of social care need to be regorously scrutinised and evaluated. [Hicks, 1976]

Though the literature on the nature of the social worker's function and activities is large and confusing, there is general agreement on the high proportion of emotional problems in social work, and the controversial issue of "casework" points to the part played by psychotherapeutic concepts in social work theory and practice [Prins and Whyte, 1972]. However, despite these close links with mental disorder and the acknowledged place of the specialist psychiatric social worker in the management of the mentally sick patients in hospital, there has been very little descriptive or evaluative work on the social worker's role in relation to the extra-mural burden of mental illness. To undertake this task with any semblance of conviction it is necessary to meet at least two criteria: namely, a reasonably homogeneous patient-population and a mode of evaluation based on independent assessment.

Both these criteria were met in the present investigation which, despite the small numbers involved, sheds some light on the management of the notoriously intractable group of chronic neuroses. It must, of course, be emphasized that the naturalistic conditions of the experiment were inevitably modified to some extent by the research setting in which it was conducted and, in particular, by the collaboration of the two psychiatrists who were available for not only assessment but also intervention if required. To some extent a degree of distortion is introduced by such a procedure, but this is attendant on any community study of this type and here even facilitated the yield of further information. In particular, the presence of the psychiatrists made it possible to observe the degree of overlap between themselves and the social worker: in 6 cases they worked closely together and in a further 3 cases the psychiatrist undertook a supporting role which could equally have been allocated to the social worker if the initial contact had been with her. It is also relevant that 16% of the cases expressed a disinclination to see the social worker and opted for either the psychiatrist or the general practitioner.

Finally, and not least in importance, there is the fact that for this unequivocally psychiatric population much the greater part of the social worker's time was devoted to practical tasks, coordinating services and disseminating information. The tendency to equate the work-load of the social worker with that of the social caseworker is widespread, even though though the evidence for the theory and practice of social casework remains dubious [Fischer, 1973]. By contrast, it is the various forms of "environmental" treatment [Hollis, 1972] and what has been termed social "brokerage" [Baker, 1976] rather than "casework" in the strict sense, which loom largest. The same trend can be detected in other studies which have analysed the activities to the social worker in general practice [Collins, 1965; Forman and Fairbairn, 1968; Ratoff and Pearson, 1970; Cooper, 1971; Goldberg and Neill, 1972]. The precise nature and specificity of social work roles clearly calls for enquiry.

From the overall results of this experiment it is not possible to pin-point the factors associated with the benefits of social worker attachment to the management of chronic neurosis in the community. The differences between Groups A and B preclude the assumption that because Group B was denied the attentions of the social worker it can be regarded as a smaller, more intensively studied microcosm of the original control group. Nor does a direct evaluation of the social worker's activities in relation to outcome establish any specific therapeutic associations. On the available evidence the likeliest explanation would appear to be that the social worker's personal activities supplement the resources which she mobilizes and facilitate a more positive approach by the general practitioner towards the social orbit of morbidity. Stimson [1977] has pointed out that the global notion of the social element in general practice embraces several themes: the social relationships between doctors and their patients; the awareness of social factors in disease and in illness-behaviour; the social causes of disease; the social consequences of diseases; social welfare problems; and the socio-psycho-therapeutic role of the doctor. The presence of a social worker as part of a primary care team may be expected to catalyse all these activities and so diffuse his or her influence at various points of professional contact. How far this function can be related to the professionalization of social work as it is currently taught remains uncertain, but the evidence suggests that some such role is necessary for the rational management of chronic mental ill-health at the level of primary care.

### Acknowledgements

This study formed part of programme of research supported by the Department of Health and Social Security. We acknowledge gratefully the help provided in various ways by Professor A. B. Cooper, Miss D. Rockett, Mr

H. N. Grindrod, Mrs R. Fitzgerald, Mrs V. Howard, Dr B. Armstrong, Dr J. Armstrong, Dr J. Booth, Dr T. Duffy, Dr A. Rapoport and Dr M. Rapoport.

## Appendix: Sample Case-Histories

### 1. Example of the social management of a psychiatric case

Mr B. was included in the survey because he was thought by his doctor to be depressed. He was not a frequent surgery attender and had never consulted with psychological symptom, but was known to be an odd, shy man and to have a good deal of unhappiness in his personal life.

A bachelor of 50, he lived with his widowed mother who was still suffering from the after-effects of a severe psychiatric illness. He received a certain amount of support from his two sisters, but the responsibility of caring for his mother rested on him. Although he did not blame his mother for his situation, insisting that the cause was in himself, the fact remained that he was living a very restricted life; he had no regular interests or hobbies, no close friends or relationships with the opposite sex.

At interview he presented as a diffident, rather gauche individual with a highly obsessional outlook. He was only mildly depressed, but exhibited a good deal of tension and anxiety. He was troubled by his solitary existence and celibate habits; he realized that he had come to the time of life when "if anything is going to be done, it has got to be done now", but felt powerless to do anything to alter his situation for himself.

Accordingly, the social worker tried to help him to widen his social life. In a series of interviews he was encouraged, first, to plan a holiday, and then to join a social club. The patient became very enthusiastic about the club, attended regularly, and succeeded in overcoming to a certain extent his natural diffidence, even with regard to the female members. Unfortunately, at this point his mother had an accident and was taken to hospital. With the strain of constant visiting he attended the club less regularly and, when his mother returned home, now quite disabled, his increased domestic responsibilities worsened the situation. Interviews then concentrated on trying to overcome his reluctance to seek more help in his home, both from his family and from social agencies.

In spite of this set-back, a definite improvement was seen in the patient when he was interviewed a year later. He was no longer on drugs and his morbid anxiety had remitted.

### 2. Example of the Social Management of Marital Disorder

Mrs G., a smart, rather forbidding woman of 40, was first seen because, when consulting her doctor for a mild physical ailment, she confessed to being worried and depressed about a marital problem. She had always enjoyed good physical health, but had been diagnosed as suffering from an anxiety state about 13 years previously, at the time of the break-up of her first marriage. She was now living with her second husband, their 3-year-old daughter and the 18-year-old daughter of her first marriage, whose relations with her stepfather were very good. After a lapse of 4 years she was just resuming work, where she was able to command a considerable salary. Her attitude to her second husband seemed largely governed by resentment of the fact that he had, she felt, very little affection for her, and valued her only for her earning capacity and her efficiency as a housewife.

It also transpired at interview that she suffered from long-standing phobic anxiety, particularly with regard to travelling. The husband, when seen, confirmed this phobia, and also agreed that she suffered from periodic bouts of depression and emotional disturbance. He maintained that he was willing to do anything to help her, but his assurances did not ring entirely true. The couple had consulted the local Marriage Guidance Counsellor.

The patient was relieved to talk about her problems with the social worker. She disclosed her resentment towards her husband and also complained of the lack of communication between them. The situation was worsened when the patient discovered that there had been infidelity on her husband's part. There followed many "talking out" sessions, with the patient ventilating her grievances and the social worker endeavouring to assist her to come to terms with her situation and make decisions for the future. The patient's condition, meanwhile, improved and worsened according to changes in the family atmosphere.

When the patient was seen again about a year later, there was little basic change in her general condition. It was noted, however, that she set great store by her contacts with the social worker, especially as she seemed to have no close friend or relative in whom she could confide.

## 3. Example of the Medico-Social Management of a Psychiatric Illness

Mr H., aged 49, had been consulting his doctor with a strained back, following an injury at work. During the previous 12 months he had had about 80 days off work with pains in his back, often associated with depression and irritability. The GP had treated him with tranquillizers and anti-depressant drugs, and eventually referred him to hospital. There was no previous history of psychiatric illness.

Prior to this episode, Mr H. had been a carefree and somewhat irresponsible individual. His marriage, although presenting some underlying difficulties, had been superficially adjusted. He had now become irritable with his wife, and she had become exasperated with his depression. Their social life, always limited by the fact that both partners worked on shifts, had become virtually non-existent.

At interview it became evident that the patient's depression centred on his dissatisfaction and anxiety concerning his work. Before his injury he had been transferred to a new location, where he felt he had a less desirable position. Added to this, the transfer had heightened his fear of redundancy and subsequent loss of pension rights. He had seriously considered changing his job, but this, again, would involve loss of pension rights, and the difficulty of making a decision had increased his anxiety and worry.

The patient was eager to discuss his employment difficulties with the social worker and proposed his own solution. If the doctors would support his application, he could be retired on medical grounds and re-trained for more interesting work. The GP was approached, agreed to the suggestion, and the patient was subsequently retired on pension. An appointment was then made for him with the Disabled Resettlement Officer. There was a set-back when his application for retraining was turned down, and none of the jobs offered appealed to him. However, he eventually accepted a job and settled happily in it. He was discharged from the hospital clinic, and no longer needed the support of the social worker.

When seen again a year after referral he was found to be well and symptom-free.

## 4. Example of the Medico-Social Management of a Psychogeriatric Illness

When recommended for supervision, Mrs G., a widow of 72, had been in failing health for some time. More recently she had complained of failing memory and depression. She had always been a healthy woman, and was active until 7 years previously, when her husband's declining health had forced them to give up the shop they had run together for over 30 years. A few months after retirement her husband had died. She was now finding it difficult to adjust from her busy life to her present isolation. She had a married son living at a distance who was rarely seen, and a widowed sister living locally who was seen rather more often.

At interview Mrs G. presented as a spirited, independent woman with an awareness of her failing powers. She was suffering from a fairly severe dysmnesic state, and there was evidence of an early dementing process. It seemed, however, that she was still able to take care of herself reasonably well and to go about the streets without undue risk.

At the social worker's first visit the patient tried hard to disguise her severe memory loss. However, she readily accepted the visits and the prospect of ideas for combating her loneliness. Unfortunately, the patient became too depressed at this point to take advantage of the suggestions made and when, after medication, her depressive episode abated, she refused to consider any ideas for change. Meanwhile, the social worker had contacted the patient's sister, who agreed to see more of the patient and to try to arrange more contact between the patient and her son.

Supported by the social worker's visits, the patient continued to lead her routine life quite successfully, until one day she collapsed in the street and had to be taken home. It was then arranged for her to attend a Day Hospital. During this time the social worker ensured that the patient could look after herself in the evenings and provided practical help. Eventually, the patient became so confused that she was admitted to hospital. The social worker visited her there and arranged for the patient's sister to take over the management of her flat and financial affairs.

Finally, the patient was transferred to an Old Peoples' Home. When she was seen there about a month after admission it was noted that her depression had lifted with the end of her loneliness, although she was by this time very amnesic and only approximately orientated.

## References

Baker, R. (1976). The multirole practitioner in the generic orientation to social work practice. *British Journal of Social Work* 6, 327—352.

Clare, A. W. and Cairns, V. E. (1978). Design, development and use of a standardized interview to assess social maladjustment and dysfunction in community studies. *Psychological Medicine* 8, 589—604.

Collins, J. (1965)."Social Casework in a General Medical Practice". Pitman Medical, London.

Committee on Local Authority and Allied Personal Social Services (Seebohm Committee) (1968). Report (Connd. 3703), para. 699. HMSO, London.

Cooper, B. (1971). Social work in general practice: the Derby scheme. *Lancet* i, 539—542.

Cooper, B., Harwin, B. G., Depla, C. and Shepherd, M. (1975). Mental health care in the community: an evaluative study. *Psychological Medicine* 5, 372—380.

Fischer, J. (1973). Is casework effective? — a review. *Social Work* 18, 5—20.

Forman, J. A. S. and Fairbairn, E. M. (1968). "Social Casework in General Practice: a Report on an Experiment Carried Out in a General Practice". Oxford University Press, London.

Goldberg, E. M. and Neill, J. E. (1972). "Social Work in General Practice". George Allen and Unwin, London.

Hicks, D. (1976). "Primary Health Care", p. 396. HMSO, London.

Hollis, F. (1972). "Casework: a Psycho-social Therapy". Random House, New York.

Prins, H. A. and Whyte, M. B. H. (1972). "Social Work and Medical Practice". Pergamon Press, Oxford.

Ratoff, L. and Pearson, B. (1970). Social case-work in general practice: an alternative approach. *British Medical Journal* ii, 475—477.

Stimson, G. (1977). Social care and the role of the general practitioner. *Social Science and Medicine* 11, 485—490.

World Health Organization. (1967). "Manual of the International Statistical Classification of Diseases, Injuries, and Causes of Death" (8th revision). WHO, Geneva.

# THE EFFECTIVENESS OF SOCIAL WORK INTERVENTION IN THE MANAGEMENT OF DEPRESSED WOMEN IN GENERAL PRACTICE

ROSLYN H. CORNEY

## Introduction

While there have been a number of favourable subjective and descriptive accounts of the feasibility and usefulness of locating social workers in general practice [Goldberg and Neill, 1972; Bowen et al., 1978; Williams and Clare, 1979] there has been a lack of objective evaluation of the advantages these schemes bring to general practice patients. These evaluations are not easy to obtain, as clinical trials pose very many difficulties in their execution and few have been carried out in this country [Goldberg et al., 1970; Berg et al., 1978; Gibbons et al., 1978]. Only one has involved a social worker attached to general practice [Cooper et al., 1975]. This paper describes the execution and outcome of a clinical trial of social work carried out on *depressed women* in general practice *aged between 18–45*. This group of women were chosen as they represent a high proportion of the referrals to attached social workers [Corney and Briscoe, 1977; Corney and Bowen, 1980] and are therefore considered by the primary care team as appropriate cases for the social worker's help. Research evidence also indicates that maternal depression has a detrimental effect on family life and the children involved [Rutter, 1966; Wolff and Acton, 1968; Weissman et al., 1972].

## Previous Work

The previous clinical trial of social work in general practice was carried out on chronic neurotic patients [Cooper et al., 1975; Shepherd et al., 1979], which included the depressed, anxious and phobic, of both sexes and of all ages over 18. Two groups of patients were obtained, 92 experimental subjects were selected from one group practice and 97 controls referred from a number of different practices in the same neighbourhood. First, the two groups were assessed initially by means of standardized psychiatric and social interviews. The experimental group were then referred to a special service operating which included an attached social worker, while the controls were referred back to the doctor for routine treatment.

After one year, both groups were reinterviewed using the same instruments. Although the initial scores for both groups were essentially similar, when the patients were reinterviewed one year later, there were marked differences indicating that the patients referred to the special services had benefited from it.

This study, however, evaluated a service which also included research psychiatrists although the social worker was the key worker in nearly two-thirds of the cases. Thus, the effectiveness of the social workers' involvement is difficult to assess in isolation from the effects of the other professional involved.

As the study on chronic neurotic patients showed that it was possible to carry out a trial of social work in general practice, this further study was initiated to evaluate the effects of social work on more acutely ill women.

## Method

The outline of the method is shown in Fig. 1. The main study involved the participation of six doctors, five of which were based in a health centre with a social work attachment scheme involving four part-time social workers. This scheme had been in operation for two years when the study started and was therefore well established. The sixth doctor was from a single-handed practice and had been involved in previous studies with the General Practice Research Unit at the Institute of Psychiatry.

The doctors were asked to refer women aged 18–45 years presenting with "acute" or "acute on chronic" depression. The duration of symptoms of depression in the former group was operationally defined as three months or less; in the latter group the symptoms may have been present for a longer period but had intensified in the preceding trimester. Women suffering from major physical ill-health and those already seeing a social worker were excluded.

All referrals were initially interviewed by a psychiatrist, using the Clinical Psychiatric Interview [Goldberg et al., 1970] and then by a social research worker using the Social Maladjustment Schedule [Clare and Cairns, 1978]. Patients were then allocated to the experimental or control group by a research assistant who was not involved in the assessments. In order that the two groups were matched in certain characteristics, patients were allocated into 1 of 8 groups according to 2 categories of age, married or single status and whether they were suffering from an "acute" or "acute on chronic" depression. The first patient in any of these categories was assigned to the experimental or control group by the toss of a coin, the second patient was automatically assigned to the alternative group, the third patient randomly allocated and so on. Those allocated to the experimental group were referred to one of four attached social workers for treatment while the controls were referred back to their doctor for routine treatment.

After six months, the women were reassessed by means of the same instruments. The research staff involved in these assessments were unaware of any intervening treatment. Additional information was obtained by placing a card in the general practitioner's notes. The date of any clinical improvement or deterioration, was recorded from the initial psychiatric assessment to one year later as well as the number of visits the patients made

METHOD

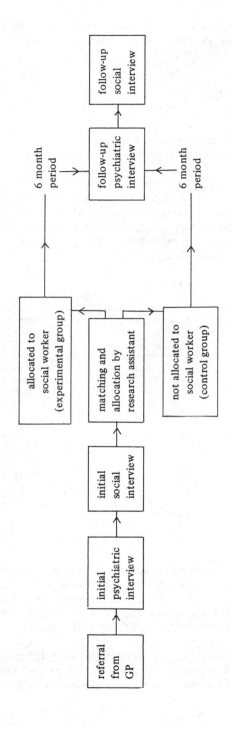

Data collected from the: i) initial and follow-up psychiatric interviews
ii) initial and follow-up social interviews
iii) medical notes for a 1½ year period
(6 months prior to referral to 1 year after)
iv) social work forms regarding treatment

Fig. 1

to the doctor and psychotropic drug prescription. Details were also collected from the attached social workers who completed specially designed forms regarding each client referred to them.

## Results

### 1. Characteristics of Cohort

Eighty patients were included in the study, 41 being allocated to the experimental group and 39 to the control group. Although 6 patients refused to see the social workers, these were still included in the experimental group, in line with the recommendations of Armitage [1979]. At the time of the initial assessment, the experimental and control groups were closely similar in respect of their demographic characteristics, psychiatric, physical ill-health and social ratings. There were no statistically significant differences between them. Approximately 80% of both groups were taking psychotropic drugs. Table 1 shows some of the initial characteristics of both groups.

TABLE 1
Summary of initial characteristics of experimental and control groups

|  | Experimental group (n = 41) % | Control group (n = 39) % |
|---|---|---|
| Married and cohabiting women | 75.6 | 69.2 |
| In employment | 61.0 | 64.1 |
| Social class I and II | 17.0 | 10.3 |
| III | 68.3 | 79.5 |
| IV and V | 14.7 | 10.3 |
| British by birth | 87.8 | 89.7 |
| Housing: Owner occupied | 68.3 | 69.2 |
| Council/rented | 31.7 | 30.8 |
| Duration of illness: |  |  |
| "Acutely" depressed | 39.0 | 48.7 |
| "Acute on chronic" | 61.0 | 51.3 |
| Mean age (in years) | 31.0 | 28.6 |

### 2. Outcome

Six months later, when the women were reinterviewed approximately two-thirds of both groups were assessed by the psychiatrist as improved (Table 2). Although a slightly higher proportion of the experimental group had improved, this was not statistically significant. All other measures of clinical outcome all failed to show a statistically significant difference between the experimental and control groups.

The patients also made some degree of social improvement, especially those who improved clinically. However, the experimental group did not improve significantly more than the control group on any of these social variables.

TABLE 2
Severity ratings at follow-up interviews experimental and control groups

| | Experimental group | | Control group | |
| | No. | % | No. | % |
| --- | --- | --- | --- | --- |
| Improved (follow-up severity rating of 0 or 1) | 28 | 68.3 | 24 | 61.5 |
| Not improved (follow-up severity rating 2 or 3) | 13 | 31.7 | 15 | 38.5 |
| | 41 | 100.0 | 39 | 100.0 |

The data collected from the medical notes also revealed no major differences between groups either with regard to the number of visits the patients made to the doctor or the length of time they were taking psychotropic drug. In addition, the experimental group did not recover any more quickly than the controls and similar proportions were considered by their doctor to be ill one year after referral. Only a few patients were referred by the doctor to other agencies. In the six month period between assessments 3 patients in each group were referred to the psychiatric services for treatment. One patient in the experimental group was referred to a child guidance clinic for her son's problems. Thus, the patients in the control group did not receive much additional professional help from elsewhere.

## 3. Effects of Intervention Certain Subgroups of Women

In other studies investigating social work and psychotherapy, the results have indicated that certain patients benefit from the treatment while others do not, depending on the patient's characteristics or those of the therapists [Truax and Carkhuff, 1967; Fischer, 1976]. As this study found no major differences between groups, the data were then analysed to investigate whether certain subgroups of women benefited from seeing a social worker or whether there were differences between the social workers in determining outcome.

These analyses revealed that the *chronicity* of the patient's depression and the *quality of the patient's relationship* with her husband or with the opposite sex were important factors in determining outcome of social work treatment. Interactions were statistically significant for a multivariate analysis of covariance and univariate analyses of clinical scores. These findings suggested that one subgroup of patients benefited from the social worker's interventions, these included women who were assessed initially as having major marital or boyfriend problems and were suffering from "acute on chronic" depression (Group 2, Table 3). With this particular group of women, 80% of the experimental group were assessed as improved clinically at follow-up in comparison with only 31% of the controls (Table 3). This difference still held one year after referral when the medical notes were

## TABLE 3

Numbers improved at 6 months for "acute" and "acute on chronic" patients in the experimental and control groups according to the quality of their relationship with spouse or boyfriend

| | Acute on chronic/ good relationship | | Acute on chronic/ poor relationship | | Acute/good relationship | | Acute/poor relationship | |
|---|---|---|---|---|---|---|---|---|
| | E Group | C Group | E Group | C Group | E Group | C Group | E Group | C Group |
| Improved (severity rating of 0 or 1) | 6 | 4 | 12 | 5 | 5 | 12 | 5 | 3 |
| Not improved (severity rating of 2 or 3) | 4 | 0 | 3 | 11 | 0 | 0 | 6 | 4 |
| Total | 10 | 4 | 15 | 16 | 5 | 12 | 11 | 7 |

Key: E Group = experimental group   C Group = control group

## TABLE 4

Differences between social workers: numbers improved for the four groups of patients studied

| Social worker | Group 1 (acute on chronic/ good relationship) | | Group 2 (acute on chronic/ poor relationship) | | Group 3 (acute/ good relationship) | | Group 4 (acute/ poor relationship) | |
|---|---|---|---|---|---|---|---|---|
| | Number improved | Number not improved | Number improved | Number not improved | Number improved | Number not improved | Number improved | Number not improved |
| A | 1 | 2 | 3 | 1 | 1 | 0 | 1 | 1 |
| B | 0 | 0 | 4 | 1 | 0 | 0 | 1 | 1 |
| C | 4 | 1 | 3 | 1 | 1 | 0 | 0 | 3 |
| D | 0 | 0 | 1 | 0 | 2 | 0 | 1 | 1 |
| Total | 5 | 3 | 11 | 3 | 4 | 0 | 3 | 6 |

examined. Fifty-seven per cent of the experimental group were judged by the doctor to be well in comparison with 18% of the controls. However, in contrast, women assessed as "acute on chronic" who had a good relationship fared less well in the experimental group than the controls but there was no difference in outcome one year after the initial assessment (Group 1, Table 3).

For the "acutely" ill patients, there were fewer differences in outcome between the experimental and control groups, all those with a good relationship improved (Group 3) while over 50% of those with a poor relationship failed to get better (Group 4).

The majority of women who had improved clinically also made some improvement in their social adjustment, thus "acute on chronic" depressed patients with marital difficulties who were referred to a social worker made more social adjustment than the controls in this category. However, the 3-way interactions for social work interventions were not statistically significant either for social scores in general or those scores measuring marital adjustment [Corney, 1981].

### 4. Social Worker's Activities

As the results suggested that social work intervention may be more beneficial to certain patients than others, the social workers' activities were analysed taking into account the four groups of patients outlined in Table 3.

*a) Differences between Social Workers*   Patients in the experimental group were referred to the social workers on a rota basis. Exceptions were made only when one of the social workers was on holiday or ill. Three social workers were employed during the first half of the study; one social worker (D) was only involved in the second half of the study (see Table 4).

The social workers differed according to the numbers of their patients who improved, but this difference was not very large and was not statistically significant (Table 4). For example, the best rates of improvement were 80% for social worker (D) in comparison with the worst rates of 60% for social worker (A). Although the numbers are very small, the social workers did not differ markedly in their rates of improvement for each of the four groups of patients studied.

The number of interviews given by the social workers with these patients varied from 1 to over 20. There was no general relationship between clinical improvement and the number of interviews given but in many cases only a few interviews were given as the patient improved and further interviews were considered unnecessary.

Just over 60% of the patients seen by the social workers were interviewed alone. This was not usually the social worker's choice as the spouses of the patients often resisted involvement, or the patient herself was reluctant for her spouse to be interviewed. These joint interviews, however, did not bring about any additional improvement on ratings measuring marital adjustment or clinical scores.

*b) The Social Worker's Interactions*   The social workers also recorded in detail their activities performed either with the client or on behalf of the client. The social workers worked in a number of ways with these clients; they were not given any specific guidelines as to how they should work with these clients as the needs of the clients were remarkably varied. Some women had few social problems, others had many. While some women had problems which were mainly practical in nature, others had mainly interpersonal problems. The social workers were asked, however, to try to see their clients on a regular basis and to make a "contract" with the client, specifying frequency of interviews and to agree on a "plan of action" regarding their work in the following months. They were also asked to limit their time of contact to the six months between assessments.

Communications with the clients were classified by the social workers according to the typology developed by Hollis [1964]. The social workers used "sustaining" and "exploring" techniques with all the clients they interviewed, investigating the reasons why the patient was depressed as well as offering support and reassurance. The social workers also considered that in 90% of cases, they tried to develop their client's awareness and understanding of the dynamics of her personal situation, behaviour and attitudes (termed "reflective consideration").

In addition, the social workers tried to help the clients using "behavioural techniques", for example, helping the client manage her depression by setting her a number of tasks to perform each day or devising a "contract" setting tasks between husband and wife to increase co-operation between them.

In addition to the interventions, the social workers also gave some form of help concerning practical matters to over 40% of their clients (Table 5). This included the provision of information, advocacy and the direct provision of materials or services. Financial aid, material improvements, holidays, day nursery placements and permanent council accommodation were some of the items obtained either through the social services department or through other agencies.

Although similar proportions of patients in all four groups received the different types of counselling identified, a higher proportion of patients in Groups 2 and 3 received practical help. A larger number of outside agencies were contacted by the social worker on behalf of patients in Group 2 than for patients in the other three groups.

*c) Motivation*   At the end of their contact with each client the social workers were asked to rate the client's motivation to be helped by them. Some of those who were not so well motivated were beginning to feel better at the beginning of the social worker's contact and, therefore, probably felt that no help was necessary. More patients in Group 2 were considered to be highly motivated, the social workers assessed nearly 60% of these women as "highly motivated" in comparison with only 15% of the women in the other groups (Table 6). This term was used by social workers when clients were willing not only to accept help but also to alter their behaviour or situation accordingly. The highest rate of improvement was found among the clients

TABLE 5

Type of social work given: numbers improved for the 4 groups of patients studied

| Type of social work | Group 1 (acute on chronic/good relationship) | | Group 2 (acute on chronic/poor relationship) | | Group 3 (acute/good relationship) | | Group 4 (acute/poor relationship) | |
|---|---|---|---|---|---|---|---|---|
| | Number improved | Number not improved | Number improved | Number not improved | Number improved | Number not improved | Number improved | Number not improved |
| Counselling only | 3 | 2 | 4 | 2 | 1 | 0 | 2 | 6 |
| Counselling and practical help | 2 | 1 | 7 | 1 | 3 | 0 | 1 | 0 |
| Total | 5 | 3 | 11 | 3 | 4 | 0 | 3 | 6 |

TABLE 6

The patient's motivation to be helped: numbers improved for the 4 groups of patients studied

| Motivation | Group 1 (acute on chronic/good relationship) | | Group 2 (acute on chronic/poor relationship) | | Group 3 (acute/good relationship) | | Group 4 (acute/poor relationship) | |
|---|---|---|---|---|---|---|---|---|
| | Number improved | Number not improved | Number improved | Number not improved | Number improved | Number not improved | Number improved | Number not improved |
| Highly motivated | 1 | 0 | 7 | 1 | 1 | 0 | 0 | 1 |
| Motivated | 2 | 2 | 2 | 1 | 3 | 0 | 2 | 4 |
| Not motivated | 2 | 1 | 2 | 1 | 0 | 0 | 1 | 1 |
| Total | 5 | 3 | 11 | 3 | 4 | 0 | 3 | 6 |

who were assessed as highly motivated; over 80% of this group had improved at follow-up.

## 5. The Clients' Assessment of Help Obtained

At the end of the second follow-up interview after the social assessment had been made, the patients were asked if anyone had helped them and were given time to spontaneously mention one or more individuals. They were then asked "who had helped most" and were questioned in further details about whether they received help from their general practitioner or social worker.

Nearly 70% of the experimental group spontaneously mentioned one or more people as helpful (including spouse, friends etc.) in comparison to only 45% of the controls. Two-thirds of those who saw a social worker spontaneously mentioned that she had helped them. When asked who had help most, just less than 60% of the 35 patients who saw a social worker indicated that she had, particularly patients in Group 2 and 3. Of the 13 clients in the experimental group who felt no one had helped, 4 had refused to see a social worker. In the control group, the doctor, husbands, friends and relatives were more often mentioned by this group as being the most helpful than by patients in the experimental group.

When the patients were asked specifically whether they had seen a social worker and whether it had been helpful, a further 6 patients thought she had been helpful who had not spontaneously mentioned her. All but 1 of the 35 patients had considered that the social worker had been understanding and only 2 patients found difficulty in talking to her.

Patients were asked about the type of help given. They were likely to mention all types of help, practical, advice support and counselling and ranged from mentioning one type of help to ten. More patients in Group 2 mentioned the practical help given, a reflection of the greater amount of this type of help given to these patients.

## Discussion

Why did one subgroup of women benefit from the involvement of a social worker while the others did not? The differences in outcome could not have been due to any initial differences in social scores between the experimental and control groups as these were examined in close detail [Corney, 1981]. The results suggest that a combination of the following factors were important:

(1) the duration of the client's depression,
(2) the quality of her relationship with her spouse and others including the amount of support she receives from them,
(3) her motivation to be helped, and
(4) the nature of her social problem.

The patients who gained most benefit were those who had been depressed for some time and who had a poor relationship with spouse or boyfriend.

The results especially when considered in conjunction with those of Cooper and colleagues, suggest that doctors should refer to social workers patients with more longstanding depressions and neuroses, as these will be helped more than those whose symptoms have a recent onset. When the patient's depression becomes "chronic" or "acute on chronic", there is less chance of spontaneous recovery [Cooper *et al.*, 1969; Kedward, 1969] and help from an outside agency may be necessary to bring about change. The patient may also be more likely to accept such help and act upon it.

Patients with "acute" depression appear more likely to recover without outside help. The additional help of a social worker may be unnecessary or even harmful, the social worker interfering with the individual's own mechanisms of coping or the support received from others. The patient may also be less motivated to receive the help offered; having only very recently become depressed and be less inclined to accept outside help or regard it as necessary. Although it is often assumed that the earlier the patient sees a social worker after the onset of his or her difficulties the more effective she will be, it is possible that *very* early intervention may be inefficient, inappropriate or even harmful.

The results also suggest that women with poor relationships with their spouse or boyfriend may benefit more from the help of a social worker. These women have been shown by other studies to be particularly vulnerable to episodes of depression [Miller and Ingham, 1976; Brown and Harris, 1978]. Many of these women also had inadequate social contacts and possibly had no-one they could talk to, confide in and discuss their problems with and thus readily accepted the emotional support given by a social worker. Possibly, the lack of a difference in general between the outcome of the experimental and control groups could have been due to the support the control patients received from relatives, husband and friends. The information obtained from patients support this; more patients in the control group mentioned the help of friends and relatives than patients in the experimental group. The reason why the control patients in Group 2 did so badly could have been due to their lack of support from others, over 70% felt no-one had helped them. In contrast only one-quarter of the experimental patients in Group 2 felt no-one had helped them.

The clients' motivation to be helped by a social worker, therefore appears related to the length of time she has been ill and the help she receives from others. However, it is possible that the nature of the patient's social problems is another important factor affecting motivation. Patients in Group 2 (both the experimental group and the controls) had more social problems than the others; many of these were practical matters which may have been why many of this group were eager for help.

The social workers also carried out more practical help on behalf of the clients in Group 2 and contacted more agencies on their behalf. In the earlier study on chronic neurotics, where a substantial difference was found between the experimental and control groups, the majority of the social work carried out was practical in nature [Shepherd *et al.*, 1979]. These findings suggest that the emotional support and practical assistance given by social workers may be of more importance than the social worker's technical skills and activities in counselling. Studies obtaining the clients' views of social work support this, clients appreciating most the combination of practical help with emotional support [Butrym, 1968; Meyer and Timms, 1970; Sainsbury, 1975]. Certainly the clients in this study were more likely to mention the supportive and practical help received from the social worker rather than other types of intervention.

This study suggests that the primary care team should be very selective when referring depressed patients to a social worker as not all will benefit from the additional help. It points to the need for future studies with different patient groups. The results could be used to guide the general practitioners and others on which patients should be referred so that the most optimal use can be made of the social worker's time.

## Acknowledgements

This study was carried out as part of a research programme planned by the General Practice Research Unit and the Institute of Psychiatry, under the direction of Professor Michael Shepherd and with the support of the DHSS.

I would like to thank Dr A. Clare, Dr B. Harwin and Dr P. Williams for help in conducting the psychiatric interviews; the social workers, Mrs B. Bowen, Mrs Y. Davies, Mrs A. Rushton and Mrs J. Winny; Dr G. Dunn, Dr V. Cairns and Mr D. Wiggins for statistical advice; the general practitioners at Woodside Health Centre and Dr and Mrs J. Fletcher.

## References

Armitage, P. (1979). The analysis of data from clinical trials. *The Statistician* **28** (3), 171–183.

Berg, I., Consterdine, M., Hullin, R., McGuire, R. and Tyrer, S. (1978). The effects of two randomly allocated court procedures on truancy. *British Journal of Criminology* **18**, 3, 232–244.

Bowen, B., Davis, Y. A., Rushton, A. and Winny, J. (1978). Adventure into health. *Update* **6**, 1512–1515.

Brown, G. W. and Harris, T. (1978). "Social Origins of Depression: A Study of Psychiatric Disorder in Women". Tavistock, London.

Butrym, Z. (1968). "Medical Social Work in Action". Bell, London.

Clare, A. W. and Cairns, V. E. (1978). Design, development and use of a standardized interview to assess social maladjustment and dysfunction in community studies. *Psychological Medicine* **8**, 589–604.

Cooper, B., Fry, J. and Galton, G. (1969). A longitudinal study of psychiatric morbidity in general practice population. *British Journal of Preventive and Social Medicine* **23**, 210–217.

Cooper, B., Harwin, B. G., Depla, C. and Shepherd, M. (1975). Mental health care in the community: an evaluative study. *Psychological Medicine* **5**, 4, 372–380.

Corney, R. H. (1981). The Effectiveness of Social Work in the Management of Depressed Women Patients in General Practice. Unpublished Ph.D. Thesis (1981), University of London.

Corney, R. H. and Bowen, B. A. (1980). Referrals to social workers: A comparative study of a local authority intake team with a general practice attachment scheme. *Journal of the Royal College of General Practitioners* **30**, 139–147.

Corney, R. H. and Briscoe, M. E. (1977). Social workers and their clients: A comparison between primary health care and local authority settings. The Team — 2. *Journal of the Royal College of General Practitioners* 27, 295–301.

Fischer, J. (1976). "The Effectiveness of Social Casework". Charles C. Thomas, Springfield, Illinois.

Gibbons, J. S., Butler, J., Unwin, P. and Gibbons, J. L. (1978). Evaluation of a social work service for self-poisoning patients. *British Journal of Psychiatry* 133, 111–118.

Goldberg, D. P., Cooper, B., Eastwood, M. R., Kedward, H. B. and Shepherd, M. (1970). A standardized psychiatric interview for use in community surveys. *British Journal of Preventive and Social Medicine* 24, 18–23.

Goldberg, E. M. and Neill, J. (1972). "Social Work in General Practice". George Allen and Unwin, London.

Hollis, F. (1964). "Casework: A Psychosocial Therapy". Random House, New York.

Kedward, H. (1969). The outcome of neurotic illness in the community. *Social Psychiatry* 4, 1, 1–4.

Meyer, J. E. and Timms, N. (1970). "The Client Speaks". Routledge and Kegan Paul, London.

Miller, P. Mc. and Ingham, J. C. (1976). Friends, confidants and symptoms. *Social Psychiatry* 11, 51–58.

Rutter, M. (1966). "Children of Sick Patients: An Environmental and Psychiatric Study". Institute of Psychiatry, Maudsley Monographs, No. 16. Oxford University Press, London.

Sainsbury, E. (1975). "Social Work With Families". Routlede and Kegan Paul, London.

Shepherd, M., Harwin, B. G., Depla, C. and Cairns, V. (1979). Social work and the primary care of mental disorder. *Psychological Medicine* 9, 661–669.

Truax, C. and Carkhuff, R. R. (1967). "Towards Effective Counselling and Psychotherapy". Aldine, Chicago.

Weissman, M. M., Paykel, E. S. and Klerman, G. L. (1972). The depressed woman as a mother. *Social Psychiatry* 7, 98–108.

Williams, P. and Clare, A. W. (1979). Social workers in primary care. *Journal of the Royal College of General Practitioners* 29, 554–558.

Wolff, S. and Acton, W. P. (1968). Characteristics of parents of disturbed children. *British Journal of Psychiatry* 114, 593–601.

# CLIENT PERSPECTIVES IN A GENERAL PRACTICE ATTACHMENT

ROSLYN H. CORNEY

## Summary

In this study, 50 clients of social workers in an attachment scheme were interviewed and their views compared with the assessments made by the social workers. The results were very favourable for the attachment; the clients were well satisfied with the service given and the majority of clients felt that they had been helped, especially with their emotional problems. However, there was much disagreement between the social worker's assessment and that made by the client, especially regarding the type and number of problems helped.

In order to evaluate the effectiveness of social work attachments to general practice, a number of studies have asked the views of all the professionals involved (Williams and Clare [1], Corney [2], Bowen et al. [3], Forman and Fairbairn [4], Ratoff and Pearson [5], and many others). However, only one study has asked the clients what they felt about the service (Munro and Hillier [6]). In the present study, clients were asked to given their assessments and these were compared with those of the social workers involved.

Fifty clients who had been referred to four social workers in a general practice scheme were interviewed. This attachment covered four group practices, three of which were housed in a health centre. The social workers filled out forms on each client including an assessment of their problems and a detailed account of their interventions. This made it possible to compare the views of the clients with those of the social worker.

## Method

Referrals were monitored over a period of four and a half months. Clients who had no previous contact with any of the attachment social workers were selected for interview so that their accounts of help would only cover their recent contact with the social worker. All clients were eligible for the study as long as they had seen the social worker at least once. Before a letter requesting a research interview was sent to the client, the attachment social worker had to agree to the client being interviewed. In a number of cases,

Reprinted, with permission, from the *British Journal of Social Work* 11, 159–170, 1981.

clients were considered not suitable for interview, for example, demented clients or those in hospital. Normally the client referred was contacted, but if the social worker's main contact had been with another member of the family (if the client was very old or very young) this other person was interviewed.

All clients were interviewed approximately two weeks after their case was closed or six months after referral if the case was still open. A letter was sent to the client explaining the purpose of the study and arranging an appointment. A stamped addressed postcard was included for the clients to send back if they wished to arrange another time for the interview. The letter emphasised the independence of the research organisation carrying out the study and the confidentiality, stressing that the social workers would not know what any one individual said. These issues were again emphasised at the beginning of the interview when it was added that complaints and dissatisfactions were as important as favourable remarks. The questionnaire was mainly a series of open-ended questions to encourage individual comments.

Some clients were not at home when visited and these were contacted again to arrange another time. If still not at home for this appointment, they were visited again unannounced.

All the forms completed by the social worker for each client interviewed were collected. They included initial forms containing demographic details and the social worker's assessment of the client's problems, a diary sheet with information on contacts made with the client and other agencies and a closure sheet outlining the client's circumstances when the case was closed. Forms on clients still being seen after six months were filled up according to the circumstances at the time of the "consumer" interview.

## Results

The social workers received 131 referrals during a period of four and a half months; 37 were re-referrals and were accordingly excluded, leaving 94 referrals for the study. Table 1 outlines the reasons why some of the new referrals were excluded from the study.

Thirty-nine of the clients were women, 11 men. Twenty-three were aged 44 or under, nine clients were between 45 and 64, and 18 clients over 65. Nearly 60% of the clients owned their own homes, 25% were council tenants and the remainder were in other rented accommodation. As can be seen from Table 2, the majority of clients were referred by members of the primary health team.

Self referrals were not encouraged and the social work service was not openly published except by a sign on the door of the office used by the social workers.

Eighty per cent of the clients visited the referral agent primarily because of their social and emotional problems. The remainder had visited the doctor or health visitor either routinely or because of physical illness when discussion of their problem occurred. In most cases it was the referral agent who suggested that the client should see a social worker and either contacted the social worker himself or personally took the client to see her.

TABLE 1
Breakdown of new referrals and reasons for exclusion from the study

|  | No. | % |
| --- | --- | --- |
| No personal social work contact with client | 15 | 16.0 |
| Client moved, died or taken into hospital before the interview | 10 | 10.6 |
| Some difficulty in interviewing client (e.g. child abuse case or client demented) | 7 | 7.4 |
| Client refused to participate in the study or not in when interviewer called | 12 | 12.8 |
| No. of clients interviewed | 50 | 53.2 |
|  | 94 | 100.0 |

TABLE 2
Referral agent

|  | No. | % |
| --- | --- | --- |
| GP | 37 | 74.0 |
| Health visitor | 6 | 12.0 |
| District nurse | 2 | 4.0 |
| Self | 3 | 6.0 |
| Relatives/friends | 1 | 2.0 |
| Other agency | 1 | 2.0 |
|  | 50 | 100.0 |

Few clients knew there were social workers attached to their doctors' surgery before referral. However, three-quarters of the clients had heard about social workers in general and just less than half the clients knew of them because a friend, relative or member of the family had had some contact with them.

Although most of the clients had heard about social workers, they were unclear about the help that could be provided or the type of problems dealt with. Some clients had heard that social workers were often involved in child and wife battering cases and could take children into care but often social workers were confused with health visitors. The elderly and the disabled were more knowledgeable about the services social workers could provide for them.

Only 30% of clients had considered that their problems were appropriate for a social worker's help before being referred to her. The elderly were most likely to regard their problems as appropriate and the younger clients least likely. Clients were also asked if they had considered going to the local authority social services department with their problems. Only 10% of the clients (with a variety of problems) said that they would have done so if they had not been referred to the attachment social workers. The rest either did not think of going or did not regard the agency as appropriate.

Most clients said that before they saw the social worker they had no clear hopes of how she would try to help them. However, nearly a quarter expected advice, information or advocacy from the social worker and 35% some form of practical help. Only just over 10% expected emotional support or discussion of problems, whilst the remainder had no idea at all of what to expect.

### Reason for Referral

The clients were asked why they were referred or had referred themselves and their replies were classified by the author into one or more of 20 categories of problems, using a modified version of a research classification (Fitzgerald [7]). The reasons for referral noted on the social workers' forms were also recorded according to the same classification.

Clients were referred with a wide range of problems. When the 20 types of problems were condensed into two groups (practical or relationship/emotional problems), most clients considered that they had been referred with difficulties in either group. Thirty-four per cent were referred for practical problems (including those associated with physical disability), 46% with relationship or emotional problems (including mental ill-health) and the remainder for a combination of these problems.

The social worker was limited to only one reason for referral for each case. In the majority of cases, the social worker's opinion of why the client had been referred was the same or very similar to the client's. In six cases, there were differences in opinion. These were due to the clients having more than one problem and the reason for referral chosen by the social workers being different from that chosen by the client.

Eighteen clients were referred for emotional problems or problems of minor mental ill-health. Most of these clients were depressed but four clients had other disorders such as alcoholism of agoraphobia.

Clients were also asked about problems other than the reason why they were referred. For this enquiry, the clients were read out the list of 20 problems and asked if any had caused them recent worry. Problems considered severe enough by the author to merit the attention of an outside agency were recorded, for example, financial problems where there were severe rent arrears or a marital problem where a doctor or other professional had been consulted. The social worker also assessed the problems of each client and recorded them on a form according to the same categories.

On average, clients had three problems each but they ranged from two problems to seven. Although most clients were referred either for practical problems or relationship problems, three-quarters of the clients had a combination of the two.

The social workers also assessed each client as having three problems each. Although there were differences between the social workers' and clients' assessments of problems, the majority of these were due to the social worker and client classifying the same problem under different headings, for example, an elderly person who cannot cope at home may regard her problem as a practical one whilst the social worker may regard it as a problem associated with physical disability.

TABLE 3
Problems identified by the clients and social workers and reasons for referral
(using a condensed version of problem classification)

| | *Reasons for referral**| | *Presence of problem**| |
|---|---|---|---|---|
| | *Client No.* | *Social worker No.* | *Client No.* | *Social worker No.* |
| *Practical/material problems* | | | | |
| 1. Housing | 6 | 5 | 11 | 13 |
| 2. Financial | 9 | 4 | 18 | 15 |
| 3. Employment | 2 | 1 | 7 | 7 |
| 4. Practical | 4 | 3 | 10 | 5 |
| 5. Problems associated with physical disability | 8 | 5 | 18 | 21 |
| *Relationship, emotional problems/ mental illness* | | | | |
| 6. Marital/family break-up | 5 | 7 | 13 | 15 |
| 7. Child care | 8 | 3 | 10 | 9 |
| 8. Other relationships | 2 | 2 | 11 | 14 |
| 9. Social isolation | 3 | 4 | 12 | 9 |
| 10. Bereavement | 1 | 1 | 7 | 5 |
| 11. Emotional problems/mental illness in client or close family | 18 | 15 | 25 | 29 |
| 12. *Other* (including education problems, reproductory problems, delinquency) | 0 | 0 | 5 | 7 |

* The social workers and clients usually identified more than one type of problem so numbers do not add up to 50. Sixteen clients also had more than one reason for referral.

The clients were asked who or what was responsible for their problems. The social workers recorded their view of who was responsible plus their own assessment of what the client thought. It can be seen from Table 4, that clients are more likely to blame others, their ill-health or the practical situation for their problem whilst social workers were more likely to consider the client at fault or her relationships with others. The social workers, however, were aware of this difference and their assessments of the clients' viewpoints reflect this.

## The Social Workers' Interventions

The majority of clients were interviewed more than once, ranging from two to 27 interviews. Most of the interviews were conducted with the client alone; in only nine cases was the client's spouse or another member of the family actively involved. The social workers also contacted the majority of their clients by telephone and letter. The telephone was often used to discuss problems and letters were written to give advice and information.

Much of the social work involved contacting other agencies on the client's behalf. These were contacted in over 70% of cases, varying from one to nine agencies. Other local authority departments were contacted most commonly but the DHSS, voluntary agencies, hospital and child guidance were also

TABLE 4
Responsibility for problems

|  | Client's view | Social worker's view | Social worker's assessment of client's view |
|---|---|---|---|
| 1. Client's own behaviour | 6 | 11 | 8 |
| 2. Behaviour or attitudes of spouse | 7 | 2 | 6 |
| 3. Relationship between client and spouse | 1 | 7 | 3 |
| 4. Behaviour of children | 3 | 2 | 3 |
| 5. Behaviour or attitudes of family as a whole | 2 | 5 | 3 |
| 6. Behaviour of others | 2 | 1 | 2 |
| 7. Difficulties due to practical situation | 8 | 5 | 10 |
| 8. Difficulties due to physical ill-health | 18 | 13 | 14 |
| 9. Combination of influences* | 2 | 4 | 1 |

* The social worker and clients were asked to avoid this category where possible.

involved. The social workers usually contacted other members of the primary care team regarding their clients, especially the member who referred the client. The GP was contacted in the majority of cases, the health visitor in nine cases and the district nurse in another nine.

The clients were asked what the social worker had done on their behalf. They were first given time in which to spontaneously mention the social worker's activities (condensed into four categories for Table 5) and then prompted by the author reading out aloud a list of 20 activities that social workers could engage upon on behalf of their clients.

TABLE 5
Social workers' interventions identified by clients and social workers

| Type of activity | Identified by social worker | | Identified by client | |
|---|---|---|---|---|
|  | No. | % | No. | % |
| Advice/information | 38 | 76.0 | 31 | 62.0 |
| Practical help (including advocacy, referral) | 34 | 68.0 | 32 | 64.0 |
| Supportive help (listening, sympathy, support) | 46 | 92.0 | 38 | 76.0 |
| Casework techniques (e.g. increasing clients' awareness of personality and relationship problems) | 37 | 74.0 | 17 | 34.0 |

As more than one intervention was usually given, percentages do not add up to 100% or numbers to 50.

Clients spontaneously mentioned a wide variety of social work interventions. Over half mentioned how supportive the social worker had been and how she had helped by listening to their problems. One-third spontaneously mentioned her role as advocate, contacting agencies on their behalf. Slightly smaller proportions mentioned the giving of advice and information, the provision of services and the social worker's help with clarifying the reasons for their problems and difficulties.

The types of techniques identified by clients when prompted is shown in Table 5 and is compared with the social worker's own categorisation of her interventions. Social workers identified the use of more techniques than clients, especially casework techniques. The social workers considered that they used these techniques in three-quarters of the cases, while only one-third of clients recognised the social worker's use of these techniques. Casework techniques usually aim to modify the client's behaviour, feelings, attitudes or social functioning and are used in interviews with the clients alone, with their spouse or child, or in family interviews. The techniques usually involve discussion of the client's problems and an investigation into how and why they developed, encouraging the client's insight.

Only 14% of the clients felt that the social worker had only used one of the four types of techniques outlined in Table 5 and nearly half felt the social worker had used three or more types of techniques in their case.

## Helpfulness of Interventions

As well as asking which specific problems had been helped by the social worker, clients were also given a series of questions on how the social worker had helped in general. The results compared with the social workers' assessments to help given are shown in Tables 6 and 7.

The social workers overestimated the helpfulness of their interventions for almost every category of problem and felt that their involvement had changed their clients' lives and relationships much more than the clients did. There was also a considerable amount of disagreement between the client and the social worker about the type of help given; those clients who considered a certain problem had been helped were not always the same as those assessed by the social worker as having been helped.

Seventy-four per cent of the clients felt that one or more of their problems had been helped with the aid of the social worker. In addition to helping these specific problems, nearly 60% of clients felt that the social worker had made them happier and less worried about their situation. Ninety per cent of clients said that the social worker had been understanding, easy to talk to and that they had experienced great relief in talking over their problems. It had also helped to be able to talk to someone independent outside the family as they could speak to her of topics which otherwise would not have been discussed. This independence also enabled the social worker to take a detached view of the situation and to see the problems in a different way from that of the client.

Four clients felt that their marriage had improved with the social worker's aid. Three of these clients had been interviewed with their spouse and they considered that these joint interviews had made communication easier, encouraging them to talk about their problems. Seven clients, all with emotional and relationship problems, felt that the social worker had helped them to improve their social functioning. They considered the social worker had made significant changes to their lives. Two former agoraphobics, for

TABLE 6
Specific problems helped or solved by the social worker's assistance

| Type of problem | Client's opinion<br>No. of clients<br>helped | Social worker's<br>opinion<br>No. of clients<br>helped |
|---|---|---|
| *Practical/marital problems* | | |
| Housing | 1 | 7 |
| Financial | 8 | 12 |
| Employment | 1 | 1 |
| Practical problems | 5 | 6 |
| Problems associated with physical disability | 4 | 8 |
| *Relationship and emotional problems/mental illness* | | |
| Marital/family break-up | 4 | 8 |
| Child care | 2 | 8 |
| Other relationships | 2 | 12 |
| Social isolation | 2 | 4 |
| Bereavement | 0 | 3 |
| Emotional problems/mental illness in client or close family | 23 | 28 |
| *Other* (includes educational problems, reproductory problems, delinquency) | 0 | 3 |

TABLE 7
Type of help given

| Type of helpfulness | Client's opinion<br>No. of clients | Social worker's<br>opinion<br>no. of clients |
|---|---|---|
| No help | 7 | 3  (1) |
| Helped how client felt about his situation | 29 | 27 (20) |
| Modification of client's attitudes, behaviour, etc. | 7 | 11  (3) |
| Minor practical changes | 17 | 19 (11) |
| Major practical changes | 2 | 4  (2) |
| Modification in client's marital relationship | 4 | 8  (2) |

* The figures in brackets correspond to the number of cases where there was agreement between the client and social worker on the type of help given.

example, had been able to conquer their fears and go out alone. These changes in the clients' lives or relationships were not always brought about by a large number of interviews with the social worker; nine out of these eleven clients were seen less than six times.

Some clients felt they had been helped by techniques similar to those used in behaviour therapy. One girl with a problem with her young son had been set tasks to do each week with him. The social worker would visit weekly to see how they had worked and to set new tasks. The two agoraphobics had been handled in a similar way. Another lady had found it helpful to have been taught how to manage her anxiety using relaxation techniques.

Nearly 85% of the clients were satisfied with the help they received. The remainder were either neutral or dissatisfied. When the clients were asked who they would approach with future problems, over 60% would re-contact the practice social worker and a further 15% the doctor.

Most of the eight clients dissatisfied or neutral about the social worker's involvement were referred for practical problems and only one received help for any specific problem. Five of these clients felt the social worker could have done more to help them; two of them said that the social worker had not taken enough details of their case and one client had been referred to another agency which had not helped.

Not all of the clients not helped in any specific way were dissatisfied. Six of the 13 clients not helped were satisfied and considered that the social worker had done all she could on their behalf.

Clients were also asked who had been the most help to them with their problems. Although members of the family and other informal contacts were mentioned as having given help, professional contacts were named as being the most helpful in 80% of the cases. The social workers tended to overestimate informal help and underestimate their own and the doctor's helpfulness. There was no strong relationship between who had given the most help and the type of problem but the four clients who felt no one helped were referred for housing and financial problems.

*Views on the Social Work Attachment*

The great majority of clients were enthusiastic about the attachment of social workers to general practices. Although they knew their doctors were busy, they had visited them (or health visitors, district nurses) with their problems because they did not know where else to go. They considered that the social worker service was therefore in a good position as their doctor could easily refer these types of cases to the social worker. Many also felt that this type of attachment would also increase co-operation between social workers, doctors and other health care staff. This was helpful as doctors often had a considerable knowledge about their patients and their circumstances.

Discussion

The results from this study indicate that the social workers' assessments are not always a reliable guide to the clients' views. The social workers not only overestimated the help they gave but there were also discrepancies between the social workers and clients as to which problems had been helped.

With practical problems, the clients may regard a problem as helped only when the desired outcome has been reached. A social worker may feel she had helped if her interventions have brought the client closer to this outcome.

Only a few clients considered their relationship problems were helped.

This could be due partly to the views of the social workers and clients on who was responsible for the problem and partly to the way in which the social workers worked. The social workers normally considered the client or her relationships to be responsible and mostly interviewed the client alone, trying to change her behaviour and attitudes. Clients usually blamed others and would therefore consider that their problems had not been helped if the behaviour of these others had not been changed. This may be why most of the clients who felt their marital problems had been helped were interviewed jointly with their spouse.

The clients' feelings regarding responsibility for their problems may also affect the way in which they regard social work interventions. Most clients recognised that the social worker was sympathetic and supportive but many fewer realised that the social worker was also trying to change their behaviour or attitudes by her interventions. Clients who blamed others for their problems were less likely to mention "casework help" or to regard themselves as having changed as a result of the social worker's intervention. The client's view of who is responsible for the problem also appears to be a useful estimate of whether the problem is helped; all 13 clients in this study who had not been helped with any specific problem had blamed others, their practical situation or their ill-health for these problems.

The results were very favourable regarding the attachment. Most of the clients were enthusiastic about the scheme and were satisfied with the service. The social workers' interventions were most effective in helping emotional problems. When problems are difficult to solve, such as with the chronically ill, the social worker's aims may be directed towards making the client feel happier with his situation. Thus, although many problems were not solved or improved, nearly 60% of clients felt the social worker had made them feel happier and more content with their life.

## Acknowledgements

This study was carried out as part of a research programme planned by the General Practice Research Unit and the Institute of Psychiatry, under the direction of Professor Michael Shepherd and with the support of the DHSS.

I would particularly like to thank the social workers involved in the study: Mrs B. Bowen, Mrs Y. Davis, Mrs A. Rushton and Mrs J. Winny.

## References

1. Williams, P. and Clare, A. W. (1979). Social workers in primary health care: the general practitioner's viewpoint. *J. Roy. Coll. Gen. Practitioners* **29**, 554–558.
2. Corney, R. H. (1980). Health visitors and social workers. *Health Visitor* **53**, 409–413.
3. Bowen, B., Davis, Y., Rushton, A. and Winny, J. (1978). Adventure into health. *Update*, 1512–1515.
4. Forman, J. A. S. and Fairbairn, E. M. (1968). "Social Casework in General Practice". Oxford University Press.
5. Ratoff, L. and Pearson, B. (1970). Social casework in general practice: an alternative approach. *Br. Med. J.* **2**, 475–477.
6. Munro, J. E. and Hillier, U. F. (1976). "Social Problems and Primary Health Care". A report of the Liverpool General Practice Study. Unpublished.
7. Fitzgerald, R. (1978). The classification and recording of "social problems". *Soc. Sc. and Med.* **12**, 255–263.

# SECTION 5

# SOCIAL WORK AND PRIMARY CARE

# SOCIAL WORK AND PRIMARY CARE PROBLEMS AND POSSIBILITIES

ANTHONY W. CLARE and ROSLYN H. CORNEY

The demonstration of a significant social component in ill-health raises difficult questions concerning how best to respond. The premise upon which this book rests is that one of the places where the social worker should be located is within the primary care team. We do not, however, argue that this is the only place for social workers. But it is an important setting and particularly so for the health care of people living in inner city areas where the quality of general practice is recognized to be poor and where social problems are ubiquitous [RCGP, 1981].

But, as is clear from the literature on social work attachment schemes which we have reviewed in this collection, collaboration between social workers and general practitioners is not without its hazards. Such schemes as are currently functioning well represent, in numerical terms, but a tiny proportion of the social workers and the general practitioners working in Britain at the present time. Obviously, with careful selection and matching, properly motivated and open-minded representatives of both professions can work together harmoniously and effectively. But how safe is it to extrapolate from such pilot and *ad hoc* initiatives and argue for a compre-hensive and integrated health and personal social service on a national basis? We readily acknowledge the fact that many social workers, perhaps even a majority, fear the loss of personal autonomy and professional inde-pendence which might be involved in any move out of the social service department and into the health centre. General practitioners, for their part, value their independent status within the National Health Service structure and view with suspicion any suggestion that they should work on a salaried and geographical basis from combined health and social service facilities. Not surprisingly, such professional and political reservations have led some, such as Dingwall (page 000) to conclude that short of a Royal Commission and a political initiative closer and statutory collaboration between health and social service personnel is inconceivable.

If this somewhat pessimistic assessment is correct then we are left with a choice between muddling on with a service which is fragmented and partial, a prospect which, in the light of the evidence reviewed in this book, we regard with dismay, or pressing for a process of piecemeal development involving attachment and liaison arrangements of differing kinds, such arrangements being instituted as and when the necessary inter-professional goodwill, confidence and enthusiasm make it possible. Such a process, however, will inevitably be slow and the resultant scale and volume of attachment schemes seem hardly likely to make more than a modest impact on either the pool of psychosocial morbidity existing in primary care or on the attitude, ability and interest of the general practitioners themselves.

Officially, the two organizations which represent general practice and social work endorse collaboration. Representatives of the British Association of Social Workers and the Royal College of General Practitioners have proposed that courses for the two professions should include opportunities for joint training and syllabuses should be altered so as to encourage the teaching of each other's roles and skills [BASW/RCGP, 1978]. In Holland, such a course has been implemented with trainee GPs and social workers, the emphasis being placed upon the sharing of information and the acqui-sition of practical skills through role-play [Schenk, 1979]. Unfortunately, there is no evidence that the participants' original prejudices were in any way altered. However, such courses can change attitudes according to one British GP trainer and his social work colleague on the basis of work under-taken with 17 trainee GPs and 18 community and hospital based social workers (Samuel and Dodge, 1981). Clearly, this is an area where much more work and evaluation needs to be undertaken. A recent survey of practice in London boroughs [Corney, 1982] has also revealed that a number of schemes have been set up in which social workers, usually relatively senior in rank, visit general practices and discuss the social worker's role without taking referrals directly. As yet there is little published evidence of the effectiveness of such arrangements but the general literature concerning "attachment" and "liaison" schemes does indicate that the former approach, although more time-consuming for the social worker, may actually be more successful [Corney and Briscoe, 1977; Jenkins, 1978; Corney, 1980].

However, while there are many voices within social work calling for further involvement within primary care, others loudly remind us that many of the most demanding and intractable social problems do not arise from and are unrelated to a medical condition. Obviously priorities have to be determined when it comes to deciding how best to deploy the available social work manpower. In emphasizing the needs and the opportunities involved in social work in primary care, we are not ignoring or under-estimating the very real demands placed on social work elsewhere. But we do not feel that we should be pusillanimous in drawing attention to an area of social work which tends to be neglected or, when it is considered, tends to be included as something of an afterthought or as an area which neatly illustrates the sorts of difficulties social workers tend to encounter in collaborating with other professionals [Parsloe and Stevenson, 1978].

We do wonder too at the too ready insistence by both the GP and the social worker that each is already over-committed. How much of the load currently borne by both professionals is due to the inefficiency and dis-organization inherent in the system? How many patients who repeatedly return for sick-notes and prescriptions might make less demands on busy GPs if a more appropriate response were to be made to the psycho-social difficulties with which they struggle to cope? How many clients whose notes oscillate backwards and forwards between "open" and "closed" status would use the social services in a more responsible and rational way if the professionals they encountered were more familiar with their general health and social status as well as their statutory needs?

Of course while there is this gap within the primary care team, professionals other than the social worker are tempted to fill it. The large area of overlap between the knowledge and skills possessed by the health visitor and by the social worker, together with the fact that large numbers of health visitors are already working alongside general practitioners, make these professionals obvious candidates for the task of bearing a greater portion of the psychosocial burden [Jefferies, 1973]. In this respect, it is interesting to note that the training base of the health visitor has been noticeably widened in recent years. The syllabuses approved by the Council for Health Visitor Training now include courses on the social and psychological aspects of child development, parental and family relationships, and on the social factors influencing these relationships in early, adolescent and adult life. The health visitor is better equipped than before to recognize and manage social aspects of ill-health in clients. But, in the absence of data, it is necessary to strike a note of caution. These educational developments have been and are being superimposed on a fairly sizeable foundation of nursing, child care and infant health training. Whether the foundations can stand this additional strain remains to be seen. Nor is it clear whether newly trained health visitors regard social problems as requiring not merely detection but management too or whether they see their role purely as screening agents who quickly pass on to others such problems as they uncover. Detecting social problems alone is not likely to assist the GP. Most GPs are only too aware of the impact of social problems upon the health of their patients; what they require is some assistance in their management. Knowing that there are even more social problems to be discovered is of scant interest unless there is some indication of how they might be dealt with more appropriately. At the moment there are any number of questions concerning the future role of the health visitor in this area and research is currently underway at our own unit, the General Practice Research Unit, which is aimed at just such a clarification. In the meantime, however, it does seem likely at the present time that in areas of high social need, the health visitor, already heavily committed, cannot take on the time consuming work of tackling social problems.

Directly related to such considerations is the issue of what it is that social workers do and how effective is such activity. There are those who argue that the most appropriate skill that a social worker should possess is an ability to know a considerable amount about social rights and services and be able to guide the client and the other members of the primary care team through the labyrinthine and ever-changing maze of social welfare legislation [Wootton, 1975; Hicks, 1976]. Indeed, Wootton is taken by the idea of being able to go directly to a social work professional "who being trained to function as a talking encyclopaedia, could deal forthwith with all the practical issues involved". However, while to some this may seem an eminently sensible use of social workers' skills and an appropriate way of ensuring the mobilization and co-ordination of the health and social welfare services in the interests of the individual within the community, not everyone takes such a view. Indeed, one critic has seen in the Scottish Social Work Act of 1968, with its emphasis on the social worker's remit to "promote social welfare", an opportunity merely for social workers to be developed into "a class of general dogsbodies" [Gammack, 1982].

Throughout this collection we have tended to avoid discussions of social work theory not because we consider it irrelevant but because we tend to agree with two recent commentators that there is a "hiatus" between theory and social work practice [Hardiker and Barker, 1981]. Social work in the setting of primary care does appear to be pragmatic and eclectic from the viewpoint of theory though whether this is a desirable state of affairs is for others to say. It is interesting to note that much of the social work practised within general practice attachments is of the kind endorsed by Wootton. However, much is not for the very good reason that the spectrum of social problems presented in this setting is very wide, wider indeed than that presented to social workers working in social service departments. Research data derived from comparative studies indicate the high proportion of emotional and interpersonal problems compared with such material problems as finance and housing which clients in general practice attachments present to social workers. Clearly primary care attachments offer social workers plenty of opportunities to undertake "counselling" and "casework". It is worth noting, however, that if such "casework" is regarded as an intervention requiring training, expertise and knowledge, then attention needs to be given to establishing the effectiveness of such approaches. Greater attention too needs to be given to matching specific forms of casework and specific kinds of social problems.

It is interesting to note in this regard that, despite the casework emphasis in the training of many social workers, the realities of working in social service departments do not permit much in the way of casework being undertaken. Social service departments struggle to cope with the very real material and statutory needs of their clients. The primary care setting, on the other hand, offers opportunities for both Wootton's social attorney and for the casework social worker interested in modifying and influencing the personal and psychological functioning of the client. There may of course be those who would argue that deploying social workers in primary care takes them away from those clients that need them most, namely the most deprived and materially impoverished. Such an argument merits respect. However, it may well be too simple. The greater emphasis on emotional and interpersonal problems in primary care may reflect the fact that social workers in this setting are involved in their clients' problems before these have developed to such an extent that statutory interventions are required. Certainly, there is the possibility that placement in primary care might offer the opportunity to the social worker to intervene earlier in and even to prevent the so-called "cycle of disadvantage" [Rutter and Madge, 1976]. However, we recognize that such an argument is more in the nature of being a hypothesis to be tested than a fact to be believed.

Related to this viewpoint is the argument that social workers should be involved more in effecting change at a local, regional or even national level and that greater involvement in primary care will merely tie them down to limited, largely palliative responses focused on the individual. It is of course true that modern medicine is strongly individualist and it is understandable, therefore, that the more radical exponent of the view of the social worker as a catalyst for political and social change should view the prospect of a more intimate relationship between medicine and social work with suspicion. But it is doubtful that medicine's social dimension and its sensitivity to local and national political issues can be strengthened if social workers remain aloof from its activities. Primary care health centres in Britain are positioned strategically within the community and are well-placed to function as foci for community interests and actions. They can certainly provide a base for the middle level or range of social change [Rothman, 1964; Meyer, 1970].

The "patch" system of working within social work, an approach which is growing in popularity [Hadley and McGrath, 1980] fits neatly into the health centre model. Most patch teams have divided the hitherto large social service areas into patches covering between 4000 and 10,000 people, populations very similar to those served by the average group practice of 3–4 GPs. Such patch teams are organized on a variety of bases and while several are on record as sharing premises with other professional and voluntary services there is as yet no published account of a social work "patch" team in active collaboration with general practitioners [Hadley and McGrath, 1981]. However, the intentions behind the "patch" deployment of social workers, which include a desire to strengthen the community links between such social workers and the population they serve, are very much in line with those which underpin the various social work attachment arrangements undertaken in various parts of the country. The foundations of a future integrated health and personal social service within the community may well be formed out of the health centre programme within primary care and the "patch" system within social work. All that is needed is some imagination, flexibility and ingenuity and the experiment of social workers and family doctors serving the same small and manageable population could be undertaken. It is in a sense, the next logical step forward from the attachment initiatives of the past decade.

Whatever the ultimate pattern of collaboration of social workers and GPs in primary care, there is a pressing need for a better, more detailed description of what it is that social workers do in this setting. There is a pressing need too to discover what general practitioners and other primary health care team members define as those social problems appropriate for referral to a social worker. What is it that distinguishes those clients so referred from the many more general practice patients who are never referred for social work assessment and intervention? What evidence, if any, is there for the suggestion that social workers in an attachment are involved at an earlier stage in the life history of social problems? What are the "suitable client groups" which the DHSS Working Party on Research in Social Work identified as the appropriate target for social work experimental studies? [Working Party Report, 1980]. A number of patient groups come to mind including those experiencing marital problems, depression, recent family disharmony and disruption, and serious, acute and chronic ill-health.

But all such research stands or falls on the quality of the basic foundations underpinning it. There is an urgent need for the existence of a small yet reasonably representative group of practising social workers, similar to the corps of research-minded general practitioners which, over the years, has paid particular attention to careful case recording, data collection and analysis. Such general practitioners have been the mainstay of the major epidemiological and clinical studies of psychosocial morbidity in primary care [Shepherd et al., 1966, 1981; Hicks, 1976; Cartwright and Anderson, 1981]. A comparable group of social workers would routinely utilize recording systems such as that advanced by Goldberg and her colleagues [Goldberg et al., 1976] and would work in collaboration with an academic social work department in the analysis and publication of results. The evaluation of the effectiveness of different social work interventions, mentioned earlier, would be facilitated too by such practitioner-based research expertise and interest. But such clinical research, whether it involves client groups [Cooper et al., 1975] or is based on a single case-design [Fischer, 1978] needs to be founded securely on accurate case records.

We readily acknowledge the difficulties involved, difficulties which include the high workload, the problems of measuring efficacy and outcome in such a complex and ill-defined area, the differing ideological views concerning the nature of social work, the lack of motivation and ability to undertake research ventures, and the interprofessional rivalries and anxieties which threaten to abort research before it can begin to bloom. But it is because we believe that social work can only advance by way of clarification of its nature and functions that we strongly favour such developments. It is also because we believe that the greater involvement of social work in medicine and in particular in primary care would do much to restore the social dimension to the theory and practice of medicine that we argue for the continuation of the experiment of attaching social workers alongside their colleagues in primary care medicine, nursing and health visiting.

At the present time, doubts are being expressed as to the wisdom of "encouraging" the presentation of social problems in the GPs surgery [Cartwright and Anderson, 1981; Parish, 1982]. It is argued that general practitioners are fundamentally organic in their orientation and it is useless indeed pointless to expect that they can be transformed into more eclectic and holistic practitioners. Social work leaders too, if the recently published and disappointing Barclay Report is a true guide, appear to rank co-operation with the medical services very low down on their list of priorities. In the circumstances, therefore, it is perhaps not surprising to find a critic such as Kathleen Jones arguing that the community mental health centre programme of the United States represents a "major breakthrough in mental health theory" and is a better blueprint for the future delivery of efficient and integrated health care in Britain than any revamped system of primary care [Jones, 1979]. The US CHMC programme is a 15 year investment for the provision of comprehensive specialty mental health services to individuals who reside in a defined geographic or "catchment" area [Sharfstein, 1980]. Quite apart from the fact that the American initiative is not without serious headaches of its own [Borus, 1978; Fink and Weinstein, 1979; Clare, 1980], it does seem to us somewhat hasty to reject the British primary care system given what has been termed "the groundswell of international opinion" [Shepherd, 1980] favouring the conclusion reached some years ago in a WHO Working Group report [WHO, 1973] that "the primary medical care team is the cornerstone of community psychiatry". It is perfectly true that the division between the primary care and social work services constitutes a serious obstacle to the proper functioning of community health and social services in Britain but it does seem to us that this is a reason for arguing for the strengthening of the primary care team in its social role rather than for dismantling or bypassing it and establishing a completely new system altogether.

Nor do we share Jones's pessimism concerning the abilities and interest of GPs in psychological and social matters. The development of group practice and the health centre approach, the growing popularity of general practice as a professional career for some of the best medical graduates and the increasing emphasis given to psychiatric and social aspects of health and disease in the vocational training programmes all constitute encouraging signs in our view. The issue is not whether social workers and general practitioners should collaborate in providing a truly integrated system of health and social care but rather whether they can afford not to do so.

## References

Barclay Report (1982). "Social Workers: Their Role and Tasks". National Institute for Social Work. Bedford Square Press, London.

BASW/RCGP. (1978). Some suggestions for teaching about co-operation between social work and general practice. *Journal of the Royal College of General Practitioners* 28, 96, 670–673.

Borus, J. F. (1978). Issues critical to the survival of community mental health. *American Journal of Psychiatry* 135, 1029–1035.

Cartwright, A. and Anderson, R. (1981). "General Practice Revisited". Tavistock, London.

Clare, A. W. (1980). Community mental health centres. *Journal of the Royal Society of Medicine* 73, 75–76.

Cooper, B., Harwin, B. G., Depla, C. and Shepherd, M. (1975). Mental helath care in the community: An evaluative study. *Psychological Medicine* 5, 5, 372–380.

Corney, R. H. (1980). Factors affecting the operation and success of social work attachment schemes to general practice. *Journal of the Royal College of General Practitioners* 30, 149–158.

Corney, R. H. (1982). "Attachment and liaison schemes in Greater London". Internal Document. General Practice Research Unit. Institute of Psychiatry.

Corney, R. H. and Briscoe, M. E. (1977). Social workers and their clients: A comparison between primary health care and local authority settings. The Team – 2. *Journal of the Royal College of General Practitioners* 27, 295–301.

Fink, P. J. and Weinstein, S. P. (1979). Whatever happened to psychiatry? The depersonalization of community mental health centres. *American Journal of Psychiatry* 136, 406–409.

Fischer, J. (1978). "Effective Casework Practice: An Eclectic Approach". McGraw Hill, New York.

Gammack, G. (1982). Social work as uncommon sense. *British Journal of Social Work* **12**, 1, 3—22.

Goldberg, E. M. and Fruin, D. J. (1976). Towards accountability in social work in a case review system for social workers. *British Journal of Social Work* **6**, No. 1, 3—22.

Hadley, R. and McGrath, M. (1980). Patch-based social services teams. Bulletin No. 1. January 1980. Social Administration Department, Lancaster University.

Hadley, R. and McGrath, M. (1981). Patch systems in SSDs: More than a passing fashion? *Social Work Service* **26**, May, 13—19.

Hardiker, P. and Barker, M. (1981). "Theories of Practice in Social Work". Academic Press, London.

Hicks, D. (1976). "Primary Health Care". DHSS, London.

Jefferies, M. (1973). The social worker and the health visitor. *Health Bulletin* **XXXI**, 2, 72—75.

Jenkins, M. E. (1978). "The Attachment of Social Workers to GP Practices". Research Section. Mid Glamorgan County Council.

Jones, K. (1979). Integration or disintegration in the mental health services. *Journal of the Royal Society of Medicine* **72**, 640—648.

Meyer, C. (1970). "Social Work Practice: A Response to the Urban Crisis". Free Press, New York.

Parish, P. (1982). The use of psychotropic drugs in general practice. *In* "Psychiatry and General Practice" (Ed. A. W. Clare and M. Lader). Academic Press, London.

Parsloe, P. and Stevenson, O. (1978). "Social Service Teams: The Practitioner's View". HMSO, London.

Report to the DHSS Research Liaison Group for Local Authority Social Services: Directions for Research in Social Work and the Social Services. (1980). *British Journal of Social Work* **10**, 2, 207—217.

Rothman, J. (1964). An analysis of goals and roles in community organization practice. *Social Work* **9**, 24—31.

Royal College of General Practitioners. (1981). "A Survey of Primary Care in London". Occasional Paper No. 16, Royal College of General Practitioners, London.

Butter, M. and Madge, N. (1976). "Cycles of Disadvantage". Heinemann, London.

Samuel, O. W. and Dodge, D. (1981). A course in collaboration for social workers and general practitioners. *Journal of the Royal College of General Practitioners* **31**, 172—175.

Schenk, F. (1979). A course on collaboration between social workers and general practitioners during their vocational training. *Medical Education* **13**, 31—33.

Sharfstein, S. S. (1980). Community Mental Health Centres. *Journal of the Royal Society of Medicine* **73**, p. 219.

Shepherd, M. (1980). Mental health services and primary medical care. *Journal of the Royal Society of Medicine* **73**, 219—220.

Shepherd, M., Brown, A. C., Cooper, B. and Kalton, G. W. (1966). "Psychiatric Illness in General Practice". O.U.P., London.

Shepherd, M., Brown, A. C., Cooper, B., Kalton, G. and Clare, A. (1981). "Psychiatric Illness in General Practice". 2nd Edition. O.U.P., London.

Wootton, B. (1975). A philosophy for the social services. *Socialist Commentary*, January, pp. ii—iii.

World Health Organization. (1973). "Psychiatry and Primary Medical Care". WHO, Copenhagen.

# INDEX

Age
  and contact with social workers 154–155
  range in group work 242–243
  and sex distribution, referrals 25, 33–34
  monitoring study 48–49
Ageing
  referrals, client "survival" 57
  help received 58, 59
  monitoring study 50, 51, 52, 53
Agencies contacted by social workers 156, 301
Alcoholism, as reason for referral 26
Amitriptyline in treatment of depression 266, 267
Analytic conceptualization in psychotherapy 200–201
Anxiety, as reason for referral 26
  see also Mental health care
Appendicectomies, and social factors 15–16
Assertive training in behavioural therapy 188
Attachment schemes, see General practice attachment schemes
Autism, behaviour therapy 196


Behaviour modification (therapy)
  in family settings 179–198
    anchoring to natural environment 186
    approach 181
    assertive training 188
    assessment 183–184
    autism 196
    case reports 187–188
    commonsense and familiar aspects 185
    conduct disorders 189

covert sensitization 192
    criticisms 180–181, 191
    definitions 179
    distancing the problems 187
    dyadic model 186
    ethical considerations 180, 196
    extinction procedures 190
    focus on overt problems 184–185
    genetic disposition 183
    hyperactivity 190–191, 193–194
    in institutionalised settings, 191
    'Micawber syndrome' 195
    modeling 188
    morality 195–196
    operant conditioning 188–189
    psychodynamic approach 194
    relationships 197
    role of insight 182–183
    self-control procedures 192
    sharing with parents 186
    systematic desensitization 187
    techniques 185
    triadic model 186
    value base 179–180
  and the social worker 146–147
Bradford Health Centre Study 92, 96


Case review system
  method of data collection 46
  setting 47
Casework
  definition 199
  methods of intervention 66
  psychotherapy and social work 199–212
  see also Psychotherapy: Tasks
  see also Tasks
Child Guidance, referral to by health visitors 138

Children
    problems 56, 61—63, 66
    protection cases, doctors and social
        workers attitudes 96—97
Child Treatment Research Unit 179, 182
    *see also* Behaviour modification
        (therapy), family settings
    behaviour therapy 182, 184, 185, 186
    conduct disorders 189
Citizens' Advice Bureau, referral to by
    health visitors 138
Clients, *see* Referrals to social workers
Conduct disorders, behaviour therapy 189
Consumer's viewpoint of group social work
    237—244, 253
Council for Education and Training of
    Health Visitors /CETHV/ 91
    inadequacies of communications with
        doctors 92
    liasion with social workers 93—94
    limitation of others' perspectives 97
Council for Education and Training in
    Social Work 94
Covert sensitization in behaviour therapy
    192


Data collection, method, for monitoring
    survey 46
Deanery 136
Delinquency, referrals
    client "survival" 57
    help given 64
    monitoring study 49, 50, 53
Dementia, senile 26
Depression
    as reason for referral 26
    evaluation of social work 249—250,
        251—252
    health visitors' role 135, 137
    referrals, monitoring study 51
    and self-poisoning 258—259
    treatment effects on social adjustment
        265—281
        assessment 269—270, 275—276
        comment on design of treatment 275
        completion rates 271
        data analysis 269—270
        drug, with psychotherapy 265—266
        drug treatment 268
        maintenance 271—274
        methods of study 266—270

psychotherapy 268—269, 276—279
    results 270—274
social work intervention 311—323
    assessment, client's 320
    characteristics of patients 314
    conclusions 320—322
    differences between social workers
        316, 317
    effects of intervention 315—317
    social worker's activities 317—320
    *see also* Mental health care, community
Discussion meetings, attitudes to 74
Doctors
    attitudes to discussion meetings 74
    attitudes to social work 95—97
    and health visitors, relationships 72
    and social workers, relationships 72, 74
    and teamwork 86—91
    and leadership 86—87
    relationships with other members
        87—89
        class structure 87—88
        hospital background 88—89, 92
        and sex equality 90—91
        and status of health visitors 91—94
        and status of social workers 87—89
    *see also* General practice: General
        practitioners: Primary Health Care
        team
Drinking problems, evaluation of social
    work 248
Dyadic model in behaviour therapy 186


Elderly patients' illness and social factors
    16
Emotional problems
    evaluation of social work 252—253
    health visitors' role 137
    reasons for referral 36—37
    referral, client "survival" 57
        help given 59, 63—64
        monitoring study 49, 50, 51, 53
Employment problems as reasons for
    referral 36—37
    status 37
Ethics of behaviour therapy 196
Evaluation, social work 247—254
    depression 249—250
    drinking problems 248
    emotional problems 252—253
    mental health care 251

primary care 247, 251–252
psychoanalysis 203–206
psychotherapy 205, 206–210
self-poisoning 249, 255–264
  *see also* Self-poisoning
transactional analysis 208
Extinction procedures in behaviour
  therapy 190

Family
  problems 62–63
  settings, social work method 179–198
  social work method
    *see also* Behaviour modification
    (therapy)
Financial problems
  as reasons for referral 36
  referrals, client "survival" 57
  help given 58, 59, 61
  monitoring study 49, 51, 53
Flow of clients referred during one year
  54–55

General practice attachment scheme
  client perspectives 326–334
    *see also* Referrals to social workers
    from GP attachment
  compared with local authority social
    workers, intervention 151–161
    *see also* Interventions, social workers
  referrals 31–43
    *see also* Referrals, to social workers,
    comparative study
  doctors' perceptions 107
  problems 125–127, 130
  social workers, referrals to 23–29
  role 144–146
  psychiatric referral rates from 9
General practitioners' viewpoint, social
  workers in primary health care
  105–114
  role of social worker compared with
    health visitor 109, 110
    *see also* Doctors: GP attachment scheme
Group work single or separated parents
  229–236
  helpfulness 238–239
Gingerbread 137

Harvard Davis Committee Report 138
Health Centres, health visitors' and social
  workers' roles 136, 138
Health Visiting and Social Work (Training)
  Act 93
Health visitors
  and doctors, relationships 72
  functions 75
  functions, overlap with social work 76
  overlap with social worker 133–134,
    137–138
  referral by GP compared with social
    worker referral 109, 110, 111
  referrals to social workers 134–135
  types of disorders referred 136
  role 133, 135
  and social workers, overlap 339
  relationships 133–139
  and teamwork 91–94
  attitudes 92–93
  relationships with doctors 92–94
  relationships with social workers
    93–94
  responsibilities 91
Housing problems
  as reason for referral 36, 37
  help given 58, 59, 61, 65
Hyperactivity, treated by behaviour
  modification 190, 193–194

Insight, role in behavioural therapy 182–
  183
Inter-professional co-operation 72, 74, 75
Interventions, social workers, attachment
  team and local authority compared
  151–161

Length of contact with client social
  workers 154, 157–158
Local authority(ies)
  classification of referrals 27
  financial assistance in attachment
    schemes 123
  with social work schemes 117
Local authority social workers
  compared with GP attachment team
    31–43, 151–161
    *see also* Interventions, social workers
  contacts with health visitors 135–136
  helpfulness to health visitors 136

Local authority social workers (contd.)
  referrals to  23–29
    compared with those of GP attach-
      ment scheme  31–43, 151–161
    to by health visitors  136–139
  role  144

Marital
  adjustment and mental disorder  300–
    301
  problems, health visitors' role  135
  relationships and task-centred social
    work  164–170
Marriage Guidance Council, referrals by
  Health visitors  135, 137
Material help given to referral clients  61–
  62, 64–67
Maudsley-Tavistock psychotherapy study
  selection criteria  208–209
Menninger Foundation's Psychotherapy
  Project  203
Mental
  health care, evaluation  251, 283–295
    experimental service,  284–286
      assessment  286
      control group  285
      selection  285
      social adjustment  291–292
  ill health, primary care, social work
    297–310
    conclusions  303–306
Meta-analysis
  definition  206–207
  effect sizes  207
Monitoring one years' intake to area office
  45–67
  area policy  54
  case review system  45–46
    see also Case review system
  flow of clients through system  54–55
  help received by clients  58–64
    social characteristics  50–51
  referral route  52
  request of referer  52–53
  type of disposal  54
Morals of behaviour therapy  195–196

Neurosis, and social work  311–312
  see also Mental health care,
    community

Old age, referrals, help received  58, 59
  see also Ageing
Operant conditioning in behaviour therapy
  188–189

Parasuicide, outcome of secondary
  prevention  255–256
  see also Self-poisoning
Penn Psychotherapy Project  204
Physical
  disability, referrals  56
  as reason for referral  36, 37–38, 41–42
    referrals, help received  58, 59
  ill-health, extent, referrals to social
    workers  23–28
    as reason for referral  37–38
  social factors, morbidity  14–16
Primary health care team
  composition  77
  social work, evaluation  247, 251–252
    GP's viewpoint  105–114
    mental disorder  297–310
      see also Mental disorder, primary
        care, social work
    problems and possibilities  337–344
      see also Social work attachment
        schemes, assessment
    teamwork  teamwork problems  81–103
      see also General Practice Attachment
        scheme: Teamwork
Problem search by social workers  166
Psychiatric
  Day Centres  225
  ill-health general practice, social factors
    10–11
    morbidity  12–14
    statistics  10
    treatment  11–12
    and social factors, management  16–19
  referral rates from general practice  9
    see also Referrals
  treatment and community mental
    health care  288–293
Psychoanalysis
  definition  203–204
  comparative treatments  205–206
  evaluation  204–205
  and the social worker  147
  techniques  201
Psychoanalytically oriented psychotherapy
  204, 205

Psychodynamic approach in behaviour
   therapy 194—195
Psychotherapy
   casework and social work 199—212
      analytic conceptualization 200—201
      necessary skills 201—210
      psychodynamic techniques 201—202
      types of psychotherapy 203
   definition 202—203
   in depression 268—269, 276—279
      characteristics 277
      combined with drugs 265—266,
         278—279
      specificity 277—278
      timing of benefits 278
   dynamic 200—201
   evaluation and criteria 208—209,
      275—276
   meta-analysis 206—207
   and the social worker 147
   symptomatic or dynamic recovery
      204—205
   types 203
      effects of different therapies 208—210
Puerperal depression, and social factors 16

Referrals to social workers 31—43
   assessment of information 39—42
   mental ill health 37—38
   physical ill health 37—38, 41—42
   reasons for referral 35—38
   re-referrals 35
   similarities between groups 41—42
   social workers' assessments 38—39
   who is the client 39—40
   depressed patients 322
      client perspectives 325—334
      problems identified 329
      reasons for referral 328—329
      responsibility for problems 330
      results 326—333
      specific problems and type of help
         given 332
      social workers' interventions 329, 330
      helpfulness 331—333
      views on 107, 333
   mental disorders 300—301
   monitoring one year's intake 45—67
      problems presented 49—51
      *see also* Monitoring one year's intake
         to area office

problems 125—127, 130
psychiatric, assessment of information
   28
   client's problems 27
   health status data 24
   local authority classification 27
   mental illness status 26—28
   methods of investigation 24—25
   reasons for 27
   results of investigations 25—26
requests of referrers, types 52—53
route 52
single and separated parents 229—230
sources 124
types 124, 130
*see also* Health visitors: Social work:
   Social workers
Rehabilitation Centres 225
Relationship problems
   evaluation of social work 251—252
   health visitors' role 135, 137
Royal Commission on the Integration of
      Health and Personal Social Services
      100
Royal Commission on the NHS 99

Schizophrenia
   as cause for referral 26
   treated at home 213—227
      co-ordination of services 223—227
      finance 226—227
      medical 224—225
      psychiatric day centres 225—226
      problems caused by patient's behaviour
         delusions 218
         depression 219
         doing nothing 216
         embarrassment 217—218
         mixing with others 215
         neglected appearance 216
         odd meal behaviour 216
         persecution 218
         restlessness 217
         suicide 219
      problems caused by relatives reactions
         219—220
         anxiety 219
         frustration 219
         guilt 219
         in the wider community 220
      social work 220—223

Schizophrenia, social work (contd.)
    discussing idea 222–223
    reducing effects of isolation and
        ostracism 223
    reducing likelihood of relapse 222–
        223
    stimulation of interest 221
Seebohm Report 16–17, 93, 105, 248
Self-control procedures in behaviour
        therapy 192
Self-poisoning, evaluation of social work
        249, 255–264
    criteria of outcome 258
    depression as cause 258–259
    discussion of results 262–263
    experimental service, nature 256–
        257
    experimental study results 259–262
    follow up 258–259
    methods of study 257–258
    psychiatric examination and diagnosis
        257
    service input 259
    social problems causing 258–259
    social problems, change after service
        261–262
    secondary prevention, outcome 255–
        256
Senile dementia 26
Separated parents, group work with 229–
        236
    *see also* Single and separated parents
Sex equality and teamwork 90–91
Single or separated parents, group work
        with 229–236, 237–244
    aims 230
    attendance 237
    changes necessary 240
    consumer's viewpoint 237–244
    contacts between group members 241
    content and discussions 223–233
    feelings about joining 238
    future running 241–242
    group development 233–235
        intimacy/superficiality 234–235
        power/powerlessness 233–234
    group leaders 240–241
    helpfulness 238–239
    male and female content 240
    marital status of members 242
    need for social worker 241, 243–
        244

Single or separated parents
    previous experience 238
    psychotherapeutic or social 243
    referrals 229–230
    selection 230–231
    social relationships 235, 240
    structure 231
Social
    adjustment, and depression treatment
        265–281
        *see also* Depression, treatment effects
        mental health care 291–292
        *see also* Mental health care, com-
            munity evaluation
    factors and physical ill-health,
        morbidity 14–16
    and psychiatric illness, general practice
        10–11
        GP morbidity 12–14
        management 16–19
    and self-poisoning 258–259
        change after services 261–262
        *see also* Self-poisoning
Social work
    casework and psychotherapy 199–212
        *see also* Psychotherapy
    general factors 247–254
        *see also* Evaluation, social work
    in general practice 115–131, 284
        appointments' schemes 123, 129
        attitudes 128
        communication 120, 128, 130, 131
        discussion 128–131
        doctors and social workers' meetings
            123
        initiation of scheme 117
        local authorities with schemes 117
        local authority financial assistance
            123
        number of doctors in general-practice
            centres 119
        number of social workers 117
        organization 120
        other settings for social work 119
        other situations involving social work
            responsibilities 121
        problem areas 125–127, 130–131
        qualification and background of social
            workers 125
        receptionist's services 122, 129
        referrals, sources and types 124, 130
            *see also* Referrals

room arrangements 121, 129, 131
secretarial help 122, 129, 131
telephone availability 121, 122, 129, 131
types of scheme 117, 118
intervention, general factors 143–150
task-centred 146–147
*see also* Task-centred social work
mental disorder and primary care 301–306
case histories 307–309
clinical and social outcome 303
monitoring one year's intake 45–67
with patients and their families 213–227
and primary care, problems and possibilities 337–344
*see also* Social work attachment schemes assessment
tasks, definition 179
Social worker
attachment schemes assessment 337–344
argument concerning deployment of work 340–341
difficulties to be overcome 342–343
health visitor and social worker overlap 339
'patch' system 341
role of social worker 339–340, 341–342
and doctors, collaboration, 18
co-operation problems 76
relationships 72, 74, 105–114
functions 75
and health visitor, overlap 133–134, 137–138, 339
relationships 133–139
in primary health care, GP's viewpoint 105–114
*see also* General practitioner's viewpoint
referrals to
*see* Referrals
role 133, 143–146
attachment to primary teams 144–146
local authority 144
status problems in primary care 87–89
and teamwork 95–97
child protection cases 96–97
relationships with health visitors 93–94

status 95–96
*see also* Teamwork
Structured approach to social work 163–164
Suicide, attempted 249, 255–264
Surgical conditions, social factors 15–16

Target problems, assessing 167–168
Task-centred social work 146–147, 149, 163–178
further crises 173–174
initial contact 164–166
marital relationships 164–170
problem search 166–170
self-poisoning 256–264
*see also* Self-poisoning, social work evaluation
structured approach 163–164
task selection 170–171
termination and time limit 174–176
work on tasks 172–174
*see also* Tasks
Tasks
selection in task-centred social work 170–171
social work, definition 179
working through with client 172–173
*see also* Casework
Teamwork
class structure 87–89
as a concept 81–83
doctors' relationships and attitudes 86–89
hospital background 88–89
division of labour 84
and the future 99–100
and health visitors 91–94
responsibilities 92
need for 83–86
occupational boundaries 85–86
problems in primary care 71, 81–103
sex equality 90–91
social equality 85–86
and social work 95–97
social workers' status 87–89
work of 98–99
Termination of interviews, 174–176
Time factor in social work 148
limits of interviews 174–176
Triadic model in behaviour therapy 186

Warwick Medical Sociology Workshop 100
Workloads, social workers 157–159